The Conflict of Laws in India

The Conflict of Laws in India

Inter-Territorial and Inter-Personal Conflict

Second Edition

V.C. Govindaraj

OXFORD
UNIVERSITY PRESS

OXFORD
UNIVERSITY PRESS

Oxford University Press is a department of the University of Oxford. It furthers the University's objective of excellence in research, scholarship, and education by publishing worldwide. Oxford is a registered trade mark of Oxford University Press in the UK and in certain other countries.

Published in India by
Oxford University Press
2/11 Ground Floor, Ansari Road, Daryaganj, New Delhi 110 002, India

First Edition published in 2011
Second Edition published in 2019

ISBN-13 (printed edition): 978-0-19-949560-3
ISBN-10 (printed edition): 0-19-949560-2

ISBN-13 (eBook): 978-0-19-909781-4
ISBN-10 (eBook): 0-19-909781-X

Typeset in Adobe Garamond Pro 11/13.2
by The Graphics Solution, New Delhi 110 092
Printed in India by Nutech Print Services India

To

my dear wife, (late) Lakshmi Govindaraj,
as a token of my gratitude to and appreciation of
her lifelong service and sacrifice for her family

Contents

Annexures

Foreword

Professor Govindaraj is a legal scholar who had a long stint at the University of Delhi, where he taught conflict of laws to several generations of students. Conflict of laws is a tough branch of jurisprudence, and only a master of jural scholarship, can write, with authority, on any branch of the subject. Professor Govindaraj is among those few erudite scholars who have chosen to write a book on the subject. The book is voluminous and deals with several dimensions of this complicated subject. No law person can claim to be a competent jurist without a fair knowledge of the conflict of laws, which, in modern international jurisprudence, is gaining greater relevance. The subject itself is so important that several universities have made it compulsory for law students to specialize in some facets of this jurisprudence.

I am happy to write a brief foreword to this learned work. While I pay a tribute to the author for the excellent handling of the subject, I have condensed my thoughts hoping that the reader would be persuaded to read the book in whole. My brief preface is meant only to initiate him into this very important work. As one reads on, the appreciation of the quality of the book grows. Surely the Indian universities will be grateful to Professor Govindaraj for the contribution he has made in so lucid and learned a manner that a difficult subject has become accessible to the average student of law.

Laws vary with countries, communities, and sovereignties, and differ with regions and sometimes even with personalities. So the laws conflict with each other, particularly private laws. Therefore, in a given case, what law governs a person is a complicated question engaging both lawyers and courts alike. In theory, law is the same for all people under the same jurisdiction. However, jurisprudence differs in different jurisdictions, and conflicts arising in individual cases, for instance, in matrimonial and property disputes, where more than one party is involved, are governed by different personal laws. Laws are often confusing and conflicting, thus making the conflict resolution even more difficult. Therefore, I would strongly plead for comprehensive legislation on this subject which will prevail over different discordant notes. This objective can be achieved only by elimination of conflicts and convergence of laws.

16 January 2011 V.R. KRISHNA IYER

Preface and Acknowledgements

A case-oriented study of *The Conflict of Laws in India: Inter-Territorial and Inter-Personal Conflict* has assumed importance in the new millennium we have embarked upon. The legitimacy of Private International Law as a subject of study is borne out by the fact that travel across frontiers by individuals and legal transactions that take place among them transnationally have become so common and so frequent that we need norms to regulate their rights and duties through the instrumentality, primarily of courts, for a resolution of conflicts between the laws of countries. On the other hand, treaties between countries and international conventions are inadequate, coupled with the fact that states are not so enthusiastic in becoming parties to the conventions that have emerged through the instrumentality of the United Nations Organization.

Laws regulating the rights and duties of persons differ from state to state and, interestingly enough, inter-personal law conflicts, as in India, call for resolution by the application of appropriate norms to render justice to the parties before courts. Broadly speaking, there are three areas in Conflict of Laws which call for treatment. They are, respectively, the Law of Obligations, consisting of the law relating to contracts and law relating to torts, the law of persons, which encompasses marriage and divorce, and the law relating to children.

The present work lays greater emphasis on case law rather than on an exclusive dependence on rules and principles, which are open to multiple interpretations, creating uncertainty even in matters like commercial transactions, not to speak of family law relationships such as marriage and divorce and allied personal law subjects, besides, of course, the law of obligations and law relating to property.

As per the treatment of the subject, particularly in the area of law of property, the author had recourse to the *Halsbury's Laws of England, Conflict of Laws* (2003), for which he expresses his profound gratitude.

It is customary for an author, based on propriety, to thank all those who had a role to play in bringing this work to a successful conclusion. His first and foremost thanks are to be extended to the Indian Council of Social Science Research, New Delhi, for funding the project. Also, the author's gratitude needs to be extended to the Indian Society of International Law, New Delhi, for auditing the accounts. It is virtually impossible for the author to name all those who contributed to the success of the project. All the same, the author chooses to name Dr T.C. Gupta, the research associate of the project, whose assistance in successfully bringing out the present work cannot adequately be expressed in words. He had chiefly been instrumental in casting the chapter on marriage and divorce. The author extends his deep debt of gratitude to his colleagues in the Indian Society of International Law, and, in particular, to Mr C. Jayaraj, advocate, Supreme Court of India, whose constant help and advice contributed in no small measure to accomplishing the task the author had set for himself. In this connection, mere words of thanks may not suffice to express the author's gratitude to (late) Mr Ram Niwas Mirdha, former president of the Indian Society of International Law, for his concern and encouragement that he gave all along for the success of the project. Thanks-giving may become no more than a formality if the author fails to express his gratitude to (late) Mr V.K. Krishna Menon, the founder president of the Indian Society of International Law, who introduced teaching of Private International Law in the Society's Academy and insisted that the author should shoulder the responsibility of teaching the subject in the Academy. The author is highly grateful to Oxford University Press, New Delhi, for publishing this work, which, goes without saying, enhances its value. The author is beholden to Mr Amresh Chadha, who, despite his other commitments, social and official, gave his best in typing the work on the computer.

To conclude, the author is immensely grateful to the commissioning and editorial departments at Oxford University Press, India, for favorably considering his request to bring out a second edition of the textbook, *The Conflict of Laws in India: Inter-Territorial and Inter-Personal Conflict*, in view of the recent developments that had taken place in the laws relating to Muslims and guardianship of children born out of wedlock.

V.C. Govindaraj
Professor (Retired), Faculty of Law, University of Delhi, India
March 2019

Introduction to the Second Edition

It has been more than seven years since the first edition of my work on Conflict of Laws bearing the title *The Conflict of Laws in India: Inter-Territorial and Inter-Personal Conflict* was published by Oxford University Press, India. Significant developments have taken place since then in the two areas of the subject, namely Muslim Law and the law relating to guardianship, which necessitate incorporation in the textbook.

As for Muslim Law, the passing of the Dissolution of Muslim Marriage Act, 1939, gave a Muslim woman the right to seek a dissolution of her marriage from her Muslim husband in pursuance of Section 2 of the Act, which, undeniably, is a progress, in view of the fact that prior to its passage, she remained helpless, even if she was subjected to domestic violence, cruelty, and humiliation by her husband and his other family members, despite attempted legislative reforms, such as the Prevention of Domestic Violence Against Women Act, 2005, as also her right to seek maintenance under Section 125 of the Indian Criminal Procedure, 1973. A Muslim husband enjoyed an uncontrolled right to seek termination of his marriage by pronouncing *talaq* without having to assign any reason for so doing.

Section 2 of the Dissolution of Muslim Marriage Act, ironically enough, confers only a right to seek by a Muslim wife a divorce from her Muslim husband, but does not contain any provision to seek maintenance from him. This lacuna was remedied by the Supreme Court in the case *Mohammad Ahmed Khan* v. *Shah Bano Begum and Others*, AIR 1985 SC 945, by laying down the rule that a magistrate can grant maintenance to a divorced Muslim wife or, as the case may be, enhancement of maintenance under Section 125 of the Code of Criminal Procedure, 1973, even beyond the *iddat* period. The Shah Bano ruling of the Supreme Court was sought to be overcome by the government by the passing of the Muslim Women (Protection of Rights on Divorce) Act, 1986. But the said enactment did not deter the Supreme Court to forge ahead in its endeavour to secure the interests of the hapless Muslim wife. It laid down the rule in the case *Danial Latifi and another* v. *Union of India*, AIR 2001 SC 3988, a Constitution Bench of the Court, that the statutory obligation under Section 3(1)(a) of the Act, which is of an inclusive character, imposes upon a Muslim husband the duty to discharge his maintenance obligation to his divorced wife during the iddat period, but also make him liable to provide her 'a reasonable and a fair provision and maintenance for the future of the divorced wife to be made and paid to her within the period of *iddat*' (per Rajendra Babu, J. as he then was). In view of the fact that the said Section 3 commences with a *non obstante* clause, the judicial interpretation in respect thereof overrides all other pre-existing laws and decisions of courts.

A Constitution Bench of the Supreme Court in the case *Khatoon Nisa* v. *State of U.P. and Others*, 2002(6) Scale 165, held the view that as the parameters and consideration are the same under Section 5 of the Muslim Women (Protection of Rights on Divorce) Act, 1986, as under Section 125 of the Criminal Procedure Code, even if the Muslim husband and his divorced wife fail to invoke the option under Section 5 of the Act, a magistrate can still exercise his powers to grant maintenance to the Muslim wife on the strength of the ruling in Danial Latifi's case. Subsequently, in the case *Shabana Bano* v. *Imran Khan*, AIR 2010 SC 305, a Division Bench of the Supreme Court observed that the cumulative reading of the relevant portions of the judgements of the Court in *Danial Latifi and Iqbal Bano* v. *State of U.P. and Another* will make it 'crystal clear' that even a divorced Muslim woman would be entitled to claim maintenance from her divorced Muslim husband, as long as she does not remarry.

In a very recent case, namely *Shamim Bano, Appellant* v. *Asraf Khan, Respondent,* (2014) 12 SCC 636, a Division Bench of the Supreme Court, speaking through Justice Dipak Misra (as he then was), endorsed the dictum in Khatoon Nisa's case, namely the seeking of option by a Muslim wife for divorce under Section 3(2) of the Muslim Women (Protection of Rights on Divorce) Act, 1986, will not in any way affect her right to seek maintenance under Section 125 of the Criminal Procedure Code.

It is no exaggeration to comment that the recent decision of the Supreme Court, dated the 22 August 2017, in the writ petition, C0 No. 118 of 2016, titled *Shayara Bano, Petitioner* v. *Union of India and Others, Respondents*, and similar other writ petitions, setting aside by a 3–2 majority the practice of '*talaq-e-biddat*' (that is, triple talaq) is truly epochal.

As for the law relating to guardianship, the recent classic decision of the Supreme Court of India in the case *ABC, Appellant* v. *The State (NCT of Delhi), Respondent*, AIR 2015 SC 2569, invites attention. The Court, while dismissing the Delhi High Court's judgment, laid down the rule that an unwed mother is the natural guardian of her child born out of wedlock, and that she is under no legal obligation whatsoever to disclose the name and address of the putative father of her child. Her refusal to do so gets strengthened in the context of Section 6 of the Hindu Minority and Guardianship Act, 1956, and Section 19 of the Guardians and Wards Act, 1890. In this connection, the Court cited with approval of the proposition laid down by an earlier Bench of the Supreme Court in the year 1985, namely *Laxmi Kant Pandey* v. *Union of India*, (1985) SCC 701, which, though not under the Guardians and Wards Act, 1890, categorically laid down the proposition that the welfare of the child takes precedence over everyone else's, including the rights of the parents. Accordingly, the refusal of the unwed mother to notify the putative father as per Section 11 of the Guardians and Wards Act, 1890, ensued from the intention of protecting the child from 'social stigma and needless controversy'.

In this connection, it is interesting to draw the attention of the readers to the colourful observation of Justice Vikramajit Singh Sen, in whose opinion Laxmi Kant Pandey does not exclusively enjoy the pride of place as regards safeguarding the welfare of the child. Even in the absence of Laxmi Kant Pandey, in his view, we are not 'like mariners in unchartered seas', in that in an earlier three-judge Bench of the Supreme Court in the case *Githa Hariharan* v. *Reserve Bank of India*, (1999) 2 SCC 228, by its ruling, strengthened the hands of an unwed mother to claim sole guardianship rights over her child. The

Court in this case overruled the refusal of the Reserve Bank of India to accept an application, signed solely by the unwed mother, for a fixed deposit in the name of her child. This ruling of the Supreme Court, needless to say, was in accord with Section 6 of the Hindu Minority and Guardianship Act, 1956, as also Section 19 of the Guardians and Wards Act, 1890, as stated earlier.

Section 6(b) of the Hindu Minority and Guardianship Act, 1956, even as the Mahomedan Law, accords custody of the illegitimate children to the mother. Section 8 of the Indian Succession Act, 1925, which is applicable to Christians in India, lays down the rule that the domicile of origin of an illegitimate child is the country where, at the time of his/her birth, the mother is domiciled.

The principle of according sole guardianship to the mother of a child born out of wedlock to the exclusion of the putative father is prevalent in Great Britain, the Irelands, the United States of America, Europe, and the Philippines and New Zealand in the far east.

The Supreme Court in the present Civil Appeal had recourse to the Convention on the Rights of the Child, acceded to by India on 11 November 1992 to highlight the principle to know the identity of his/her parents, which, needless to say, is basic to its welfare.

While allowing the appeal, the Supreme Court bemoaned the failure of the Guardian Court and the High Court to discharge their *parens patriae* jurisdiction to safeguard the child born out of wedlock.

These developments in the law relating to Muslims and the law relating to guardianship have ben elaborated in this second edition. This edition also addresses the printing and typographical errors identified in the first edition.

V.C. Govindaraj
March 2019

1

Introduction

The *raison d'etre* for this branch of law to have its own separate and exclusive existence, although an integral part of the private law of a country, is due to the fact that the world is composed of territorial states which are sovereign and independent, each having its own system of law different from the others. Legal transactions or, as the case may be, issues arising out of such transactions have, more often than not, particularly in the context of the globalized world, a significant relationship to more than one state. This warrants that courts devise and systematically develop a distinct body of rules and principles, known as conflict of laws or private international law, for resolving disputes arising out of such transactions. Accordingly, conflict of laws comes into operation if, and only if, a case contains a foreign element. The phrase 'foreign element' signifies a contact with some system of law other than the law of the forum. Such a contact is discernible, *inter alia*, in the following cases:

(i) a contract is entered into or to be performed in a foreign country, or that a tort is committed in a foreign country;

(ii) a marriage is contracted between nationals of different states or, as is the case with India and some of the African countries, between different religious or ethnic groups within them;

(iii) a property is situated in a foreign country; and

(iv) the parties belong to different countries.

Frederic Harrison aptly describes the nature and importance of the subject in the following words:

> It starts unexpectedly in any court and in the midst of any process. It may be sprung like a mine in a plain common law action, in any administrative proceeding, in equity or in a divorce case, or a bankruptcy case ... The most trivial action of debt, the most complex case of equitable claims, may be

suddenly interrupted by the appearance of a knot to be untied only by Private International Law.[1]

If in Frederic Harrison we have a publicist who is expressive and articulate in pointing out how private international law emerges in any action, whether it be one of common law, or of equity, one of administrative, or any proceeding whatsoever, Walter Wheeler Cook gets down to the brasstacks and offers an issue-based counsel, presumably addressed to courts, that 'the problems in the field under consideration (that is, contracts) need to be broken down into smaller groups and dealt with so as to meet the needs of society.'[2] Morris endorses the words of wisdom of Cook which, if translated into action, would enable courts to avoid the mistake of treating the subject under consideration, be it a contract, a tort, a marriage, or a property right, or any, as an all-purpose concept instead of, as is the right course to adopt, according proper weight in a particular case, depending upon the facts and the circumstances of the case, as Morris puts it, 'to factors of varying significance like the place of contracting, the place of performance, the nationality of the ship, the *situs* of the land, the domicile, residence and place of business of the parties, reasonable expectations, the currency in which the obligation is expressed, and countless others.'[3]

Also, in the second place, he argues, 'the rule enables attention to be concentrated not so much on the question, what law governs the validity of the contract, as on the question what law governs the particular issue before the court' that would enable the court to give different answers to such questions as, for instance, 'offer and acceptance, reality of consent, formalities, necessity for consideration or cause, agency, capacity of the parties, essential validity, illegality, interpretation, scope, performance, discharge, remedies and so forth.[4]

To the same effect Willis Reese argues that the validity of a marriage in great majority of situations may have to be treated merely as incidental to the determination of another issue and not, as courts do, treat marriage like an 'all purpose concept' and that it would be advisable to determine the validity of a marriage in the light of the particular issue involved that may render the validity of a marriage incidental.[5]

Conflict of laws, by virtue of its being essentially, though not wholly, judge-made, is part of the common law of a country. The rules of conflict of laws, like any other branch of common law, are subject to the constitution and the statutes of a country, besides obligations arising out of treaties to which the said country is a party.

Rules of choice of law, devised and applied by courts with the avowed objective of resolving conflicts between the laws so as to render justice to the parties, are, perforce, subject to constitutional limitations and statutory directives of the concerned state. In the absence of such statutory directives, factors that influence courts in evolving appropriate choice of law rules include, as set out in the *Restatement (Second) of Conflict of Laws* of the American Law Institute, 1971, the following namely,

(a) the needs of the interstate and international systems,

(b) the relevant policies of the forum,

(c) the relevant policies of other interested states and the relative interests of those states in the determination of the particular issue,

(d) the protection of justified expectations,

(e) the basic policies underlying the particular field of law,

(f) certainty, predictability and uniformity of result, and

(g) ease in the determination and the application of the law to be applied.[6]

APPROPRIATENESS OF THE TITLE 'CONFLICT OF LAWS'

Between the two terminologies that are in vogue to designate this branch of the law, namely 'conflict of laws' and 'private international law', the former is preferred because of the fact that municipal laws with respect to legal relationships differ from state to state, thus giving rise to conflict. This phenomenon is brought out clearly by employing the phraseology 'conflict of laws'. If, on the contrary, we choose the other expression to designate the subject, namely 'private international law', it is likely to confuse the uninformed who may mistake this subject for international law which can only be public, not private.

Of course, there is the twilight zone where rules of choice of law bow to uniform rules of law that emerge from international treaties and conventions such as, for example, the United Nations Convention for the International Sale of Goods, 1980. This convention sets out uniform law for certain aspects of international sales. It is interesting, in this connection, to advert to the Rome Convention on Contractual Obligation, 1980, of the European Community which finds incorporation into the body of the law in England by the British Parliament's passing of the Contracts (Applicable Law) Act, 1990. Strange as it may seem, the said Act adopts a dual standard in that, on the one hand, it replaces common law rules in respect of foreign contracts and, in particular the proper law doctrine, in respect of cases arising under the convention binding on the European Community, and on the other, it retains the common law rules in respect of non-convention cases arising outside the European Community.

More and more modern writers opt for the phrase 'conflict of laws' in preference to the other competing phraseology 'private international law', presumably to obviate the confusion that the employment of the phrase 'international law' prefixed by the word 'private' may entail. The preference for the title 'conflict of laws', doubtless, stems from its simplicity and pragmatism. The same may not be the case with expressions equally short and simple, such as 'transnational litigation' and the like or, for that matter, titles more accurate and exact, though long and clumsy, such as the one employed by Professor Von Mehren of the Harvard Law School, namely 'the law of multistate problems'.

Professor Joseph Beale of the Harvard Law School opted for the phrase 'conflict of laws', as it was inspired by the great Anglo-American publicists, Story, Wharton, Dicey, and Minor. Even while associating with the said greats as to the choice of the title of the subject, Beale imparts a vein of humour to it as is evident from the following passage of his magnum opus, *A Treatise on Conflict of Laws*, acknowledging the wise and witty remarks of Vereilles-Somieres:

> The warlike expression 'conflict of laws' is used to describe the pacific work of settling by fixed bounds the line of separation between two legislative jurisdictions. The only conflict is among the legal scholars who are doing this work. Yet since the expression is consecrated by good use and is simple we may well make use of it.[7]

Further, the title acquires greater legitimacy viewed in the light of the Indian legal system. Here, in India, the conflict in certain cases, particularly in regard to the Law of Persons, is inter-personal rather than inter-territorial, and that encompasses marriage, adoption, legitimacy and legitimation, et cetera inasmuch as each of the religious communities inhabiting the subcontinent, namely the Hindu, the Muslim, the Christian, the Parsi, the Buddhist, the Sikh, and the Jain (though the last three categories are deemed to be part of the Hindu community) is governed by its own personal law, legislative, or customary. Such a diversity of personal laws gives rise to conflicts in certain cases of family and succession law which result from the conversion of a spouse from one faith to another, usually by marriage, even without any change in the domicile of the concerned spouses. In the case of a Hindu woman, for instance, her conversion to Islam may subject her to two systems of law instead of one, namely her pre-conversion Hindu law and her post-conversion Muslim law. Courts in India, as we shall see from the succeeding chapters, have to resolve conflicts of this kind. Thus, the Indian choice of law rules in the area of personal laws add influence to the ardent supporters of the term 'conflict of laws'.

AVOIDANCE OF CONFLICTS: WAYS AND MEANS

Conflicts, perhaps, may be minimized, though not altogether eliminated, by a conscious effort on the part of states aimed at unifying their internal laws in certain areas of vital concern to all—such as carriage of persons and goods across frontiers—by means of concluding suitable regional treaties and conventions. Alternatively, countries may seek to unify rules of conflict of laws in respect of matters of greatest importance such as capacity and status touching matrimonial relations, adoption and child welfare, succession to property (both testate and intestate), essential validity of contracts, and matters of procedural concern such as service of summons abroad for which the Hague Convention on the Service Abroad of Judicial and Extra Judicial Documents in Civil or Commercial Matters, 1965, stands as exemplar.

UNIFICATION OF INTERNAL LAWS

So long as the world stands sharply divided into two divergent groups—namely those governed by the common law, which include the Anglo-American and the Commonwealth countries, and those governed by the civil law which, in the main, encompass the European countries, apart from others such as Japan which embraced the latter, unification of the internal laws is a far cry, so it appears, unless it be confined to such areas of common concern.

Two such areas of common concern are international transport and contracts for the sale of goods, both relating to movement of persons, goods and effects across frontiers. Illustrative of such an attempt to unify the internal laws of countries is the Warsaw Convention of 1929, as amended at the Hague, 1955, further supplemented by the Guadalajara Convention, 1961, which sought to regulate rules of jurisdiction and the applicable law with respect to carriage of persons or goods by aircraft for reward. The said convention forbids parties from altering the rules of the convention, declaring such alterations null and void. The British Parliament enacted the Carriage by Air Act, 1961, to give effect to the convention. Likewise, the enactment by the British Parliament of the Carriage of Goods by Sea Act, 1924, was necessitated by the Hague rules which had to be amended subsequently by the British Parliament by its enacting the Carriage of Goods by Sea Act, 1971, to incorporate the Brussels Protocol, 1968. Similarly, road transport, too, was regulated by the British Parliament by the passing of the Carriage of Goods by Road Act, 1965, the Carriage of Passengers by Road Act, 1974, the International Road Transport Convention Act, 1983, as well as the Merchant Shipping Act, 1995. The enactment of all the aforesaid Acts was to give effect to conventions concluded at international conferences.[8]

The Berne Convention of 1886, since amended several times, established an international union to give protection to authors over their literary and artistic works or, more appropriately, to give protection to intellectual property rights. Mention may also be made, in this connection, of the United Nations Convention on Contracts for the International Sale of Goods, 1980, under the auspices of the United Nations Committee on International Trade Law (UNCITRAL). Simultaneously, there had been attempts at regional levels, too, for the unification of various aspects of international laws, albeit confined to the Scandinavian and the Latin American countries.[9]

UNIFICATION OF RULES OF CHOICE OF LAW

So long as the world stands divided, as mentioned before, on the basis of systems of law that regulate human relationships, namely the common law which originated in England and like a banyan tree spread to the United States and the Commonwealth countries as against the civil law which with its seat on the Continent of Europe influenced, and found acceptance with, far off countries like the Latin American States and Japan in the far east, any talk of unification of the rules of conflict of laws, as of now, sounds no more than a promise to the ear. Viewed against this background, efforts on the part of the Hague Conference on Private International Law to bring about uniformity, as far as may be, on a number of topics where rules of choice of law differ, are indubitably laudable.

The drafting of a charter in the year 1951 designed to place the Hague Conference on a firm footing by the creation of a Permanent Bureau composed of a Secretary-General and two Assistant Secretaries-General belonging to two different countries, is an event of great significance.[10] The said charter has been accepted by many countries, including the United Kingdom. Its functions are chiefly to examine and prepare proposals for the unification of the rules of choice of law while, at the same time, maintaining a close touch with other governmental and non-governmental organizations such as the Commonwealth countries and the International Law Association. The Bureau works under the general direction of the Standing Government Commission of the Netherlands established by a Royal Decree in 1897 with the avowed objective of promoting the codification of the rules of choice of law. Various laws that had recently been enacted by the British Parliament on the subject of choice of law rules are a sequel to the acceptance by the United Kingdom of the Hague Conventions on Private International Law. We need make mention here of the multilateral convention concluded in the year 1969 by Benelux States, that is, Belgium, the Netherlands, and Luxembourg, which brought about unification of the rules of choice of law on vital matters such as capacity and status, succession to property upon death and the essential validity of contracts.[11]

The Rome Convention on contractual obligation concluded by the European Community in the year 1980 and adverted to earlier, is of great significance to the business world. This became part of the law of England by being incorporated into the body of the law by the passing of the Contracts (Applicable Law) Act, 1990, by the British Parliament.

So are the Brussels and Lugano Conventions of the EEC, concluded in the years 1968 and 1988 respectively, on the subjects of jurisdiction of courts in conflicts cases as well as recognition and enforcement of judgments in civil and commercial matters.

As India is not a party to any of the conventions set out above, with the solitary exception of the Hague Convention on Inter-Country Adoptions, 1993, besides three other Hague Conventions[12] and as the existing legislations in India, leave alone the constitutional mandate of ushering in a uniform civil code, are out of tune with the felt needs of the community in respect of family law, the responsibility of evolving appropriate choice of law rules in respect thereof is squarely upon the superior courts.

CONFLICT OF LAWS: ITS EVOLUTION IN RETROSPECT AND IN PROSPECT

Strange as it may seem, the science of conflict of laws failed to grip the minds and imagination of courts and publicists in England till the dawn of the nineteenth century. Even so, during the eighteenth century, certain basic principles touching the law of obligations had been adumbrated in a rudimentary form by Lord Mansfield through his judicial pronouncements that are mentioned below.

The law to govern a contract is the law of the place where the contract is made (that is, *lex loci contractus*), unless it be that the parties while concluding the contract had in their contemplation a law other than the *lex loci contractus* to govern their contract.[13] Elsewhere, he observes that a law to govern a foreign contract is the law where the cause of action arose.[14] The law to govern a foreign tort in a conflicts case, according to Lord Mansfield, is the law of the place where the tort occurred (that is, *lex loci delicti commissi*), and, that, according to him, what would constitute a justification by the law of the place of the tort could be pleaded as a defence to an action in England.[15] The said principle, it appears, might have influenced Willis, J. in propounding the 'double actionability' doctrine as a conflicts rule in foreign torts, attributed to him, however doubtful its authenticity be.[16]

Presumably this doctrine was given a seeming burial by the British Parliament by enacting the Private International Law (Miscellaneous Provisions) Act, 1995[17] as were certain other rules of choice of law such as that the formal validity of a marriage is governed by the *lex loci celebrationis*;[18] that for the purpose of succession the law of the domicile of the owner governs movables of the owner[19] (which holds good equally to bankruptcy distribution[20]), and that courts in England should not sustain actions that touch and concern foreign immovables.[21]

Concededly, courts in England are to be credited with laying down choice of law rules in respect of contracts, torts, and legitimation in the years 1865, 1869, and 1885. As a matter of fact, it was not until 1895 that courts in England could exercise jurisdiction for dissolution of marriages based on domicile. On the contrary, other matters relating to capacity to marry, choice of law rules in respect of nullity, and legitimacy remained unresolved. As compared to the relatively impressive case law that we find in England on subjects like contracts and torts, English decisions in other areas on choice of law rules are scanty. This, coupled with the movement of favouring unification of choice of law rules by conventions and the resultant establishment of Law Commissions, led to a flurry of legislative activity in England in the area of conflict of laws towards the last quarter of the twentieth century.[22]

As contrasted with the tardy growth of the science of conflict of laws in England, scholary exposition of the theories and methods of conflict of laws in the United States, coupled with the three Restatements on the subject, are nothing but awesome. This prompted Morris, unquestionably one of the greatest English conflict lawyers of the twentieth century, to comment that nothing like it had been seen in any other country or in any other period of the centuries-long history of the subject.[23] Viewed in the light of the phenomenal growth of the subject in the western world, the Indian conflict of laws is in its state of infancy.

Only recently have there been certain legislative measures, and that, too, confined to the Hindus, on topics such as marriage and matrimonial causes, succession, minority and guardianship, and adoptions and maintenance, by the passing of legislations by the Parliament of India like the Hindu Marriage Act, 1955, the Hindu Succession Act, 1954, the Hindu Minority and Guardianship Act, 1956, and the Hindu Adoptions and Maintenance Act, 1956, respectively. Besides, we have in India the Parsi Marriage and Divorce Act, 1936, the Special Marriage Act, 1954, and the Foreign Marriage Act, 1969.

As for Christians in India, they are still governed by the colonial legislation of the third quarter of the nineteenth century, namely the Indian Christian Marriage Act, 1872 and the Indian Divorce Act, 1869, which, needless to say, are hopelessly out of tune with the present day needs of the Indian Christian community, despite cosmetic amendments they are subjected to from time to time. Reforms for the Indian Muslim community are taboo, despite the presence of a pre-Independence solitary legislation of a peripheral kind, namely, the Muslim Marriage Dissolution Act, 1939, which, in the name of secularism, is a constitutional directive reflecting the need to usher in a uniform civil code.[24]

Case law on inter-personal law conflicts, as we shall see in the chapters devoted to the subject, are few and far between; a significant part of the existing case law is not backed by a sound *ratio decidendi* contrary to the dictum *ratio legis est anima legis* (that is, the reason of the law is the soul of the law). The Indian legislature, too, it is no exaggeration to say, has so far remained insensitive to usher in reformist measures, though there are or have been committees and commissions apart from the Indian Law Commission—a standing law reform body—to recommend wholesome legislative measures designed to secure the interests of the teeming millions that beckon social justice and equal protection of the laws.

Courts in India and, in particular, the higher judiciary to whom is entrusted the unenviable task of evolving appropriate choice of law rules, have not so far been able to live upto the expectations, due presumably to their slavish adherence to the rules of English conflict of laws as expounded by Dicey and Morris, and by Cheshire.

All the same, there is no room for skepticism about the future of conflict of laws in India. Also there is no denying the fact—and there can be no two opinions in this regard—that the Indian judiciary has ample opportunity to evolve its own impressive choice of law rules in keeping with our native ethos. If, as is expected of them, courts in India play their rightful rôle in evolving appropriate choice of law rules to facilitate a healthy growth and evolution of this area of legal discipline, and if the Indian legislature, too, acts in tandem by enacting timely legislative measures, the Indian conflict of laws is sure to acquire its own identity and respectability.

MODERN THEORIES OF CONFLICT OF LAWS: A BRIEF SURVEY

One wonders what useful purpose will be served by projecting theories and methods employed by publicists in dealing with a branch of law, popularly known as 'conflict of laws', that is predominantly, though not exclusively, judge-made, which can aptly be described as 'lawyers' law'. Courts do more often than not have recourse to the views of publicists to fortify the ratio they employ in deciding cases. Such recourse by courts to the writings of jurists is more pronounced in the area of conflict of laws than in other branches of the law.

As has earlier been pointed out, conflict of laws is still in its state of infancy. We may in vain try to trace the subject beyond the second quarter of the seventeenth century for any meaningful survey of the subject. The said period was marked by a flurry of writings on the subject by jurists of eminence, chief among whom was Ulrich Huber (1635–94), a Dutch jurist-cum-judge. His writings on conflict of laws which, in the words of Morris, are no more than five quarto pages, are to be found under the title '*De Conflictu legum diversarum in diversis imperiis*' (vol. III, Book 1, title 3). His influence on the Anglo-American world, however, is more pronounced than that of any other foreign publicist. His formulations are simple but precise. They are as under:

(1) The laws of each state have force within the limits of that government, but bind all subject to it, but not beyond.
(2) All persons within the limits of a government, whether they live there permanently or temporarily, are deemed to be subjects thereof.
(3) Sovereigns will so act by way of comity that rights acquired within the limits of a government retain their force everywhere so far as they do not cause prejudice to the power, or rights of such government or its subjects.

The first two formulations of Huber clearly and unequivocally emphasize the territoriality of laws that bind citizens and foreigners alike by virtue of their residence within the jurisdiction of a state, whether permanently or temporarily. The said formulations constitute the foundation, as it were, of the science of conflict of laws on which the Anglo-American jurisprudence is built. The third formulation mixes up three doctrines, namely the doctrine of comity, the doctrine of vested or acquired rights, and the doctrine of public policy. The first and the third, namely the doctrine of comity and the doctrine of public policy, do not call for any elaborate treatment or comment and, as such, can be summarily disposed of.

The Doctrine of Comity

Comity or courtesy sounds more a political rather than a legal concept which, of course, is familiar to international lawyers. It gained currency through the writings of Joseph Story, simultaneously a judge of the Supreme Court of the United States and a Professor of Law at the Harvard Law School. Admittedly, Story repeated, *mutatis mutandis*, the maxims of Huber.[25] However, his influence on the scholarly writings on the subject of conflict of laws and on courts in England and in the United States can hardly be overemphasized.[26] He expounded Huber's doctrine of comity which was central to his system as under:

> The true foundation on which the subject rests is that the rules which are to govern are those which arise from mutual interest and utility; from the sense of inconveniences which would arise from a contrary doctrine; and *from a sort of moral necessity to do justice in order that justice may be done to us in return* [emphasis added].[27]

Story's theory of comity was subjected to a good deal of criticism by continental writers, based as it is on Huber's formulation of comity with its attendant political connotation, instead of, as Lorenzen contends, with a sense of duty on the part of courts to do justice.[28] Dicey is one of the most unsparing critics of Story's theory of comity. He dismisses Story and his theory of comity on a contemptuous note such as this:

> Is, or is not the enforcement of foreign law a matter of 'comity'? This is an inquiry which has greatly exercised the minds of jurists ... If the assertion that the recognition or enforcement of foreign law depends upon comity means only that the law of no country can have effect as law beyond the territory of the sovereign by whom it was imposed, unless by the permission of the state where it is allowed to operate, the statement expresses, though obscurely, a real and important fact. If, on the other hand, the assertion that the recognition or enforcement of foreign laws depends upon comity is meant to imply that, to take a common case, when English judges apply French law, they do so out of courtesy to the French Republic, then the term 'comity' is used to cover a view which, if really held by any serious thinker, affords a singular specimen of confusion of thought produced by a laxity of language. The application of foreign law is not a matter of caprice or option; it does not arise from the desire

of the sovereign of England, or of any other sovereign, to show courtesy to other states. If follows from the impossibility of otherwise determining whole classes of cases without gross inconvenience and injustice to litigants, whether natives or foreigners.[29]

The theory of comity may lead to such ridiculous results drawn from judicial disposition to it, such as we notice in cases like *Hilton* v. *Guyot*[30] and *Ritchie* v. *Mc Mullen*.[31] In the first of the two cases, the Supreme Court of the United States, speaking through Justice Gray, refused to give effect to a French judgment in favour of a French firm against an American citizen on the ground of want of reciprocity on the part of France to give effect to English and other foreign judgments. In the second case, the Supreme Court of the United States held that an Ontario judgment should be enforced without examining its merits based on the ground that Canadian courts would give conclusive effect to judgments of courts in the United States.

As Morris points out here, perhaps, the one and only useful outcome of the doctrine of comity is to make subjects shed their parochialism and to make judges more internationalist in outlook and more tolerant of foreign law than otherwise they might have been.[32] Often we notice judges invoking comity to justify their extending recognition to foreign judgments. The classic example for such recognition of foreign decrees based upon a so called comity is the case of *Igra* v. *Igra*,[33] where the court, speaking through Pearce J., while extending recognition to a German decree of divorce obtained during the Second World War at the instance of the Gestapo (perhaps on racial grounds) observed that 'the interests of comity are not served if one country is too eager to criticise the standards of another country or too reluctant to recognise decrees that are valid by the law of the domicile'.

To conclude, if the courts of one state or jurisdiction will give effect to the laws and judicial decisions of another, not as a matter of obligation but out of deference and respect,[34] the science of conflict of laws, whose aim is to render justice to the parties in a litigation on the basis of law and facts, is sure to suffer a setback.

The Doctrine of Public Policy

The doctrine of public policy has usually been invoked in cases pertaining to foreign contracts or foreign status. Public policy is a tool that calls for restraint and circumspection in its application by courts. It is a wild horse, if we may say so, that needs to be entrusted to a skilled jockey to be tamed and pressed into service. I mean, by this metaphor, that we need judges who are endowed with a keen perception and sound judgment to choose to apply suitable concepts such as comity or public policy to grant or withhold recognition to foreign judicial determinations. Judges not so endowed are apt to either endorse foreign laws or foreign judicial determinations on the touchstone of the so called comity or respect, or refuse to recognize such foreign laws or foreign judicial decrees altogether based on their own notions of public policy. It is interesting, in this connection, to recall the words of wisdom of an eminent American judge as to the scope and ambit of the doctrine of public policy. He remarks: 'The courts are not free to refuse to enforce a foreign right at the pleasure of the judges, to suit the individual notion of expediency or fairness. They do not close their doors unless help would violate some fundamental principle of justice, some prevalent conception of good morals, some deep-rooted tradition of commonweal.'[35] We may have to, once again, dwell upon public policy while dealing with preliminary topics like prohibition against enforcement of foreign penal laws or revenue laws or, foreign policies that are internal to the exercise by foreign sovereigns of the rights or jurisdictions.

Theory of Vested or Acquired Rights*

The vested rights theory was decorously dropped by the judiciary both in England and the US in the latter half of the twentieth century. Instead, courts in deciding cases employed norms based on policy, value, and interests which, unlike the vested or acquired rights theory, may not necessarily yield uniformity of results.

* See Chapter 15, first three paragraphs under section 'Rule Selection Rule in Conflict of Laws: A Critique of the So-called American Revolution'; see also section 'A Complementary Resume'.

NOTES

1. Frederic Harrison, *On Jurisprudence and the Conflict of Laws*, with annotations by A.H.F. Lefroy (Oxford: Clarendon Press, 1919), p. 101.
2. Walter Wheeler Cook, *Logical and Legal Bases of Conflict of Laws*, p. 431 (1942); see also pp. 417–18.

3. J.H.C. Morris, 'The Proper Law of a Tort', *Harvard Law Review*, Vol. 64 (1951), pp. 881 at 883.

4. Ibid, p. 882

5. Willis L.M. Reese, 'Marriage in American Conflicts of Laws', *The International and Comparative Law Quarterly (ICLQ)*, Vol. 26 (1997), p. 952.

6. Section 6, *Restatement (Second), the Conflict of Laws* of the American Law Institute (St. Paul, Minnesota: American Law Institute Publishers, 1971), p. 10.

7. Joseph H. Beale, *A Treatise on Conflict of Laws*, First Edition, Reprint (The Lawbook Exchange Ltd.: New Jersey, 2004), p. 15.

8. *Cheshire and North's Private International Law*, Thirteenth Edition (Butterworths: London, Edinburg, Dublin, 1999), p. 10.

9. Ibid.

10. Ibid., p. 12

11. Ibid.

12. Subsequent to India becoming a party to the Hague Convention on Inter-Country Adoptions, 1993, with effect from 1 October 2003, India embraced three other Hague Conventions on Private International Law, namely the Convention Abolishing the Requirement of Legalisation of Foreign Public Documents, 1961, the Convention on the Service Abroad of Judicial and Extra-Judicial Documents in Civil or Commercial Matters, 1965, and the Convention on the Taking of Evidence Abroad in Civil or Commercial Matters, 1970.

13. Wm. Bl 234 at pp. 258–9

14. 2 BURR 1077, p. 1078

15. *Mostyn* v. *Fabrigas*, (1774) AMB 25.

16. *Phillips* v. *Eyre*, (1870) LR 6 QB1.

17. The rule in *Philips* v. *Eyre* has been abolished in respect of all torts committed after 1 May, 1996, (vide Section 10 of the Act), but is preserved as respects defamation (vide Section 13 of the Act), although it continues to apply to all torts committed before 1 May, 1996, for no law can have retrospective operation.

18. *Scrimshire* v. *Scrimshire*, (1752) 2 Hag Con 395.

19. *Pipon* v. *Pipon*, (1774) Amb 25.

20. *Solomons* v. *Ross*, (1764) Hy B1 131n. See *Cheshire and North's Private International Law*, Thirteenth Edition, 1995.

21. *Shelling* v. *Farmer*, (1726) 1 Strange 646.

22. Ibid.

23. J.H.C. Morris, *The Conflict of Laws*, Second Edition (London: Stevens and Sons, 1980), p. 499.

24. Article 44, Part IV, The Constitution of India, 1950.

25. Lorenzen, 'The Theory of Qualifications and the Conflict of Laws', 20 *Columbia Law Review*, (1920), p. 247.

26. Commenting on his work, Frederic Harrison observes:

> This famous work which was first published in 1834 (it has now reached the eighth edition, 1883); and from the date of its appearance hardly a single case on this subject in America or in England, perhaps few on the Continent, have ever been decided without some reference to this learned book. A new era in the History of Private International Law may be traced from it.

Frederic Harrison, *Jurisprudence and the Conflict of Laws*, (1919), p. 119.

27. Joseph Story, *Commentaries on the Conflict of Laws*, Eighth Edition, (1883).

28. Lorenzen, 'The Theory of Qualifications and the Conflict of Laws', p. 19.

29. A.V. Dicey, *Conflict of Laws*, Third Edition, p. 10.

30. (1895) 159 US 113, 16 SCC 139, 40 LEd 95

31. 159 US 235 (1895)

32. Ibid.; Morris, *Conflict of Laws*, Second Edition, p. 501.

33. (1951) pp. 404, 412; Cf. *Travers* v. *Holley*, (1953) pp. 246, 257, where the court, speaking through Hodson L.J., observed: '... It would be contrary to principle and inconsistent with comity if the courts were to refuse to recognize a jurisdiction (based on residence) which *mutatis mutandis* they claim for themselves.'

34. See *Black's Law Dictionary*, Sixth Edition, p. 267, where judicial comity is defined.

35. *Loucks* v. *Standard Oil Co.*, (1918) 224 N.Y. 99, 111; 120 NE 198, 202, per Cardozo, J.

2

Exclusion of Foreign Law

FOREIGN LAW, FOREIGN JUDICIAL DECREES, AND INDIAN COURTS

Based on the rules of choice of law, an Indian court will generally apply the appropriate foreign law in order to render justice to the parties before it. An Indian court will do this even if the acceptance and application of a foreign law under the circumstances of the case may prove to be contrary to a policy of Indian law which the court would ordinarily apply in a purely domestic case.[1] In insolvency proceedings, an Indian court would accept the status of insolvency as determined by a foreign court with respect to property situated within its jurisdiction, immovable property excepted.[2] Courts in England, too, have exhibited a cosmopolitan and a constructive approach by their readiness to enforce generally a contract valid by its governing law, even if the contract is without consideration,[3] is champertous,[4] is one that ousts the jurisdiction of a foreign court,[5] or is for a loan irrecoverable under the English domestic law.[6]

Likewise, English courts have shown the same liberal attitude of recognizing polygamy,[7] marriage by proxy,[8] marriage within prohibited degrees (as per English Law),[9] and marriage below the age of consent.[10]

Public Policy

Section 23 of the Indian Contract Act, 1872, forbids an Indian court from recognizing or enforcing a contract where, on the facts of the case, such recognition or enforcement would be opposed to Indian public policy, or where such contract was obtained by fraud. The common law of India, even as the statutory injunction as highlighted in the Indian Contract Act set out above, upholds the principle that an Indian court will not recognize or enforce a right based on a foreign judgment when such recognition or enforcement of the right is opposed to justice or morality,[11] is unconscionable,[12] or where the judgment is obtained by fraud.[13]

Public policy is an inclusive concept based on which the Indian Contract Act, 1872, declares void the following transactions: a contract in restraint of marriage,[14] trade,[15] or legal proceedings,[16] an agreement the meaning of which is not certain or capable of being made certain,[17] a wagering contract,[18] et cetera.

However, where a contract is subject to two jurisdictions, the parties to the contract are at liberty to choose one or the other of the two. Such an exercise of choice is not opposed to public policy and the contract, accordingly, is valid.[19] Furthermore, in the event the parties to a contract have chosen a forum, recourse may be had to yet another forum provided it be backed by balance of convenience,[20] or it be instrumental in promoting international trade and commerce.[21]

Foreign Penal Law

It is a well known principle of conflict of laws that a court will not enforce a foreign penal law, either directly or indirectly.[22] A penal law is to be distinguished from a remedial law. While a penal law imposes punishment for breach of duty to the state, a remedial law is designed to compensate a private person for the damage he suffers due to a breach of duty owed to him.[23] The question of whether a foreign law is penal in character is to be determined by the local court irrespective of whether the foreign court would agree with it or not.[24] A sum of money that a plaintiff may claim to be due to him under the provisions of foreign law is not deemed to be a penalty unless it be recoverable at the instance of the foreign state concerned, by one of its officials, or by a common infomer.[25]

In case the foreign law in question is partly penal and partly remedial, a court of law would choose to enforce only the rights arising under that part which is remedial to the exclusion of the other that is penal.[26] Notwithstanding the fact that a court will not enforce a foreign penal law, it may, however, recognize it for other purposes such as not to enforce a contract which required the commission of a crime in that state[27] or, for that matter, any foreign confiscatory law that is discriminatory on grounds of race, religion or the like, constituting as it were a grave threat to human rights.[28]

Foreign Revenue Law

Foreign revenue laws are comparable to foreign penal laws from the standpoint of enforceability. They both signify exercise by the concerned state of its sovereign power over its subjects which is inconsequential so far as third states are concerned. A foreign revenue law could neither impose a burden[29] nor confer a benefit[30] on the subjects of another state. Nevertheless, states do recognize the revenue laws of third states and even show respect to them, based on comity.

Courts will refrain from enforcing a foreign revenue law, either directly or indirectly such as collection of capital gains tax as in *Government of India, Ministry of Finance (Revenue Division)* v. *Taylor*.[31] However, assisting a foreign court to obtain evidence for proceedings to enforce a revenue law in the foreign country would not constitute enforcement, direct or indirect, as was held in Re State of Norway's application.[32] An action to collect taxes of a foreign country will not be entertained by a court, whether it be a claim by a liquidator in winding up of company as in *Peter Buchanan Ltd. and Macharg* v. *McVey*,[33] or it be a garnishee order in respect of tax due from the plaintiff, as in *Rassano* v. *Manufacturers' Life Insurance Co. Ltd.*[34]

In the case of a foreign penal law, a court will not enforce a foreign revenue law, although it may recognize it for other puposes.[35]

Foreign Public Law

As a matter of principle, a court will not enforce the public law of a foreign country, though the scope and ambit of this principle remains nebulous.[36]

NOTES

1. *(Gummideli) Anantapadmanabhaswami* v. *Official Receiver of Secunderabad*, AIR 1933 PC 134, 142 IC 552, (1933) All LJ 645, (1933) 37 CAL WN 553; *Lakhpat Rai Sharma* v. *Atma Singh*, AIR 1962 PUNJ 228, (1961) ILR PUNJ 166.
2. *Magadhu Pillai Rowther* v. *Asan Muhammadhu Rowther*, AIR 1920 MAD 934, 51 IC 38, (1919)9 MAD LW 535.

3. Re Bonacina, *Le Brasseur* v. *Bonacina*, (1912) 2 Ch. 394, CA.

4. Re Trepca Mines Ltd. (No. 2), (1963) Ch. 199 at 218, (1962) 3 ALL ER 351 p. 354, CA (litigation in foreign country); *Trendtex Trading Corpn.* v. *Credit Suisse*, (1982) AC 679, (1981) 3 All ER 520, HL (litigation in England).

5. *Addison* v. *Brown*, (1954) 2 ALL ER 213 p. 217, (1954) 1WLR 779 p. 784.

6. *Saxby* v. *Fulton*, (1909) 2 KB 208, CA (betting loan) *Shrichand & Co.* v. *Facon*, (1906) 22 TLR 245 (Loan at rate of interest in excess of that permitted by English Money-Lenders Acts).

7. *Baindail* v. *Baindail*, (1946) p. 122, (1946) 1 All ER 342, C.A. Indian courts, too, it may be said to their credit, recognize polygamous marriages when giving relief. (See *Khambata* v. *Khambata*, AIR 1935 BOM 5, (1935) ILR 59 BOM 278, (1934) 36 BOM LR 1021. *A contrario*, an Indian court will not recognize a polygamous marriage contracted by Christians domiciled in India. (See *William Hudson* v. *K.M. Webster*, AIR (1937) MAD 565 pp. 567, 169 IC 516, (1937) MAD WN 363. Such non-recognition is based on the Indian Christian Marriage Act, 1872, as read with the Indian Divorce Act, 1869.

8. *Apt.* v. *Apt*, (1948) p. 83, (1947) 2 ALL ER 677, CA.

9. Re Bozzelli Settlement, *Husey-Hunt* v. *Bozzelli*, (1902) 1 Ch. 751; *Cheni* v. *Cheni*, (1965) p. 85, (1962) 3 ALL ER 873.

10. *Alhaji Mohamed* v. *Knott*, (1969) 1 QB1, (1968), 2 ALL ER 563. See V.C. Govindaraj, *Conflict of Laws*, Halsbury's Laws of India Series, Vol. 10 (New Delhi: LexisNexis Butterworths, 2001), p. 212.

11. *Smt. Satya* v. *Teja Singh*, AIR 1975 SC 105, (1975) 1 SCC 120, (1975) SCC (Cr) 50.

12. *Y. Narasimha Rao* v. *Y. Venkata Lakshmi*, (1991) 3 SCC 451, (1991) 2 SCR 821, (1991) SCC (CR) 626.

13. Ibid., *Smt. Satya* v. *Teja Singh*.

14. Section 26, The Indian Contract Act, 1872.

15. Section 27, The Indian Contract Act, 1872.

16. Section 28, The Indian Contract Act, 1872.

17. Section 29, The Indian Contract Act, 1872.

18. Section 30, The Indian Contract Act, 1872.

19. *Ajmera Bros.* v. *Suraj Mal Naresh Kumar Jain*, AIR 1968 PAT 44, (1967) ILR 46 PAT 753, (1967) BLJR 164.

20. *Union of India* v. *Navigation Maritime Bulgare*, AIR 1973 Cal 526; *Black Sea SSUL Lastochkina Odessa, USSR* v. *Union of India*, AIR (1976) AP 103, (1975) ILR AP 805, (1975) 2 ANDH WR 339.

21. Ibid.

22. *Huntington* v. *Attrill*, (1893) AC 150, P.C.
23. Ibid.
24. Ibid.
25. Ibid.
26. *Raulin* v. *Fischer*, (1911) 2 KB 93.
27. *Regazzoni* v. *K.C. Sethia Ltd.*, (1958) AC 301, (1956) 2 QB 490.
28. *Oppenheimer* v. *Cattermole*, (1976) AC 249.
29. *Commissioner of Income Tax, Bombay City, Bombay* v. *Nandlal Gandlal*, AIR (1960) SC 1147, (1960) 3 SCR 620, (1961 Bom LR 208.
30. *Kumar Jagdish Chandra Singh* v. *Commissioner of Income Tax, West Bengal*, AIR (1956) CAL 48.
31. 1955 AC 491, (1955) 1 ALL ER 292, HL
32. 1990 1 AC 723, (1989) 1 ALL ER 745
33. 1955 AC 516 n (1954) IR 8
34. (1963)2 QB 352, (1962)2 ALL ER 214
35. *Regazzoni* v. *K.C. Sethia*, (1958) AC 301 at pp. 319–22, (1957) 3 ALL ER 286 at 290–2.
36. See V.C. Govindaraj, Halsbury's Laws of India, *Conflict of Laws*, Vol. 10 (New Delhi: LexisNexis Butterworths, 2001), pp. 211–14.

3

Consecutive Stages of Conflict of Laws

DETERMINATION OF CONFLICTS

As has been stated earlier, conflict of laws comes into operation if, and only if, an issue or issues in a dispute presented before a municipal court for adjudication contain(s) a foreign element. The phrase 'foreign element', to repeat that which has already been said, refers to the presence of a foreign law or laws in the dispute other than the law of the forum and to the universally accepted fact that the two are in conflict with each other. Then, in that case, the adjudicating court chooses the appropriate rule of law that is directly relatable to the issue or issues to be resolved, and applies the same in order to render justice to the parties before it. There are four distinct stages in the conflict resolution process. They are:

(i) determination by the adjudicating court of its jurisdictional competence;

(ii) classification or characterization of the cause of action with a view to determining the legal category to which the disputed issue, which has a conflict element, can appropriately be allocated: for instance, whether the issue is one of breach of contract or of tort, whether it is one of matrimonial rights between the spouses or of succession, or, as the case may be, whether it is one of administration of the assets of the deceased or of succession in which case the governing law will be *lex fori* if it relates to the former or *lex domicilii* or *lex situs* depending upon whether the assets are movable or immovable;

(iii) identification by the court of the *lex causae* (that is, the law that governs the cause of action) based on which judgment is rendered; and

(iv) recognition and enforcement of the judgment by the concerned court, if that be warranted, for its due execution.

JUDICIAL JURISDICTION

The concept of jurisdiction in the context of its exercise by a court of law varies with the nature of the dispute, depending upon whether it is purely local (*in personam* or *in rem*) or transnational (having one or more foreign elements). Both local and transnational issues warrant an issue-based approach to resolving the dispute. If it be the former, namely local, due process of law requires (1) notice, (2) opportunity of being heard, (3) orderly procedure, and (4) a fair trial. However, in case there is a foreign element or elements, mere notice without giving an opportunity to the defendant to appear before the foreign court and put forth his or her defences is sure to render the judgment *brutum fulmen*. Besides, in conflict cases, *forum conveniens* plays a preponderant role in imparting respectability to the foreign judgment for it to be recognized and given effect to by the court in the other country to which it is addressed, seeking its recognition and enforcement.

If the court of forum renders judgment in a case involving a foreign element or elements without proper basis—in the sense that it lacks jurisdictional competence over the person or the thing (tangible or intangible), that the law of the state of forum does not authorize the court to exercise the state's judicial power, or, that the forum court exercises jurisdiction and renders judgment founded on an erroneous 'jurisdictional fact'—that judgment is not worth the paper on which it is written.[1] If the court is invested with jurisdiction in a conflicts case but fails to choose to apply the appropriate *lex causae*, that is, the law that governs the cause of action as determinable by reference to the substantive law that establishes the parties' legal relationships, such judgment, is nothing short of an exercise in futility.[2]

The bases of exercise of judicial jurisdiction by a state over individuals, as set out in the *Restatment (Second) of the Conflict of Laws* of the American Law Institute, 1971,[3] are the following: (a) presence; (b) domicile; (c) residence; (d) nationality or citizenship; (e) consent; (f) appearance in an action; (g) doing business in the state; (h) an act done in the state; (i) causing an effect in the state by an act done elsewhere; (j) ownership, use or possession of a thing in the state; (k) other relationships to the state which make the exercise of judicial jurisdiction reasonable.[4]

Further, the above mentioned criteria for the exercise of judicial jurisdiction by a court of forum ought to be read and understood reasonably and judiciously so as to render the said exercise meaningful. Such a meaningful exercise of judicial jurisdiction is brought out in bold relief in the explanatory Sections 28 to 39 of the *Restatement (Second) of American Conflict of Laws*. For instance, the presence of the defendant that invests the court with jurisdiction ought to be genuine, not fraudulent. The presence of the defendant is, again, subjected to two exceptions viz; (a) that such presence is not obtained by force or fraud or, (b) that the sovereign immunity available to certain persons like the heads of states, ambassadors, or instrumentalities of international organizations under public international law may divest the court of its jurisdiction, unless they choose to waive their sovereign immunity or, (c) that, to add yet another, the presence of the defendant within jurisdiction is not ephemeral, transient or fleeting. Needless to say, such an exercise of judicial jurisdiction, based on a transient or fleeting presence of the defendant within jurisdiction, is sure to render the judgment in the action *brutem fulmen* and to ensure its certain rejection by the foreign court to which it is sent for recognition and enforcement. We may here recall the words of wisdom of Justice Holmes, namely that 'the foundation of jurisdiction is physical power.'[5]

Presumably, such usurpation of jurisdiction is an outcome of purely domestic procedural law norm relating to the writ of summons.

Strange as it may seem, such usurpation of judicial jurisdiction, taking advantage of a fleeting presence within the jurisdiction of the defendant, a bird of passage, was given a clean bill of health by a court in England well over two hundred years ago.[6] More astonishing is that such an anachronistic basis of exercise of judicial jurisdiction should receive endorsement or reaffirmation, not too long ago, by Courts of Appeal in England![7]

Presumably, the English courts in the aforementioned cases failed to distinguish between presence and residence, the latter of which, *inter alia*, could serve as basis for the exercise of judicial jurisdiction. Judicial jurisdiction based on residence ought to stand a qualitative and a quantitative test. Equally, the outmoded English courts' approach to determining domicile which, in a majority of cases, rendered domicile uncertain throughout one's life is to be discarded as unworthy of a place in the private international law of the new millennium we have embarked upon. The concept of 'habitual residence', devised and nurtured by the Hague Conference on Private International Law, would serve as a suitable substitute for the twin concepts of residence and domicile.

Exercise of judicial jurisdiction based on nationality or citizenship, which is a political concept, may, perhaps, render such exercise of jurisdiction unreasonable or uncalled for in situations where the defendant establishes his or her domicile/habitual residence in a foreign state.

Once the judicial jurisdiction is established over a party to an action, the same continues throughout all subsequent proceedings which are the outcomes of the original cause of action. As is stated in Section 26 of the *Restatement (Second) of the Conflict of Laws* of the American Law Institute, 1971, reasonable notice and reasonable opportunity to be heard ought necessarily to be given to the party at every step of the subsequent proceedings arising out of the original cause of action. The bases of exercise of judicial jurisdiction, which according to the *Restatement (Second)* are eleven in number, call for illustration through cases for the benefit of the legal community.

The first four bases of jurisdiction set out in the *Restatement (Second)*, namely presence, domicile, residence, and nationality or citizenship have already been dealt with. As for the remainining seven, they call for a case-oriented approach which, as far as may be, is adhered to in this work, depending upon the availability of Indian case law in respect thereof. In the absence of Indian case law, academic integrity demands that classic decisions of courts of the common law world concerning any of the bases for the exercise of judicial jurisdiction should unreservedly be resorted to so as to lend respectability to the treatment.

Consent

Consent to submit to the jurisdiction of a foreign court may be (1) express, when the defendant contracts to submit to the jurisdiction or (2) implied, when the defendant presents himself before the court and contests the action brought against him on merits or, so to say, puts forth his defences to the action by filing a formal written statement.

Appearance in an Action

The phrase 'appearance in an action' calls for clarification. As implied consent overlaps with appearance in an action, namely entering defences, case law illustrations in respect of both seem to be coincident. If, on the contrary, the so-called appearance is solely directed to contesting the jurisdiction of the court, such appearance of the defendant before the court rules out any notion of submission to it.[8]

Closely following on the heels of appearance of the defendant before the court, conferring upon it jurisdiction is the common law basis for the exercise of jurisdiction adopted and applied by courts in India, namely that the cause of action arose within its jurisdiction coupled with presence of the defendant within the country at the time of the commencement of the action.[9]

The Restatement (Second), The Conflict of Laws, 1971, of the American Law Institute lays down the proposition that courts in the United States could exercise jurisdiction based merely on the cause of action arising within their jurisdiction, irrespective of the presence of the defendant in the United States at the commencement of the action. This proposition of the *Restatement* contradicts the view held by Justice Holmes of the Supreme Court of the United States in *Macdonald* v. *Maybee*, adverted to earlier, namely that the foundation of jurisdiction is physical power. Long before Justice Holmes's pronouncement of physical power serving as the basis for the exercise of judicial jurisdiction, the Privy Council in *Sirdar Gurdyal Singh* v. *Raja of Faridkot*, speaking through Lord Selborne, declared:

> In a personal action ... a decree pronounced *in absentem* by a foreign court, to the jurisdiction of which the defendant has not in any way submitted himself is by International Law an absolute nullity. He is under no obligation to obey it, and it must be regarded as a mere nullity by the court of every nation except [when authorized by special local legislation] in the country of the forum by which it was pronounced.[10]

Submission to a court's jurisdiction in conflicts cases includes the appearance of the defendant before the court in the character of a plaintiff in the forum in which he is afterwards sued.[11] However, it appears that it would not amount to submission even if he has appeared as a plaintiff in the same forum but in a different case.

WHAT AMOUNTS TO SUBMISSION?

If a defendant to an action pleads that the court in which he is sued lacks jurisdiction but, all the same, engages a counsel and allows himself to be cross-examined on issues that have a bearing on the merits of the case, such a conduct on the part of the defendant amounts to submission. The Madras High Court, in a case similar to the factual situation set out above, observed that, if the defendant's plea as to the lack of jurisdiction of the trial court found acceptance with the court that is likely to result in the dismissal of the case, such conduct on the part of the defendant clearly establishes his submission to the count's jurisdiction.[12]

Executing a power of attorney in favour of another empowering him to conduct on the executant's behalf litigation in a foreign court, also amounts to submission to the jurisdiction of that court and, accordingly, its judgment is binding on the executant.[13] In addition, in case the power of attorney holder fails to appear before the court and an *ex parte* decree is passed, such a decree will bind the executant.[14]

Voluntary appearance of the defendant before a court in a suit filed against him, followed by his defending the case would amount to submission.[15] Filing a written statement by the defendant to an action brought against him, even if he subsequently withdraws, would equally amount to submission.[16] When a suit is brought on a foreign judgment, it is not open to the defendant to plead that the court which passed the judgment had no jurisdiction, when he himself had submitted to the jurisdiction of the court that passed the decree and had not challenged it there.[17]

Filing a review petition also amounts to submission.[18]

WHAT DOES NOT AMOUNT TO SUBMISSION?

The court in the above mentioned case, namely *Sheo Tahel Ram* v. *Binack Shukul*, speaking through Sulaiman, C.J., observed that the submission of the defendant to an action before a foreign court must be prior to the passing of a decree by the court. Subsequent conduct does not retrospectively confer jurisdiction upon the court. The dissenting judge Niamatullah, J. disagreed with Sulaiman, C.J., on the issue of what would constitute submission. In the learned judge's view, even such subsequent conduct of the defendant has a bearing on his submission, if it appears that his staying away from his defence as such gives rise to the assumption that he had really felt that the plaintiff's claim was just and not resistable. In that case, according to the learned judge, he should be treated as having submitted to the jurisdiction of the court. In his view, part payment of the decretal amount could amount to submission.

The above reasoning of Niamatullah, J., so to say, is specious. Understandably, the Nagpur High Court in *Ramkisan Janakilal and another* v. *Seth Harmukharai Lachminarayan*,[19] rejected the *obiter* of Niamatuallah, J. and observed:

> The observation of Niamatuallah, J. was *obiter* because the learned judge did not hold in that case that the defendant had submitted to the jurisdiction of the foreign court by reason of any intention on his part to submit to that jurisdiction. It is difficult to subscribe to the view that mere intention on the part of the defendant to submit to the jurisdiction of the foreign court tantamounts to submission to that jurisdiction. The law does not normally take note of intention which is not translated into action.

Actually both Sulaiman Ag, C.J., (p. 692) and Niamatullah, J. (p. 694) acted on the rule that in order that a foreign judgment or decree should be binding on the defendant, the submission to jurisdiction must be before the passing of the judgment or the decree.

The four stages in the conflict resolution process are as under:

Jurisdiction of an Indian Court

This aspect of the matter has already been discussed elaborately with reference, particularly, to Indian cases. Therefore, it may not be necessary to quote English or other foreign cases on the preliminary question of assumption of jurisdiction by a municipal court in a matter involving conflict of laws.

CLASSIFICATION OF THE CAUSE OF ACTION

Having assumed jurisdiction, the stage is set for an Indian court to classify or categorize the cause of action. Here there are two hurdles to be crossed before the court spells out the nature of the dispute brought before it for resolution. In the first place, the case may be such that the legal category to which it belongs may pose a problem, especially when the dividing line between two legal categories in which the matter may fall is thin as, for instance, whether the suit is for breach of contract or for tort, whether it is one of succession to land or of matrimonial rights between the spouses or, again, whether it is one of administration of the estates of the deceased or of succession, and so on. The second hurdle may arise in cases where the Indian law and the foreign law hold diametrically opposed views on the classification of the subject matter of litigation such as, for instance, where the question of whether a will is revoked by marriage may be deemed by the forum as a question of matrimonial law but by the foreign legal system as a testamentary matter. But, these two hurdles are only apparent but not real for, the court of forum invariably classifies the cause of action based on the so-called 'essential general principles of professedly universal application of analytical jurisprudence and comparative law', unless there be agreement in the shape of a convention to which countries by and large are parties. This aspect of the matter is brought out in bold relief in the historic *Maltese Marriage Case*[20] decided by the court of appeal at Algiers in 1889, which served as exemplar for classification of the cause of action. The facts of the case as set out below are simple.

A husband and wife, both Maltese domiciliaries at the time of their marriage, acquired a French domicile. The husband bought land in France. After his death, his widow brought an action in France claiming, as per French law, a usufruct in one quarter of this land. The choice of law rules of France and Malta happened to be uniform in the sense that succession to land was governed by the *lex situs* and matrimonial rights by the *lex domicilii* at the time of the marriage. The issue that called for determination by the French court was whether the facts of the case raised a question of succession to land or of matrimonial rights. Whereas French law would characterize the matter as one of succession, Maltese law would, on the contrary, view it as one of matrimonial rights. Thus, the two countries' views on this question were diametrically opposed to each other. Even so, the French court, contrary to the prevailing practice of a court applying its own rule of classification that would only encourage forum shopping, displayed judicial statesmanship by applying the matrimonial law of Malta.

English courts, too, have exhibited from time to time the same kind of judicial statesmanship in matters of classification as borne out by two examples set out below. The first example is *De Nicols* v. *Curlier*.[21]

The facts of the case are briefly as follows: A husband and wife, both French nationals and domiciliaries, were married in Paris without making an express contract as to their proprietary rights. Accordingly, their property, present and future, became subject to the system of *communaute des biens* (that is, community of property) as per French law. The husband died domiciled in England and left a will disregarding his widow's rights under the French doctrine of community. The widow took proceedings in England to recover her community share.

As per English private international law, the proprietary rights of a spouse to movables are governed primarily by any contract, express or implied, that the parties may have made before marriage. In the absence of a contract the rights are determined by the law of the matrimonial domicile of the parties. Thus, the court was called upon to classify the right claimed by the widow as contractual or testamentary, depending upon which the choice could be exercized between the French law governing the contract and the English law governing testamentary questions. As per English internal law, *ex facie*, there was no contract entered into between them. Even so, the House of Lords ruled that the absence of an express contract between the spouses notwithstanding, the French rule of community of property applied on the basis of an implied contract between them. By this gesture of recognizing a foreign concept, the House of Lords widened the category of contracts as understood by English internal law.

Yet another instance of English courts exhibiting a truly international spirit in respect of classification is their readiness to abandon the English internal law distinction between realty and personalty in favour of the more universal distinction between movables and immovables.

Yet, again, the English internal law rule of regarding land in England subject to a trust for sale but not yet sold as one of personalty instead of realty by using the operation of the domestic doctrine of conversion, was supplanted by the universally accepted principle of categorizing it as immovable property governed by the *lex situs* and not as movable property governed by the *lex domicilii*.

However, the one and only exception of an English court not classifying a matter on the basis of *lex fori* is a situation where the *lex causae* is either the law of X or the law of Y both of which would classify it in the same manner, though differently from that of England.[22]

Selection of the *Lex Causae*

After allocating a matter to its correct legal category, the stage is set for the selection of the *lex causae* (that is, the law that governs the cause of action), which is vital to determine the rights and obligations of the parties. The court seized of a matter involving a foreign element is expected to faithfully honour the rules of conflict of laws in order to render justice to the parties before it. Such an approach on the part of the court is peremptory if miscarriage of justice is to be avoided. In this context, the performance of the English courts, barring a few exceptions, leaves much to be desired. Indian courts, too, are not above blame in this regard.[23]

The decision in *Leroux* v. *Brown*[24] is a classic example of miscarriage of justice where the English court invalidated a contract valid by the French law by applying an English procedural law namely the Statute of Frauds. That was an oral agreement between an English employer and a Frenchman by which the latter was to be employed for a period longer than a year. The Statute of Frauds, an English procedural law, required that an action shall not lie upon a contract not to be performed within the space of one year unless the agreement or some note or memorandum thereof was in writing signed by the defendant. The startling decision by the English court based on a purely domestic procedural law, turning a blind eye to the *lex causae* (that is, the French law) according to which, as aforesaid, the contract was valid, was nothing short of travesty of justice. This, as Cheshire rightly observes, strikes at the root of private international law and defeats one of its cardinal objects, namely of upholding rights duly acquired under the law that governs the cause of action. The decision of the English Court of Appeal in *Ogden* v. *Ogden* is yet another instance of making a mockery of rules of private international law that rights acquired or obligations incurred under the law that governs the cause of action (that is, *lex causae*) are to be recognized and given effect to wherever an action is brought in pursuance thereof. This fundamental rule of conflict of laws was, once again, set at naught by the court of appeal in this case. The facts of the case are briefly as follows:

A domiciled Frenchman, a minor aged nineteen, married an Englishwoman in England without obtaining the consent of his only surviving parent in contravention of Article 148 of the French Code which was prohibitive in nature. The Frenchman obtained an annulment of this marriage in a French court based on the said Article 148 of the French Code. The English wife subsequently married in England a domiciled Englishman. The Englishman brought an action before the court of appeal in England seeking a decree of nullity of his marriage with the respondent on the ground that her prior marriage with the Frenchman was still subsisting.

The court of appeal, strangely enough, construed article 148 of the French Code as a mere formality despite its being prohibitive in nature, rendering the marriage between the French minor and the English woman void for lack of parental consent. Any comment is surely superfluous. A decision such as this which strikes at the cardinal rule of private international law is not worth the paper on which it is written. At the same time, a decision of the English court in *Simonin* v. *Mallac*,[25] forty-eight years before *Ogden* v. *Ogden* was decided, correctly construed yet another provision of the Code Napoleon as no more than a formality, which was to the effect that the intending French minor spouses were to only approach their parents for their advice three times, each separated by a month; and if the parents were opposed to the marriage, at the end of the fourth month the marriage might take place despite parental disapproval. On a petition by the wife seeking a decree of nullity from the English court on the ground of want of parental consent, the court dismissed it holding thereby that the provision in question of the Code Napoleon was just a formality and nothing more.

The one and only classic decision of the English court was in Re Maldonado's Estate.[26] Here, a person domiciled in Spain died intestate, leaving assets to the extent of some £ 26,000 in England. As per Spanish law, the Spanish state would succeed to the assets in the absence of relatives.

This is in contrast to the English law which enables the state to take over the assets of the deceased as *bona vacantia* (that is, ownerless goods). Here the English court, true to the spirit of conflict of laws, selected the Spanish law as the *lex causae*.

We may, in conclusion, state the performance of the courts of England in the selection of the *lex causae* is a mixture of mingled sunshine and cloud.

I may here suggest that the Indian courts may learn to be discernible in the matter of selection of *lex causae* and not repeat the mistakes of the courts in England.

The Incidental Question

It is appropriate here to deal with the so-called 'incidental question' or 'preliminary question' in the context of determining the *lex causae* that governs the main issue. Courts ought to be more than satisfied before they come to the conclusion that after the determination of the main issue by recourse to the relevant choice of law rule, there is also an incidental question of equal importance that calls for the application of the forum's choice of law rule. The relevance of discovering a so-called 'incidental question' after determining the *lex causae* is suspect and for that reason only is to be approached with utmost caution. As to the relevance of an incidental question, one is reminded of the terminology used in the Section 6 of the Indian Evidence Act, 1872, which runs thus:

> Facts though not in issue are so connected with the fact in issue as to form part of the same transaction is relevant, whether they occurred at the same time and place or at different times and places. Rightly Ehrenzweig characterizes this so-called incidental or preliminary question, which necessitates the application of the forum's choice of law rule, as 'another miscreant of a conceptualism gone rampant.[27]

Professor Cheshire illustrates the concept of the incidental question by citing two decisions, one from England and another from Canada. The English case is *Lawrence* v. *Lawrence*.[28] The facts of the case are briefly as follows.

The first husband and his wife both Brazilian domiciliaries, were married in Brazil and lived there until 1970. In the same year the wife obtained a divorce in Nevada, USA, which was not recognized in Brazil, and married again the second husband in Nevada. On a petition by the second husband, addressed to a court in England seeking nullity of the second marriage, the English court dismissed the petition, thereby upholding the Nevada decree of divorce—an incidental question, based on the divorce recognition rules of England[29] as against the Brazilian law, the law of domicile of the wife and also the *lex causae* as per the main issue, by which she lacked capacity to marry again a second husband. The court of appeal, by upholding the validity of the second marriage, in effect gave primacy to the divorce recognition at the expense of that of capacity to marry. Curiously enough, in *Schwebel* v. *Ungar*[30] the Supreme Court of Canada on a more or less similar factual situation upheld the validity of the second marriage, thus giving primacy to capacity to marry at the expense of divorce recognition, even though, as per the choice of law rules of Ontario, the divorce would not be recognized.

In conclusion, we are persuaded to remark how dangerous it is to unearth a so-called incidental question and apply a choice of law rule on that basis.

Depeċage

As a corollary to the incidental question arises the question of depeċage (that is, picking and choosing). This, again, leads to manipulation by the party concerned in a dispute by recourse to forum shopping that may help characterize the main issue as an incidental issue and vice versa. This could be exemplified by reference to automobile accidents caused by either of the spouses in a third state, not the state of which they are domiciliaries. Such accidents may be viewed as negligence in the third state giving rise to liability in tort, whereas the law of domicile governing their status may, by the application of interspousal immunity, deny one spouse recovery, she/he being guilty of contributory negligence. In sum, the same remark that we made with reference to the incidental question equally applies to depeċage.

Application of the *Lex Causae*: *Renvoi*

The doctrine of *renvoi* (that is, remission or transmission), which manifests itself in the form of either partial *renvoi* or total or double *renvoi*, is a legal fiction which may sooner or later become extinct even in countries like England where it flourished in a limited area. With the emergence of international conventions in the private law area like the Hague Conventions on Private International Law or, as for that matter, the Rome Convention on the Law Applicable to Contractual Obligations, the doctrine of *renvoi* surely will become a thing of the past.

When there is a reference to a foreign law in the conflict resolution process, prudence and common sense would tell us that the reference is to the internal or domestic law of the country referred, and not to the rules of choice of law of the chosen country. However, even in countries like France which subscribes to the partial *renvoi*[31] or England which has adopted the double or total *renvoi*, which is also known as the foreign court theory, the doctrine may find its honourable exit once countries become parties to international conventions, as aforesaid, and suitable legislations are enacted by them incorporating the conventions. Here, it is appropriate to quote from *Cheshire and North's Private International Law* to highlight the very limited area of its applicability. It runs thus:

> [The] review of the principal decisions discloses that the total *renvoi* doctrine is not of general application. Its scope appears to be limited to certain matters concerning either status or the disposition of property on death. In countless cases dealing with such matters as torts, insurance, sale of movables, gifts *inter vivos* or *mortis causa*, mortgages, negotiable instruments, partnerships, dissolution of a foreign company and so on the English courts, when referred to the law of a foreign country, have never had the slightest hesitation in applying the internal law of the country.[32]

Cheshire and North's Private International Law sets out the limited area where the *renvoi* doctrine may, perhaps, find its relevance. They are in respect of the determination of the essential validity of a will[33] or intestate succession to movables[34] and the right or claim to foreign immovables.[35] However, in the matter of a disputed title to movables referred by the forum court to the law of their *situs*, the internal law that the court of the *situs* would apply in the particular circumstances of the case, and not the rules of choice of law of that court, would probably apply.[36]

In family law matters, the *renvoi* doctrine holds good in England with respect to recognition by the common law of legitimation by subsequent marriage (that is, *legitimatio per subsequens matrimonium*).[37] However, it is doubtful, according to Cheshire and North, whether the doctrine of *renvoi* applies to recognition of foreign legitimation under the Legitimacy Act, Section 3. Also the view is held by Cheshire and North that there is some authority for the application of the doctrine of *renvoi* to matrimonial property issues,[38] and to both formal[39] and essential[40] validity of marriage.

After all the exercise, pros and cons done heretofore on the subject of *renvoi*, taking note of the authentic views of publicists of renown, it is but appropriate to conclude on the following note. The decision of the English court of the Chancery Division in Re O'Keefe, foisting on the deceased the domicile of a country (that is, the so-called domicile of origin) in the matter of intestate succession, of whose succession laws she was no doubt 'profoundly and happily ignorant', does no credit to the foreign court theory. Cheshire, here, characteristically remarks: 'Comment is surely superfluous. A decision that is so out of touch with the realities of life and so calculated to defeat the expectations of the deceased is not a good advertisement for the foreign court theory.'[41]

Indian Courts and the Doctrine of *Renvoi*

The doctrine of *renvoi* does not form part of the conflicts resolution process in India. Courts in India have chosen to apply the domestic or internal law of the country, if that be the *lex causae* that calls for application for resolving the dispute where there is a foreign element.

The proper law of contract, which may be either the *lex loci contractus* or *lex loci solutionis*, means the domestic rules of the chosen legal system to the exclusion of its rules of choice of law.[42] The doctrine of *renvoi* was categorically rejected by the Supreme Court of India with reference to the law of contract in the leading case of *National Thermal Power Corporation* v. *Singer Company*.[43] It is a fundamental principle of conflict of laws that questions relating to rights over immovables are governed by the *lex situs* (that is, the law of the country where the immovable is situated).[44] *Lex situs* can only mean the domestic law of the country where the immovable is situated to the exclusion of the country's rules for choice. This clearly shows that the doctrine of *renvoi*, partial or total, has no place whatsoever in the Indian conflict of laws.

Even in matters of succession, testate or intestate, as determined by the choice of law rules, the reference is to the internal or domestic law of the chosen country's legal system to the exclusion of *renvoi*, partial or total.[45]

NOTES

1. *Schibsby* v. *Westenholz*, (1870) LR 6QB 155.
2. *Y. Narasimha Rao* v. *Y. Venkatalakshmi*, AIR 1991 SC 821.
3. *Restatement (Second), Conflict of Laws*, American Law Institute (St. Paul, Minnesota: American Law Institute Publishers, 1971).
4. Section 28 of the *Restatement (Second)*.
5. *Macdonald* v. *Maybee*, (1917) 243 US 90, 91.
6. *Carrick* v. *Hancock*, (1895) 12 TLR 59.
7. See the decisions in *Colt Industries Inc.* v. *Sarlie*, (No. 1) (1966) ALL ER 673; (1966) WLR 440 and *Maharanee of Baroda* v. *Wildenstein*, (1972) 2 QB 283; (1972) 2 ALL ER689.
8. *Molony* v. *Gibbons*, (1810), 2 camp 502; *Guard* v. *Clermont* (1914) 3 KB 145; *Mladinich* v. *Kohn*, 250 MISS 138; 164 SO 2d 785 (1964); Tex. Rules Civ. Proc. 120 a (Vernon's supp. 1962).
9. *Chormal Balchand* v. *Kasturi Chand Seraogi and Another*, 1.LR LXiii CAL 1033; 40 CWN 591; *Schibsby* v. *Westenholz*, (1870) LR 6Q B158; *Rousillon* v. *Rousillon*, (1880) 14 Ch. D351.
10. (1894) AC 670; (1894) LR 211. A.171; 1.LR 22 CAL 222; 4 MLJ 267. The prevalent practice in the United States relating to special appearance directed to questioning the jurisdiction of the court is not to treat such appearance as submission, although in *York* v. *Texas*, 137 US 15 (1890), the Supreme Court of the United States had held to the contrary.
11. *Chormal Balachand* v. *Kasturichand Seraogi and Another*, ILR LXiii 1042.
12. *Subramania Aiyer* (Appellant) v. *Annaswami Iyer* (Respondent), AIR (1948) 35 MAD 203.
13. *Janno Hassan Sait* v. *Mahamad Ohuthu*, AIR 1925 MAD 155; *Ramanathan Chettiar* v. *Kalimuthu Pillai*, ILR (1940) 37 MAD 163; and *Asanalli Nagoor Meera & others* v. *K.M. Mahadu Meera & Others*, AIR 1926 MAD 259.
14. *Ramkisan Janakilal and another* (Appellants) v. *Seth Harmukhari Lachminarayan* (Defendant-Respondent), AIR 1955 NAG 103.
15. *Rama Iyer (died) Lakshmana Iyer* v. *Krishna Pattar*, (1915) MLJ 148.
16. *T. Sundaram Pillai* v. *Kandaswami Pillai*, AIR 194 MAD 387.
17. *Ganga Prasad and another* (Defendants) v. *Ganeshi Lal and Others* (Plaintiffs), ILR (1913) ALL 119. The Allahabad High Court in the course of its judgment quoted with approval the English case of *Emanuel* v. *Symon*, (1908) 1 K.B. 302 at p. 309.

18. *Sheo Tahel Ram* v. *Binack Shukul*, AIR (1931) ALL 689.

19. AIR 1955 NAG 103 p. 105

20. *Anton* v. *Bartolo, Clunet*, (1891), 1171. See also Robertson, *Characterization in the Conflict of Laws*, pp. 158–162, as also Beckett (1834), 15 BYBIL 46, 50, note 1 and Wolff, *Private International Law*, Second Edition, (1950), p. 149.

21. (1900) AC 21

22. See *Cheshire and North's Private International Law*, Thirteenth Edition, (London, Edinburg, Dublin: LexisNexis Butterworths, 1995), pp. 38–9.

23. See *Y. Narasimha Rao* v. *Y. Venkatlakshmi*, AIR 1991 SC 821 p. 831.

24. (1852) 12 CB 801; see also *Mahadevan* v. *Mahadevan*, (1964) p. 233, (1962) 3 ALL ER 1108.

25. (1860) 2 SW&TR 67

26. (1954), p. 223, (1953) 2 ALL ER 300

27. A.A. Ehrenzweig, *A Treatise on Conflict of Laws*, (1962), p. 340.

28. (185) FAM 106

29. Recognition of Divorces and Legal Separations Act, 1971; the result would now find legal justification under Section 50 of the Family Law Act, 1986.

30. (1963) 42 DLR (2d) 622; affd 48 DLR (2d) 644; Lysyk (1965) 43 CAN BR 363; Webb (1965) 14 ICLQ 659

31. Forgo's case, (1883) 10 clunet 63.

32. *Cheshire and North's Private International Law*, Thirteenth Edition, p. 64.

33. Re Annesley, (1926) Ch. 692; Re Ross, (1930) 1 Ch. 377; Re Adams, (1967) IR 424.

34. Re O'Keefe, (1940) Ch. 124, (1940) 1 All ER 216; Re Thom, (1987) 40 DLR (4th) 184.

35. Re Ross, (1930) 1 Ch. 377; Re Duke of Willington (1947) Ch. 506, Re Bailey, (1985) 2NZLR 656; Re Schneider's Estate, 96 NYS 2d 652.

36. *Winkworth* v. *Christie, Mason and Woods Ltd.* All the same, in *Macmillan Inc.* v. *Bishopgate Trust*, (No. 3) 1996 1 WLR 387, it was said at (p. 405) that *renvoi* did not apply to the choice of the law to determine who has title to shares in a company.

37. Re Askew (1930) 2 Ch. 259.

38. *Vladi* v. *Vladi*, (1987) 39 DLR (4th) 563.

39. *Tazanowska* v. *Tazanowski*, (1957) p. 301, (1957) 2 ALL ER 563; *Hooper* v. *Hooper*, (1959) 2 ALL ER 575.

40. *R* v. *Brentwood Superintendent Registrar of Marriages.* According to Cheshire and North, the actual decision in this case would now be different by reason of Section 50, Family Law Act, 1986.

41. G.C. Cheshire, *Private International Law*, Fourth Edition (Oxford and Clarendon Press, 1952), p. 80.

42. *National Thermal Power Corporation* v. *Singer Co.*, AIR 1993 SC 998, (1992) 3 SCC 551 at 562, (1992) 1 Scale 1034.

43. Ibid. The Supreme Court of India opined that the expression 'proper law' refers to the substantive principle of the domestic law of the chosen system and not its conflict of law rules; the law of contract is not affected by the doctrine of *Renvoi*.

44. *Chutta Veettil Puthu Parambil Muhammad Koya* v. *Panmanichandakath Katheessa Bi*, (1944) 2 MAD LJ 305 p. 365.

45. *R. Viswanathan* v. *Rukn-ul-Mulk Syed Abdul Wajid (dead)*, AIR 1963 SC 1, (1963) 3 SCR 22.

4

Domicile and Residence

MEANING AND FUNCTION OF DOMICILE

Questions relating to the personal status of an individual are governed by his personal law. The purpose behind the determination of a person's country of domicile is to identify his personal law. The country of domicile of a person defines the legal relationship between the individual concerned and a territory with a distinctive legal system which governs his personal law.[1]

The domicile of a person is in that country in which he either has or is deemed by law to have his permanent home.[2] In *Central Bank of India Ltd.* v. *Ram Narain*,[3] the Supreme Court of India observed that every individual is regarded as belonging, at every stage in his life, to some community consisting of all persons domiciled in a particular country; the rules as to domicile are such that this legal idea may not correspond to social reality. The Allahabad High Court in *Sharafat Ali Khan* v. *State of Uttar Pradesh*[4] made a significant observation, namely that although a person may have no permanent home, the law requires him to have a domicile and law may attribute to him a domicile in a country which, in reality, he has no domicile in. Even if a person has more than one home, he may be credited with only one domicile for any purpose.[5] Likewise, a person may have his home in one country, but may be deemed to be domiciled in another.[6]

Domicile denotes a relationship between a person and a country, but can never arise from membership of a group as distinguished from the country in which the group is domiciled; however, the municipal law of the country of domicile, as is the case with India, may itself distinguish between different classes of its subjects such as Hindus, Muslims, Christians, et cetera, and apply different rules based on religion. Consequently, even after the domicile has been ascertained, it becomes necessary to ascertain the religious identity.

LIMITS OF DOMICILE AREAWISE

On the question of the area of domicile, Chagla, C.J., of the Bombay High Court in *State* v. *Narayandas Mangilal Dayame*[7] observed: '... all those persons who have, or whom the law deems to have their permanent home within the territorial limits of a single system of law, are domiciled in the country over which the system extends; and they are domiciled in the whole of that country although their home may be fixed at a particular spot within it.' In a federal union, such as India, certain subjects may be under the competence of the Union Parliament and, accordingly, the whole federation will be subject to a single system of law and an individual within the federation may be spoken of as domiciled in the federation as a whole; certain other subjects may be under the competence of the states constituting the federation and the individual, in that case, will be deemed to be domiciled in the concerned state in respect of the subjects so allotted to it under the constitution.[8]

DETERMINATION OF ACQUISITION OF DOMICILE

If a question as to the acquisition of Indian domicile presents itself for resolution before an Indian court, it will exclusively fall back upon principles of Indian law governing choice of law rules.[9]

DOMICILE IS A MUST FOR EVERYONE

No person can be without a personal law. Similarly, no one by choice *vel non* can remain without a domicile. There are two kinds of domiciles, namely domicile of origin which he acquires at birth and domicile of choice which he acquires by volition. The domicile of origin of a person will remain with him and govern his legal status until and unless he acquires a new domicile (that is, a domcile of choice).[10]

DOMICILE OF ORIGIN AND DOMICILE OF CHOICE: NATURE AND CHARACTER

The domicile of origin of a person is determined by operation of law, in the sense that the law attributes to him a domicile through the father, if legitimate, or through the mother, if illegitimate.[11] *A contrario*, an individual acquires a domicile of choice by moving to another country and setting up a home there with the intention of living there indefinitely.

Secondly, the domicile of origin is retained until the person concerned acquires a new domicile called the domicile of choice, as aforesaid, by taking up a fixed habitation in a country which is not the domicile of origin[12] and which the author would choose to designate as his 'habitual residence' by making that country his permanent home *animo et facto*.[13]

By virtue of Section 13 of The Indian Succession Act, 1925,[14] the English doctrine of the revival of the domicile of origin *proprio vigore*[15] does not form part of, and may we say is rejected by, the Indian conflict of laws.[16]

The English doctrine of indestructibility of domicile of origin, it being only kept in abeyance and never destroyed, thus transcending even the European concept of *lex patriae* (that is, law of nationality), is rejected not only in India but also in New Zealand,[17] in Austrialia[18] in matters of matrimonial proceedings, and in Canada.[19]

Therefore, we may say that the doctrine of revival of domicile of origin established in *Bell* v. *Kennedy*[20] is, if we may say so, given a seeming burial. It has no place either on the Continent of Europe or in the United States of America.

DOMICILE OF DEPENDENT PERSONS

There are three categories of dependent persons, namely married women, minors and mentally retarded persons. Law, as we all know, is slow to come to grips with social realities. In the absence of legislative reforms, common law, which is the prerogative of courts, cannot conceivably render justice that is remedial, prompt, and efficacious in keeping with the changing structure of the society and the felt necessities of the times. Even in advanced countries like England, not to talk of Third World countries to which India belongs, reforms were ushered in rather belatedly, to be exact, only in the last quarter of the twentieth century. The tyranny of the husband, based on the outmoded rule of law—namely the domicile of a married woman being considered the same as, and changing with, the domicile of the husband—manifested itself in the shape of matrimonial adventures on the part of the husband, inflicting untold miseries on the forlorn wife. It is high time that civilized countries wake up from their slumber and come to the rescue of the hapless married woman and her offspring, in case nature also conspires against her in the shape of children being born of her marriage.

The first significant legislative reform in England to alleviate 'the last barbarous relic of a wife's servitude'[21] is the British Parliament's passing of the Domicile and Matrimonial Proceedings Act, 1973, which came into force on 1 January 1974. Two sections, in particular, invite attention that liberated a married woman and a minor from the outmoded legal concept of their domicile being inexorably linked to the husband in the case of the married woman and the father in the case of the minor. Section 1(1) provides that the domicile of a married woman, instead of being the same as her husband's by virtue only of marriage, be ascertained by reference to the same factors as in the case of any other individual capable of having an independent domicile. Though a minor attains majority at the age of eighteen, Section 3(1) of the Act provides that a person becomes eligible to have an independent domicile when he attains the age of sixteen or marries under that age.

Married Woman

As for a married woman, Section 1(1) of the Act provides that the Act applies to her whether she is married before or after 1 January 1974, thus making the Act retrospective in one sense. Section 1(1) is accompanied by Section 1(2), which is of a transitional character, by which it is provided that a married woman whose marriage had taken place before 1 January 1974, acquires her husband's domicile of dependence, which is to be treated as her domicile of choice, if it is not also her domicile of origin, unless and until it is changed by her acquiring another domicile either on or after that date.[22]

From the above, it appears, that her own domicile prior to her marriage is left unaddressed. In order to overcome this lacuna, the Law Commission recommended that the domicile of any person at any date after the enactment of the new rules should be determined on the basis of the new rules as if they had always been in force. In the absence, therefore, of the reformulation of the law of domicile in respect of any person at any date and on the strength of the Law Commission's recommendation, the old law is still in force and, accordingly, Section 1(1) of the Act is not retrospective in any other sense.

Minors

The law, as it stood in England before the passing of the Domicile and Matrimonial Proceedings Act, 1973, was that the domicile of a minor (that is, a person under the age of sixteen) was that of his father if he be legitimate, or that of his mother if he be illegitimate or a fatherless child, as compared to a legitimate child whose father is alive, was not clear. On this point, there is no authority barring a solitary decision of the nineteenth century, namely Re Beaumont.[23] That was a case of a Scottish widow, domiciled in Scotland, who, after her remarriage to an Englishman, left for London to live with her second husband, taking alongwith her all but one of her minor children. The question arose as to the domicile of the minor child left behind her in Scotland and taken care of by an aunt. The court held that the domcile of the child left behind in Scotland continued to be Scottish. It appears, however, that the domicile of a legitimated child, may be by a subsequent marriage between the parents, would be dependent on that of his father.

However, in the case of a minor girl, her dependency on her father or mother, as the case may be, would be only upto her marriage, after which she would take on the domicile of her husband.

As has already been mentioned under section 'Domicile of Dependent Persons', Section 3(1) of the Domicile and Matrimonial Proceedings Act, 1973, lays down the rule that a child could acquire an independent domicile when he attains the age of sixteen or marries under that age. Though, as per the English domestic law, marriage between persons either of whom is below sixteen is void,[24] it is not the case with countries like Austria and Hungary on the Continent of Europe where such marriages are valid. An anomalous situation would emerge if after marriage which is valid as per the *lex loci celebrationis*, the parties choose to set up their matrimonial home in England where the marriage as per its domestic law is void. In case the validity of the marriage itself is in issue, an English court may have to hold the marriage void. If that be not the case, in the sense that the validity or otherwise of the marriage becomes an incidental question, then the English domestic law by which the marriage is void can be given a go by.[25]

Domicile of Dependent Children: The 1973 Act vis-à-vis The Common Law Rules

The common law rules relating to domicile of dependency have undergone a sea change, viewed in the light of the Domicile and Matrimonial Proceedings Act, 1973. Section 4 of the Act imparts flexibility to the common law rules. In particular, Section 4(2)(a) of the Act provides that the domicile of a dependent child whose parents are alive but living apart shall be that of his mother if he has his home with her and no home with his father. Section 4(2)(b) provides further that the child would take on the domicile of the mother if he has acquired his mother's domicile as contemplated in Section 4(2)(a) and has not since then had a home with his father. We infer from the latter provision that a child who has his home with his mother would retain his mother's domcile, though he may cease to live with her, provided he does not later have a home with his father. Section 4(3), which we may deem as a corollary to the aforesaid provisions, lays down the rule that a child who has acquired his mother's domicile, in pursuance of the aforesaid provisions, would retain it even after her death unless and until he has a home with his father. Section 4(4), however, retains the previously existing rules, namely that an illegitimate child and a child whose father is dead takes on the mother's domicile.

An adopted child under the common law, which has been given statutory fiat, is equated with a child born in lawful wedlock.[26] Accordingly, it follows that the domicile of an adopted child under sixteen years of age is the same as that of a legitimate child of his adopted parent or parents.

Morris infers from the above—which appears to the author incontrovertible—that the domicile of a legitimate child whose parents are both dead or of an illegitimate child whose mother alone is dead, cannot be changed at all.[27]

The domicile of a dependent child, which, as a result of a change in his parents' domicile or of legitimation, is a domicile of dependency and not a domicile of origin.[28] Morris, by recourse to the English doctrine of revival of domicile of origin, which is rejected under the Indian conflicts rules, as aforesaid,[29] here argues that if the child were to abandon later in his life one domicile of choice without at the same time acquiring another, his domicile at birth, and not his domicile of dependency, will revive. He further argues from the above, that if the domicile of origin of an adopted child be deemed to be the domicile of the adoptive parent or parents at the time of his adoption and not his original domicile of origin, it leads to the conclusion that it is one instance in English law under which a domicle of origin can be changed.[30]

Mentally retarded persons

A mentally retarded person under the English common law cannot, as a general rule, acquire a domicile of choice and would, therefore, retain the domicile he had when he became insane. Lacking as does his own independent will, he can neither acquire nor lose a domicile. His domicile cannot be changed either by the person in whose charge he is.

Lunacy or insanity is a question of fact which has to be ascertained by a formal inquiry. A lunatic is not to be equated with a dependent person. The issue of whether or not he could acquire or lose a domicile is to be treated as a question of fact.

Morris spells out an exception to the rule that a mentally disordered person retains the domicile he had when he became insane. If in case a dependent child becomes insane and remains so even after attaining the age of sixteen, the appropriate parent has power to change his domicile even after he attains that age. Whether the power is exercised or not is a question of fact.

The English Law Commission, in Part VI of its treatment of the Law of Domicile, proposed that an adult lacking the capacity to form the requisite intention to acquire a domicile would be treated as having acquired the domicile of the country with which he was for the time being most closely connected. When he regains his capacity, he would retain the domicile he had at that time and, thereafter, be legally competent to acquire a new domicile as per the rules applicable to adults in general.[31]

DOMICILE OF CORPORATIONS

The concept of domicile is more appropriate if applied to individuals than to corporations which are in essence fictitious entities created by law and subjected to legal controls. Such legal controls take the shape of sending summons by courts to corporate entities behind which are only individuals who act on their behalf, to file a return of the income earned by them, to sue and be sued for contravening the law mostly in the area of civil wrongs and to bring them within the ambit of law, substantive and procedural, when there takes place amalgamation among them, or emergence of subsidiaries, or, as for that, their dissolution or their winding up.

PRESENCE

The presence of a corporation within a country, as has been pointed out above, enables courts to serve summons on it and exercise jurisdiction over it for the purpose of resolving any dispute to which it is a party. This aspect of the matter has thoroughly been examined earlier in Chapter 3 under section 8 'Judicial Jurisdiction'.

RESIDENCE

The residence of a company is of great importance in the field of taxation. As Lord Loreburn of the House of Lords observes, '... a company cannot eat or drink but it can keep house and do business'.[32] Our endeavour, therefore, is to find out where it keeps house and does business. Under the common law, a company is regarded as having residence in the country where the centre of control exists, that is, where the seat and directing power of the affairs of the company abide. This aspect of the matter came up for judicial consideration and resolution in an early case of the Exchequer Division in England in *Cesena Sulphur Co.* v. *Nicholson*.[33] The ruling in this case based on the central control test has repeatedly been approved and followed, with the result that it has become a binding precedent.

The Cesena Company was incorporated in England under the Companies Act for the purpose of taking over and working sulphur mines at Cesena in England. But the actual manufacture and sale of sulphur took place in Italy under the administrative direction and control of an Italian delegation, including the managing director, who was permanently resident in Cesena. The products were never sent to England. Besides, various elements appertaining to the company such as the registration of the company, keeping of books of accounts, and the residence of two-thirds of the shareholders were all in Italy. As against these preponderent factors connected with the business of the company, the London connection of the company was evidenced by its memorandum of association that set up a Board of Directors in London which controlled the 'sale, order, direction and management' of 'the working of the company's mines, the mode of disposal thereof, and the general business of the company'. Added to these, the meetings of the shareholders took place in London and it was there that dividends were declared.

Taking note of the fact that every act of the company relating to management was done in London which served as the main place of business for the company, the court adjudged that the company was resident in England and that, therefore, it was liable to pay income tax upon the whole of its profits, wherever earned.

The above ruling of the Exchequer Division based on the central control test was reaffirmed by the House of Lords thirty years later in the leading case *De Beers Consolidated Mines Ltd.* v. *Howe*. The House of Lords, speaking through Lord Loreburn, declared that 'the real business is carried on where the central management and control actually abide.'[34] The rulings of the Exchequer Division in the Cesena case and the House of Lords in the *De Beers case* upholding the central management and control test found its echo in two other cases, namely *Swedish Central Rail Co. Ltd.* v. *Thompson*[35] and *Egyptian Delta Land and Investment Co.* v. *Todd*.[36] Lord Atkinson of the House of Lords entered a caveat to the ruling in the Swedish case, namely that the company was resident both in England and in Sweden. According to His Lordship that since

> the residence is where the central control and management abide, then, unless a thing can have two or three different and separate centres, it would appear to me to be quite impossible, according to the ordinary use of language, that the 'central control and management' of a company can at the same time abide in two or more different and separated places.[37]

On the analogy of an individual—that he cannot at any time be without a domicile—corporations which possess corporate personality also have a domicile and their domicile is in their places of incorporation. Unlike an individual, the domicile of a corporate entity remains unchanged, even if it carries on business elsewhere.[38] The nationality of a corporate entity, likewise, is the place of its incorporation.

DOMICILE, NATIONALITY, AND RESIDENCE

Ordinary Residence and Habitual Residence

The concept of 'domicile', as interpreted and applied by courts in England, has, in many instances, led to uncertainty, incongruity, and, may we say, with due apologies, bordering on absurdity. It might have appeared simple to Lord Cranworth to define domicile when he observed: 'By domicile, we mean home, the permanent home,' and added, 'if you do not understand your permanent home, I am afraid that no illustration drawn from foreign writers or foreign languages will very much help you to it.'[39] It is easier said than done. We may only have to turn to decisions such as *Winans* v. *A.-G.*[40] and *Ramsay* v. *Liverpool Royal Infirmary*[41] to learn that whatever may be the length of stay of a person in a country, courts would choose to go into the entire gamut of his life with a view to elicit his intention, the most elusive factor, and credit that person with a domicile in a country which he might have abandoned for good; or, for that matter, by a whimsical reading of his animus coupled with factum of residence foisted on him a domicile in a country, even though his stay in that country may be no more than an overnight stay.[42] Equally amusing is the concept of 'domicile of origin' which would stage a comeback when the person concerned has given up a domicile of choice and has not yet chosen another to substitute for it.[43] On top of it all, the decision in *Re O'Keefe*[44] is astounding; may we say a laughing stock, in that a person was credited with a domicile in a country which was neither her country of birth nor the country where she resided for the best part of her life, but the country of domicile of her father at the time of her birth of whose succession laws, as Chesire remarks, 'she was profoundly and happily ignorant'; and 'under the law of which it was impossible in the circumstances for her to claim citizenship.'[45]

NOTES

1. See V.C. Govindaraj, *Conflict of Laws*, Halsbury's Laws of India Series, Vol. 10 (New Delhi: LexisNexis Butterworths, 2001), p. 215. In the case *State* v. *Narayandas Mangilal Dayame*, AIR 1958 BOM 68 p. 72, (1957) 59 BOM LR 901 (FB), the Bombay High Court observed:

> In India, the personal law which applies to a Hindu or a Muslim is not based upon domicile. His personal law is not the result of a particular part of India in which he happens to reside. He carries his personal law with him wherever he goes. Personal law is the result of certain precepts in his religion or in his sacred books which apply to him by reason of the fact that he follows a particular religion. Therefore the expression 'domicile' used in any state or provincial law is a misnomer and it does not carry with it the implication which that expression has when used in (the) context of international law.

Chagla, C.J., observed in the case quoted above, namely *State* v. *Narayandas Mangilal Dayame*, AIR 1958 BOM 68 p. 71, that: '... All those persons who have, or whom the law deems to have their permanent home within the territorial limits of a single system of law, are domiciled in the country over which the system extends; and they are domiciled in the whole of that country although their home may be fixed at a particular spot within it.' See also the following cases: *Michael Anthony Rodrigues* v. *State of Bombay*, AIR 1956 BOM 729 pp. 729–30; *Central Bank of India Ltd.* v. *Ram Narain*, AIR 1955 SC 36, (1954) Cr LJ 331.

2. AIR 1955 SC 36, (1954), Cr. LJ 331

3. *Sharafat Ali Khan* v. *State of Uttar Pradesh*, AIR 1960 All 637, (1959) ILR 1 All 729.

4. AIR 1960 ALL 637, (1959) ILR 1 All.729

5. *Thomas Edmond Teignmouth Shore* v. *Hugh Carey Morgan*, (1935) ILR 47 CAL 869.

6. Ibid.

7. AIR 1958 BOM 68 p. 71 (FB) per Chagla, C.J.

8. Despite the fact the Republic of India is defined as a Union of States, giving us the impression that India is multi-domiciliary, in reality it is apt to describe India as uni-domiciliary. See judicial opinion on the subject of Indian domicile is inferable from decided cases such as *Kamlabai* v. *Devram*, AIR 1955 BOM 300 p. 302, (1955) ILR BOM 749, (1955) 57 BOM LR 768. In that case Justice Gajendragadkar (as he then was) observed: '... whether or not the Constituion of India permits a plea of dual citizenship and dual domicile in dealing with the question of application of laws passed by different states, it would be permissible to resort to the theory of domicile, though different domiciles to which resort would be taken may in a sense be

fictitious,' at p. 305 (AIR, p. 305). Justice Shah, J., in his individual judgment of the abovementioned case observes: '... Strictly speaking the rules of private international law apply when there is a conflict of different sovereign states; but there is authority for the proposition that where the law of one province in India is different from (the) law in another province, the two provinces must be regarded as analogous to two sovereign states.'

9. *Smt. Satya* v. *Teja Singh*, AIR 1975 SC 105, (1975) SCC (Cr.) 50.

10. *Carolina Das Santos* v. *Dominic Joseph Pinto*, (1971) ILR 41 BOM 687; *Michael Anthony Rodrigues* v. *State of Bombay*, AIR 1956 BOM 729, (1956) ILR BOM 954, (1956) 58 Bom 825; *Thomas Edmund Teignmouth Shore* v. *Hugh Carey Morgan*, (1933) ILR 42 CAL 869.

11. Ibid.

12. Section 10, The Indian Succession Act, 1925.

13. *Carolina Das Santos* v. *Dominic Joseph Pinto*, AIR 1916 BOM 167, (1917) ILR 4 BOM 687, 36 IC 227.

14. Section 13, The Indian Succession Act, 1925: 'A new domicile continues until the former domicile has been resumed, or another has been acquired.'

15. *Santos* v. *Pinto*, 41 BOM 687.

16. The rejection of the doctrine of revival of the domicile of origin under the Indian conflict of laws is the outcome of Section 13 of the Indian Succession Act, 1925.

17. Section 11, Domicile Act, 1976.

18. Domicile Act, 1982

19. The Domicile and Habitual Residence Act, 1983, of Manitoba.

20. (1868) LR 1 Sc. & Div 307, 5 SLR 566, 6 Macq 69, HL

21. *Gray* v. *Formosa*, (1963) p. 289, 267, per Lord Denning M.R.

22. *I.R.C.* v. *Duchess of Portland*, (1982) Ch. 314.

23. (1893) 3 Ch. 490

24. Section 2, Marriage Act, 1949. See *Pugh* v. *Pugh*, (1951) p. 482 where the marriage between an English colonel and an Austrian girl under sixteen was held void. Interestingly enough, in *Mohamed* v. *Knott*, (1969) 1 QB 1 where a marriage between a thirteen-year-old Nigerian girl and a Nigerian twice her age was held valid as per the Nigerian law, Nigeria being the prenuptial domicile of both the parties.

25. See Willis L.M. Reese, 'Marriage in American Conflict of Laws', *The International and Comparative Law Quarterly*, Vol. 26 (1977), p. 952.

26. Section 39(1)(5), Adoption Act, 1976.

27. J.H.C. Morris, *The Conflict of Laws*, Fourth Edition (Sweet & Maxwell, 1993), p. 28.

28. *Henderson* v. *Henderson*, (1967) p. 77.

29. Section 13, The Indian Succession Act, 1925.

30. Ibid. See also Sir Peter North and J.J. Fawcett, *Cheshire and North's Private International Law*, Thirteenth Edition (London, Edinburgh, Dublin: LexisNexis Butterworths, 1999), pp. 153–6. The Law Commission in England proposed new rules to replace those incorporated in the 1973 Act. A child should be domiciled in that country with which he is, for the time being, most closely connected. A child's domicile would be presumed to be the country of domicile of his parents if that be the same, and that, besides, he had his home with either or both of them. The child in that case is presumed, unless the contrary be shown, to be domiciled in that country with which he is most closely connected. If, on the other hand, his parents were not domiciled in the same country and he had his home with one, and not the other, the presumption is that the child is most closely connected with the country in which the parent with whom he had his home was domiciled. There is no room for presumption in cases where the parents were domiciled in separate countries as the child had his home with both of them, nor where the child had his home with mother. For the purposes of these rules, 'parent' would include parents who are not married to one another; there would be no longer separate rules applicable to legitimate, illegitimate and legimated children. Further, no rules were proposed in respect of adopted children whose adoptive parents will be the parents to whom the rules will refer (see Morris, pp. 28–9).

31. See Morris, p. 29.

32. *De Beers Consolidated Mines Limited* v. *Howe*, (1906) AC 455 at 458.

33. (1876), 1 EX.D. 428

34. De Beers caset p. 458

35. (1925) AC 495 p. 508

36. (1929) AC 1

37. Swedish Case, p. 274.

38. *Gasque* v. *I.R.C.*, (1940) 2 KB 80.

39. *Whicker* v. *Hume*, (1858), 7 HL Cas. 124, p. 160.

40. (1904) AC 287

41. (1930) AC 588

42. *Hoskins* v. *Mathews*, (1856), 8 De GM & G 13, p. 28.

43. *Udny* v. *Udny*, (1869) LR 1 SC & Div. 441, *H.L. and Bell* v. *Kennedy*, (1868), LR 1 SC & Div. 307, H.L.

44. (1940) Ch. 124, (1940) 1 All ER 216

45. North and Fawcett, *Cheshire and North's Private International Law*, Thirteenth Edition (London, Edinburgh, Dublin: LexisNexis Butterworths, 1999), p. 59.

5

The Law of Obligations

FOREIGN CONTRACTS

The law of obligations consists of the law of contracts and the law of torts. The law of obligations, whether it be contract or tort, is the outcome of the act of parties which gives rise to a legal obligation. Whereas in the case of a contract the legal obligation is retrospective, in the case of a tort, on the other hand, it is prospective and pathological, as Professor Morris would prefer to characterize it.

Foreign Contracts and the Conflicts Resolution Process

The traditional approach to resolving conflicts in the area of foreign contracts was based on the vested or acquired rights theory propounded by Dicey in England and Beale in the United States. This theory held sway over courts in the common law world and, more particularly, in the United States, till the first half of the twentieth century. According to Professor Beale, the Reporter of the Original (that is, First) *Restatement of Conflict of Laws* of the American Law Institute, 1934,

> issues of the validity of a foreign contract are determined by the law of the place of contracting, which was the place where occurred the last act necessary under the forum's rules of offer and acceptance to give the contract binding effect, assuming, hypothetically, that the local law of the place where the act occurred rendered the contract binding; and that in respect of 'issues of performance [they] are determined by the local law of the place of performance.

The above enunciation of Professor Beale, *ex facie*, is attractive in that it is endowed with the twin qualities of simplicity on the one hand and certainty, predictability, and ease of application on the other, whether or not it caters to the expectation of the parties to the contract, express or implied.

Firstly, Beale's enunciation, with respect to foreign contracts, rules out altogether the intention of the parties as being the determinant of the applicable law—a stand which is contrary to the prevailing practice subject, of course, to certain limitations.[1]

Secondly, Beale's enunciation with respect to the validity of a contract based exclusively on the local law of the place of contracting, is replaced by the modern approach under which the validity of a contract is to be determined by the local law of the state which, considering the particular issue, has the most significant relationship to the transaction and the parties.[2]

Thirdly, the distinction that Beale drew between matters of validity of a contract and matters of performance such as damages, sufficiency of performance, and excuse for non-performance, was that that the latter, namely matters of performance, are governed only by the local law of the place of performance rather than by the local law of the place of contracting. This, again, is not borne out by the prevailing practice of courts under which both matters of validity and matters of performance are governed by the local law of the state which, with respect to the particular issue, has the most significant relationship to the transaction and the parties.

Lastly, the original *Restatement I* of Beale laid down a rule of the thumb that the entire field of contracts except, of course, matters relating to performance, is governed only by the *lex loci contractus*.

The abovementioned approach of Professor Beale overlooks particular kinds of contracts for the transfer of interests in land, contractual duties arising from transfer of interests in land, contracts to sell interests in chattels, life insurance contracts, contracts of fire, surety or casualty insurance, contract of suretyship, contracts for repayment of loan, contracts for rendition of services, contracts of transportation, and so on and so forth. These omissions are generally governed by an explicit exercise of choice of law by the parties or, in the alternative, by the local law of the state which, with respect to the particular issue, has the most significant relationship to the contract and to the parites.[3]

Professor Cavers of the Harvard Law School, in a ground breaking article that he subscribed to the *Harvard Law Review* in the year 1933 under the caption, 'A Critique of the Choice of Law Problem,'[4] ably advocated the employment by courts of the 'rule selection' rule to the abandonment of the time-honoured 'jurisdiction selection' rule. According to him, courts of law in conflicts cases would be well advised to have recourse to selecting the rule of law in order to render justice to the parties before them, rather than selecting the jurisdiction or the country whose law is sought to be applied by them for resolving conflicts. Selecting the rule, not the jurisdiction, would help avoid false conflicts, besides affording the courts knowledge of the contents of the law prior to their application, if justice in the real sense is to be rendered to the parties before them.

Walter Wheeler Cook added yet another dimension to the conflicts resolution process by advocating an issue-based approach to resolving conflicts, be it contract or tort, or even law relating to persons, law relating to property, and any other arising within the scope of the subject of conflict of laws. His advice to courts engaged in resolving conflicts between the laws is that 'the problems in the field under consideration [that is, contracts] need to be broken down into smaller groups and dealt with so as to meet the needs of society'.[5]

Professor Morris combines the 'rule selection' rule of Professor Cavers and the issue-based approach to resolving conflicts of Professor Cook into a philosophic doctrine of the 'proper law'—a generic concept, if I may say so, for the resolution of disputes relating to the Law of Obligations in order to achieve results which are 'commercially convenient and sound' in respect of contracts and 'socially convenient and sound' in respect of torts. Courts in England have unreservedly embraced the proper law doctrine of Morris as exemplified in a catena of cases in respect of foreign contracts, the classic instance being the decision of the House of Lords in International Trustee for the *Protection of Bond Holders Akt* v. *R.*[6] The same cannot be said of foreign torts vis-à-vis English courts as we gather from the decision of the House of Lords in *Chaplin* v. *Boys*,[7] where Their Lordships tenaciously clung to a so-called flexible interpretation of Willis, J.'s 'double actionability' doctrine based on the decision in *Phillips* v. *Eyre*.[8] The said doctrine has since beeen abolished by an enactment of the British Parliament, namely Private International Law (Miscellaneous Provisions) Act, 1995,[9] subject to an only one exception, namely defamation.[10]

It appears that many a scholarly writing on the subject of the proper law doctrine cannot but be influenced by Professor Morris who expounded the said doctrine in a thought–provoking article that he contributed to the *Harvard Law Review* in the year 1951, entitled 'The Proper Law of a Tort'.[11] Therein he acknowledges his gratitude to Professor Walter Wheeler Cook who advocated an issue-based approach to resolving conflicts. I may here hazard a guess that Professors Cheatham and Reese of the Columbia Law School were no exception to being influenced by Professor Morris which is evident from the tone and tenor of their article published in the *Columbia Law Review* in the year 1952, entitled 'Choice of the Applicable Law'.[12] The latter of the two, namely Professor Willis L.M. Reese, turned out to be the pioneer of the *Restatement (Second) of the Conflict of Laws* of the American Law Institute, 1971. Therein Professor Reese, the Reporter of the *Restatement (Second)*, embraced the 'grouping of contacts' or the 'centre of gravity' rule for resolving conflicts between the laws, generally as the choice of law principle.[13] The said principle, in the absence of exercise of choice of law by the parties, finds its echo in the *Restatement (Second)* in Sections 145 and 187 with regard to foreign torts and foreign contracts.

The proper law doctrine, according to the *Halsbury's Laws of England*, is determinable in the three ways, namely

(i) by express selection by the parties;
(ii) by inferred selection from the circumstances; or
(iii) by judicial determination of the system of law with which the transaction has the closest and the most real connection.

Express Choice of Law

In the event the proper law of a contract is based on express selection by the parties, which is popularly known as the 'subjective theory' or the 'doctrine of autonomy', such an express selection by the parties as to the applicable law, in order to acquire the legal status of the proper law of the contract, ought to be explicit, emphatic, unambiguous, *bona fide*, legal, and not opposed to the public policy.[14] So is the case even if it be that the selected legal system to govern the contract has no real connection with the transaction.[15]

Informed or Implied Intention

If, however, the express choice of law clause is fanciful or whimsical, rendering it virtually meaningless, the court is free to disregard it and ascertain the proper law by recourse to the inferred or implied intentions of the parties.[16] If in a commercial contract the parties exercise their option as to the applicable law of arbitration, the presumption is that arbitration is to take place in the country of the applicable law,[17] subject, of course, to balance of convenience.[18]

Inferred Choice of Law

The Supreme Court of India in the leading case *National Thermal Power Corporation* v. *Singer Company* quoted with approval Dicey's Rule 180, Sub-rule (2) in laying down the proposition that in the absence of an express statement about the governing law, the inferred intention of the parties determines that law.[19] The Court further observed, on the strength of an old English case of the Queen's Bench Division,[20] that in the absence of an express selection, the intention of the parties has to be discovered by applying 'sound ideas of business, convenience and sense to the language of the contract itself.'[21] Therefore, in the opinion of the Court, 'selection of courts of a particular country as having jurisdiction in matters arising under the contract is usually, but not invariably, be the indication of the intention of the parties that the system of law followed by those courts is the proper law by which they intend their contract to be governed.'[22] Accordingly, as laid down by the Supreme Court in the *Shanmughavilas Cashew Industries case* that, in the absence of an express choice by the concerned parties to a case as to the proper law of the contract, the law of the country of the chosen court will, as aforesaid, usually, but not invariably, be the proper law.[23]

Inference as to the Validity of a Contract in Case of Conflict

If there be a conflict between the systems of law that govern a contract, in the sense that the contract or the terms employed therein happen to be valid and good under one and invalid under the other, the inference as to the intention of the parties is that the contract is to be treated as valid. However, the said presumption is not irrebuttable but only serves as a pointer indicative of the intentions of the parties.[24]

Absence of Express or Inferred Choice of Law

In the absence of an express selection by the parties or inferred selection from the circumstances, the law to govern a contract in a conflicts case is the proper law of the contract. By 'proper law of a contract' we mean that system of law with which the transaction relating to the contract has 'the closest and most real connection'. In other words, the proper law of a contract, viewed in the light of judicial pronouncements, is 'the law of the country in which its elements were most densely grouped and with which factually the contract was most closely connected.'[25] That would require ascertainment by the court of factors such as 'where the contract was made and how and where it was to be performed and by the nature of the business or transaction to which it refers.'[26]

In yet another case, a decision of the Calcutta High Court,[27] the issue that arose for consideration was as to the validity of an assignment of an insurance policy, a chose in action, from a father to his son, both residing at Calcutta at the time of the assignment, notice of the assignment having been promptly communicated to the Life Insurance Corporation of India, the debtor, with its Head Office at Bombay, and registered with it as required under the Indian Law. Just a few elements call for consideration of the law of Pakistan, namely that the father happened to be a permanent resident of Rajshahi which became part of Pakistan on partition of the Indian subcontinent in 1947, but that he was paying his insurance premia in Indian rupees at Rajshahi, and that the register relating to the policy was attached to the Dhaka branch, which also became part of Pakistan, and now the capital city of Bangladesh, wherefrom servicing for the insurance policy was provided. Similarly, a contract relating to bank accounts is governed by the law of the country where the account is held and not of that where the bank's head office is situated.[28] By the same token, the law to govern a contract of performance entered into in the course of trade shall be the law of the country that governs the contract of performance, which we may designate as the principle of 'characteristic performance', by which we mean the law of the country where the bank's account is kept and where the performance is due as per contract[29] or, as the case may be, of a performance bond given by a bank to secure payment on a contract in favour of the beneficiary.[30] The said doctrine of 'characteristic performance' finds incorporation in Article 4(2) of the Rome Convention, 1991.

A classic illustration of the said doctrine of 'characteristic performance' is the case of *Bank of Baroda* v. *Vysya Bank*.[31] The facts of the case are briefly as follows:

Certain Indian buyers instructed the Vysya Bank, an Indian bank, to issue a letter of credit in favour of certain Irish sellers with an office in London. The credit provided it should be advised to the sellers through the Baroda Bank, also an Indian bank, at its London branch. The Baroda Bank confirmed the credit and paid the sellers under it. The Vysya Bank withdrew its authorization to the Baroda Bank to claim reimbursement from the former before the due date. Thereupon, the Baroda Bank sought permission to serve the Vysya Bank out of jurisdiction on the ground, *inter alia*, that the contract between the two banks was governed by the English law.

Mance, J. held that the contract between the issuing and the confirming banks was governed by the English law. The contract was one of agency; the characteristic performance was of the confirming bank (that is, the Baroda Bank). Since that was to be effected through the London branch ('a place of business other than its prinicipal place' of business), by Article 4 (2) of the Rome Convention, 1991, English law was the applicable law.

It is but appropriate here to highlight the view held by Dicey and Morris on the legal effects of 'performance bonds'. It reads: 'Broadly speaking, a performance bond is a contractual undertaking, normally made by a bank, to pay a specified sum of money in the event of a default by a party to a contract with a third party.'[32]

The Calcutta High Court, in *Rabindra N. Maitra* v. *Life Insurance Corporation of India*, discussed earlier, applied the proper law doctrine, a generic concept, even as the Supreme Court did in the case of *Delhi Cloth and General Mills Co. Ltd.* v. *Harnam Singh*, based on the grouping of elements of the insurance contract at Bombay. Such grouping of elements in a single country may lead one to believe, as did the Supreme Court of India in the Delhi Cloth Mills case, that it is the *lex situs* that is the governing law which, obviously, is a misnomer in our search for an issue-based proper law. It becomes all the more so where the elements in a foreign contract are evenly distributed between two or more countries as in the English case, The Assunzioni,[33] where pragmatism, and not a doctrinaire approach, may lead to a commercially desirable result.

Presumptions Relating to the Proper Law Doctrine

The contemporary approach to ascertaining the proper law of a foreign contract, in the absence of any intention of the contracting parties, is to weigh and consider all the relevant factors without recourse to specific presumptions as to their intention.[34] When such presumptions are absent, the law of the place of performance (that is, *lex loci solutionis*) may justifiably be regarded as the proper law.[35] Only when the place where the contract is negotiated or made happens to be the place where it is to be performed, or that it is to be performed in another country, can the presumption that the *lex loci solutionis* is the proper law, hold good.[36]

Does the Proper Law Signify Connection with a Country or with the System of Law?[37]

Indian courts in their search for the proper law with reference to a foreign contract have applied the norms of connection with a country[38] or, as the case may be, the 'grouping of elements' test[39] as the determinants. What actually courts have in mind in their search for the proper law is connection with the system of law rather than connection with the country, for a country may have more than one system of law.[40]

Time Factor as an Aid to Interpretation[41]

Whether it be the ascertainment of the intention of the parties to a contract or it be the ascertainment of the connection the transaction has with a country or system of law, it is to be determined with reference to the time the contract was made.[42] Subsequent conduct of the parties cannot be pressed into service as an aid to interpreting the contract, unless the parties themselves have agreed to vary the original contract, or have actually entered into a new contract.[43]

The Doctrine of *Renvoi* vis-à-vis the Proper Law[44]

The proper law of a contract, as interpreted and applied by a foreign court exercising judicial jurisdiction, is confined merely to laying down a rule of decision based on its substantive law as if the dispute presented before it for its adjudication is purely local or domestic. It is evident, therefore, that a foreign court determining the proper law of a contract is not expected to employ its rule for choice of law (*renvoi*). The Supreme Court of India, in a leading case on the subject, observed that the expression 'proper law' refers to the substantive principle of the domestic law of the chosen system and not to its conflict of law rules; the law of contract is not affected by the doctrine of *renvoi*.[45]

In fact, the doctrine of *renvoi*, it is no exaggeration to say, is anachronistic and for that reason alone deserves to be discarded even without obsequies.

The proper law doctrine yields a satisfactory result only if our approach to resolving conflicts is issue-based that does not bring in there the law that governs the validity of the contract which, as Professor Reese observes, *mutatis mutandis*, in a majority of situations may have to be treated merely as incidental to the determination of another issue and not, as courts do, treat contract as 'an all-purpose concept', if our aim and objective is to achieve in respect of foreign contracts commercially desirable results.[46]

The contemporary trend to determine the proper law of a contract under the common law calls for, as aforesaid, an issue-based approach which requires, as Professor Cook urges, and as stated earlier, that the contract needs to be 'broken down into smaller groups and dealt with so as to meet the needs of society.' Such a course would enable courts, in the words of Professor Morris which needs to be re-emphasized, 'to accord proper weight in a particular case to factors of constantly varying significance like the place of contracting, the place of performance, the nationality of the ship, the *situs* of the land, the domicile, residence and place of business of the parties, their reasonable expectations, the currency in which their obligation is expressed and countless other.'[47] Also in the second place, according to Morris,

> the rule enables attention to be concentrated not so much on the question, what law governs the validity of the contract, as on the question what law governs particular question before the court that would enable the court to give different answers to such questions as, for instance, offer and acceptance, reality of consent, formalities, necessities for consideration or 'cause', agency, capacity

of the parties, essential validity, illegality, interpretation, scope, performance, discharge, remedies and so forth.[48]

To conclude, we may recall the words of wisdom of Lord Wright in *Mount Albert Borough Council* v. *Australasian Temperance and General Mutual Life Assurance Society Ltd.*[49] and *Lord Simonds in Bonython* v. *Commonwealth of Australia.*[50] Lord Wright in the Mount Albert case defined the proper law as 'that law which the English or other court is to apply in determining the "obligation" under the contract',[51] thus drawing a distinction between obligation and performance. Lord Symonds, in the Bonython case, defined the proper law as 'the system of law by reference to which the contract was made or that with which the transaction has its closest and most real connection.'[52]

FOREIGN TORTS

The Civil Procedure Code of India, 1908, deals only with the subject of the remedy available to a person in a local court for any wrongful act done to him or to his movable property. However, the C.P.C. does not contain any provision for resolving conflicts in respect of foreign torts.

Section 9 of the C.P.C. lays down the following proposition on the issue of exercise of jurisdiction by a local court.

> Where a suit is for compensation for a wrong done to a person or to movable property, if the wrong was done within the local limits of the jurisdiction of one court and the defendant was resident, or carried on business, or personally worked for gain, within the local limits of the jurisdiction of another court, the suit may be instituted at the option of the plaintiff in either of the courts.[53]

For a tort committed abroad, a suit for compensation for the wrongful act may be brought before an Indian court which may entertain the said action against the defendant who resides or carries on business, or personally works for gain in India provided, in keeping with the procedural due process, he has been effectively served with a summons.[54] As for the choice of law, in the absence of a legislative directive, an Indian court before which a suit for compensation for a tort committed abroad is brought, may, as instanced by a solitary decision in this area, namely *Kotah Transport Limited, Kotah* v. *Jhalawar Transport Service Limited,*[55] fall back upon the so-called English 'double actionability' doctrine,[56] which is no longer the law even in England consequent upon the enactment by the British Parliament of Private International Law (Miscellaneous Provisions) Act, 1995. Section 10 of the Act abolishes the general rule laid down by Willis, J. in *Phillips* v. *Eyre* in respect of all torts committed abroad after 1 May 1996. Section 13 of the Act, curiously enough, preserves the general rule in *Phillips* v. *Eyre* in respect of defamation.

In retrospect, the English courts, for well over a century, tenaciously clung to the Willis, J. formula, presumed to have been laid down in *Phillips* v. *Eyre* in respect of a suit for a tort committed abroad, namely that it shall be actionable in tort under *lex fori* (that is, the law of the forum) and that it shall also be actionable as per the *lex loci delicti commissi* (that is, the law of the place where the tort occurred). This the English courts did in utter disregard of the ratio that Willis, J. employed under the peculiar circumstances of the case before him, namely the wrong committed by the ex-Governor of Jamaica of assaulting and falsely imprisoning the plaintiff during an emergency was exonerated by the local legislature by passing an act of indemnity. With a view to discourage forum shopping and to eliminate adventitiousness, Willis, J. while dismissing the action against the ex-Governor of Jamaica ratiocinated thus:

> As a general rule, in order to found a suit in England for a wrong alleged to have been committed abroad, two conditions must be fulfilled. First, the wrong must be of such a character that it would have been actionable if committed in England. Secondly, the act must not have been justifiable by the law of the place where it was done.

The first condition of Willis, J. obviously relates to the jurisdictional competence of an English court to entertain an action against a defendant for a tort he is alleged to have committed elsewhere. The second condition emphasizes the legal requirement that the said act of the defendant ought to be actionable in tort as per the law of the country where it is committed.

Strange as it may seem, courts in England for nearly a century misconstrued the so-called 'general rule' of Willis, J. in *Phillips* v. *Eyre*. The said condition was, in fact, designed to discourage 'forum shopping'. By employing the phrase 'not justifiable', Willis, J. only emphasized that the act complained of must be actionable in tort at the place where it was committed.

The classic instance of such misconception is the decision of the Queen's Bench Division in *Machado* v. *Fontes*.[57] That was an action brought before an English court for a libel published by the defendant in Brazil. The defendant's plea that by Brazilian law libel was a crime, not a tort, for which he could be prosecuted at the instance of the plaintiff was rejected by the court of appeal. Lopes, L.J., speaking for the court, came forward with a startling proposition that the criminal act of the defendant was not innocent and therefore not justifiable in the country where libellous matter was published. Rigby, L.J., while agreeing with Lopes, L.J., added yet a new dimension to the ratio by observing that the change of language from 'actionable' to 'justifiable' in *Phillips* v. *Eyre* was deliberate.

Needless to say, the kind of ratio bordering on absurdity that the court of appeal employed in *Machado* v. *Fontes*, construing the phrase 'not justifiable' of Willis, J. as 'actionable' as one would expect, is, to say the least, execrable. It may not amount to transgression of academic propriety, if one ventures to remark that the decision in *Machado* v. *Fontes* deserves a place in the Hall of Fame, if an institution of that kind were to be established in recognition of outstanding decisions rendered by courts, as is done in the area of sports! No wonder, therefore, the House of Lords, in *Chaplin* v. *Boys*,[58] had no hesitation in overruling by a majority the unfortunate decision in *Machado* v. *Fontes*. Lord Donovan, in the abovementioned case of *Chaplin* v. *Boys*, observed that the decision in *Machado* v. *Fontes* is a clear case of 'blatant forum shopping'. Though the House of Lords could take credit for shutting out the unhealthy practice of forum shopping in respect of foreign torts, it failed to carry its judgment to its logical conclusion, namely that the law to govern a foreign tort is the proper law of the tort as is the case with a foreign contract, to the disownment of the much maligned 'double actionability' doctrine.[59] To set things right, it required legislative intervention in the name of Private International Law (Miscellaneous Provisions) Act, 1995.[60]

To conclude, if the proper law doctrine makes inroads into and finds acceptance with courts with respect to foreign torts in conflicts cases, as is the case with foreign contracts, and at the same time, it does not let go an issue-based approach to resolving conflicts, there is no scope whatsoever to deal with maritime torts and torts in aircraft any differently, as Halsbury or, as for that matter, Dicey and Morris, would choose to do in the traditional mould.

NOTES

1. See Section 187, *Restatement (Second) of the Conflict of Laws* of the American Law Institute (St. Paul, Minnesota: American Law Institute Publishers, 1971).

2. Section 188, *Restatement (Second).*

3. Section 189–97, *Restatement (Second).*

4. *Harvard Law Review*, Vol. 47, (1933), p. 173.

5. Walter Wheeler Cook, *Logical and Legal Bases of the Conflict of Laws*, (1942), pp. 417–18.

6. (1937) AC500; (1937)2 ALL ER 164, H.L

7. (1969) 2 ALL ER 1085

8. LR 6 QB 1. See V.C. Govindaraj, 'Foreign Torts in Conflicts Cases: A Plea for a Viable Social Environmental Theory—The English Double Actionability Dortrine', *Columbia Journal of Transnational Law*, Vol. 9 (1970), p. 152.

9. See Section 10 of the Act.

10. See Section 13 of the Act.

11. J.H.C. Morris, The Proper Law of a Tort, *Harvard Law Review*, Vol. 64 (1951), pp. 881–3.

12. Elliott E. Cheatham and Willis L.M. Reese, 'Choice of the Applicable Law', *Columbia Law Review*, Vol. 52 (1952), p, 959.

13. Section 6, *Restatement (Second).*

14. *National Thermal Power Corporation* v. *Singer Co.*, AIR 1993 SC 998, (1992) 3 SCC 551 at 560; (1992) 3 SCR 106.

15. *Vita Food Products Inc.* v. *Unus Shipping Co. Ltd.*, (1939) AC 277 at 290; (1930) ALL ER 513 at 521. However, English courts in a catena of cases held to the contrary following the ruling in *Boissevain* v. *Weil*, (1949) 1 KB 482 pp. 490–1; (1949) ALL ER 146 pp. 152–3.

16. See the classic case of *Compagnie D'Armament Maritime S.A.* v. *Tunisienne De Navigations S.A.*, (1971) AC 572; (1970) 3 ALL ER 71, H.L. The case was about a contract for the shipment of oil from one Tunisian port to another, concluded in Paris between French shipowners and a Tunisian company. The contract was in the English form and language and clause 13 provided that the

contract was to be governed by 'the laws of the flag of the vessel carrying the goods', indicating thereby that the French law was the proper law. In addition, clause 18 also provided for arbitration in London. The court of appeal held clause 13 prescribing the law of the flag as the proper law 'meaningless' as the contract of shipment of oil was entered into with different ships flying different flags. The House of Lords, however, overruled the finding of the court of appeal by a bare majority, holding thereby that clause 13 was not meaningless. As for the arbitration clause 18, the House of Lords opined that such a clause may often be decisive, though not necessarily always conclusive.

17. *National Thermal Power Corporation Appellant* v. *Singer Company and others* (Respondents), AIR 1993 SC 998 pp. 1000–1; (1992) 3 SCC 551; (1992) 3 SCR 106.

18. *Naviera Amazonica Persuana S.A.* v. *Cia Internacional de Seguros del Peru*, (1998) 1 Lloyd's Rep 116, CA. See *Black Sea, SS UL Lastochkina Odessa, USSR* v. *Union of India*, AIR (1976) AP 103, p. 107.

19. Ibid., p. 1006.

20. *Jacobs, Marcus & Co.* v. *The Credit Lyonnais*, (1884) 12 QBD 589, 601 (CA).

21. Ibid.

22. Ibid. See also *British India Steam Navigation Co. Ltd. Appellant* v. *Shanmughavilas Cashew Industries and others Respondents*, (1990) 3 SCC 481 p. 492; (1990) 1 Scale 462; (1990) 2 Comp. LJ1.

23. Ibid.

24. Ibid.

25. *Delhi Cloth and General Mills* v. *Harnam Singh*, AIR 1955 SC 590; (1955) ILR PUNJ 1127; (1955) 2 SCR 402; (1955) 2 MAD LJ (SC) 141.

26. Ibid.

27. *Rabindra N. Maitra* v. *Life Insurance Corporation of India*, AIR 1964 CAL 141. Also see for insurance contracts the English cases namely *Rossano* v. *Manufacturers Life Insurance Co.*, (1963), QB 352 and Crédit Lyonnais New Hampshire Insurance Co., (1997) 1 LIR at 6CA.

28. *X AIG* v. *A Bank*, (1983) (2 ALL ER 464; *Libyan Arab Bank* v. *Bankers Trust Co.*, (1989) QB 728; *Libyan Arab Foreign Bank* v. *Manufacturers Hanover Trust Co.*, (1988) 2 LIR 494.

29. *Sierra Leone Telecommunications Co. Ltd.* v. *Barclays Bank Plc*, (1998) 2 ALL ER 821. Also see with respect to reinsurance contracts, *AIG Group (U.K.) Ltd.* v. *Ethnicki*, (1998) 4 ALL ER 301 p. 310.

30. Likewise, a banker's credit has been held to be governed by the law of the country in which the beneficiary can draw on it, like a performance bond given by a bank to secure payment on a contract. *Offshore International SA* v. *Banco*

Central SA, (1997) 1 WLR 399, approved in *Power Curber International Ltd.* v. *National Bank of Kuwait*, (1981) 1 WLR 1233 CA; *Attock Cement Co. Ltd.* v. *Romanian Bank for Foreign Trade*, (1989) 1 WLR 1147 CA.

31. (1994) 2 LIR 187

32. Dicey, Morris & Collins (Sir Lawrence), p. 1796 (33–4). See Chitty on Contracts, (Twenty Eighth Edition (1999), Vol. 2, para. 44–014). For a detailed account, see O'Donovan and Phillips, *The Modern Contract of Guarantee*, Third Edition, (1996), Ch. 15.

33. (1954), p. 150; (1954) 1 ALL ER 278

34. *Delhi Cloth Mills case.*

35. Ibid., see also *Raman Chettiar* v. *Raman Chettiar*, AIR 1954 MAD 97 p. 98.

36. *Brij Raj Marwari* v. *Anant Prasad*, (1942) ILR 1 CAL 505.

37. See V.C. Govindaraj, *Conflict of Laws*, Halsbury's Laws of India Series, Vol. 10 (New Delhi: LexisNexis Butterworths, 2001), p. 252.

38. *Black Sea SS UL Lastochkina Odessa USSR* v. *Union of India*, AIR (1976) AP 103 at 107; (1975) ILR AP 805; (1975) 2 AND Hr WR 339.

39. *Delhi Cloth Mills case.*

40. *Juggilal Kamalapat* v. *Internationale Crediet-En-Handels Vereeninging Rotterdam (alias Rotterdam Trading Co. Ltd.)*, (1954) 58 CAL WN 730.

41. Ibid.; Butterworths.

42. *Raman Chettiar* v. *Raman Chettiar*, AIR (1954) MAD 97.

43. *Delhi Cloth Mills case.*

44. See Govindaraj, *Conflict of Laws*, Holsbury's Laws of India Series, Vol. 10 (New Delhi: LexisNexis Butterworths, 2001), p. 253.

45. *National Thermal Power Corporation* v. *Singer Co.*, AIR 1993 SC 998; (1992)3 SCC 551 at 562; (1992) 3 SCR 106; (1992) 1 Scale 1034.

46. Willis L.M. Reese, 'Marriage in American Conflict of Laws', *The International and Comparative Law Quarterly* (ICLQ), Vol. 26 (1977), 952.

47. J.H.C. Morris, 'The Proper Law of a Tort', *Harward Law Review*, Vol. 64 (1951), pp. 881–3.

48. Ibid.

49. (1938) AC 204 (A)

50. (1951) AC 201

51. *Mount Albert case*, supra 240.

52. *Bonython case*, supra 219 (B). See also *Delhi Cloth and General Mills Co. Ltd.* v. *Harnam Singh*, AIR (1955) SC 590, at 596–7.

53. Section 9, The Civil Procedure Code, 1908.

54. *Haveli Shah* v. *Painda Khan*, (1926) 96 IC 887, PC.

55. AIR 1960 RAJ 224;[1960] ILR 10 RAJ 705

56. The English 'double actionability' doctrine, presumed to be the outcome of the decision in *Phillips* v. *Eyre*, (1870) 6LR QB1, received endorsement by the House of Lords in England, albeit flexibly interpreted, in the leading case of *Chaplin* v. *Boys*, (1971) AC 356; (1969) 2 ALL ER 1085, HL, in preference to the American 'grouping of elements' or 'centre of gravity' test which was employed by Fuld, J. (as he then was) in *Babcock* v. *Jackson*, 12 NY 2d 473; 191 NE 2d 279; 240 NY 2d 143 (1963) in order to achieve justice, fairness and best practicable result.

57. (1897) 2 QB 231

58. (1969) 2 ALL ER 1085

59. See V.C. Govindaraj, 'Foreign Torts in Conflicts Cases: A Plea for a Viable Social Environmental Theory—The English Double Actionability Doctrine', *Columbia Journal of Transnational Law*, Vol. 9 (1970), 152. See also J.H.C. Morris, 'The Proper Law of a Tort', *Harvard Law Review*, Vol. 64 (1951), pp. 881–3.

60. See Sections 10 and 13 of the Act.

6

Negotiable Instruments

THE MAKING AND ASSIGNMENT OF NEGOTIABLE INSTRUMENTS

The legal requirements and the legal effects of a negotiable instrument such as a bill of exchange or a promissory note or cheque are governed by the Negotiable Instruments Act, 1881.

Section 134 of the Act lays down the rule that in the absence of a contract to the contrary in respect of a negotiable instrument, the liability of the maker or drawer of a promissory note, bill of exchange, or cheque is regulated in all essential matters by the law of the place where he made the instrument. The respective liabilities of the acceptor and indorser are regulated by the law of the place where the instrument is made payable, which is also the law that governs dishonour.

Section 134 of the Indian Negotiable Act, 1881, speaks of the liability of the drawer and the respective liabilities of the the acceptor and indorser in regard to essential matters. There is no mention as to what law would govern the formalities of making the instrument, its acceptance, and its indorsement. This is in contrast to its British counterpart, namely the Bills of Exchange Act, 1882, which draws a distinction between form and substance, the governing law in respect thereof albeit the same both as respects formal validity and essential validity. The choice of law rule is *locus regit actum* in regard to all the transactions, be it making of the instrument, acceptance, indorsement, or acceptance supra protest of the instrument.

We may, therefore, draw the inference that the said Section 134 of the Indian Negotiable Instruments Act, 1881, does not only distinguish between matters of form and matters of substance, but also does not adhere to the English rule of *locus regit actum* as the governing principle behind all these transactions.

As pointed out by Morris, even the provisions of the (British) Bills of Exchange Act, 1882, 'are open to serious criticism in that they are ambiguous and at times unintelligible, and they do not deal with all matters that can arise but only with formal validity, interpretation, the duties of the holder, and the due date of payment.' Morris further observes: 'The section does not deal in terms with such matters as capacity, essential validity or illegality, or with the proprietory as opposed to the contractual aspects of bills and notes.'[1] The Indian counterpart, namely The Negotiable Instruments Act, 1881, needless to say, seems to suffer from the similar defects Morris points out with reference to the (British) Bills of Exchange Act, 1882.

NEGOTIABILITY

An instrument negotiable in the country of origin acquires negotiability in another country, if so recognized under the law of the latter or by the custom of the mercantile world of that country. There are only two old English decisions to exemplify the proposition stated above. In *Goodwin* v. *Robarts*,[2] scrip issued by the Russian government containing a promise of full payment to issue a bond in respect of a loan, was treated as negotiable on the strength of the custom of merchants in England. On the contrary, in *Picker* v. *London and County Banking Co.*[3] bonds issued by the Russian government were not treated as negotiable in England due to the absence of legislation or custom of merchants in England to treat them as negotiable. The defendant company's plea that they had taken delivery of the bonds bona fide and for value, though the said bonds deposited with them happened to be stolen, did not find favour with the court of appeal for the reason that nothing could pass as cash in England unless it be so deemed either by statute or by a custom of merchants. This decision of the court of appeal, however, does not run counter to the well known principle that a negotiable instrument, even if stolen, would confer a good title on a person who takes delivery of it bona fide and for value.

NEGOTIABLE INSTRUMENTS: THE GOVERNING LAW

LIABILITY

Section 134 of the (Indian) Negotiable Instruments Act, 1881, as stated above, provides for the respective liabilities of a maker or drawer as well as the acceptor and indorser. According to the said section, the respective liabilities of the acceptor and indorser are determined by the law of the place where the instrument is made payable. But under the (British) Bills of Exchange Act, 1882, there is no clear indication as to which law determines the respective liabilities of the acceptor and indorser. However, Section 72(2) of the British Act seems to offer guidance in this regard generally. Section 72(2) reads: 'The interpretation of the drawing, indorsement, acceptance, or acceptance supra protest of a bill is determined by the law of the place where such contract is made.'

According to Morris, the word 'interpretation' used in Section 72(2) has a usually wide meaning so as to embrace the respective obligation created by the Act of drawing, indorsing and accepting the bill.[4] This interpretation of the English law has, in the Indian context, no relevance whatsoever.

Transferability

The (Indian) Negotiable Instruments Act, 1881, in Section 134, dealing with the liability of the maker, acceptor or indorser of a foreign instrument, lays down the rule that the liability of the acceptor or indorser shall be governed by the law of the place where the bill is payable. In the absence of any other provision regarding transferability, it appears, this rule also governs the acceptability or the indorsement by the law of the place where the bill is made payable. However, adherence to this rule may restrict the negotiability of the instrument. It is likely that an indorsement made in a foreign country according to the law of that country may not be honoured in India, if it happens to be payable in India. The outcome of it all may so work out as to restrict its negotiability. Therefore, it appears that with a view to offset this limitation, the section begins with the phrase 'in the absence of a contract to the contrary ...' This clearly implies that the parties are free to choose any other law to govern the instrument.

To sum up, the foregoing analysis of Section 134 of the (Indian) Negotiable Instruments Act, 1881, dealing with transferability of foreign negotiable instruments, shows that the provision is restrictive from the standpoint of negotiability in that it prescribes the law of the place where the instrument is made payable as the law to govern the respective liabilities of the acceptor or indorser. This may give rise to conflict if the law of the acceptor or the indorser were to be different from the law of the place where the instrument is made payable. This may be the reason, perhaps, that the Act allows the parties concerned to choose the law to govern the liability of the maker or drawer of the instrument on the one hand and the respective liabilities of the acceptor and indorser on the other.

We may, therefore, suggest that the legislator may give the said Section 134 of the Negotiable Instrument Act, 1881, a second look with a view adequately safeguard the interests of the mercantile world.

NOTES

1. J.H.C. Morris, *The Conflict of Laws*, Fourth Edition, first Indian Reprint (Delhi: Universal Law Publishing Co. Pvt. Ltd., 2004), p. 327.
2. (1875) LR 10 Exch. 337 p. 494. See the House of Lords decision in the leading case *International Trustee for the Protection of Bond Holders* v. *R.*, (1936) 3 ALL ER 407.
3. (1887), I8 QBD 515;56 L.J.Q.B. 299; 35 W.R.469; 3 TLRTLR 444, C.A.
4. J.H.C. Morris, *The Conflict of Laws*, Fourth Edition, first Indian Reprint (Delhi: Universal Law Publishing Co. Pvt. Ltd., 2004), p. 329.

7

Law of Persons

Marriage and Divorce

INTRODUCTION

Conflict of laws in the matrimonial field might have existed in India even in the earliest stage[1] of its civilization, but it emerged in a recognizable form only during the Muslim period due to the existence of two sects in the Muslim community, namely Shia and Sunni which were each subject to a different law but, all the same, could inter-marry. The conflict became sharper during the last days of the Muslim rule when Shia nawabs ruled the Oudh area of India. According to Ronald Wilson[2] (in *Baillie's Digest of Shia Law*), during the rulership of Shia nawabs, Shia law was invariably applied by courts even if only one party happened to be Shia. The conflict became more pronounced with the advent of the British into this country since, then, a new community, namely the Christian, also emerged. This community, though numerically negligible, had a formidable claim to a separate legal status as it was backed by the new rulers. The rulers had now to deal with three communities and the result was the advent of a complex matrimonial system with each of the three communities having its own marriage law different from the others. For example, Christian law allowed the right to divorce to both the spouses whereas Muslim law restricted it to the male spouse only, and Hindu law denied it to both. To compound the matter further, the right to conversion from one faith to another was not only guaranteed but, in fact, encouraged (if it was to Christianity). Conversion raises manifold complex questions such as, for example, whether or not the changed religious identity of a spouse makes him/her subject to a different law. Does the nature of a marriage change in consequence of change of religion on the part of the spouses? Does the nature of the marriage remain unchanged and is the converted spouse entitled to all the rights available to his/her new co-religionists, even though practice of such right was not permitted under the pre-conversion law? Also, what law would govern a marriage celebrated abroad between parties following different religions, et cetera?

Satisfactory answers to all these questions needed a well thought out legislation for which the English rulers were not prepared. They were unacquainted with these types of problems which did not arise under the English judicial system, and they were still struggling to settle down. However, in their anxiety to do something in the matter, they came out with the Regulating Act, 1781, which laid down that, whenever parties before the court professed different religions, the applicable law was that of the defendant. It was a very rudimentary sort of legislation. Though it produced rather satisfactory results in some cases of marriage—such as when one of the parties was a Shia[3] and other a Sunni—it broke down in cases of succession as we notice from *Prasannamayee* v. *Sarkies*,[4] inasmuch as it tended to produce bizarre results. Thereafter, it went into hibernation from which it emerged only as late as 1948 when it was invoked by the defendant in *Ayesha Bibi* v. *Subhodh Chandra*,[5] a case of conversion of a Hindu wife to Islam and her petition for divorce under Muslim law. Obviously, Hindu law which forbade divorce was applicable, being the defendant's law; Ormond, J. bypassed it in favour of the doctrine of justice, equity, and good conscience as, in his opinion, application of the defendant's law was likely to produce undesirable results. The next occasion calling for the application of this rule followed soon in *Rakeya Bibi* v. *Anil Kumar Mukherji*;[6] but again the rule failed to find acceptance with the court. Since then, it has not been invoked although, it has neither been expressly repealed by the government. Apart from this, there is no statutory general provision for any solution of conflicts, although provisions exist in some statutes for avoiding conflicts. For example, the Hindu Marriage Act, 1955, permits marriage between followers of certain different religions such as between Hindus and Sikhs, each religion prescribing its own solemnization ceremony. Conflict would have certainly resulted but for Section 7 of the Act, according to which a Hindu marriage may be solemnized in accordance with the customary rites and ceremonies of either party thereto.[7]

However, courts have given rulings on points of conflict that had arisen in different cases. Unfortunately, these rulings suffer from various drawbacks. In some cases, the court has taken a one-sided view by treating them as non-conflict cases. For example, in *Govardhan* v. *Jasodamono Dassi*,[8] a case of conversion of both the Hindu spouses of a non-dissoluble Hindu marriage (as Hindu marriage then was) to Christianity and then their petition for dissolution of the marriage under the Divorce Act, 1869, the court dissolved the marriage on the basis of the then Christian identity of the spouses without considering the other aspect, namely the subsistence of the Hindu marriage. Another drawback, attributable to the existing multiplicity of high courts, is the disagreement in the rulings of different high courts on the same point. For instance, in *Periyanayakam* v. *Pottukanni*[9] and in *Peter Thapita* v. *Laxmi Thapita*,[10] both cases identical in all respects with *Govardhan* v. *Jasodamono Dassi*, the Madras High Court dismissed the petitions on the ground that a Hindu marriage, even though the spouses had since converted to Christianity, could not be dissolved under (Indian) Divorce Act, 1869, which applies only to monogamous marriages. Instances of such differing opinions are manifold and make the law uncertain and unclear, a defect which jeopardises not only a community's faith and belief that courts of law are verily the dispensers of justice and upholders of equality, but also the equal protection of the laws itself. These rulings have been discussed topic-wise in the following sections. A marriage involves many topics/processes as, for example, celebration, divorce, nullity, et cetera. Each one is accorded a different treatment by the concerned law. The following sections deal with these topics/processes under each matrimonial law.

SECTION I: PRE-SOLEMNIZATION REQUISITES

Before the solemnization of a marriage, it is essential to see whether (i) the intending parties can invoke the applicable/chosen law for getting married and (ii) whether they fulfill the requirements laid down by the applicable/chosen law. Since provisions of these matrimonial laws differ from each other, we may have to consider the matter Act-wise or Law-wise.

The Hindu Marriage Act, 1955

The question was raised in *Prem Singh* v. *Dulari Bai,*[11] as to whether a Hindu who is not domiciled in India can get married under this Act. The Calcutta High Court ruled that no domiciliary qualification is needed for marriage under this Act. The Act (vide Section 1(1) extends to the whole of India except the state of Jammu & Kashmir, and any Hindu who is in India except in the state of Jammu & Kashmir can invoke this Act. Domciliary qualification is needed only when the parties are outside India (vide Section 2 (1)).

Christian Law: The Indian Christian Marriage Act, 1872

The Act, vide Sub-section 1(2), extends to the whole of India except the state of Jammu & Kashmir. This means any Christian who is in India, except in the state of Jammu & Kashmir, is entitled to marry under this Act. This is also corroborated by the preamble which states that this is 'an Act to provide for the solemnization in India of the marriages of persons professing the Christian religion.'

Muslim Law

In terms of The Muslim Personal Law (Shariat) Application Act of 1937, if a Muslim makes a declaration that he desires to be governed by the Muslim Personal Law (Shariat) Application Act, 1937, then, in all matters excluding questions regarding agriculture but including those relating to all aspects of marriage, the Shariat law shall be the governing law. However, in terms of Section 3 (c), only those Muslims who are resident in India (except the state of Jammu & Kashmir) are entitled to make such a declaration with the result that Muslims who want to get married under the Shariat law have to be resident in India. For those not keen on Shariat law, the qualification of residence in India is not needed and the marriage, in their case, would take place under the non-shariat law prevalent in this country.

The Parsi Marriage & Divorce Act, 1936

It is clear from Section 4 of the Act that marriage under it can be solemnized even if one of the parties has changed his/her religion. Thus, unlike the Hindu Marriage Act, 1955, this Act does not insist on both the parties professing the same faith. It is also clear from this section that a marriage can take place under this Act even if one of the parties has changed his/her domicile. Further, it appears that a marriage can be solemnized even if both the intending spouses have changed their domicile, since (i) like other enactments this Act purports to extend to the whole of India and (ii) that there is no provision in this Act which seeks to restrict its applicability only to the parties domiciled in India for the solemnization of the marriage.

Special Marriage Act, 1954

The Act extends to the whole of India except the State of Jammu & Kashmir and provides for solemnization of marriage between any two persons. Domicile as such does not appear to be necessary for getting married under this Act.

We infer, therefore, that none of the matrimonial laws of India (except Muslim law) contain any provision barring a non-domiciliary/non-resident party from getting married under one of them. Only Muslim law insists upon residence qualification if the party opts for the application of the Shariat law. Such an inference is in accord with the rules of conflict of laws.

Further, there is no rule of private international law which forbids a non-domiciliary from contracting a marriage. In England, marriage could be solemnized between non-domiciliaries visiting England just for a while.[12] In India, marriage was solemnized between parties one of whom was domiciled in the erstwhile native State of Hyderabad, a foreign state at that time.[13]

The next question that invites our attention is whether the intending parties fulfill the requirements laid down by the matrimonial law applicable to them. The parties may be domiciled in India or they may be domiciled abroad. The location of their domicile determines which country's law applies to them. To those domiciled here in India, the Law of India is applicable and it is the personal law appropriate to their religion in case they intend to have a religious marriage; for those desiring a secular marriage, the Special Marriage Act, 1954 applies.

All these laws differ from each other. The Hindu Marriage Act, 1955 provides for marriage only between two Hindus and insists upon monogamy, whereas the uncodified pre-1955 Hindu law allows a Hindu to marry a non-Hindu and permits polygamy.[14] The Indian Christian

Marriage Act provides for marriage not only between two Christians but also between a Christian and a non-Christian.[15] In fact, such a marriage can be solemnized only under this Act. The Act allows only monogamy.[16] The Parsi law, while providing for marriage between Zoroastrian Parsis, also allows matrimonial alliance between a Zoroastrian Parsi and a non-Zoroastrian Parsi and ensures through appropriate provisions[17] that the spouses of a Parsi marriage remain monogamous until the marriage has been duly dissolved. Muslim law, on the other hand, allows polygamy permitting the husband to have as many as four wives at a time.

In the case of parties domiciled abroad, the law(s) of the domicile(s) of the parties lay down the necessary requirements. Since the decision in *Brooke* v. *Brooke*,[18] these requirements are split into two categories namely, (i) essential or substantive requirements such as consanguinity, whether neither party has a spouse living (in case the concerned law allows only monogamy), et cetera. and (ii) the procedural requirements such as parental consent (only when non-availability of such consent is not an absolute bar), parties' capacity to give consent to the marriage, et cetera.[19]

While there is complete unanimity on the point that the procedural requirements are governed by the law of the place where the marriage is to be solemnized, that is, by the *lex loci celebrationis*, disagreement exists in regard to the choice of law which should govern the substantive requirements. There are two theories on this point, namely (i) the dual domicile theory of Dicey, and (ii) the intended matrimonial home theory of Cheshire. These theories are discussed below.

THE INTENDED MATRIMONIAL HOME THEORY

Under this theory, the parties' capacity is tested with reference to the law of the place where they intend to establish their home after marriage. The theory attributes to the parties the intention to settle down in the place of the husband's domicile and therefore it can, in fact, be treated as the one of husband's domicile.

As the name suggests, the intention of the parties is the key to the application of this theory but it is not clear whether intention, which is just presumed (and not investigated and proved), is good enough by itself, or whether it is necessary to translate it into action. Judgments on this point differ as set out below.

The other theory requires the parties to have capacity with reference to *lex domicilii* of each of the parties. Which of these two is to be adopted depends upon the wisdom of the court. In India, the case law on this subject is very sparse and therefore we have to turn to English case law to ascertain which of the two theories finds favour with courts in England.

The English case law is the obvious option since our courts have followed that law exclusively during the pre-Independence era and also mostly during the post-Independence period, too. Unfortunately, however, English case law on this point is ambivalent. There are cases to support one theory, others to support the other and still others, which are compatible with both, as discussed hereunder.

(1) In *Mette* v. *Mette*,[20] a domiciled English man contracted in Germany marriage with his deceased wife's sister domiciled in Germany. The marriage was prohibited by English law but valid by German law. An English court declared the marriage void, but, the *ratio decidendi* was equivocal. The court observed that there could be no valid marriage unless each party was competent to marry the other according to its respective *lex domicilii* but, nevertheless, concluded that the validity of the marriage could not be upheld since the parties contracted it with a view to subsequent residence in England. Apparently, the case supports both the theories.

(2) In the Will of Swan,[21] a marriage was celebrated in Scotland between parties domiciled in the State of Victoria when the parties were in Scotland on a temporary visit. The marriage was void by the Scottish law though only voidable by the law of the State of Victoria. The English court while upholding the validity of the marriage observed: 'The validity of marriage as to ceremonial and so forth depends upon the place of the marriage but the policy of the occurrences of such marriages and their results, should depend, I think, upon the laws of the country of the parties in which they are afterwards probably to live.'

(3) In *De Reneville* v. *De Reneville*,[22] Lord Greene M.R. made the following observation:

> Validity of a marriage so far as regards the observance of formalities is a matter for the *lex loci celebrationis*. But this is not a case of form. It is a case of essential validity. By what law is that to be decided? In my opinion by the law of France

either because that is a place of husband's domocile at the date of marriage or preferably in my view because at that date it was the law of the matrimonial domocile in reference to which the parties may have been supposed to enter into the bonds of marriage.

The views of Bucknill, LJ, on this point were forthright.

To hold that the law of the country where each spouse is domiciled before the marriage must decide as to validity of the marriage, specially in this case might lead to the deplorable result if the laws happened to differ, that the marriage would be held valid in one country and void in the other country. For this reason, I think it is essential that the law of one country should prevail and that it is reasonable that the law of the country where the ceremony of marriage took place and where the parties intended to live together and where in fact they lived together should be regarded as the law which controls the validity of their marriage.

(4) In *Kenward* v. *Kenward*,[23] in view of Lord Denning's unambiguous affirmation, we need not go into the details of this case. He declared substantial validity of a marriage contracted between persons domiciled in different countries is governed by the law of the country where they intend to live and on the basis of which they have agreed to marry. A classic decision governed by this theory is *Radwan* v. *Radwan*[24] where the validity of a bigamous marriage of a female domiciled in England with an Egyptian Muslim male governed by Muslim polygamous system was in question. Bruce, J. held that the capacity to contract a polygamous marriage is governed by the law of the intended matrimonial home.

(5) In paine Re—W[25], a British subject domiciled in England, married in Germany her deceased sister's husband, a German subject, who had lived in England for sometime before the marriage. W was to receive a legacy absolutely in case the marriage was valid. The marriage was valid under German law but invalid under English law since the latter forbade marriage with one's deceased sister's husband.

An English court held the marriage invalid since it adopted the dual domicile theory. However, the same result would have been reached in case the other theory namely, 'the intended matrimonial home' theory had been adopted since the husband had been resident in England for sometime before marriage and continued to be there till his death. The case is, therefore, compatible with both the theories.

(6) In *Padolecchia* v. *Padolecchia*,[26] the husband, domiciled in Italy but resident in Denmark, married in England, during his one day's visit to that country, the respondent who was resident and domiciled in Denmark. They both returned to Denmark to live there and the husband petitioned an English court for the grant of decree of nullity of marriage on the ground that, at the time of this marriage, he was still married since his divorce from his earlier marriage would not have been recognized by an Italian court. In this case, the law of the intended matrimonial home was Danish, but the judgment did not try to investigate whether the marriage was valid or invalid under that law suggesting that the court had no intention of applying the intended matrimonial home theory. The court's focus was only on the law of the husband's domicile, the Italian law, and, therefore, this case is a clear endorsement of the dual domicile theory.

(7) In *Pugh* v. *Pugh*,[27] the marriage took place in Austria between an English officer domiciled in England but stationed in Austria and a girl of Hungarian origin but residing in Austria. Because the girl was only fifteen years of age, the marriage was void under English law though valid by both Austrian law and Hungarian law.

The wife petitioned an English court for the grant of a decree of nullity on the ground that the marriage was invalid by English law which was the *lex domicilii* of the husband as well as the law of the intended matrimonial home. Lord Pearce, while granting the decree of nullity, said that the essential validity was determinable by English law as being either *lex domicilii* or the law of the intended matrimonial home. In fact, the Judge relied here on Re Paine,[28] suggesting that the court depended mainly on the dual domicile theory.

Do all these conflicting decisions add up to a system of justice in the matter of choice between these two theories? A cursory glance would portray the English court as vacillating between the two theories, unrestrained by any principle or being guided, so to say, simply by their whims. However, a critical analysis reveals a perceptible consistent trend which has changed with the progress of time. As can be noticed, the tendency in the earlier cases[29] was to follow the intended matrimonial home theory, but there has been a perceptible change with Padolecchia.[30] This change seems to be the outcome of the Marriage

(Enabling) Act, 1960 which brought about a change in the prohibited relationship. Prior to this enactment, one could marry one's wife's sister only after the death of one's wife, or one's brother's wife only after the death of the husband of such wife. The Act of 1960 eliminates this condition of death but significantly adds that 'no such marriage shall be valid if either party to it is, at the time of marriage, domiciled in a country outside the U.K. and under the law of that country there can't be a valid marriage between the parties.' Such a marriage, in case the husband is domiciled in UK, is valid under the intended matrimonial home theory, but invalid under the dual domicile theory.

The Act of 1960, by treating such a marriage invalid if either party to it is, at the time of the marriage, domiciled in a country outside Great Britain, the law of which country forbids such an alliance, declares in unequivocal terms that the dual domicile theory is the ruling one now and the intended matrimonial home theory is *passe*. The English courts seem to have taken notice of this development in law and switched over to the dual domicile theory, as is evidenced from the post-1960 judgments.

The Act of 1960, it may be noted, was never discussed in Parliament as a rule of private international law, but its role in reshaping these rules is undeniable. It is to be treated as part of English rules of private international law. The outcome of it all is that in Great Britain, the present practice is to opt for the dual domicile theory.[31]

Position in India

The Indian case law on this point is based solely on *Parwathawwa* v. *Channawwa*,[32] the facts of which are reproduced below.

Siddhalingiah, a domiciliary of the erstwhile native State of Hyderabad (a foreign state at that time) married Channawwa, domiciled in Bombay, while he was already married. Bigamy was prohibited in terms of the Bombay Prevention of Hindu Bigamous Marriage Act (which had no counterpart in Hyderabad State). On Siddhalingiah's death, dispute arose with regard to succession to his property which, in turn, raised the question of the validity of his second marriage with Channawwa. The marriage was void if the dual domicile doctrine was to be applied since the wife's *lex domicilii*—the Bombay law—did not permit this bigamous matrimonial alliance. But the marriage was valid in terms of the intended matrimonial home theory as the parties were supposed to set up their home in Hyderabad where polygamy was not prohibited.

Somnath Iyer, J. opted for the intended matrimonial home theory and upheld the validity of the marriage and observed as follows:

What emerges from this discussion is that on the question as to what law should govern the capacity of marriage there are at least three streams of thought. One view is that it is the law of the place of celebration which overlooks the distinction between formality and capacity. The second is that it is the law of the domicile of each party before the marriage which is demonstrated by the latter pronouncement to be a conservative and orthodox view. The third is that the law of the intended matrimonial home is what governs capacity which has been explained as the best.

The discussion made so far is about the law which governs capacity, and in my opinion, that law is the law of the husband's domicile if not the law of the intended matrimonial home which was in the case before us, the Mitakshara School of Hindu law in force in the erstwhile State of Hyderabad which bestowed capacity on both the spouses to marry one another. That it is so would be end of the defendant's contention that the plaintiff was not the wife of Siddhalingiah.

The law of Siddhalingiah's domicile which was also the law of intended matrimonial home did not prohibit polygamy. So Siddhalingiah could take a second wife and the plaintiff could be his wife.

The court also referred to *De Reneville* v. *De Reneville*[33] and observed that a marriage which was celebrated in the State of Bombay does not fall outside the principle pronounced by the Master of Rolls in that case. De Renville, the court felt, covered the case before it since the plaintiff and Siddhalingiah both intended to live together in the husband's home in Hyderabad State which was the country of their matrimonial home. The Hyderabad law, therefore, applied and validated the marriage, even though it was polygamous and, as such, prohibited by Bombay law. It is, thus, clear that India has adopted the intended matrimonial home theory. However, it is likely that Indian courts may in future follow English courts in the resolution of this conflict by adopting the latter's post-1960 approach—that is, by adopting the dual domicile theory.

From the foregoing discussion, it appears that the problem of choice of law for testing the capacity of intending spouses has been neatly solved—one opts either for the intending matrimonial home theory or for the dual domicile theory. However, this solution is not so simple and straightforward as it appears to be. The matter defies such a neatly defined solution on account of the presence of another factor, namely the *lex loci celebrationis*. It has been stated earlier that this law is there only to govern the formal requirements and has nothing to do with the capacity of the parties; but this rule is not always observed in England. In *Breen* v. *Breen*,[34] a case of marriage solemnized in Ireland between two England domiciled parties, the question of capacity was referred to the Irish law. Further, an English registrar of marriages would not allow solemnization to go through unless all the requirements of English law were satisfied. As Cheshire puts it

> an English registrar, for instance, cannot be required to sanction a marriage if it would be void for incapacity by English law and an English court is unlikely, for policy reasons, to uphold such a marriage. It is probably true to say that all marriages in England must comply with English law not only as to formal validity but also as to matter of essential validity.[35]

Breen has been widely criticized and can be dismissed as a freak, but what about insistence of English law on compliance with all its requirements? Cheshire's justification of this approach of English law as conditioned by reasons of policy seems to be flawed. There can certainly be some requirement so fundamental that it has to be satisfied in all cases: for example, monogamy is so fundamental to the English social system that its violation on the English soil cannot be tolerated and therefore solemnization of a bigamous marriage cannot be allowed in England even though permitted by the *lex domicilii* of the parties. However, to assert that all requirements of English law (even as to capacity) should be satisfied, is to set the rule at naught which may engender conflict.

There is no case law on this point in India; but it appears that we can follow the rule whereby the capacity is governed by the dual domicile theory or the intended matrimonial theory, with *lex loci celebrationis* allowed to step in only when some fundamental social norm/basic tenet is violated.

It may be stated that this insistence by English courts on compliance with all requirements of English law is confined only to cases where the *lex loci celebrationis* and *lex fori* coincide. In cases where the marriage has been solemnized outside the UK, there is no such insistence, as is illustrated by *Reed* v. *Reed*.[36] The parties were first cousins, domiciled in British Columbia, the law of which did not allow marital alliance between them for the reasons that the female party, being below 18, needed parental consent which had been refused. They, therefore, got married in the State of Washington where all the formal requirements stood satisfied even though alliance between two first cousins was not permitted.

The wife petitioned an English court for nullity on the ground of lack of parental consent. The court characterized this requirement as one of formal validity referrable to the *lex loci celebrationis* and dismissed the petition. As is evident, the court did not insist on compliance with English law as regards the formal requirements since the marriage had been solemnized in a country outside the UK.

Ambiguity in the Concept of the Intended Matrimonial Home Theory

As its name suggests, the parties' intention[37] to set up their home in the place of the husband's domicile is the key to the application of this theory. However, it is not clear whether intention alone is sufficient or whether it has to be supplemented by something else—the translation of this intention into reality. Let us revert to case law on this point:

(1) In *Mette* v. *Mette*,[38] the court relied on the fact that the husband had remained domiciled in England and marriage was with a view to subsequent residence in England. Domicile in the past, that is, before the solemnization of the marriage, can only strengthen and reinforce the presumption about the intention; but it cannot substitute for actually settling in that place.

(2) In Sean's Will,[39] the word 'probably' employed by the court in its observation that the 'law of the country of the parties in which they are afterwards *probably* to live', suggests not only that intention is enough, but that there is no obligation on the part of the parties to actually settle down in the place of husband's domicile.

(3) In *Kenward* v. *Kenward*,[40] there is a clear affirmation by Lord Denning that intention alone is sufficient.

(4) In *De Renville* v. *De Renville*,[41] according to Lord Green MR, the governing law is the law of the husband's domicile on the day of

marriage because it is the law by reference to which the parties are supposed to have entered into the marriage. This, at the most, points to the intention of the parties (since the parties are supposed to enter into marriage with this law in view). There is no obligation to actually set up their home in the place of the husband's domicile. However, in the same case, Lord Bucknill, LJ emphasized, while applying the doctrine of intended matrimonial home, the fact of the marriage ceremony as having taken place and the parties as having lived together in that very place. This gives the impression that actually setting up a home there is necessary.

As shown above, it is evident that there is no consensus on this important point. In that event, all that can be done is to make presumptions and to see what consequences flow from them.

Presumption I: Mere intention is enough. If so, can the validity of marriage be challenged on the ground that such intention was absent on the date of the marriage. Intention is a conscious mental act which can be ascertained by reference to the facts of the case and the surrounding circumstances as is done in the case of determining one's domicile. For the application of the intended matrimonial home theory, it is only a presumption and that makes it an unreliable basis.

Presumption II: Mere probability should suffice as is evident from 'In the Swan's Will', such probability is derivable from the fact of the husband's domicile, and even intention does not appear to be necessary.

Presumption III: Parties must not only have the intention[42] but must actually settle down in the place of husband's domicile.

In conclusion, we may state that courts cannot reasonably be expected to ascertain the intention of the parties, the most elusive factor, as to the place of their matrimonial home.

To sum up, the view held by courts on what qualifies for the application of the intended matrimonial home theory differs and it is not possible to arrive at a consensus on this point.

SECTION II: SOLEMNIZATION

Solemnization is the first and foremost step in the chain of matrimonial events and is a necessary stipulation in three out of five matrimonial laws of India, namely Hindu law, Christian law (only in the case of Church marriage) and Parsi law. This is discussed below:

Christian Law

There are two types of marriage under the Indian Christian Marriage Act, 1872, namely (i) the religious and (ii) the secular. A religious marriage is to be solemnized in a church appropriate to the denomination of the spouses, to the accompaniment of a religious ceremony. A secular marriage is performed in a registrar's office in the presence of a marriage officer, just by taking the prescribed oath in the name of God and Jesus Christ. It was held in Re Kolandaivelu[43] that a marriage between a Christian and a Hindu can, in terms of Section 4 of the Indian Christian Marriage Act, 1872, be solemnized only under this Act (although there was dissent on this point). Further, by prescribing a compulsory Christian ceremony in all cases where only one party is a Christian, the Indian Christian Marriage Act clashes with the Hindu Marriage Act and the Parsi Marriage and Divorce Act and there is no reason why this Act should be allowed to be what it is in this regard.

Muslim Law

Marriage under this law is not a sacrament but a contract and as such no religious ceremony is needed. Marriage is gone through as if it is entering into a contract.

Parsi Law

The Parsi Marriage and Divorce Act, 1936, prescribes a religious ceremony—*ashirwad*—for the solemnization of a Parsi marriage and in terms of Section 3 of the Act, no Parsi marriage is valid unless solemnized in accordance with the ashirwad ceremony which is to be performed by a priest in the presence of two Parsi witnesses other than the priest. There is no possibility of conflict arising.

Special Marriage Act, 1954

Marriage under this Act is secular and there is no solemnization. The marriage can be entered into before the marriage officer by signing a declaration evidencing the intention of the parties to get married under this Act. There is no possibility of conflict.[44]

Hindu Law

A Hindu marriage cannot be deemed to be conclusive until it has been duly solemnized in accordance with the procedure laid down in Section 7 of the Act. This requirement cannot be dispensed with on the ground that a marriage under the Hindu Marriage Act, 1955 partakes of the character of a contract as it insists on compliance with certain conditions laid down in Section 5 of the Act. A marriage without the solemnization is a nullity.[45]

With the Act providing for marriage between persons following certain different faiths—namely Hinduism, Buddhism, Sikhism—and with each religion having its own solemnization ceremony, the potential for conflict exists. However, this has been forestalled by the provisions contained in Section 7, itself, which says that a marriage under this Act may be solemnized in accordance with the customary rites and ceremony of either party.[46]

For entering into a Hindu Marriage, solemnization (as prescribed in Section 7 of the Hindu Marriage Act, 1955) is essential; at the same time, certain conditions (as laid down in Section 5) have also to be complied with. While the former requirement imparts to a Hindu marriage the character of a sacrament, the latter makes it a contract. It has been felt that these two characteristics cannot go together and one must yield to the other. Thus, in *Parwathawwa* v. *Channawwa*, in which the validity of a Hindu marriage was challenged on the ground of alleged failure to comply with one of the conditions laid down in Section 5, the Mysore High Court observed as follows: 'The doctrine against incapacity in either of the two parties to the marriage is influenced by the theory that a marriage is a contract' and therefore, the court felt doubtful if insistence on the existence of such capacity is possible in the case of a Hindu marriage which is not a contract but a sacrament. The court was of the opinion that 'if the basis of the requirement of capacity in both the parties is the contractual character of the marriage and that basis is not a safe foundation in the case of a marriage between two Hindus, the incapacity in the plaintiff, if any, should not affect the validity of the marriage.'

The court further observed:

> Assuming that the Bombay Act when it came into force divested plaintiff of that capacity to marry a person who had his first wife living and in consequence,

there was incapacity in the plaintiff to marry Siddalingiah,—and on that question,—I do not express any opinion; in this case the question is whether the plaintiff who married Siddalingiah in whom there was no incapacity with the intention of following him to the place of his domicile, where the spouses desired to establish their matrimonial home and of the existence of such intention which is fully established by their subsequent conduct, there can scarcely be any doubts, did not thereby acquire the status of a wife by reason of her own capacity.

It is clear from the observation that the court felt that a Hindu marriage, being a sacrament, cannot be subjected to such legal conditions (as have been laid down in Section 5 of the Hindu Marriage Act, 1955) as applied to a contract. It felt that mere intention on the part of the wife to go to the place of the husband's domicile, be willing to settle down there with him in a domestic framework, and the translation of this intention into reality are good enough to impart validity to the marriage and to enable the plaintiff to acquire the status of a wife.

In this connection, we may also refer to *Ravinder Kumar* v. *Kamal Kanta*[47] wherein the parties refused to go through the solemnization ceremony as prescribed in Section 7 of the Act on the ground that a Hindu marriage is a contract, since contract-like conditions (as laid down in Section 5) have to be complied with and, therefore, mere consent is enough for the validity of a marriage. The Bombay High Court negatived this contention holding that a Hindu marriage remains a sacrament inspite of the requirement of compliance with certain conditions and therefore solemnization ceremony is a must for the validity of a Hindu marriage.

As the Mysore High Court finally decided the case on the basis of the intended matrimonial home doctrine, the conditions of which were fulfilled by the parties, it appears that the court's observations regarding superfluity of the need to comply with the contract-like conditions laid down by Section 5 of the Hindu Marriage Act, 1955, should be treated as *obiter dicta* and the decision delivered by the Bombay High Court in *Ravinder Kumar* v. *Kamal Kanta* should be regarded relevant.

SECTION III: DIVORCE

Each matrimonial law lays down grounds upon which marriage can be dissolved through divorce. However, there is an important omission, whether deliberate or inadvertent, in all these laws except in the Christian law: these laws do not state whether domiciliary/residence qualification is needed for getting a divorce. In fact, before it was amended in 1926, the Indian Divorce Act, 1869, was also silent on this point, with the result that decrees of divorce were made by courts in India in respect of Christian spouses whether or not domiciled in India. It was only after this Act was so amended as to prescribe domiciliary qualification, that Christian spouses became subject to the condition that they had to be domiciled in India. With other Acts/Laws, namely The Hindu Marriage Act, 1955, The Parsi Marriage and Divorce Act, 1936, Muslim Law and the Special Marriage Act, 1954, still remaining silent on this point, we have to look outside for guidance.[48]

In *Smt. Satya* v. *Teja Singh*, a case of grant of divorce by a Nevada court (USA), the Supreme Court of India refused to recognize the divorce on the ground that the husband had not duly acquired domicile in the State of Nevada and, therefore, the divorce in question lacked legality. This case clearly establishes the proposition that domicile in the state from the court of which divorce is sought is considered essential by courts in India.

However, the concept of domicile has been very demanding and even erratic, if we may say so, and has produced bizarre results. This led to a search for an alternative which appeared in the form of 'habitual residence'—a whittled down version of domicile. The British Domicile and Proceedings Act, 1973, replaced domicile by 'residence in UK for at least 18 months.' There is no explicit acceptance of this change, either legislative or otherwise, in India; but it is presumed that courts in our country should also switch over to habitual residence rather than sticking to domicile while granting divorce.[49]

Each law provides for divorce on the grounds specified therein. We are not concerned with all of those grounds but with only those which may create conflict. One such ground not specified in any law is conversion from one faith to another by a spouse followed by his/her petition for divorce on that ground. We may have to consider this aspect on the basis of matrimonial legislations of each of these communities besides the Special Marriage Act, 1954, which is secular.

The pre-1955 Hindu Law

This law did not permit divorce. However, cases of divorce occurred when Hindu spouses converted to another faith. These cases are discussed below:

In *Govardhan* v. *Jasodamono Dassi*,[50] Hindu spouses of a Hindu marriage converted to Christianity and sought dissolution of their marriage under the Indian Divorce Act, 1869. The Calcutta High Court did not consider the matter from the conflicts point of view, but, focusing on the then Christian identity of the spouses, granted divorce.

Both *Peter Thapita* v. *Lakshmi Thapita*[51] and *Periyanayakam* v. *Pottukanni*[52] were identical to *Govardhan* v. *Jasodamono Dassi*. However, the approach of the Madras High Court was different. The court considered the matter from the conflict of laws angle. The parties were married under the polygamous Hindu law (as the pre-1955 uncodified Hindu law was) and in the court's view, this characteristic of the marriage being polygamous was still operative despite the parties' conversion to Christianity. The Indian Divorce Act, which applies only to monogamous marriages, therefore could not be invoked in this case and the petitions were dismissed. Thus, the two high courts delivered contradictory decisions and it is difficult to arrive at any general conclusion on this point. It may be noted that the aforesaid rulings of the high courts have now become no more than academic with the coming into force of the Hindu Marriage Act, 1955.

Hindu Law: Hindu Marriage Act, 1955

The Act (vide Section 13) prescribes the grounds upon which divorce can be granted. These grounds do not seem to have any potential for conflict; and what concerns us is the ground not specified in this section, namely conversion of one or both the spouses to another faith.

Cases of divorce on this ground are set out below.

Aiyesha Bibi v. *Subhodh Chandra*[53]

The Hindu wife of a Hindu marriage converted to Islam and petitioned for divorce on the ground that her new law—the Muslim law—did not allow her to remain married to a non-Muslim and therefore, the marriage stood dissolved under Muslim law. In terms of the Regulating Act, 1781, Hindu law being the defendant's law, was applicable, and consequently the marriage could not be dissolved; but Ormond. J. did not apply Hindu law holding it inapplicable on the ground that a marriage is not a contract. He opted for the rule of justice, equity, and good conscience and, accordingly, dissolved the marriage. What carried weight with the judge was the unenviable position of the wife in case she was forced to stay with her Hindu husband who was certain to treat her with cruelty for having converted to Islam and then sought dissolution.

Rakeya Bibi v. *Anil Kumar Mukherji*[54]

This case is identical with Aiyesha Bibi and Chakravarty, J. agreed with Ormond, J. in that case and dissolved the marriage.

Vilayati Raj v. *Sunila*[55]

A Hindu husband of a Hindu marriage who converted to Islam, petitioned for divorce under Section 13 of the Hindu Marriage Act. The petition was dismissed by the district court on the ground that the petitioner, being no longer a Hindu, could not invoke the Hindu Marriage Act, 1955. However, on appeal, the decision was reversed by the Delhi High Court which held as follows:

(i) a Hindu spouse of a Hindu marriage remains a Hindu for the purpose of his/her Hindu marriage despite his/her conversion to another faith;

(ii) since he/she remains a Hindu despite his/her apostasy from Hinduism, his/her marriage can be dissolved only under the Hindu Marriage Act, 1955; and

(iii) the above position holds good even if the conversion to another faith is by both the spouses.

Promila Khosla v. *Rajneesh Khosla*[56]

The parties were married under the Hindu Marriage Act, 1955, and therefore had to be treated as Hindus on the date of marriage (although it seems the wife professed Christianity even at that time). Later on, the wife declared herself a convert to Christianity and sought divorce under Section 2 (read in conjunction with Section 19) of the Divorce Act, according to which a court can make a decree of dissolution of a marriage when the petitioner or the respondent is a Christian and the parties are domiciled in India. Both the conditions were fulfilled and apparently the Indian Divorce Act was applicable. However, what was not reckoned with was the ruling in Vilayat Raj (discussed above) which ruled out the application of the Indian Divorce Act to this case. Thus, there is a head-on collision between Vilayat Raj and Promila Khosla. The judge resolved the conflict by holding that when one of the spouses is a Christian and the other a Hindu, relief is available under both the laws. The decision, it may be noted, is confined to those cases only where the two religions, namely Hinduism and Christianity, are involved. Subscription to another faith by either spouse shall not attract this ruling.

We may consider what all these rulings, put together, add up to. Of course, the decision in Aiyesha Bibi and Rakeya Bibi can be ignored as they are applicable only in exceptional circumstances; even so justice, as meted out in normal circumstances, may cause extreme hardship to one of the parties. This leaves us with Vilayat Raj and Pramilla Khosla. Are they reconcilable? We shall discuss this aspect later on.

Section 2 of the Indian Divorce Act, 1869, contains provisions regarding grant of divorce. The said section which defines the scope of its applicability, states that a decree of dissolution can be granted under it if (i) the petitioner or the respondent professes Christianity at the time when the petition is presented and (ii) the parties are domiciled in India at the time presenting the petition. This makes its ambit very wide, since any marriage, irrespective of which law it had been solemnized under and despite what faith the party professed when entering into the marriage, can be dissolved under Christian law provided only that one of the parties is a Christian at the time when the petition is presented.

That the ambit of this section is really so wide has been confirmed by *Khosla* v. *Khosla*[57] in the context of a Hindu marriage the wife of which converted to Christianity and then sought divorce under the Indian Divorce Act, 1869. The court declared that when one is a Hindu and the other a Christian, relief is available under both the laws. Accordingly, relief is available under the Christian law/Hindu law, to a

(i) Hindu spouse of a Hindu marriage who converts to Christianity,

(ii) Hindu spouse of a Hindu marriage who remains Hindu, but the other spouse embraces Christianity,

(iii) Christian spouse of a Christian marriage who converts to Hinduism, and

(iv) Christian spouse of a Christian marriage who remains a Christian but the other spouse switches over to Hinduism.

It is submitted that (i) & (ii) above contradict *Vilayat Raj* v. *Sunila*[58] in which it has been decided that a Hindu marriage can be dissolved only under the Hindu Marriage Act, 1955, even if both the parties have embraced some other faith.

Further, (iii) & (iv) establish that two laws now control the marriage and this may also create conflict.

Christian Law

Section 2 of the Indian Divorce Act, 1869, states that a court may grant a decree of dissolution of a marriage in case (i) the petitioner or the respondent professes Christianity and (ii) the parties are domiciled in India at the time of presenting the petition. This section does not state whether this applies to marriages solemnized under this Act only or whether it extends also to other marriages solemnized under other Acts between non-Christian parties one of whom has, since the solemnization of the marriage, converted to Christianity, although the relevant part of this section seems to suggest that it applies irrespective of the original nature of the marriage.[59] Further, it has been held in *Promila Khosla* v. *Rajneesh Khosla* that when one of the spouses is a Christian and the other a Hindu, then relief is available under both the laws.

Muslim Law

Muslim law authorizes a Muslim husband to divorce his wife extrajudicially by pronouncing the word '*talaq*', without having to assign any reason. There is no conflict as long as a Muslim wife remains a Muslim but the situation becomes confusing when a Muslim wife becomes an apostate from Islam. In terms of Section 4 of the Dissolution of Muslim Marriage Act, 1939, a Muslim marriage does not get dissolved in consequence of the wife's apostasy. According to *Sayeeda Khatun* v. *Obadiah*,[60] the new law of the convert also exercises control over her in some respects, but the extent of control has not been defined in the judgment. In cases of conversion to Hinduism, it can be argued that the marriage, having been contracted under Muslim law, remains subject to the control of that law for the purpose of dissolution. There is no conflict as long as a Muslim wife remains a Muslim, but the situation becomes confusing when she becomes an apostate from Islam in view of Section 4 of the Dissolution of Muslim Marriage Act, 1939, which lays down the rule that a Muslim marriage does not get dissolved in consequence of the wife's apostasy. According to *Sayeeda Khatun* v. *Obadiah*,[61] the new law of the convert also exercises control over her in some respects, but the extent of control has not been defined in the judgment. In cases of conversion to Hinduism, it can be argued that the marriage, having been contracted under Muslim law, remains subject to the control of that law for the purpose of dissolution.

Contrary to the ruling in *Sayeeda Khatun* v. *Obadiah*,[62] as also the ruling in *Robasa Khanum* v. *Khodadad Bomanji Irani*,[63] relating to apostasy on the part of a Muslim wife, the Delhi High Court in the case *Munavvar-ul-Islam* (Appellant) v. *Rishu Arora @ Rukhsar* (Respondent),[64] dated 9 May 2014, upheld the decree of divorce granted by the trial court to the Muslim wife, who aposthetised to Hinduism, which was her original fold prior to her conversion and her marriage to her Muslim husband. The Court, a Division Bench headed by Justice S. Ravindra Bhat and Justice Najmi Waziri, speaking through Justice Waziri, while upholding the decree of divorce granted by the trial court to the Muslim wife, made the following significant observation:

> In the light of the above discussion, and the admitted fact that the Respondent was originally a Hindu, who converted to her original faith from Islam, this Court holds that she falls within the second proviso to Section 4 of the Act (namely The Dissolution of Muslim Marriage Act, 1939), which is properly described as an exception to the Section. Her marriage is, accordingly, regulated not by the rule enunciated in Section 4 of the Act, rather by the pre-existing Muslim personal law, which dissolves marriage upon apostasy ipso facto.

Prior to the passing of the Dissolution of Muslim Marriage Act, 1939, a Muslim woman was denied the basic right of seeking dissolution of her marriage from her Muslim husband, even if she be subjected to domestic violence, cruelty, and humiliation by him and his other family members. Legislative reforms such as the Prevention of Domestic Violence Against Women Act, 2005, and the right to seek maintenance by a deserted Muslim wife, whose marriage has been terminated unilaterally by her husband by pronouncing the word 'talaq', without him having to assign any reason for so doing, under Section 125 of the Code of Criminal Procedure, 1973, is of recent happening.

Ironically enough, Section 2 of the Dissolution of Muslim Marriage Act, 1939, confers upon a Muslim wife the right to seek a divorce from her Muslim husband, but does not contain any provision to seek from him maintenance. This hiatus was remedied by the Supreme Court of India by its classic decision in the *Mohammad Ahmed Khan* v. *Shah Bano Begum and Others*,[65] by laying down the rule that a magistrate can grant maintenance or, as the case may be, enhancement of maintenance under Section 125 of the Code of Criminal Procedure, 1973 even beyond the *iddat* period.

However, when conversion is to Christianity, such assertion is not sustainable in view of Section 2 of the Indian Divorce Act, 1869, according to which a marriage can be dissolved under it if at least one party is a Christian. Does it mean total control of the Christian law to the exclusion of Muslim law in the matter of dissolubility? Continued control of Muslim law renders the Indian Divorce Act, 1869, redundant in respect of a Muslim marriage with a Christian wife and a control-sharing arrangement does not seem to be feasible. The husband may divorce his Christian wife through talaq; but she may contest it on the strength of her right to be divorced only judicially under the Indian Divorce Act, 1869, or the Christian wife may invoke this Act for getting a divorce which the Muslim law is not likely to recognize.

A head-on collision seems inevitable. There is no authority on this point. Conflict may also occur in the matter of grant of divorce through talaq as discussed below:

(i) It is not known whether some domiciliary qualification is needed for pronouncing talaq. A Pakistani Muslim husband, while on a short visit to India, may pronounce talaq against his wife living in Pakistan. Is the talaq valid in Pakistan or in India?

(ii) Given the fact that the procedural requirements for pronouncing talaq differs from country to country, the law of which country shall govern the validity of a talaq pronounced in a country other than that in which the husband is domiciled. For example, a Pakistani husband, while on a visit to India, pronounces talaq against his wife living in Pakistan without going through the quasi-judicial formalities prescribed by the Pakistani law. There appears to be no authority on these points. The recent decision of the Supreme Court, dated 22 August 2017, in the writ petition (C) No. 118 of 2016, titled *Shayara Bano, Petitioner* v. *Union of India and Others, Respondents* and similar other writ petitions, in which the Supreme Court by a 3–2 majority set aside the practice of '*talaq-e-biddat*'.

Parsi Law: The Parsi Marriage & Divorce Act, 1936

Provisions regarding divorce/dissolution under this law are embodied in Sections 31, 32, 32A, 32B, and they don't seem to create any conflict. However, one additional ground of dissolution of a Parsi marriage has been sought to be introduced by *Robasa Khanum* v. *Khoda Dad Bomanji Irani.*[66] A Parsi Zoroastrian wife embraced Islam and sought dissolution of the marriage on the ground that her new law did not allow her to remain married to a non-Muslim (the same ground as urged in *Aiyesha Bibi* v. *Subhodh Chandra*). The court rejected her plea for two reasons, namely (i) there is no rule of law under which a marriage solemnized under one law can be dissolved under another law just because one of the spouses has converted to another faith, and (ii) under the rule of justice, equity, and good conscience, which rule has to be applied in the absence of any other being available to meet this situation, dissolution of the marriage is not justified. The petition was dismissed.

The rule which emerges from this case, is, therefore, that a Parsi marriage does not automatically stand dissolved merely on the ground that one of the spouses has switched over to another faith.

The Special Marriage Act, 1954

The provisions relating to grant of divorce are contained in Section 27 of the Act. They do not seem to have any potential for conflict. The Bombay High Court in *Abdul Rahim* v. *Shrimati Padma Abdul Rahim*[67] applied it to a case of marriage solemnized in England in a secular form between two citizens of India describing it as the *lex domicilii* in respect of the marriages solemnized abroad.

Marriages with Foreign Elements

So far, we have limited our discussions to conflict involved in purely domestic cases. The conclusions arrived at may not be valid in cases with foreign elements. As held in *Prem Singh* v. *Dulari Bai*,[68] rules of private international law come into play in such a situation. For ascertaining these rules, we may refer to the Foreign Marriage Act, 1969. This Act envisages the presence of foreign elements for solemnization of marriages abroad between parties at least one of whom is an Indian citizen and, therefore, its provisions must have been formulated taking into consideration the rules of private international law and the requirements of marriage where foreign elements are involved. In Sub-section 4 of the Foreign Marriage Act, 1969, with respect to marriages solemnized abroad, divorces can be granted under the relevant provisions of the Special Marriage Act, 1954, subject to the condition that, in cases of marriages not solemnized under the Foreign Marriage Act, 1969, relief under Special Marriage Act, 1954 shall be provided only if not available under any other law (vide sub-Sections (1) and (4) of Section 18 of Foreign Marriage Act, 1969.

Nullity

Each matrimonial law lays down the reason for which a marriage governed by it can be declared null and void. Each has its own reasons for such declaration. This is shown below in respect of each matrimonial law.

Hindu Law

In terms of Section 11 of the Hindu Marriage Act, 1955, a marriage may be declared null and void if it contravenes any of the conditions laid down in Sub-sections (I), (II), and (V) of Section 5 of the Act, that is, if either party has a spouse living, the parties are within the prohibited degrees of relationship, or are sapindas. It has been held in *Kanwal Ram* v. *HP Administration*[69] that a marriage is not valid unless the essential ceremonies required for its solemnization are proved to have been performed. If a marriage is not proved, what is its legal status? Is it to be equated with nullity with the same consequences as follow nullity under Section 11 of the Act, that is, is it void or voidable? Presumably, from a reading of the language employed in this section of the Act, the marriage is *ab initio* void.[70] There does not appear to be any room for conflict under this head.

Muslim Law

There appears to be no provision in the Muslim law for declaring a marriage null and void. For breach of or non-compliance with the conditions of marriage, the marriage may be irregular, but not null and void.

Christian Law

The matrimonial law of each Christian denomination lays down conditions, the fulfilment of which is necessary before a marriage can be solemnized. The most common of these conditions are:

(i) attainment of the prescribed age by both the parties;
(ii) being out of the degrees of prohibited relationship; and
(iii) not having a spouse living.

However, Sections 18 and 19 of the Divorce Act, 1869, which authorize a court to make a decree of nullity, mention non-fulfilment of only two of these conditions, namely (ii) and (iii) as the grounds for granting nullity; non-fulfilment of the first condition, that is attainment of the prescribed age has not been mentioned. Does it mean that even when the parties have not attained the requisite age, the marriage is valid?

It is not clear whether, for a marriage to be deemed void under Sections 18 and 19, a declaration to this effect by a court is necessary, or whether a marriage is automatically void on the grounds mentioned under Section 19 of the Act.

It is also not clear whether a marriage covered by one of the Sub-sections (1) to (4) is a nullity only if declared so under Sections 18 and 19, that is, is voidable, or whether it is a nullity even when a declaration under Sections 18 and 19 has not been obtained in respect thereof, that is, it is void *ab initio* (as a Hindu marriage under Section 11 of the Hindu Marriage Act, 1955, is). Being voidable means that even a bigamous marriage can subsist, if not challenged.

Besides, Section 88 of the Indian Christian Marriage Act, 1872, also has a bearing upon the validity of a Christian marriage. This section reads as follows: '88. Non-validation of marriages within prohibited degrees ... Nothing in this Act shall be deemed to validate any marriage, which the personal law applicable to either of the parties forbids him or her to enter into.'

Thus, a marriage forbidden by the personal law of either party remains invalid even though duly solemnized under this Act. In that case, is such a marriage void *ab initio* or valid until challenged as regards its validity and declared null and void? The legal status in such a case may require equating it with a voidable marriage.

Special Marriage Act, 1954

Void Marriage

Section 24 of the Act reads as follows:

24. Void Marriage: (1) Any marriage solemnized under this Act shall be null and void and may, on a petition presented by either party thereto against the other party, be so declared by a decree of nullity if

(i) any of the conditions specified in clauses (a), (b), (c) & (d) of Section 4 has not been fulfilled; or

(ii) the respondent was impotent at the time of the marriage and at the time of the institution of the suit.

It is clear from clause (i), read in conjunction with Sub-section 24(1), that a marriage not fulfilling any of the conditions specified in the clause (a), (b), (c) and (d) of Section 4 of the Act is void without being so declared by a court and that a declaration to this effect can be obtained by one of the parties by petitioning the court.

But what about nullity under the clause (ii) of Sub-section 24, that is, where one of the parties is impotent?

Sub-section 24(1) by itself suggests that no declaration is needed in this case also but the use of the words 'respondent' (instead of one of the parties) and 'at the time of the institution of the suit' in clause (ii) point to the necessity of obtaining the declaration from the court. Thus, there seems to be conflict between the first part of Sub-section 24(1) and its subsequent part constituting clause (ii).

It can, no doubt, be argued that impotency is a subjective factor which needs appraisal by a court and therefore a declaration by the court is necessary. Lunacy and other physical defects specified in clause (b) of Section 4 of the Special Marriage Act, 1954, are equally subjective but their appraisal has not been found necessary in terms of clause (i) of Sub-section 24(1) of the Special Marriage Act, 1954 (reproduced above), and a marriage suffering from non-compliance with the conditions laid down in clause (b) of Section 4 can be treated as void without the spouses having to seek a declaration to that effect. From the foregoing, we are constrained to remark that it is regrettable that the Union Parliament in its wisdom chose to bracket clauses (b) of Section 4 and 24(1)(i) along with clauses (a), (c), and (d) of the Section (4) and to treat all of them as null and void *ab initio*.

It may be noted that under the Parsi Marriage and Divorce Act, 1936, such a declaration is not necessary when nullity arises out of non-fulfilment of an objective type of defect such as prohibited degrees of relationship, age, et cetera. (Sections 3 and 4 of the Act); but when nullity results from impotency, declaration from the court is necessary (Section 3 of the Act).

The above exposition of the law on the topic of nullity, however, holds good only in respect of purely domestic cases, that is, cases free from foreign elements. Cases with foreign elements have to be dealt with under the rules of the private international law, as held in *Prem Singh* v. *Dulari Bai*. Under these rules, there are two theories, namely (i) the intended matrimonial home theory, and (ii) the dual domicile theory. These theories have already been discussed. If a marriage, invalid under the chosen theory, is void, a decree of nullity granted in respect thereof can, by petitioning a court, be obtained. If, on the contrary, it be valid, a petition seeking nullity of the marriage, doubtless, will be rejected.

Jurisdiction

We have seen above that all matrimonial laws lay down the grounds on which a decree of nullity can be granted. However, this relief (as all other reliefs) cannot be granted unless the courts are jurisdictionally competent to do so. Therefore, these laws also define the jurisdiction of the court to grant reliefs, including the relief of nullity. But this jurisdiction, unless it explicitly includes cases with foreign elements, is limited to purely domestic cases. Let us discuss the scope of the jurisdiction in respect of each law when some foreign element is involved, that is, when one of the parties happens to be domiciled outside India or when the marriage has been solemnized abroad, et cetera.

SECTION IV: MARRIAGES SOLEMNIZED UNDER THE FOREIGN MARRIAGES ACT, 1969.

Section 4 of the Foreign Marriages Act, 1969, reads as follows:

Conditions relating to solemnization of foreign marriages—a marriage between parties one of whom at least is a citizen of India may be solemnized under this Act by or before a Marriage Officer in a foreign country, if, at the time of the marriage, the following conditions are fulfilled, namely:

(a) neither party has a spouse living;

(b) neither party is an idiot or a lunatic;

(c) the bridegroom has completed the age of twenty one years and the bride the age of eighteen years at the time of the marriage; and

(d) the parties are not within the degrees of prohibited relationship.

Provided that where the personal law or a custom governing at least one of the parties permits of a marriage between them, such marriage may be solemnized, notwithstanding that they are within the degree of prohibited relationship.

Marriage in a foreign country between parties at least one of whom is a citizen of India can be solemnized in the following three ways:

(i) under Section 4 of the Foreign Marriage Act, 1969 (of India) before a marriage officer appointed by the Government of India;

(ii) under the law of the country in which solemnization takes place; and

(iii) under the law of the country in which solemnization takes place, the said solemnization being followed by registration in terms of Section 17 of the Foreign Marriage Act, 1969, with the marriage officer appointed by the Government of India. On registration such a marriage, as from the date of registration, is deemed to have been solemnized under the Foreign Marriage Act, 1969.

Matrimonial reliefs in respect of all marriages solemnized abroad between parties at least one of whom is an Indian citizen, are available under Chapters (V) and (VI) of the Special Marriage Act, 1954.[71] This includes a marriage solemnized under the law of the country in which the solemnization takes place, whether such marriage has been registered under Section 17 of the Foreign Marriage Act, 1969 or not. This is subject to the following conditions:

(i) Section 24 of the Special Marriage Act, 1954, (including Chapter (VI) of the Act and providing for grant of nullity) shall not be applicable to marriages not solemnized under this Act; or deemed to be solemnized under this Act by reason of the provisions contained in Section 17 of the Act;

(ii) Reliefs in respect of marriage not solemnized under this Act shall not be available under the Special Marriage Act, if available under any other act/law.[72] Accordingly, if the parties are co-religionists, a personal law appropriate to the religion they follow shall be there to provide them relief which therefore shall not be available to them under the Special Marriage Act, 1954. Thus, if they both are Hindus, married as per the Hindu marriage ceremony, they shall have relief under the Hindu Marriage Act, 1955, in India. However, if they marry in a secular form, it is not clear under which law, whether under the Hindu Marriage Act or under the Special Marriage Act, relief is available. In *Abdul Rahim* v. *Smt. Padma Abdul Rahim*,[73] a decision of the Bombay High Court, is rather equivocal. In this case, the marriage took place in a secular form in England between two Indian domiciliaries—the male a Muslim and the female a Hindu. The Bombay High Court rejected the husband's claim to relief under the Muslim law on the ground that the relief offered by the Muslim law—the right to divorce by talaq, is not the relief contemplated by Sub-section 18(4) of the Foreign Marriage Act, 1954, the divorce being unilateral and extrajudicial. The court applied the Special Marriage Act. In our imaginary case, relief of the type contemplated by Sub-section 18(4) of the Foreign Marriage Act is available under the Hindu Marriage Act, and it is not known whether the court could opt for the Hindu Marriage Act or the Special Marriage Act.

Similarly, if both the spouses are Parsis or Christians, and the marriage is a religious one, relief may be offered under the Parsi or the Christian law, but if, on the contrary, the marriage is a secular one, the identity of the applicable law is not known. However, if the spouses subscribe to different faiths, the conflict may become yet more complex, since the law of each party in addition to the Special Marriage

Act may contend for application. Let us consider some imaginary cases to demonstrate the nature of the likely conflict involved in foreign marriages.

1. A Hindu husband domiciled in India and having a wife living, goes to Nepal where he contracts marriage with a local girl belonging to a tribe, which follows not Hinduism but some animistic faith, which is not Hinduism in the strict sense of the word and which allows polygamy. This marriage is a foreign marriage in terms of Sub-section 18(1) of the Foreign Marriage Act, 1969, and is, therefore, governed by the Special Marriage Act, 1954. However, its validity cannot be tested with reference to this Act (the Special Marriage Act, 1954) in view of the explanation (ii) (a) to Sub-section 18(1). The marriage is valid by the *lex loci celebrationis* as well as by the second wife's *lex domicilii*. But it has to be valid by the law of the husband's domicile, whether we adopt the dual domicile doctrine or the doctrine of intended matrimonial home. However, which is the husband's *lex domicilii*? Could it be the Hindu Marriage Act, 1954, vide Section 5 of the Act which provides for marriage between two Hindus only and therefore is open to the question of whether a marriage between a Hindu and non-Hindu can also be within the scope of the Act? Furthermore, there is Sub-section 1(2) of the Hindu Marriage Act which reads as follows:

(i) It (the Act) extends to the whole of India except the State of Jammu & Kashmir and applies also to Hindus domiciled in the territories to which this Act extends who are outside the said territories.

Is this provision binding on the husband in question? The entire Act revolves around marriage between two Hindus and is not concerned with anything else. Every provision of this Act has therefore to be read in the context of this Act and there is no justification for construing this particular provision otherwise. It, therefore, cannot be treated as an independent injunction to a Hindu to practice monogamy even while marrying a non-Hindu; its mandate has to be limited to a marriage between two Hindus as laid down in Section (5) of the Act. This rules out the applicability of the Hindu Marriage Act, 1955.

In that case, which law is to govern the validity of this marriage? Could it be the pre-1955 uncodified Hindu law of marriage which has been superseded by the Hindu Marriage Act, 1955, but only in regard to those matters for which provisions are contained in the latter?[74] The Act (Hindu Marriage Act, 1955) does not provide for marriage between a Hindu and a non-Hindu and, therefore, the pre-1955 uncodified Hindu law automatically steps in. There does not appear to be any authority in this regard.

2. A Hindu male citizen of India domiciled in Nepal marries in Nepal a Hindu girl, a citizen and a domiciliary of Nepal, under the Foreign Marriage Act, 1969. In terms of Sub-section 19(2) of the Act, he stands barred from taking an additional wife even in Nepal but he is well within his right to do so under the Nepalese law which allows polygamy. The husband remarries in Nepal and the wife seeks redress. Since none of the parties is domiciled in India, nor has the marriage been solemnized in India, an Indian court has no jurisdiction in the matter (vide subclause 3(c), (i) & (ii) of Sub-section 18 (3) of the Act). A Nepalese court has jurisdiction; but it may hold the marriage valid under the Nepal's polygamous marriage law on the strength of the Nepalese domicile of the concerned parties. However, the wife may come to India and after becoming a resident here in India petition an Indian court, which has jurisdiction in terms of the sub-section quoted above. In such an eventuality what will be the forces ranged against each other? On the one hand, we have the rules of private international law under which the marriage is valid whichever of the two theories, namely the dual domicile theory and the intended matrimonial theory, is applied. Besides, the marriage is also permitted by the *lex loci celebrationis*. On the other hand is the Foreign Marriage Act, 1969, under which the first marriage was solemnized. If the marriage is held valid, rules of private international law based on the generally accepted ground of domicile may be deemed decisive. However, if it is held invalid, statutory provisions of the Foreign Marriage Act grounded on a comparatively weak link, namely citizenship, is the winner. Most likely the court shall abide by the Foreign Marriage Act.

SECTION V: CONVERSION OF SPOUSES OF THE HINDU, CHRISTIAN, AND PARSI MARRIAGES TO ISLAM: RIGHT TO POLYGAMY AFTER SUCH CONVERSION

Three of the four personal laws, namely the Hindu, the Christian, and the Parsi, permit only monogamy. It is only the Muslim law that allows polygamy. As a result, spouses of marriages solemnized under the first three laws sometimes convert to Islam and then take additional wives. It is to be considered whether these remarriages are valid. A critical analysis of some of the important provisions of the acts/laws and cases is given below.

The Hindu Marriage Act, 1955

The leading case on this point is *Sarla Mudgal, President Kalyani* v. *Union of India*.[75] The Hindu husband of the Hindu marriage converted to Islam and then, while the Hindu wife was still living, married a Muslim woman under Muslim law. The validity of this Muslim marriage was challenged by a writ petition presented before Supreme Court.

The Court first examined the impact of this marriage on the subsistence of the Hindu marriage—whether the latter got automatically dissolved or whether it continued to subsist. The Court referred to a number of cases in which the Hindu, Christian, or Parsi wives who had converted to Islam petitioned courts for declaration to the effect that their pre-conversion marriages stood dissolved in consequence of their embracing Islam. The Court took special notice of the following two cases:

Sayeeda Khatun v. *M. Obadiah*[76]

A Jewish wife converted to Islam and then petitioned the court for a declaration that her Jewish marriage had been dissolved.

Lodge, J. while deciding this case made the following observation:

> The Plaintiff (the converting wife) has since converted to Islam and may in some respects be governed by the Mahommedan law ... I can find no authority for the view that a marriage solemnized according to one personal law can be dissolved according to another law simply because one of the two parties has changed his/her religion.

The petition seeking required declaration was dismissed.

Robasa Khanum v. *Khodadad Bomanji Irani*[77]

The case was identical with Sayeeda Khatun except that the petitioner was a Parsi lady. Chagla, J. (as he then was) observed that since there is no rule or authority for dealing with this case, the court was required, as per the Privy Council's decision in *Waghela Rajsanji* v. *Sheikh Masluddin*[78] to apply the rule of justice, equity, and good conscience.

As in the Court's view the spouses could happily live together inspite of the wife's conversion to Islam, dissolution of the marriage was uncalled for. The petition, therefore, was dismissed. It may be noted that the decisions in two similar cases, namely, *Aiyesha Bibi* v. *Subhodh Chandra*[79] and *Rakeya Bibi* v. *Anil Kumar*[80] favoured dissolution of the marriages. However, the dissolution was decreed by the courts keeping in view the special circumstances of those cases and not because the petitioners had a right to automatic dissolution sought by them. Thus, these two cases only confirm what has been decided in Sayeeda Khatun and Robasa Khanum.

The other cases, referred to by the Supreme Court also came to same conclusion and, therefore, the Court felt persuaded to accept that a marriage endures despite the conversion of the wife to Islam.

The Court then considered whether the Muslim marriage can be accommodated alongwith the subsisting Hindu marriage. It found that the Hindu law enjoins monogamy and does not admit yet another marriage. The second marriage thus is bigamous and therefore void. Consequently, it attracts Sections 494 and 495 of the Indian Penal Code.

The Court also referred (vide paragraphs 28 and 29 of the judgment) to *Attorney General of Ceylon* v. *Reid*[81] in which a Christian husband in Ceylon embraced Islam and then married a Muslim woman. The Privy Council held the marriage valid. The Supreme Court dismissed that case as not relevant on the ground that there were two personal laws operating in that case, namely the Christian law and Muslim law, the latter having become operative after the conversion; whereas, in the case under consideration only one law, namely Hindu law, governed the marriage. The Court thus impliedly reiterated the position spelt out in *Vilayat Raj* v. *Sunila* that a Hindu spouse of a Hindu marriage remains a Hindu subject to the Hindu law for the purpose of the Hindu marriage, conversion to another faith notwithstanding.

In connection with the court's finding in this case, we may refer to Section 17 of the Hindu Marriage Act, 1955 which reads as follows: 'Punishment for bigamy of any marriage between two Hindus solemnized after the commencement of this Act is void if on the date of such marriage either party had a husband or a wife living and provisions of Section 494 and 495 of the Indian Penal Code shall apply accordingly.'

According to this section, the marriage, to be void, has to be between two Hindus, whereas in the case under consideration, only one party, the husband (assuming that he remains a Hindu for the purpose of the Hindu marriage inspite of his conversion to Islam) was a Hindu, and the other, the wife, a Muslim. The condition that both the parties had to be Hindu is thus not fulfilled and therefore sections of the IPC are not attracted.

Can we approach these sections direct without the intervention of the Hindu Marriage Act, 1955? If Section 17 of the Act had not been there, there is no doubt that the two sections of the IPC would automatically apply; but with the scope of these sections having been defined, in the context of Section 17 of the Hindu Marriage Act, 1955, it seems imperative, that the Sections 494 and 495 of the IPC are interpreted and applied as ordained in Section 17.

This seems to suggest that a Hindu husband on conversion to Islam can validly marry a Muslim female (even while having his Hindu wife alive) unless Section 17 of the Act is deleted or is so amended as to drop the words 'between two Hindus.' This is contrary to what the Supreme Court has in this case decided, and, it is submitted with respect, that the court has not taken into consideration the provisions of Section 17 which insist on the Hindu religious identity of both the parties.

In this connection, we may refer to Section 4 of the Parsi Marriage and Divorce Act, 1936, the provisions of which, in clear and unambiguous language, ensure that a Parsi remains monogamous and there is no escape route such as change of religions for practising bigamy. The said section states explicitly what it means. This provision was there before the draftsmen of the Hindu Marriage Act, 1955, when they drafted the Act; and it is intriguing as to why they did not choose to incorporate similar provisions in the Act, if they wanted strict monogamy as the norm to govern Hindus.

Parsi Law

Section 4 of the Parsi Marriage and Divorce Act, 1936, lays down that no Parsi spouse even if he/she has changed his/her religion can contract another marriage unless his/her subsisting marriage, even if contracted under a law other than the Parsi Marriage & Divorce Act, 1865, or the Parsi Marriage & Divorce Act, 1936, has been duly dissolved. It is, therefore, evident that a Parsi spouse, even after his/her conversion to another faith, cannot validly practise polygamy. It is also clear from Sub-section 52 (2) that the spouses remain subject exclusively to the control of the Parsi Act.

Christian Law

In *John Jiban Chandra* v. *Abinash Sen*,[82] the Christian husband of a Christian marriage embraced Islam and contracted a second marriage. The Calcutta High Court held the second marriage valid on the ground that the husband's new personal law, namely the Muslim law, permits him to practise polygamy.

It is to be noted that the Christian law in terms of Sub-section 10(ii) of the Indian Divorce Act, 1869, allows a Christian wife to seek divorce from her husband on the ground of her husband's conversion to another faith. This suggests that (1) the wife remains subject to the Christian law and that (2) the Christian marriage remains subsisting. With the Calcutta High Court holding (as it did in John Jiban Chandra) that a Christian husband on conversion to Islam can remarry under the Muslim law, the position that emerges is that there are two laws governing the marriage,[83] namely the Christian law governing the wife and the Muslim law controlling the husband. This might lead to conflict. The husband may like to divorce his wife under Muslim law by pronouncing talaq and the wife also may counter by asserting her right under the Divorce Act, 1869, to be divorced only judicially.

2. Amongst the various requirements laid down by personal matrimonial laws, the one which is foremost and which is common to all such laws is the one insisting upon the certain religious identity of spouses. Compliance with this requirement is crucial, as failure implies non-availability of the particular law to the parties concerned. Thus, for getting married under the Hindu Marriage Act, 1955, the parties have to be Hindus as the Act is not open to non-Hindus. The question that arises is whether this requirement is an essential one referrable to the *lex domicilii* or a procedural norm controlled by the *lex loci celebrationis*.

For example, parties domiciled in Thailand and professing Buddhism may choose to get married in India under the Hindu Marriage Act, 1955. According to the Thai law they are not Hindus, but in terms of various provisions of the Hindu Marriage Act, 1955, they are to be treated as Hindus.[84] In case the validity of such a marriage is challenged on the ground that the parties are not Hindus, are we to refer to the Thai law, the *lex domicilii* of the parties, or to the Hindu Marriage Act, the *lex loci celebrationis*?

This question neatly arose in *Meera Devi* v. *Aman Kumari*.[85] In this case, the *lex domicilii* and *lex loci celebrationis* were different. The court referred the matter to the *lex domicilii* which determined the husband to be a non-Hindu. If this requirement was treated as one of essential nature, the marriage should have been declared invalid. But the court, on consideration of the fact that the husband declared himself a Hindu before the marriage officer, held the marriage valid, suggesting thereby that this requirement could also be treated as procedural. What seems to emerge from this is that this requirement is of a twin character, referable to either of the two, the *lex domicilii* and the *lex loci celebrationis*, and the marriage should be upheld if either of them supports it.

3(i). Conflict between the provisions of the Hindu Marriage Act, 1955, and those of the Foreign Marriage Act, 1969. Sub-section 1(2) of the Hindu Marriage Act, 1955, reads as given below.

It (the Act) extends to the whole of India except the State of Jammu & Kashmir, and applies also to Hindus who are domiciled in the territories to which this Act extends, who are outside the said territories.

The sub-section mandates that Hindus who are domiciled in India must, even when they are outside India, comply with the conditions laid down in Section 5 of the Act for getting married; whereas Section 4 of the Foreign Marriage Act, 1969, obligates an Indian citizen, while getting married abroad under this Act, to fulfil the conditions laid down under the said section. The conditions laid down by these two sections, namely, Section 5 of the Hindu Marriage Act, 1955, and Section 4 of the Foreign Marriage Act, 1969, are different. This may result in conflict as a Hindu domiciled in India may also be an Indian citizen. In that case which of the two sets of conditions has he to fulfill?

Perhaps the conflict may be resolved by holding that when a Hindu domiciled in India also happens to be an Indian citizen and wants to get married abroad—say in Nepal, where a Hindu marriage law is in force—he can choose to get married as a Hindu, in which case he has to comply with the conditions prescribed by Section 5 of the Hindu Marriage Act, 1955, (in addition to the conditions prescribed by the Nepalese law). However, if he elects to marry not as a Hindu domiciled in India but as an Indian citizen under the Foreign Marriage Act, 1969, then he has to comply only with the conditions laid down in Section 4 of the Foreign Marriage Act, 1969, the conditions laid down in Section 5 of the Hindu Marriage Act, 1955, notwithstanding.

3(ii). Can a marriage be validly solemnized between a Hindu and a non-Hindu and, if so, under which law/Act?

Section 5 of the Hindu Marriage Act, 1955, provides for marriage only between two Hindus and there is no other section in the Act which provides for marriage between a Hindu and non-Hindu.[86] Does this mean that under the current Hindu matrimonial regime marriage is not permitted between a Hindu and a non-Hindu? It was held in *Mrs. Chandramani Dubey* v. *Ramakant Dubey*[87] that a marriage between a Hindu and a Christian was valid. This was in terms of the uncodified pre-1955 Hindu law. That law has since been replaced by the Hindu Marriage Act, 1955, but only in respect of those matters in regard to which provisions have been made in the Act.[88] The Act provides for marriage only between two Hindus, suggesting thereby that the provisions of the uncodified pre-1955 Hindu law regarding marriage between a Hindu and a non-Hindu may be deemed to be still in force. It may be gathered therefrom that the solemnization of a marriage between a Hindu and a non-Hindu is still permitted.

3(iii). It is not known whether such a marriage can be solemnized under the uncodified pre-1955 Hindu law, but it is clear that such a marriage can validly be solemnized if some other law is available that permits such matrimonial alliance.

3(iv). The pre-1955 Hindu law permitted polygamy.[89] Does it mean that a Hindu can validly contract a polygamous marriage under a tribal law with a member of a scheduled tribe the law of which allows polygamy?

4. A marriage takes place in Great Britain in a registrar's office between two Indian domiciliaries, the male a Christian and the female a Hindu. On return to India, the husband seeks divorce. The question arises under which law he can seek remedy.

This is a foreign marriage in terms of Sub-section 18(1) of the Foreign Marriage Act and therefore the relief of divorce is available under the Special Marriage Act, but only if, in terms of Sub-section 18(4) of the Foreign Marriage Act, 1869, it is not available under any other law.

In *Abdul Rahim* v. *Shrimati Padma Abdul Rahim*,[90] a similar case of marriage with the exception that the husband was a Muslim (and not a Christian), the Bombay High Court refused to apply the Muslim law on the ground that the relief provided by that law was not the one contemplated by Sub-section 18(4) of the Foreign Marriage Act, 1869, the divorce being unilateral and extrajudicial. Does it mean that, in this case, the Christian law may be applied since that law provides relief comtemplated in Sub-section 18(4) of the Foreign Marriage Act?

5. Who is a Parsi?

Attempts have been made by courts in two cases to analyse and define a Parsi personality for the purpose of the Parsi marriage laws. These cases are discussed below:

(1) *Sir Dinshaw M. Petit* v. *Sir Jamshetji Jijibhoy*.[91] In this case, Sir Dinshaw Davar, J. was of the opinion that the Parsi community consists of:

(i) Parsis who descended from the original Persian emigrants and who are born of both Zoroastrian parents and who profess Zoroastrianism; or
(ii) the Iranians from Persia who profess Zoroastrian religion and who come to India either temporarily or permanently; or
(iii) the children of Parsi fathers from alien mothers who have been duly admitted into the religion.[92]

Sarvar Merwan Yezdiar v. *Merwan Rashid Yezdiar*[93]

In this case, the Bombay High Court was concerned with a much narrower question, namely whether Iranians who profess Zoroastrianism and who are temporarily in India can be regarded as Parsis for the purpose of the Parsi Marriage and Divorce Act, 1936. The court's findings are as follows:

(a) If the two attributes mentioned against (i) in Sir Dinshaw M. Petit case referred to above were enough to make a person a Parsi, then all the Iranians professing Zoroastrianism in Iran would have been Parsis; but this is not so;

(b) Faith in Zoroastrianism cannot be regarded as an essential attribute of a Parsi; there are many Parsi Muslims and Parsi Christians in India. The court declined to treat the parties in the case mentioned above as Parsi for the purpose of the Parsi Marriage and Divorce Act, 1936. In the course of the judgment, the court made the following observation:

(i) it (that is, the court) felt that domicile in India is the minimum condition for being a Parsi, although it refrained from expressing its view whether acquisition of domicile by the parties could make them Parsis;

(ii) the court referred to the Privy Council's view in *Sir Dinshaw M. Petit* v. *Sir Jamsetji Jijibhoy* to the effect that Parsis were racial Parsis or people deemed after a long lapse of ages to be racial Parsis. This, in the court's view, suggests that a Parsi could be a Parsi only by birth. However, by birth from whom? In the court's opinion a section of Zoroastrians from Persia who came to India many centuries ago and settled down here forming a close knit community which laid the foundation of the Parsi community and its descendents who are termed as Parsis. However, the court has not clarified whether this process of Parsization, of ripening of the Persian Zoroastrians, after the lapse of ages, into Parsis froze after the first wave of immigration or whether it is a continuum continuing even with the subsequent immigration in groups or individually and, if continuous, what time gap is permissible.

It is clear that even after two judgments by two disntinguished judges, Sir Dinshaw Davar in *Sir Dinshaw M. Petit* v. *Sir Jamsetji Jijibhoy* and M. C. Chagla, C.J., in *Yezdiar* v. *Yezdiar*, the Parsi identity for the purpose of the Parsi Marriage & Divorce Act, 1936, lacks a clear-cut definition.

Special Marriage Act, 1954

Can it be invoked for the dissolution of the marriages solemnized under it only, or can any marriage solemnized under any other Act also be brought within its scope for the purpose of dissolution? This question arose in two cases which are discussed below:

Aulvin V. Singh v. *Chandravati*[94]

The Allahabad High Court ruled that only marriages solemnized under this Act can be dissolved under it. It dismissed the petition for dissolution under this Act of a marriage solemnized under the Indian Christian Marriage Act, 1872.

Christopher Andrews Neelkantan v. *Anne Neelkantan*[95]

The marriage took place in England between two Christians, the male domiciled in India and the female in the UK. On return to India, alone without his spouse, the husband petitioned the Rajasthan High Court for a decree of divorce under the Special Marriage Act, 1954. The marriage had been solemnized in a church and, therefore, relief was available in India under the (Indian) Divorce Act, 1869. But the court granted the decree of divorce holding that the phraseology of the Special Marriage Act suggests that its applicability is wide enough to embrace all marriages irrespective of which law they have been solemnized under. Thus, according to that court, this Act is the general law of divorce in force in this country.[96]

We may, in this connection, make the following observation touching the Special Marriage Act, 1954:

The basic purpose of the Special Marriage Act, 1954, is to avoid conflict inherent in a matrimonial alliance between parties who profess different faiths. If this Act had not been enacted, parties following different religions would not have been in a position to marry, or if even they could, they would have been, in fairness to each of them, subject to their respective personal laws; the same would have been the position if the parties, co-religionists at the time of marriage, drifted away from this coincidence by one of the parties changing over to another religion.

Such a situation would have caused conflict. The Special Marriage Act, 1954, steps in in such a situation and, by providing one law biased in favour of neither governs both the spouses and averts conflict. But in this particular case, where both the parties were Christians and the marriage was solemnized in a church, the Indian Divorce Act, 1869, is more appropriate since it is common to both the spouses, besides its being their religious law. In fact in *Aulvin V. Singh* v. *Chandrawati*,[97] a case of marriage between two Christians domiciled in India, the Allahabad High Court, as aforesaid, refused to apply the Special

Marriage Act, 1954, for grant of a decree of divorce on the ground that since the marriage was solemnized under the Indian Christian Marriage Act, 1872, relief was available only under the Christian law that is, the Indian Divorce Act, 1869. However, *Neelkantan* v. *Neelkantan* having set a precedent, a Christian marriage solemnized in a religious form has become subject, for the purpose of matrimonial relief, to two laws—the Indian Divorce Act, 1869 and the Special Marriage Act, 1954.

This may lead to a conflict[98]—something which the Special Marriage Act, 1954 seeks to avert.

It may, however, be noted that the Law Commission in its 23rd Report took notice of this decision which stands negatived by the Foreign Marriage Act, 1969, enacted by the government in response to the Law Commission's Report as mentioned above. In terms of Section 18 of the Act, the matrimonial reliefs are available in respect of all the marriages solemnized abroad (including marriages solemnized under a law other than the Foreign Marriage Act) between parties of whom at least one is an Indian citizen under Chapters V and VI of the Special Marriage Act, 1954. However, this is subject to the condition that, in case of a marriage not solemnized under the Foreign Marriage Act,1969, relief under the Special Marriage Act, 1954, shall be available only if not available under any other Act/law. In this particular case, the marriage had been solemnized in a religious form in a church and therefore, the Christian law—the Indian Divorce Act, 1869, could be invoked for relief, thus barring access to the Special Marriage Act, 1954.

Abdul Rahim v. *Smt. Padma Abdul Rahim*[99]

A marriage took place in 1966 in Britain in a registrar's office between parties—a male Muslim and a female Hindu, both citizens of, and domiciled in India. The marriage was under the British Marriage Act, 1949. The spouses returned to India in April, 1969 and the husband purported to divorce the wife through talaq. The husband maintained that the talaq was efficacious because Muslim law was applicable to the marriage on two grounds, namely;

(i) it was the *lex domicilii* of the husband on the spouses' return to India, and

(ii) the wife, after their return to India, had converted to Islam.

The main issue before the Bombay High Court was which law governed the marriage on the spouses' return to India. Could it be the (Indian) Foreign Marriage Act, 1969?

The plaintiff husband in this case raised two objections to the applicability of the Foreign Marriage Act, 1969, namely:

(i) the Foreign Marriage, Act, 1969, came into force in November, 1969, after the marriage had been solemnized in 1966 and the Act could not be applied retrospectively as it has not provided for retrospective application; and (ii) even assuming that the Foreign Marriage Act, 1969, could be applied retrospectively, support for the applicability of this Act remains absent, since Sub-section 18(4) states that relief under the Special Marriage Act can be granted in respect of marriages solemnized abroad under a law other than the Foreign Marriage Act, 1969, only if it is not available under any other Act.

In this case, relief being available under Muslim law, the Foreign Marriage Act, 1969, and in pursuance of it the Special Marriage Act, 1954 could not be invoked.

The court dealt with this objection as set out below:

(i) The phraseology of the Foreign Marriage Act,1969 is so structured as to allow its retrospective application; and, besides, (ii) relief available under the Muslim law being unilateral and extrajudicial, is not the relief contemplated in Sub-section 18(4) of the Foreign Marriage Act,1969.

The court, therefore, held the Special Marriage Act, 1954, as indicated vide Sub-section 18(4) of the Foreign Marriage Act, 1969, as applicable.

In this connection, it is pertinent to observe as follows:

That the marriage had taken place under the British Marriage Act, 1949, according to which the contract in which the marriage originates becomes *functus officio* on the solemnization of the marriage.[100] Accordingly, the British Marriage Act ceased to apply on the solemnization of the marriage and a successor law taking over. Now which law could it be? This law had to be found immediately. If the spouses had been domiciled in Britain, the obvious choice would have been the British law on divorce; but since the parties were domiciled in India, it had to be an Indian law. A choice of Muslim law as the law of the husband could not be made, since it could prove to be discriminatory against the wife, while the selection of both the laws for governing the marriage could create conflict.

So the obvious choice was the Special Marriage Act which could accommodate both the parties to this secular marriage. Thus only this law could properly be fitted in here. Arguably the Special Marriage Act could have been applied even without the intervention Section 18 of the Foreign Marriage Act, 1969. It may be noted that the plaintiff, in support of his claim that Muslim law was applicable, cited *Khambatta* v. *Khambatta*,[101] which was an identical case except that the wife was a Christian. The Bombay High Court in that case held the Muslim law applicable. This finding, however, was obviously based on the fact that the Special Marriage Act, 1872, then in force, did not apply to Muslims.

CONCLUSION

The law relating to marriage and divorce, as interpreted and applied by courts in India, more than justifies the title chosen by the author, namely *The Conflict of Laws: Inter-Territorial and Inter-Personal Conflict.*

As for the Western World, which is predominantly Christian, they understand only conflicts between the laws of countries and not inter-personal law conflicts. But in the Indian subcontinent, wherein each religious community is governed by its own personal law, conflicts do arise when a person belonging to one religious community intermarries with a person belonging to another religious community. As all the Indian religious communities, barring the Muslims, profess monogamy, there is less likelihood of conflicts arising when such inter-religious marriages take place among them, except that a Hindu marriage could take place only between two Hindus as per Section 5 of the Hindu Marriage Act, 1955. On the contrary, when a Christian husband embraces Islam, it appears, he cannot only unilaterally terminate his prior marriage, but also take as many as four wives after divorcing his first wife.[102]

Courts in India, as we gather from our inquiry, rendered conflicting decisions on the legal effects of such unilateral divorces. It is no wonder, therefore, that scholars from England, to name Professor Duncan Derrett and Dr David Pearl among others, hold the view that there is nothing like *lex domicilii* or *lex loci* for the Indian communities. The falsity of such appraisal is laid bare considering that courts in India employ, *mutatis mutandis*, the self same conflict of law rules in resolving inter-personal law conflicts.

The Supreme Court of India, as its counterpart in the United States, has had very few opportunities to decide cases on conflict of laws. Even so, a few cases that the Supreme Court of India was called upon to decide in matters such as grant of maintenance to a divorced wife, recognition of foreign judgments of divorce rendered *ex parte*, or, as may be, of the case of a Hindu wife whose Hindu husband, after having embraced Islam, sought to divorce her unilaterally by pronouncing talaq, the courts' performance has hitherto been satisfactory.

The Supreme Court was categorical in its pronouncements both in *Shah Bano's case*[103] and in *Danial Latifi's case*[104] that a magistrate can grant maintenance or, as the case may be, enhancement of maintenance under Section 125 of the Criminal Procedure Code, even beyond the iddat period. The Shah Bano ruling of the Supreme Court prompted the government to usher in the Muslim Women (Protection of Rights on Divorce) Act, 1986, as a counter to the judicial challenge, but the legislative challenge through the above enactment could not deter the Supreme Court to forge ahead in its endeavour to secure the interests of the hapless divorced Muslim wife by enlarging the scope and effect of the maintenance obligation of her Muslim husband. This, as one could see, is reflected in the decision of the Constitution Bench of the Supreme Court in the case *Danial Latifi and another* v. *Union of India*.[105] The court, while dismissing a writ petition filed by Danial Latifi, a Muslim husband who divorced his wife, challenging the validity of the Muslim Women (Protection of Rights on Divorce) Act, 1986, as a violation of the Fundamental Rights guaranteed under Articles 14, 15, and 21 of the Constitution of India, ruled that a Muslim husband as per Section 3(1)(a) of the Act is obliged to make 'a reasonable and fair provision for the future of the divorced wife'. The statutory obligation under Section 3(1)(a) of the Act, according to the Supreme Court, is inclusive in its scope and effect in that it obligates the Muslim husband not only to discharge his maintenance obligation to his divorced wife during the iddat period but also to make 'a reasonable and fair provision and maintenance for the future of the divorced wife to be made and paid to her within the period of iddat' (per Rajendra Babu, J. as he then was). Besides, considering that the said Section 3 of the Act commences with a *non obstante* clause, the judicial interpretation in the case under review overrides all other pre-existing laws or decisions of courts.[106] The Constitution Bench of the Supreme Court of India in *Khatoon Nisa* v. *State of U.P. and Others*[107] held the view that as the parameters and considerations are the same under Section 5 of the Muslim Women (Protection of Rights on Divorce) Act, 1986, as under Section 125 of the Criminal Procedure Code, even if the Muslim husband and his divorced wife fail to invoke the option under Section 5 of the Act, a magistrate can still exercise his powers to grant maintenance to the Muslim wife on the strength of the ruling in Danial Latifi's case. In the case *Shabana Bano* v. *Imran Khan*,[108] a Division Bench of the Supreme Court observed that a cumulative reading of the relevant portions of judgments of the Court in *Danial Latifi and Iqbal Bano* v. *State of U.P. and Another*[109] would make it 'crystal clear' that even a divorced Muslim woman would be entitled to claim maintenance from her divorced husband as long as she does not remarry.

In a recent case, namely *Shamim Bano, Appellant* v. *Asraf Khan, Respondent*,[110] decided by a Division Bench of the Supreme Court on 16 April 2014, the Court, speaking through Dipak Misra, J., endorsed the dictum in Khatoon Nisa's case, namely that seeking of option by a Muslim wife for divorce under Section 3(2) of the Muslim Women (Protection of Rights on Divorce) Act, 1986, will not in any way affect her right to seek maintenance under Section 125 of Criminal Procedure Code. Based on the above dictum of the Constitution Bench of the Supreme Court in the Khatoon Nisa case, the Supreme Court, in the present case, observed that the High Court was not correct in holding that when the appellant-wife filed her application under Section 3 of the Act, she exercised her option. On the contrary, the magistrate still retained the power of granting maintenance under Section 125 of the Criminal Procedure Code to a divorced Muslim woman. Further, in view of the fact that the proceeding was continuing without any objection that undoubtedly would lead to the same result, whether it be an application under Section 125 of the Criminal Procedure Code or it be one under Section 3 of the 1986 Act, the High Court obviously erred in holding that the proceeding after the divorce took place was not maintainable. On top of it all, the recent decision of the Supreme Court, dated 22 August 2017, in the writ petition (C) No. 118 of 2016, titled *Shayara Bano, Petitioner* v. *Union of India and Others, Respondents*, and similar other writ petitions, setting aside by a 3–2 majority the practice of '*talaq-e-biddat*' (that is, triple talaq), is truly epochal.

The recent developments on the issue of recognition of *ex parte* decrees of divorce granted by foreign courts to errant husbands, based on the so-called domicile that they claim to have acquired by a six-week or twelve-week residence, as required under the laws of the State of Nevada and the State of New Mexico, the Supreme Court of India in *Smt. Satya* v. *Teja Singh*[111] and in *Y. Narsimha Rao* v. *Y. Venkatalakshmi*[112] was equally categorical in denouncing them. Again, on the issue of the right of a Hindu husband, a convert to Islam, to unilaterally denounce his prior Hindu marriage by pronouncing talaq, the High Court of Delhi in *Vilayat Raj* v. *Sunila*[113] and the Supreme Court in *Smt. Sarla Mudgal, President, Kalyani and others* v. *Union of India*[114] held that a marriage solemnized between two Hindus in accordance with Hindu rites and ceremonies could be dissolved only under the Hindu Marriage Act, 1955.

As case to case decisions do not add upto a system of justice, statutes need necessarily be enacted in those areas which are secular in character that would help arouse public awareness as to their rights and duties. Therefore, the Supreme Court's appeal to the Legislature must be direct and specific, offering necessary guidelines to facilitate wholesome legislative drafting. It does not further the cause that the Supreme Court stands for, if it merely suggests, as it did speaking through Justice Chanderchud (as he then was) in *Smt. Satya* v. *Teja Singh*, that the Union Parliament may seek guidance from British legislation such as The Recognition of Divorces and Judicial Separations Act, 1971, which sought to incorporate the Hague Convention on the Recognition of Divorce and Judicial Separations, 1970 which, in the learned judge's considered opinion, may serve as a model. Yet, again, Justice Kuldip Singh of the Supreme Court in *Sarla Mudgal's case* expressed his view that it is high time that the Union Parliament takes steps to ushering in a uniform civil code in deference to the constitutional mandate contained in Article 44 of the Constitution of India, 1950. In fact, the learned judge's concern in that case was limited to putting an end to a unilateral denunciation of a Hindu marriage by a Hindu husband after embracing Islam, instead of his seeking, as is the right course to adopt, dissolution of his Hindu marriage under the Hindu Marriage Act, 1955. The learned judge, it is respectfully submitted, would have acquitted himself more creditably had he, instead of his making an appeal to the Union Parliament to usher in a uniform civil code in due compliance with the constitutional mandate, which I dare say is a tall political order, simply reminded the legislative wing of the government of its social and moral obligation to enact without delay a law whose sole aim is to maintain and restore the integrity of a marriage. Such a timely reminder by the Apex Court and a prompt follow up action on the part of the legislature in a matter that is secular and of common concern would, doubtless, fulfil the legitimate expectations of the people of India.

These concluding remarks on the law relating to marriage and divorce may, in the author's considered opinion, serve as a fitting finale.

NOTES

1. The Atharva Veda says, 'This (India) is a country of many religions, many ethnicities, many castes, many languages,' B.N. Pande, a scholar of History and Comparative Culture in *Times of India* (Delhi) dated 22 August 1993.
2. Ronald Wilson, *Anglo Mohammadan Law in India.*
3. *Nusrat Hussani* v. *Hamidan Begum*, (1932) 4 ALL 205.
4. (1929) ILR 4 LUCK 168
5. (1948) ILR 2 CAL 405, 49 CWN 439
6. (1948) ILR 2 CAL 119
7. *Ashwani Kumar* v. *Asha Rani*, (1992) 1 Hindu LR 307 (P & H).
8. (1891) ILR 18 AL 252
9. (1891) ILR 14 MAD 382
10. (1894) ILR 17 MAD 235
11. AIR 1973 CAL 425

However, this case cannot be considered an authority on the point of whether the party/parties intending to get married under the Hindu Marriage Act, 1955 must be domiciled in India or not since the parties concerned in this case were found to have been residing in India for some time. Another case involving this point is *Parwatawwa* v. *Channawwa*. In that case, a domiciliary of the erstwhile State of Hyderabad (then a foreign territory) came to Bombay and validly married a local girl there. This case, again, cannot be treated as an authority on this issue since the validity of the marriage was challenged on the ground of being bigamous and the question of the husband being not domiciled in India was not raised.

12. *Padoleechia* v. *Padoleechia*, (1968) p. 314, (1967) 3 ALL ER 863.

13. *Parwatawwa* v. *Channawwa*, AIR 1966 Mys10.

14. *Smt. Chandramani Dubey* v. *Ramashankar Dubey*, AIR 1951 ALL 529

15. Section 4 of the Act.

16. This condition of monogamy may prove illusory in some cases. A Muslim male marrying a Christian female under Section 4 of the Act may validly practise polygamy. See *John Giban Chandra* v. *Abinash Sen*, (1939) ILR 2 CAL 12.

17. Section 4 & Sub-section 52(4) of the Act.

18. (1858) 3 Sm&G 481

19. Disagreement exists also on the categorization of certain requirements, that is, whether a particular requirement is substantive or procedural; for example, the requirement that the suit/claim must be filed within a certain time limit, is categorized as a procedural requirement in the U.K. but as substantive in Germany. *Huber* v. *Steiner*, (1835) 2 Bing NC 202. An English court characterized the time limit by the applicable foreign law as a procedural requirement. In this case the limit imposed by the foreign law barred remedy but did not extinguish the right.

20. (1859) 1 SW 7 Tr 416

21. (1871) 2 VR (IE &M) 47

22. 1948 100

23. 1951 124 at 144–6

24. 1973 FAM 35

25. 1940 Ch. 46, 108 LJ ch. 427

26. 1968 314; (1967) 3 All ER 863

27. 1951 482; (1951) All ER 680

28. 1940 ch. 46, 108 LJ ch. 427

29. *Mette* v. *Mette*, (1859) 1 SW&Tr 416; in the Will of Swan (1871) 2 UR (I C&M) 47; *Kenward* v. *Kenward*, (1951) p. 124 p. 144–6, et cetera.

30. *Padolecchia* v. *Padolecchia*, (1968) p. 134.

31. It is no doubt true that English courts, even before 1960 in some cases such as Re Paine, *Pugh* v. *Pugh*, et cetera, had adopted the dual domicile theory, but their approach in these cases was not a forthright assertion of this theory, since they tended to rely on the law of the intended matrimonial home. Also Padolecchia is the outright endorsement of the dual domicile theory, because

here the court considered both the laws in equal measure; obviously it is the outcome of the Act of 1960.

32. AIR 1966 MYS 100

33. 1947 168, (1947) 2 ALL ER 112

34. 1964 144, (1961) 3 ALL ER 225

35. *Cheshire and North's Private International Law*, Eleventh Edition, pp. 586–7.

36. (1969) 6 DLR (3d) 617

37. In some cases, for example in the Swan's Will, even probability alone has been treated as the basis for applying this theory. Probability is derivable directly from the fact of the husband's domicile and is not dependent upon intention—which is a conscious mental act. It, thus, dispenses with both the intention and the obligation to settle in the place of the husband's domicile.

38. (1859) SW&Tr. 416

39. (1871) 2 VR 47

40. (1950) p. 71, (1949) 2 ALL ER 959, [1951] p. 124

41. (1948) p. 100; (1948) 1 ALL ER 56

42. According to Cheshire, the presumption (the parties intended to establish their home in the country of husband's domicile) is rebutted if it can be inferred that the parties at the time of marriage intended to establish their home in a certain country and they did in fact establish within a reasonable time. The statement is incompatible with most of the cases which lay stress only on intention *Cheshire and North's Private International Law*, Eleventh Edition, p. 58.

43. (1917) ILR 40 MAD 1030

44. The Act provides for marriage between any two persons which means that it does not take cognizance of the spouses' religious identities. This enables a Muslim female to marry a non-Muslim. This is not allowed under Muslim law which forbids absolutely a Muslim female to marry a non-Muslim. This may create conflict which may, however, seem to have been avoided by the phrase 'Notwithstanding any thing contained in any other law for the time being in force relating to the solemnization of marriage' prefixed to Section 4 of the Act. This phrase gives overriding effect to this Act.

45. *Ravinder Kumar* v. *Kamal Kanta*, (1973) ILR BOM 1220.

46. A valid marriage can be performed between a Sikh and a Hindu by Anand Karaj (a Sikh ceremony) or by Saptapadi (a Hindu ceremony). *Ashwani Kumar* v. *Asha Rani*, (1992) 1. Hindu Ir 307 (P&H).

47. (1973) ILR BOM 1220

48. That domiciliary qualification is essential appears to be borne out by sub-Section 18(3) of the Foreign Marriage Act, 1969, which reads as follows:

(3) Nothing contained in this section shall authorize any court—(a) to make any decree of dissolution of marriage except where—(i) the parties to the marriage are domiciled in India at the time of the presentation of the petition; or (ii) the petitioner being the wife was domiciled in India immediately before the marriage and has been residing in India for a period of not less than three years immediately preceding the presentation of the petition.

It is clear that in respect of marriages solemnized abroad under this Act both the spouses have to be domiciled in India at the time when they present the petition for dissolution of the marriage. The only relaxation being that if the petitioner is the wife, she is required to have been domiciled in India immediately before the marriage and be residing in India for a period of not less than three years immediately preceding the presentation of the petition. What applies to a marriage solemnized abroad under an Indian law, namely the Foreign Marriage Act, 1969, should equally apply, it appears, to a marriage solemnized in India.

49. Upto 1969, that is, upto the enactment of the Foreign Marriage Act, 1969, the insistence has been on domicile as is evident from section 18 of that Act. There does not appear to be any statute since enacted which brings about any change in this qualification.

50. (1891) 18CAL252

51. (1894) MAD254

52. (1891) 14MAD382

53. (1948) ILRCAL405

54. (1949) ILR2 CAL119

55. AIR 1983 DELHI 351

56. AIR 1979 DELHI 78

57. AIR 1979 DELHI 78

58. AIR 1983 DELHI 351

59. The relevant part of Section 1 reads as follows:
'Extent of power to grant relief generally—Nothing hereinafter contained shall authorize any court to grant any relief under this Act except where the petitioner or respondent professes the Christian religion.'

60. 49 CWN 745

61. 49 CWN 745

62. 49 CWN 745

63. (1948) ILR BOM 1946

64. AIR 2014 Del. 130

65. AIR 1985 SC 945

66. (1948) Bom ILR, 1946

67. AIR 1982 BOM 341

68. AIR 1993 CAL 2125

69. AIR 1966 SC 614

70. It is rather surprising that non-performance of the ceremonies as prescribed under Section 7 of the Act has not been made a ground under Section 11 for seeking nullity.

71. Chapter (V) provides for grant of restitution of conjugal rights and judicial separation and chapter (vi) for nullity and divorce.

72. Sub-section 18(4) of the Foreign Marriage Act, 1869, reads as follows: Nothing contained in Sub (1) shall authorize any court to grant any relief in respect of such marriage (whether on any of the ground specified in the Special Marriage Act, 1954 (43 of 1954) or otherwise is provided for under any other law for the time being in force.

73. AIR 1982 BOM 341

74. Section 4, The Hindu Marriage Act, 1955.

75. JT 1995 (4) SC 331

76. 49 CWN 745

77. (1948) ILR BOM 1946

78. (1887) (14) IA 89

79. (1948) ILR 2 CAL 405

80. (1949) ILR 2 CAL 119

81. (1965) ALL ER 813

82. (1939) ILR 2 CAL 12

83. In *Sayeeda Khatoon* v. *M. Obadiah*, (1945) 19CAL12, 49CWN745, the court, while referring to the fact of Jewish wife's conversion to Islam, observed: 'The plaintiff (the Jewish wife) has since converted to Islam and may in some respects be governed by Muslim law.' The court did not spell out in what respects she will now be governed by the Muslim law and on what basis demarcation can be drawn between the Mahommedan law and other law which governed the remaining aspects. As against this, the Supreme Court in *Sarla Mudgal President Kalyani* v. *Union of India* has (vide paras 28 & 29 of the judgment) indicated that two personal laws became operative in *Attorney General of Ceylon* v. *Reid* when the Christian husband of a Christian marriage embraced Islam, although it is not clarified whether the Mahommedan law acquired only part control or full control. However, whatever may be the respective extent of the control of the two laws, the fact remains that two personal laws control the marriage when one of the spouses abandons the faith which he/she professed at the time of the marriage. This, however, does not hold true in the case of Hindu and Parsi laws, as has already been explained.

84. Although Sub-section 2 (1) (b) of the Hindu Marriage Act, 1955, recognizes a Buddhist as a follower of a religion distinct from Hinduism, Sections 5, 7 &17 use the term 'Hindu' to mean Jains, Sikhs and Buddhists also.

85. AIR 1962 MP 212

86. Marriage can be solemnized between a Hindu and a non-Hindu under the Special Marriage Act but only as individuals and not a followers of any particular religion or religions. This Act does not take cognizance of the parties' religious identities, and accordingly, any change of religion by the spouses does not affect the continuing subsistence of the marriage and the continued applicability of this Act to the marriage. On the other hand, the Indian Christian Marriage Act, 1872, provides for marriage also between a Christian and a non-Christian but only as followers of the particular religions. Consequently change of religion(s) by the spouses may bring about a change in the law governing the marriage, see *Promila Khosla* v. *Rajneesh Khosla*, AIR 1979 DELHI 78.

87. AIR (38) 1951 ALLD 529

88. Section 4 of Hindu Marriage Act reads as follows:

Overriding effect of the Act—Save as otherwise expressly provided in this Act—(a) Any text, rule, interpretation of Hindu law or any custom or usage part of that law in force immediately before the commencement of this Act shall cease to have effect with respect to any matter for which provision is made in this Act.

(b) Any other law in force immediately before the commencement of this Act shall cease to have effect in so far as it is inconsistent with any of the provisions contained in this Act.

89. *Peter Thapita* v. *Lakshmi Thapita*, (1892) MAD 254, Perianayakam Pottukanni, (1891) 14 MAD 382; the Hindu marriages contracted under the uncodified Hindu law were polygamous.

90. AIR 1982 BOM 341

91. 11 BOM LR 85

92. See page 14 of the judgment, 11 BOM LR (33) 509.

93. AIR (38) BOM 14 (CN 6)

94. AIR 1974 ALL 178

95. AIR 1959 RAJ 133

96. As stated in the judgment in *Abdul Rahim* v. *Smt. Padma Abdul Rahim*, AIR 1982 BOM 341.

97. AIR 1974 ALL 178

98. Control of a marriage by two laws is legally permissible as is apparent from *Promila Khosla* v. *Rajneesh Khosla*, AIR 1979 DELHI 78, in which the court ruled that in case one of the spouses of a marriage is Hindu and the other a Christian, relief can be had either under Hindu law or under the Christian law. In *Sayeeda Khatoon* v. *M. Obadiah*, 49 CWN 745 the court held that in consequence of a spouse converting to another faith, some aspects of the

marriage are controlled by the new law of the converting spouse. The court did not specify the particular aspects but the fact remains that this arrangement results in dual control.

99. AIR 1982 BOM 341

100. *Cheshire and North's Private International Law*, Eleventh Edition (Virginia: Lexis Law Publishing, 1987), p. 576.

101. AIR 1935 BOM 5

102. See *John Jiban Chandra* v. *Abinash Sen*, (1939) ILR 2CAL12; as also *Attorney General of Ceylon* v. *Reid*, (1965) All ER 813.

103. *Mohammad Ahmed Khan* v. *Shah Bano Begum and Others*, AIR 1985 SC 945.

104. *Danial Latifi and another* v. *Union of India*, (2001) 7 SCC 740.

105. AIR 2001 SC 3988

106. See V.C. Govindaraj, *The Conflict of Laws in India: Inter-Territorial and Inter-Personal Conflict* (New Delhi: Oxford University Press, 2011), p. 132.

107. 2002 (6) Scale 165

108. AIR 2010 SC 305

109. (2007) 6SCC 785

110. (2014) 12 SCC 636

111. AIR 1975 SC 105

112. AIR 1991 SC 821

113. AIR 1983 DEL 351

114. AIR 1995 SC 1531

8

Law of Persons

Law Relating to Children

INTRODUCTION

Courts play the role of a guardian angel in protecting the interests of children. To preserve and promote the welfare of the child has always been and will ever remain the courts' paramount concern.[1] The Guardians and Wards Act, 1890, lays down appropriate norms in respect of issues such as exercise of jurisdiction by an Indian court,[2] appointment of a guardian for a minor[3] in order to secure the welfare of the child,[4] recognition by a court in India of a foreign court's order as to the custody and guardianship of a minor and also as to the rights of a guardian[5] so appointed under the law of a foreign country, provided a foreign court's order in respect thereof meets the requirements of the (Indian) Code of Civil Procedure, 1908.[6]

An Indian court, as defined in Section 4(5) of the Guardians and Wards Act, 1890,[7] exercises jurisdiction in the matter of appointment of a guardian for a minor[8] to secure the minor's welfare.[9] The criteria to determine the welfare of a minor include the age, sex, and religion of the minor, character and capacity of the proposed guardian, and his proximity to the minor by way of kin, the wishes, if any, of a deceased parent, and any existing or previous relations of the proposed guardian with the minor or his property.[10] The intelligent preference of the minor, if he is old enough to form such a preference, may also be taken into account.[11] The court, in appropriate cases, may appoint a person as guardian residing outside its jurisdiction, if that be warranted under the circumstances of the case based on the welfare of the minor, which is of paramount importance for a court seized of the matter.[12]

Custodial Orders of Minors as Part of Matrimonial Reliefs

Courts in India more often than not, while granting matrimonial reliefs, issue orders as to the custody of minor children.[13] A child, according to Section 2 (c) of the Children's Act, 1989, is one who has not attained the age of sixteen years in the case of boys and eighteen years in the case of girls. When a court issues a custodial order, it does so taking into consideration the applicable matrimonial law of the parties. For example, a court order in respect of a Hindu minor will be based on Section 26 of the Hindu Marriage Act, 1955; as for a Muslim minor, the relevant provisions of the Muslim Law; as for a Christian minor, Section 41 of the (Indian) Divorce Act, 1869; as for a Parsi minor, Section 49 of the Parsi Marriage and Divorce Act, 1936; as for a minor born of a marriage that is secular, Section 38 of the Special Marriage Act, 1954, and so on.

Custodial Orders of Minors Independent of Matrimonial Reliefs

In a non-matrimonial case, a court in India assumes jurisdiction and issues order as to the custody of a minor on an application made to it on his behalf, based on the presence of the minor within its jurisdiction even in cases where the minor concerned is not ordinarily resident in India.[14] An Indian court would recognize and give effect to a foreign guardianship and custody order if the order is in consonance with the requirements of the Code of Civil Procedure, 1908.[15]

The Role of Courts as *Parens Patriae*

Bearing in mind that the welfare of children is of paramount importance,[16] courts keep a vigil in matters relating to the upbringing of children.[17] By so doing, superior courts like the high courts play the role of *parens patriae* in preserving and promoting the welfare of children. In this regard, the exercise of jurisdiction by a high court is not facultative and, therefore, does not permit the application of the rule of *forum conveniens*.[18] The brooding omnipresence of a high court is made manifest as and when it chooses to exercise jurisdiction, especially in the custodial matters of a child, with the avowed objective of ensuring the child's physical, moral, and religious well-being. In the case *ABC* v. *The State (NCT of Delhi)*, 2015 SCC OnLine SC 609, the

Supreme Court ruled that 'an unwed mother is the natural guardian, not the putative father.'

As stated earlier, an Indian court will recognize and give effect to a foreign court's order as to the custody of a minor child, provided the order satisfies the requirements of Section 13 of the Code of Civil Procedure, 1908.[19]

On the subject of abduction of minor children by either of the spouses, we may advert to the 1980 Hague Convention on the Civil Aspects of International Child Abduction which, in the preamble, states that, 'the interests of children are of paramount importance, in matters relating to their custody'. Furthermore, the convention states it is incumbent on member states ...

> to protect children internationally from the harmful effects of their wrongful removal or retention and to establish procedures to ensure their prompt return to the state of their habitual residence, as well as to secure protection for rights of access ... Kidnapping of a minor by either of the spouses in defiance of an order of a foreign court with some element of force or deception or secrecy is a factor that weighs against the concerned spouse in any assessment by a court of his or her competence to preserve and promote the welfare of the child, which remains the court's paramount consideration.[20]

Foreign Custody and Guardianship Order: Recognition

As stated earlier, an Indian court will recognize and give effect to a foreign court's order as to the custody and guardianship of a minor, if the foreign order satisfies the requirements of Section 13 of the Code of Civil Procedure, 1908.[21] Accordingly, the rights of a guardian appointed under the law of a foreign country will be recognized in India. Probably, an Indian court will recognize the jurisdiction of a foreign court to appoint a guardian if, and only if, the circumstances leading to the exercise of jurisdiction on the part of the foreign court correspond to those that would prompt an Indian court to exercise its inherent jurisdiction.[22]

Law Relating to Property of Children

Issues relating to the administration of property belonging to children are to be addressed keeping in view the welfare of children, which ought to be the court's preponderant consideration. *A priori*, any accrual from the property subject to the control of the court will not be paid over to children's parents or guardians, even if such payments would otherwise be proper, if to do so would be contrary to the children's interests.[23] Subject to the abovementioned limitation, the rights of the parents over the movable properties of their minor children will be governed by the law of their respective domiciles, unless it be that the parents and their minor children had, as in the past, a common domicile, which is now, in contemporary conditions, not always the case.[24] The rights of the guardians, too, will be governed by their respective domiciles.[25] It is a well known general principle of conflict of laws that rights over and title to immovable property of minors are governed by the *lex situs*, that is, the law of the country where the immovable property is situated.

LEGITIMACY AND LEGITIMATION

Declaration of Legitimacy or Parentage: Jurisdictional Competence of Courts

An Indian court[26] has jurisdictional competence to grant a declaration that a named person is or was the parent of the applicant seeking legitimacy or, as the case may be, that the applicant is the legitimate child of his parents if the applicant happens to be an Indian domiciliary on the date of the application.[27]

In making such a declaration as to the legitimacy of the applicant, the court will act in pursuance of the Indian Evidence Act, 1872.[28]

Proof of Legitimacy

The fact that a person was born during the continuance of a valid marriage between his/her mother and any man, or within 280 days after its dissolution, the mother remaining unmarried, is conclusive proof that he/she is the legitimate son/daughter of that man, unless it is shown that the parties to the marriage had no access to each other at any time when he/she could have been conceived.[29]

According to Muhammadan law, a child born six months after marriage or within two years after divorce or the death of the husband is presumed to be a legitimate offspring. This rule of the Muhammadan law has, however, been superseded by the Indian Evidence Act, 1872.[30]

The presumption as to paternity or legitimacy under the Indian Evidence Act arises only in respect of the offspring of a married couple.[31]

The provision regarding the presumption as to legitimacy under the Act, however, does not lay down a maximum period of gestation, and hence does not bar the proof of the legitimacy of a child born more than 280 days after the dissolution of marriage. The effect of the section, therefore, is that if no presumption in favour of legitimacy is raised, the question must be decided simply upon the evidence for or against legitimacy.[32]

Under the Act, a child born in wedlock should be treated as the child of the person who was, at the time of its birth, the husband of the mother, unless it is shown that he had no access to the mother at the time of its conception, irrespective of whether or not the mother was a married woman at that time.[33]

Jurisdictional Competence of Indian Courts to Grant Declarations of Legitimation

The concept of legitimation (that is, *legitimatio per subsequens matrimonium* or legitimation by acknowledgment) by a subsequent marriage between the parties is alien to the Indian legal system, whether it be Hindu law or Muhammadan law. Indian law only recognizes the concept of legitimacy of a child and not legitimation either by a subsequent marriage between the parties or by an acknowledgement by the man.[34]

As stated earlier, the Indian Evidence Act, 1872 treats a child as legitimate if it is born during a valid marriage between its mother and any man, or within 280 days after the dissolution of the marriage, the mother remaining unmarried during this period.[35]

When there arises a doubt or dispute as to the legitimacy of a child, an acknowledgment by the presumptive father under Muhammadan law is proof that the child so acknowledged is the legitimate child of the presumptive father, provided that legitimacy is possible.[36]

ADOPTION

Nature and Scope

Adoptions taking place in India are regulated by the Guardians and Wards Act, 1890. The Act is of an inclusive character in that it is applicable to all religious communities, barring Muslims,[37] and is limited to the form of guardianship of a ward. By the passing of the Hindu Adoptions and Maintenance Act, 1956, by the Parliament of the Union of India, it is only the Hindu religion that is endowed with a statutorily recognized right to adopt.[38] The Guardians and Wards Act, 1890, and the Hindu Adoptions and Maintenance Act, 1956, extend to the whole of India except the State of Jammu and Kashmir. They do not impose domicile, nationality, or residence as condition precedent to their applicability.[39] However, the requirement of domicile is essential for Hindus resident abroad.[40]

Adoption is a private act both under the Guardians and Wards Act, 1890, and under the Hindu Minority and Guardianship Act, 1956, and, by implication, does not require the intervention of a court of law, except in cases where a minor is offered for adoption by a guardian appointed by will, any other instrument, or appointed or declared by a court.[41] Both under the Guardians and Wards Act and the Hindu Minority and Guardianship Act, only a city civil court or a district court is invested with jurisdiction to entertain adoption cases.[42]

The court, in the matter of sanctioning permission to the guardian appointed by it, must be guided by what appears to it under the circumstances to be in the best interests and welfare of the minor. This the court could ascertain on the basis of the minor's intelligent preference, if he is old enough to form one, which would require the presence of the minor within the jurisdiction of the court.[43]

In foreign adoption cases where the minor is a Hindu, the Hindu Minority and Guardianship Act, 1956 applies subject to the guidelines issued by the Supreme Court of India in *Lakshmi Kant Pandey* v. *Union of India*.[44] The tone and tenor of the guidelines reflect the concern of the court as *parens patriae* to protect and to promote the welfare of the minor which is of paramount consideration overriding all other considerations.[45] Muslims, however, are governed by their personal law.

Adoption Under Foreign Law of Adoption

The court, in making an adoption order, must give its first and foremost consideration to the need to safeguard and promote the welfare of the child.[46] With this objective in view, the court must see to it that the adoption by a foreigner should be in accordance with the law of his or her country and is legally valid by that law.[47]

Adoption Orders of Indian Courts: Their Recognition

Adoption orders issued by courts in India are recognized throughout the country.[48]

Foreign Adoption Orders: Their Recognition in India

Foreign adoption orders are recognized in India subject to the provisions of the Code of Civil Procedure, 1908.[49]

Foreign Adoptions: Succession Rights of Adopted Persons

A son adopted under a foreign law, if the adoption be good and valid under Indian law, is entitled to the property of the deceased adoptive father, even if the adoption has been made by the adoptive mother after the death of the father.[50]

MAINTENANCE ORDERS

Suits for Grant of Matrimonial Reliefs

The court of competent jurisdiction to entertain suits and grant matrimonial reliefs is the district court, and the reliefs are divorce, nullity, and judicial separation which are available under each one of the following enactments, namely the Special Marriage Act, 1954,[51] the Hindu Marriage Act, 1955,[52] the Indian Divorce Act, 1869,[53] and the Parsi Marriage and Divorce Act, 1936.[54] A successful conclusion of a suit may result in an order made by the court for payment of maintenance to the wife *pendente lite* as well as on a permanent basis. The jurisdiction to grant maintenance by the court is coterminous with the jurisdiction to grant the reliefs set out above, namely divorce, nullity, and judicial separation.

Muslim law, which till today remains to a large extent uncodified, provides for one and only one matrimonial relief, namely divorce, which the husband can avail of unilaterally and extra-judicially, by pronouncing talaq. However, the codified part of Muslim law is contained in the enactment, namely Dissolution of Muslim Marriage Act, 1939,[55] which allows the wife to seek a divorce, but does not contain a provision for the grant of maintenance.[56]

The failure of the legislature to come to the rescue of the hapless divorced Muslim woman is the measure and success of the judiciary, as we shall presently see. In the sensational case *Mohammad Ahmed Khan* v. *Shah Bano Begum and Others*,[57] the Supreme Court ruled that a magistrate can grant maintenance or, as the case may be, enhancement of maintenance under Section 125 of the Code of Criminal Procedure, 1973, even beyond the iddat period.

The above ruling of the Supreme Court had since been superseded by the Muslim Women (Protection of Rights on Divorce) Act, 1986. As irony would have it, the Supreme Court, in a recent case, namely *Danial Latifi and another* v. *Union of India*,[58] while dismissing a writ petition filed under Article 32 of the Constitution of India challenging the validity of the above Act as a violation of the Fundamental Rights guaranteed under Articles 14, 15, and 21 of the Constitution, ruled that a Muslim husband as per Section 3(1)(a) of the Act is liable to make a reasonable and fair provision for the future of the divorced wife. This obviously includes the grant of her maintenance as well as a reasonable and fair provision extending beyond the iddat period to be paid by the husband within the iddat period under the terms of Section 3(1)(a) of the Act which reads that 'a reasonable and fair provision and maintenance to be made and paid to her within the period of iddat by her former husband'.[59] As Section 3 of the Act commences with a *non obstante* clause, the judicial interpretation in the case under review overrides all other pre-existing laws or decisions of courts.

In contrast, Section 18 of the Hindu Adoptions and Maintenance Act, 1956, entitles a Hindu wife who is separated from her husband on the basis of any of the grounds specified therein to seek and obtain maintenance from her husband during her lifetime which right she may forfeit in case of her unchastity or conversion to any other faith. For all the communities maintenance is available under Section 125 of the Code of Criminal Procedure, 1973, which provision, in its present application to a Muslim woman, has been liberally interpreted by the Supreme Court in Danial Latifi's case, as stated above.

It is desirable, in this context, to consider introducing a domestic legislation on maintenance obligation uniformly for all communities, bearing in mind the Hague Convention on Recognition and Enforcement of Decisions Relating to Maintenance Obligations, 1973. That would require, as pre-requisite, the enactment of a law on the pattern of Part II of the Family Law Act, 1986, enacted by the British Parliament.

Financial Provision as Part of Maintenance Obligation

A person having sufficient means must maintain his wife, children (legitimate and illegitimate) and parents who are unable to maintain themselves.[60]

Service of Process

A person may be sued for maintenance of his wife, children, and parents in any district:[61]

(a) where the husband is, or
(b) where he or his wife resides, or
(c) where he last resided with his wife, or, as the case may be, with the mother of the illegitimate child.

Courts in India, unlike courts in England, have no extended jurisdiction to entertain suits for maintenance at places other than those mentioned above.

Proof of Declarations and Other Documents

Any document purporting to be a declaration as to service of process[62] or to be a certified copy, statutory declaration, affidavit, certificate, transcript of summary made for the purposes of the award of maintenance is deemed without further proof to be the document it purports to be and to have been made in the proper manner, unless the contrary is shown.[63]

RECIPROCAL ENFORCEMENT OF MAINTENANCE ORDERS

Enforcement of Orders

A maintenance order issued by a foreign court may be enforced in India subject to the provisions of the Code of Civil Procedure, 1908.[64]

The court issuing the order for maintenance must be a court of competent jurisdiction, and the order must be final.[65] In case the decree for maintenance is issued by a court of competent jurisdiction in a reciprocating country, it may be executed in India as if it had been passed by a district court in India.[66]

NOTES

1. *Elizabeth Dinshaw (Mrs)* v. *Arvand M. Dinshaw and Another*, AIR 1987 SC 3, (1987) 1 SCC 42, (1987) MAD LW 130.
2. Section 4 (5), The Guardians and Wards Act, 1890.
3. Ibid., Section 4 (1)
4. Ibid., Section 17 (1). See *Elizabeth Dinshaw (Mrs)* v. *Arvand M. Dinshaw and Another*, AIR 1987 S.C. 3, (1987) 1 SCC 42, (1987) Mad LW 130; *Surinder Kaur Sandhu* v. *Harbax Singh Sandhu*, AIR 1984 SC 1224.
5. *Marggarate Pulparampiz Neefeldman* v. *Dr Chacko Pulparampil*, AIR 1970 Ker 1, (1969) Ker LT 174, (1969) Ker LR 753.
6. Section 13, The Code of Civil Procedure, 1908.
7. Section 7(1) (3), Guardians and Wards Act, 1890. In this connection, it is of interest to note that the Hindu Minority and Guardianship Act, 1956, applies only to Hindu minors and that its provisions are in addition to, and not in derogation of, those contained in the Guardians and Wards Act, 1890.
8. Note 3 supra. However, as per Section 17 (5) of the Act a court cannot appoint or declare any person to be guardian against his will.
9. Note 4 supra
10. Section 17(2), Guardians and Wards Act.
11. Section 17(3), Guardians and Wards Act.
12. *Pamela Williams* v. *Patrick Cyril Martin*, AIR 1970 MAD 427, (1970)2 MAD LJ 539, (1970) MAD LW 206. Re Lovejoy Patell, 1944 CAL 433, (1943) ILR 2 C 554 (a pre-Independence case in which it was held that the jurisdiction of the Calcutta High Court to appoint a guardian of person and estates of a minor was not limited to the minor residing within its ordinary, original jurisdiction but extended to any minor residing outside its jurisdiction, but not beyond the Division of Presidency, provided the minor was a British subject).
13. Such custodial orders issued by courts would include expenses relating to their maintenance and education. See V.C. Govindaraj, *Conflict of Laws*, Halsbury's Laws of India Series, Vol. 10 (New Delhi: LexisNexis Butterworths, 2001), pp. 239–40.
14. *Pamela Williams* v. *Patrick Cyril Martin*, AIR 1970 MAD 427, (1970) 2 MAD LJ 539, (1970) 83 MAD LW 206. See also Govindaraj, *Conflict of Laws*, Vol. 10 (New Delhi: LexisNexis Butterworths, 2001), p. 240.

15. The requirements of Section 13 of the Code of Civil Procedure, 1908, ought to be met for an Indian court to honour a foreign guardianship and custody order. See the following cases, namely *Elizabeth Dinshaw (Mrs)* v. *Arvand M. Dinshaw and Another*, AIR 1987 SC 3, (1987) 1 SCC 42, (1987) MAD. LW 130 and also *Jacqualine Kapoor* v. *Surinder Pal Kapoor*, AIR 1994 P&H 309, (1994) 3 PUNJ LR 544, (1994) 2 Hindu LR 97.

16. *Elizabeth Dinshaw (Mrs)* v. *Arvand M. Dinshaw and Another*, AIR 1987 SC 3, (1987) 1 SCC 43, (1987) MAD LW 130; *Surinder Kaur Sandhu* v. *Harbax Singh Sandhu*, AIR 1984 SC 1224. (Although under Section 6 of the Hindu Minority and Guardianship Act, 1956, the father is the natural guardian of a minor son, the mother may in the minor's interest be given the custody.) See Govindaraj, *Conflict of Laws*, Vol. 10 (New Delhi: LexisNexis Butterworths, 2001), p. 240.

17. Ibid.

18. R (Minors) (Wardship-jurisdiction), 1981 2 FLR 416 (CA).

19. See *Jacqualine Kapoor* v. *Surinder Pal Kapoor*, AIR 1994 P&H.309, (1994) 3 PUNJ LR 544, (1994) 2 Hindu LR 97.

20. Govindaraj, *Conflict of Laws*, Vol. 10 (New Delhi: LexisNexis Butterworths, 2001), p. 240; see also *Elizabeth Dinshaw (Mrs) v. Arvand M. Dinshaw and Another*, AIR 1987 SC 3, (1987) 1 SCC 42, (1987) MAD LW 130.

21. *Marggarate Maria Pulparampiz Neefeldman* v. *Dr Chacko Pulparampil*, AIR 1970 KER 1, (1969) Ker. LT 174, (1969) KER LR 753.

22. See Code of Civil Procedure, 1908, as to the exercise of inherent jurisdiction.

23. Re Chatard's Settlement (1899) 1 Ch. 712. See the effect of Section 13 of the Judicial Factors (Scotland) Act, 1899, in respect of guardians appointed in Scotland.

24. *Gambler* v. *Gambler*, (1835) 7 SIM 263, 58 ER 838; Re Chatard's Settlement (1899) 1 Ch. 712. See also Re Brown's Trust (1865) 12 LT 488; Re Hellmann's Will (1866) LR 2 EQ 363.

25. Re Crichton's Trust (1855) 24 LTOS267; Re Chatard's Settlement (1899) 1 Ch. 712 at 716; *Mackie* v. *Darling*, (1871) LR 12 EQ 319. All the above three footnotes are taken from Govindaraj, *Conflict of Laws*, Vol. 10 (New Delhi: LexisNexis Butterworths, 2001), p. 24.

26. The court referred to is a family court presided over by a judicial officer of the rank of a district judge.

27. Section 34, The Indian Specific Relief Act, 1963.

28. Section 112, The Indian Evidence Act, 1872.

29. Ibid.

30. Ibid. See *Mazhar Ali* v. *Budh Singh*, (1881) 7 ALL 297 (FB); *Musammat Kaniza* v. *Hasan Ahmad Khan*, (1924) 1 LUCK 71.

31. A marriage presumed from a long cohabitation is also a marriage within the meaning of the section for giving rise to this presumption: *S.P.S. Balsubramanyam* v. *Suruttayan*, AIR 1992 SC 756, (1992) Supp 2 SCC 304.

32. *Uttamrao Rajaram* v. *Sitaram*, (1962) 64 BOM LR 752 p. 759. See Ratanlal and Dhirajlal, *The Law of Evidence*, Nineteenth Edition (1999), p. 332.

33. *Palani* v. *Sethu*, (1924) 1LR 47 MAD 706; *Pai Singh* v. *Jagir*, (1926) 17 LAH 368.

34. See section 'Proof of Legitimacy', supra.

35. Section 112, The Indian Evidence Act, 1872.

36. *Sadik Husain Khan* v. *Hashim Ali Khan*, (196) ILR 38 ALL 627, PC In this conection, a passing reference may be made to a provocative, may we say anachronistic, decision of the Privy Council in *Bibi Nanyer Omissa* v. *Bibi Zainirum*, 11 WR 476, declaring a child legitimate on being acknowledged as such even in the absence of a marriage between the parties. This decision of the Privy Council was subjected to a good deal of criticism by Muslim scholars who have favourably responded to a decision of the Allahabad High Court in *Muhammad Allabdad Khan* v. *Muhammad Ismail Khan*, (1888) ILR 10 ALL 289 at 326 per Mahmmod, J., which runs thus:

> '... a child whose illegitimacy is proved beyond doubt, by reason of the marriage of its parents being either disproved or found to be unlawful cannot be legitimatised by acknowledgment: achnowledgment only has the effect of legitimation where either the fact of the marriage or its exact time, with reference to the legitimacy of the child's birth, is a matter of uncertainty'.

37. *Lakshmi Kant Pandey* v. *Union of India*, AIR 1984 SC 469 at 472, (1984) 2 SCC 244, (1984) 1 Scale 159.

38. That is, under The Hindu Minority and Guardianship Act, 1956.

39. Section 1 (2), The Guardians and Wards Act; Hindu Minority and Guardianship Act.

40. Section 1 (2), The Hindu Minority and Guardianship Act, 1956.

41. Section 9 (4), The Hindu Adoptions and Maintenance Act by implication makes adoption offered by natural parents a private act.

42. Section 7 (3), The Guardians and Wards Act, 1890.

43. Section 4(5), The Guardians and Wards Act, 1890.

44. Note 37 supra; that is, the guidelines issued by the Supreme Court of India, entitled 'Guidelines to regulate Matters Relating to Adoption of Indian Children', Ministry of Social Welfare, Government of India; see also Section 17(1), The Guardians and Wards Act, 1890,

45. Guardians and Wards Act, 1890, Section 17(3).

46. Section 9(5), The Hindu Adoptions and Maintenance Act, 1956. Also see Section 7(1), The Guardians and Wards Act, 1890.

47. Note 37 supra.

48. Article 261, The Constitution of India, 1950.

49. Section 13, The Code of Civil Procedure, 1908.

50. *Suganchand Bhikamchand* v. *Mangibai Gulbchand*, AIR 1942 BOM 201 IC 759, (1942) 44 Bom. LR 358. See also Govindaraj, *Conflict of Laws*, Vol. 10 (New Delhi: LexisNexis Butterworths, 2001), pp. 243–5.

51. Sections 36, 37, The Special Marriage Act, 1954.

52. Sections 24, 25, The Hindu Marriage Act, 1955.

53. Sections 36, 37, and 38, The Indian Divorce Act, 1869.

54. Sections 39, 40, The Parsi Marriage and Divorce Act, 1936.

55. Section 2, The Dissolution of Muslim Marriage Act, 1939.

56. The Muslim Women (Protection of Rights on Divorce) Act, 1986, Sections 4, 5. See also *Mohammad Yameed* v. *State of Uttar Pradesh*, (1992) Cr. LJ 1804 at 1807, 1808; *Syed Iqbal Hussain* v. *Syed Nasamunnissa Begum*, (1992) Cr. LJ 1823 at 1825, AP; *Usman Khan* v. *Fathimunnissa Begum*, (1990) Cr. LJ 1364, AP.

57. AIR 1985 SC 945.

58. (2001) 7 SCC 740.

59. As per Rajendra Babu, J. as he then was.

60. Section 125 (1), The Code of Criminal Procedure, 1973.

61. Section 126, The Code of Criminal Procedure, 1973.

62. As in 'Service of Process': note 61.

63. See Sections 79–86, The Indian Evidence Act, 1872.

64. Section 13, The Code of Civil Procedure, 1908.

65. Section 14, The Code of Civil Procedure, 1908.

66. Section 44-A, The Code of Civil Procedure, 1908. See Govindaraj, *Conflict of Laws*, Vol. 10 (New Delhi: LexisNexis Butterworths, 2001), pp. 245–9.

9

Validity of Marriage

Could it be Deemed an Omnific Concept in Conflict Resolution of Related Issues?

THE AMERICAN REVOLUTION

Taking the cue from the writings of Professor Morris[1] and Professor Willis Reese,[2] an attempt is made in this work to examine the inflexible, we may say the conservative attitude and approach of the courts in general, that has inexorably led them to treat marriage and its validity as omnific vis-à-vis correlative issues such as adoption, legitimacy, and rights of succession, testate or intestate, of a surviving spouse and children born of such marriage. Professor Willis Reese, in his article entitled 'Marriage in American Conflict of Laws' referred to above, pays rich tributes to Professor Morris for the groundbreaking article that he contributed to the *Harvard Law Review* in the year 1950 that revolutionized the American choice of law rules. Therein Professor Morris introduces the proper law doctrine to govern foreign torts, as is the case with foreign contracts, so as to reach results which are 'socially convenient and sound' comparable to the said doctrine's application to foreign contracts to secure results which are 'commercially convenient and sound'.

Professor Willis Reese, in his article on 'Marriage in American Conflict of Laws' makes the following preliminary observation. 'The purpose here is to express surprise that, with rare exceptions, marriage is treated by the courts as an all-purpose concept. Doubt will be expressed that the courts can "achieve socially desirable results if they apply the same conflicts rule" in all cases, where the validity of a marriage is in issue.'[3] Elsewhere, after categorizing instances where the issue of the validity of a marriage may be rendered incidental in relation to the issue that calls for judicial determination, he observes: 'The problem is whether in these situations the validity of the marriage should first be established independently of the other issue involved or whether the determination of the validity of the marriage should be made with reference to that issue.' Stated in choice of law terms, 'the problem is whether the law governing the validity of a marriage should always be the same irrespective of the other issue or whether the choice of this law should depend, at least in part, upon that issue.' If the latter is true, we are inevitably faced with a situation where a marriage may be good for the purpose of one issue and yet invalid for the purpose of another.'[4]

A question may be raised here that, if in the case of a contract or a tort the choice of the applicable law should be made in the light of the particular issue, namely the proper law, why should not the same conflicts rule be employed with respect to marriage related issues? To get an answer to the query, a case study seems necessary and proper.

Professor Willis Reese relies upon five decided cases to establish his thesis. A brief resume of the cases highlights the switch that had recently taken place in the judicial thinking that establishes the proposition that marriage cannot be treated as an all-purpose concept in respect of related issues such as adoption, legitimacy, and rights of succession of the surviving spouse and children born of a putative marriage. The approach, perforce, ought to be issue-based, which would take into consideration factors such as the validity or otherwise of a marriage under the *lex loci celebrationis*, the expectations of the parties concerned, the legislative directive or judicial precedent, if any, of the state which has the most significant relationship to the spouses and the marriage, the non-contravention of any strong public policy of that state, and the like. Only then courts can render socially desirable results.

The first of those cases, namely Re *May's Estate*,[5] is an instance where an uncle and niece by half blood, both of whom were New York domiciliaries, got married in Rhode Island whose law permitted such marriage contrary to the law of New York which declared such marriage incestuous and therefore void. Two weeks later they returned to New York, the state of their common domicile, and lived there for thirty-two years until the wife's death. Six children were born of the marriage. Thereupon, the husband sought to be appointed administrator of his deceased wife's estate which was opposed by one of his daughters on the ground of the invalidity of the marriage as per New York law. The lower court upheld the daughter's contention. Nevertheless, on appeal, the marriage was upheld by the court of appeals by a majority but with a strong dissent. The court observed that in the absence of any New York statute 'expressing clearly the legislative intent to regulate within this state [namely New York] marriages of its domiciliaries solemnized abroad', the case called for the application of 'the general rule that a marriage valid where performed is valid everywhere.'[6]

In *Wilkins* v. *Zellichowski*,[7] both the husband and the wife were domiciled in New Jersey and could not get married in New Jersey, as intended, for the girl was under 18 years of age which, as per New Jersey's law, rendered the marriage void. They, however, got married in Indiana whose law permitted such marriage, despite her being only sixteen years of age. They immediately returned to New Jersey, the state of their domicile. A child also was born of their marriage. Around this time, the husband was convicted of car theft and was placed in a reformatory. Thereupon the wife sought an annulment of her marriage in a New Jersey court despite being validly married as per the law of Indiana. The Supreme Court of New Jersey reversed the lower court's ruling and held the marriage void on the ground that Indiana's interests were at best limited to 'the formal requirements of the marriage and that New Jersey was the only state having any interest in the (marital) status.' The Court concluded 'that atleast in this situation that the "strong public policy" of New Jersey' was involved and that 'if the New Jersey's public policy is to remain at all meaningful, it must be considered equally applicable though this marriage took place in Indiana.' The Court, in the course of the judgment, also emphasized that the annulment would be in the best interest of the child in that the New Jersey law would not render the child illegitimate.

The third case which Professor Willis Reese has taken up for inquiry is *Re Ommang's Estate*.[8] In that case, both the parties were originally domiciled in Wisconsin. They could not get married in Wisconsin, the state of their common domicile, for its law would not allow the woman to get married to him based on the fact that she had received a divorce within the past year. The said impediment was got over by their getting married in Minnesota where their marriage was legal. They soon returned to Wisconsin and lived there as man and wife for about two years. They then got separated and the man moved to Minnesota. The wife, too, subsequently moved to Minnesota to live with her daughter of her former marriage. After the man's death, the woman sought to administer his estate claiming to be his widow. The move was resisted by the decedent's half-sister, based on the ground that their marriage in Minnesota was invalid as per Wisconsin's law and that their marriage in Minnesota was to evade the Wisconsin law. The court at Minnesota held the marriage valid by the application of the general rule that 'a marriage which is valid where performed is valid everywhere.'

The fourth case *Meisenhelder* v. *Chicago & N.W. Ry Co.*,[9] is to be read and understood in the context of Re Ommang's Estate, as the former was decided by a Minnesota court four years earlier to the latter. *Meisenhelder* v. *Chicago & N.W. Ry Co.* was a case of a marriage between first cousins, both domiciled in Illinois, that took place in Kentucky with a view to evading the Illinois law which prohibited such a marriage. The marriage, however, was valid in Kentucky but was void under the law of Illinois by virtue of an explicit statutory provision to that effect. Soon after the marriage, the couple returned to Illinois, as is the case with such marriages that take place elsewhere to evade the local law of domicile. Subsequently, while the parties were still domiciled in Illinois, the man was killed in that state in the course of his employment. Thereupon, the woman sued the employer in Minnesota within the meaning of the Federal Employees' Liability Act, claiming to be the widow of the deceased. Relief was denied to her on the ground that the marriage was invalid in view of the fact that the Illinois statute 'modified the rule that marriages valid where the ceremony is performed are valid everywhere', as is the case on hand where the parties domiciled in Illinois went to another state (that is, Kentucky) to get married there designed to circumvent the effect of the Illinois law on their marriage.

The fifth and last case cited by Professor Willis Reese is a Pennsylvania decision, *Re Estate of Lenherr*,[10] which he claims reflects his approach to the relevance of marriage, its validity or, as the case may be, its invalidity, to the conflicts resolution process of correlative issues. This was a case of spouses, both of whom were domiciliaries of the State of Pennsylvania and who obtained a divorce from each other on the ground of adultery on the part of both. Both of them wanted to marry but could not do so in Pennsylvania, their state of domicile, as there was a statute in the state which provided that a person who has been guilty of the crime of adultery 'shall not marry the person with whom the said crime was committed during the life of the former wife or husband.' Therefore, they were constrained to marry in West Virginia whose law imposed no such bar to their marriage, and then returned to Pennsylvania, their home state, until the death of the man in question. The issue that called for determination was whether his property could pass on to the woman, free of the Pennsylvania transfer inheritance tax. The exemption from the tax would depend on their getting validly married. The trial court held that the tax was due; but this was reversed, on appeal, by the Supreme Court of Pennsylvania. The Court viewed the prohibition imposed by the Pennsylvania statute on the parties from marrying would 'to a significant degree' depend on the particular issue involved. According to the Court, the policy behind the Pennsylvania statute was to protect 'the sensibilities of the injured and innocent husband or wife ... by being forced to witness the continued cohabitation of the adulterous pair, even under the guise of a subsequent marriage performed in another state'. The Court further observed that though the said policy might 'be quite strong with respect to cohabitation' as well as other issues, it would not significantly advance by any denial of tax exemption, since any 'affront' caused to the innocent former spouse by the cohabitation was now a thing of the past because of the man's death.

It is of interest to note, in this connection, that Section 283 of the *Restatement (Second) of Conflict of Laws*, 1971, sounds very much like the proper law of a contract or, as for that, the proper law of a tort. It reads as under:

SECTION 283: VALIDITY OF MARRIAGE

(1) The validity of a marriage will be determined by the local law of the state which, with respect to the particular issue, has the most significant relationship to the spouses and the marriage.

(2) A marriage which satisfies the requirements of the state where the marriage was contracted will everywhere be recognized as valid unless it violates the strong public policy of another state which has the most significant relationship to the spouses and the marriage at the time of the marriage.

The above formulation of the *Restatement (Second) of Conflict of Laws*, as Professor Willis Reese would himself admit, is broad and imperfect in the sense that it cannot tell a court how to decide a case. Nevertheless, it offers some guidance besides, of course, emphasizing the underlying values. In particular, it highlights three factors that are germane to the determination of the particular issue for any meaningful judicial dispensation, namely (a) the interest of the state, (b) the protection of the expectations of the parties and (c) the general policy favouring the validation of marriages.

Before winding up our discussion on the so-called American revolution that has brought about a sea change in the area of the Law of Obligations, consisting of the Law of Contract and the Law of Tort, by the introduction of the proper law doctrine, it is but appropriate we inquire into whether a similar change had taken place in the law relating to marriage and, in particular, the extent to which the validity of a marriage has any bearing on the related issue or issues that a court is called upon to adjudicate. In other words, is or is not the validity of a marriage omnific, in the sense of having its independent existence regardless of the related issue that calls for determination.

Of the first four cases discussed above, *May's Estate* and *Wilkins* v. *Zillichowski* highlight the shortcoming of placing exclusive reliance upon the law of the state of the parties' common domicile for determining the validity of a marriage, if our aim and objective is to achieve socially desirable results. That would *vel non* lead us to the one and only alternative course that is both pragmatic and socially desirable, namely that the validity of a marriage must be determined in the light of the particular issue which may render the validity of a marriage, not surprisingly, incidental. Impliedly a reading of the cases suggests, as Professor Willis Reese remarks, that a marriage, which would be held good for the purposes of succession, might nevertheless be held invalid in a suit for annulment.

As for the other two cases, namely in *Re Ommang Estate* and *Meisenhelder* v. *Chicago & N.W. Ry. Co.*, that whereas the subsequent acquisition of the domicile of Minnesota by the spouses in the Ommang case invested the widow with a right of succession as per Minnesota law, the *lex loci celebrationis*, thus rendering the law of Wisconsin (the previous *lex domicilii* of the parties) prohibiting the marriage incidental, in the *Miesenhelder case*, the explicit prohibition of marriage between the first cousins under the law of Illinois robbed the widow of her claim for compensation under the Employer's Liability Act as per the law of Kentucky, the *lex loci celebrationis*.

The fifth and the last case cited by Professor Willis Reese, a Pennsylvania Supreme Court decision, namely *Re Estate of Lenherr*, in his (the Professor's) assessment fortifies his thesis. This case, discussed earlier, relates to a Pennsylvania statute that forbade adulterous spouses from marrying elsewhere their adulterous partners. The underlying strong public policy was to protect the sensibilities of the injured and innocent husband or wife from the continued cohabitation of the adulterous pair even if their marriage be valid as per the *lex loci celebrationis* (that is, as per the law of West Virginia). Here, the widow of an adulterous union claimed a tax exemption that she might be entitled to as per the Illinois law in respect of the property inherited from her deceased husband, provided she was validly married to him. The Supreme Court of Pennsylvania upheld her claim after having reversed the lower court's decision denying her the tax exemption that she sought for. The ratio that the Court employed is convincing, though ingenious. In its view, the policy of the State of Illinois, as stated earlier, might be 'quite strong with respect to cohabitation as well as other issues; but it would not be furthered significantly by a denial of tax exemption, in the changed scenario, in that the 'affront' caused to the innocent former spouse by cohabitation was a thing of the past because of the man's death.' Accordingly, the Court declined to apply the Pennsylvania law to invalidate the marriage for this purpose.

To conclude, the decision in this case, and there can be no two opinions about it, clinches Professor Willis Reese's thesis that a marriage cannot serve as an 'all purpose concept'.

THE INSULATED APPROACH OF COURTS IN ENGLAND

Courts in England are generally conservative and slow to adapt to the changing structure, the needs, and the reasonable expectations of the society in this, our fast changing world. They tenaciously cling to rules and doctrines that govern a subject matter, be it a contract, a tort or a marriage. It is not inconceivable that the law relating to the above mentioned subjects may under certain circumstances be rendered incidental or marginal, as a case study bears out, in the determination of the law that governs a related issue.

Ironically enough, it was Professor Morris, a distinguished English academic lawyer, who, by his ground breaking article 'The Proper Law of a Tort', published in the *Harvard Law Review* during his stay at the Harvard Law School as a Visiting Professor, virtually set ablaze the American choice of law rules in the areas of contract and tort by his proper law doctrine, which we find reflected in the formulations of the *Restatement (Second) of Conflict of Laws*, 1971 in the United States. The English choice of law rules *a contrario sensu* remained resilient, impervious to any call for a change based on social good. Professor Willis Reese, the author of the *Restatement (Second) of Conflict of Laws*, extended it further to marriage with good results.[11]

Courts in England have all along treated marriage, in the words of Professor Willis Reese, an 'all purpose concept'. This is evident from a case law study in England, spread over a hundred and twenty years. We may pick and choose four English leading cases as illustrative of the comment. They are: *Shaw* v. *Gould*,[12] in *Re Paine*,[13] in *Re Bischoffsheim*[14] and *Motala* v. *A-G*.[15]

The decision in *Shaw* v. *Gould* and the ratio employed therein by the House of Lords are anachronistic, and for that reason only do not call for a searching inquiry. The facts of the case are briefly as follows:

A testator domiciled in England bequeathed funds in trust for Elizabeth Hickson for life and after her death in trust for her children. The will included English land that was devised after her death to 'her first and other sons lawfully begotten'. Elizabeth, at the age of sixteen, was induced by fraud, without the knowledge of her family, to marry one Buxton, domiciled in England, at Manchester. She, however, never lived with her husband even for a day, as her friends managed to take her away from Buxton soon after the marriage ceremony. Sixteen years later, she became engaged to one Shaw, a British domiciliary, who, after acquiring a domicile in Scotland, contrived to get Buxton there for forty days by paying him £250, and succeeded in getting Elizabeth's first marriage to Buxton dissolved by the court of Session in Scotland. Elizabeth then married Shaw in Edinburgh and had by him two daughters and a son, all of whom were born during the lifetime of Buxton. The children, then, brought an action before an English court claiming a right of succession under the will of the English testator to the funds as being the 'children' of Elizabeth and also to the land by the son as being her 'son' lawfully begotten. At the time of the action Buxton, Elizabeth, and Shaw were dead. Evidence was given in support of the validity of the second marriage and the legitimacy of the children born of a putative marriage as per Scottish law, that is, a marriage deemed regular in point of form but void owing to the prior existing marriage of one of the parties, provided it be that the parents were justifiably ignorant of the prior existing marriage.

The court, so to say, not only failed to take note of the validity of the second marriage as per Scottish law (that is, the *lex loci celebrationis*) after the dissolution of the first marriage, but was equally oblivious to the main issue that called for determination, namely the right of inheritance of the children of Elizabeth and Shaw, that would render the so-called invalidity of the second marriage, on which the subsistence of the first marriage had to feed for its sustenance, inconsequential. It is all the more so due to the death of all three of them, namely Buxton, Shaw, and Elizabeth.

The decision in *Re Paine* is all the more regrettable if not for the court's blind adherence to the House of Lords' ruling in *Shaw* v. *Gould*. That was a case where an English woman domiciled in England married her deceased sister's husband, a German domiciliary, in Germany. The marriage was valid according to the German law (that is, the *lex loci celebrationis*) though prohibited at that date under English law. The couple cohabitated in England for more than forty years till their death. The court, speaking through Bennett, J. held that the three children born of the marriage were illegitimate by the application of the dual domicile doctrine and, accordingly, denied them the right of inheritance.

Comment is surely superfluous. Even a feeble justification one may find to support the ratio employed by the House of Lords in *Shaw* v. *Gould*, namely that the Scottish divorce of the English first marriage was invalid and that the Scottish second marriage was rendered void in the wake of the subsistence of the first English marriage, is absent in the case *Re Paine*. Moreover, two other factors militate against the decision in that the marriage contracted in Germany was in accordance with the *lex loci celebrationis*, and that the German domicile of origin of the children would render them legitimate. The core issue, therefore, is the right of inheritance of the children after the death of their parents coupled with their reasonable expectations of being treated as lawful heirs, and certainly not the validity of the marriage of their parents which, in the circumstances of the case, would take a back seat and accordingly be deemed incidental.

Unlike the above two cases, in the case of *Re Bischoffsheim*, the court seems to have realized that to deny legitimacy to children born of putative parents and thereby deprive them of their entitlement to the benefit under the will of a testator who had died domiciled in England would be unconscionable and unjust from a societal standpoint. *Re Bischoffsheim* was a case where a woman married her deceased husband's brother, both British domiciliaries, in New York. Their marriage was valid under the law of New York (that is, the *lex loci celebrationis*) but void under English law. They then acquired the domicile of New York and a son was born to them subsequently. The question arose as to the son's entitlement to the benefit under the will of a testator who had died domiciled in England. Romer, J. allowed the claim of the son based on his domicile of origin (namely New York) which happened to be the domicile of his parents at birth. The learned judge employed the following ratio in decreeing favourably to the son:

> While succession to personal property depends upon the legitimacy of the claimant, the status of legitimacy conferred on him by his domicile of origin [that is the domicile of his parents at birth] will be recognized by our courts; and that, if that legitimacy is established, the validity of his parents' marriage should not be entertained as a relevant subject for investigation.[16]

The learned judge distinguished this case from *Shaw* v. *Gould*. According to him, the House of Lords in *Shaw* v. *Gould* laid stress on the invalidity of the Scottish decree of divorce which deprived the children of their legitimacy based on their domicile of origin, that is, English, whose law rendered the parents' second Scottish marriage void in view of the subsistence of the English marriage. Moreover, what prompted Romer, J. in *Re Bischoffsheim's* to uphold the legitimacy of the son was that his domicile of origin was New York, which happened to be the domicile of choice acquired by his parents prior to his birth, and that the status of legitimacy of the son in the instant case was comparable to his being legitimated by the law of the country where at the time of his birth and of the subsequent marriage his father was domiciled (that is, *legitimatio per subsequens matrimoniam*), a well established rule of English law.

Interestingly enough, even the marginal deviation from the customary attitude and approach of courts in England, such as we notice in *Re Bischoffsheim* in the matter of determining the issue relating to the legal status of children, subordinating it to the validity of the marriage of their parents as though marriage is 'an all purpose concept', is a short lived possession. It is evident from a reading of the decision in *Motala* v. *A-G.*,[17] which is not one of legitimacy and succession but legitimacy and claims to British citizenship on the part of some of the children. The facts are as under:

The spouses, both of whom Indian domiciliaries, went to live in Northern Rhodesia, now Zambia. While so, they went through a form of marriage in 1950 which was in accordance with Sunni Muslim law, but contrary to the law of Northern Rhodesia. They overcame the invalidity of their marriage by entering into a subsequent marriage in 1968 as per the law of Northern Rhodesia. The earlier marriage between them, nevertheless, was valid under Indian law. The issue of the legitimacy of the children, being one of status, was referred to the law of the children's domicile of origin (that is, India), according to which the parents' first marriage was valid. The court distinguished the instant case from *Shaw* v. *Gould* the latter of which, as we know, was concerned with the validity of the Scottish decree of divorce; and by the same token approved the ruling in *Re Bischoffsheim*.

With due respects to the English conflicts rules as interpreted and applied by courts in England, viewed in the light of the legislative measures such as the Legitimacy Acts of 1959 and 1976, the issue of the legitimacy of children and the claims arising therefrom as dealt with by courts in England, leave much to be desired. When the English system has gone so far as to recognize putative marriages, fortified by the concept of legitimation of children by subsequent marriage between the spouses, it is surprising that courts in England have failed to assign primacy to the issue of legitimacy of children and correlate it judiciously to the validity of the marriage between the spouses. By so doing, we would be able to achieve results which may prove to be socially convenient and sound, to employ Professor Morris's phrase. Consequentially, marriage would no longer be deemed an omnific concept.

It may not amount to any infringement of academic propriety if one ventures to remark that, courts in England have not learnt to shed their diehard attitude of treating marriage as 'an all-purpose concept'. It is not unlikely that circumstances may so warrant as to relegate marriage and its validity to an incidental legal status when juxtaposed with the main issue of the legitimacy of the child or the children born of such marriage. If, for the sake of argument, in the case *Re Bishchoffsheim*, the son was to be born prior to the acquisition of a domicile in New York by the parents, the son would be deemed illegitimate based on his domicile of origin which happened to be English. Similarly, in Motala's case, to seek to validate the marriage, as the court did, on the basis of the domicile of origin that happened to be Indian, which had all along been the domicile of the spouses, is questionable. The court, if we may say so, could have very well achieved the same result by relying on the subsequent valid marriage of the spouses in Northern Rhodesia in the year 1968 in accordance with the law of Northern Rhodesia, that is, *lex loci celebrationis*, in view of their continuous and habitual residence there in Northern Rhodesia from the year 1950 to the year 1968, if our aim and objective was to legitimize those of the spouses' children who sought British citizenship.

This variant approach is sure to accord to marriage its rightful legal status vis-à-vis the issue of the legitimacy of children. In other words, the proper law concept has a role to play in marriage-related issues comparable to the concept of the proper law of a contract or the proper law of a tort.

THE HIDEBOUND ATTITUDE OF INDIAN COURTS TO MARRIAGE AND OTHER PERSONAL LAW ISSUES

Courts in India, even as courts in England, need must adopt an issue-based approach to resolving conflicts if their aim and objective is to render justice to the parties before them in disputes relating to marriage and other family law issues such as legitimacy, legitimation, adoption, succession to property, testate or intestate, et cetera. Such a course will obviate the risk of denial of justice, inasmuch as the validity of a marriage is not considered independently of the issue addressed that calls for judicial determination, but that it (namely the validity of the marriage) is considered with reference to that issue. Accordingly, the validity of the marriage is not omnific but is relative to the issue addressed which may render it, and that it is not unlikely, incidental vis-à-vis the main issue that calls for determination. Admittedly, the validity of a marriage becomes the sole issue before the court if any action for annulment of marriage is brought, or a suit is instituted for a declaratory judgment that a marriage does or does not exist, or that a criminal prosecution is launched for bigamy. With this prefatory note we may examine a few Indian cases.

Even as marriage, from the standpoint of its validity, ought not to be allowed to assume 'an all-purpose character', so is the case *pari ratione* with adoption from the standpoint of its validity. We may, in this connection, cite two decisions of the Bombay High Court, reported in the years 1938[18] and 1939,[19] on the issue of a right to succession in pursuance of a marriage or an adoption respectively and also a decision of the Calcutta High Court, reported in the year 1960,[20] where the issue was one of succession by an adopted son to the property of an adoptive father.

In *Ratan Shah* v. *Bomanji*, the issue was a claim by the second wife of a Parsi husband, domiciled in the erstwhile State of Baroda, to her husband's property situated in Bombay by way of succession. The husband had earlier obtained a divorce from his first wife in accordance with the custom known as '*fargat*', then prevalent amongst the Parsis of Baroda. Such divorce by fargat was alien to the Parsis of Bombay. This factor prompted the High Court of Bombay to deny to the second wife her status as the deceased husband's wife, based on which she could claim a right of succession to his property situated in Bombay.

This decision of the Bombay High Court, needless to say, is startling, considering that the second wife's marriage to her deceased husband as well as the earlier divorce by fargat that he obtained from his first wife were in accordance with the law of Baroda, the *lex loci celebrationis* and the *lex domicilii* respectively. Logic and common sense would tell us that the second wife's legal status as the widow of her deceased husband and, accordingly, his heir ought to be determined by reference to the law of Baroda and not the law of Bombay.

The same is the case with the decision of the Bombay High Court in *Keshaji* v. *Khai Khusroo* where it was a question of a claim for succession by an adopted son of the deceased, a Parsi domiciled in the erstwhile State of Baroda, to the property situated in Bombay. The adoption took place in the State of Baroda as was required under the Parsi law of the State of Baroda. The Bombay High Court, curiously enough, refused to recognize the adoption and the consequent claim to succession based thereon by the adopted son in that the institution of adoption was unknown to the Parsi law as practised in Bomaby.

It is pertinent to remark here that a mere absence of law or custom as to adoption among the Parsi community in the erstwhile Province of Bombay could not set at naught an adoption that was valid and binding as per the *lex domicilii*, that is, the law of the State of Baroda, unless it be that the adoption was opposed to the distinctive public policy of the Province of Bombay. The issue that the Bombay High Court was called upon to determine was the right of the adopted son to inherit his adoptive father's property situated in Bombay and that, therefore, any *de novo* scrutiny of the legal effects of the Baroda adoption on the basis of the *lex fori* (that is, the law or custom of Bombay) was uncalled for. Besides, such a course runs counter to social justice which is basic to the science of conflict of laws.

Still more baffling is the decision of the Calcutta High Court in *Sukdeo Sahi and others* v. *Kapil Deo Sing and others*. The facts of the case are briefly as follows:

A Punjabi Brahmin gentleman by name Biru Maharaj belonging to thc Hoshiarpur District of the Punjab adopted a Brahmin boy by name Ramachandra Pandey, a permanent resident of Balia District of the erstwhile United Provinces (now renamed Uttar Pradesh), in Calcutta.

Subsequently, Biru Maharaj returned to his native town in the Punjab and died there in the year 1941. The issue that arose for determination by the court was the validity of the adoption of Ramachandra Pandey by Biru Maharaj, based on which, alone, the former could succeed to the latter's property.

Prior to the codification and secularization of the Hindu law in the 1950s, the practice of Hindu law by the Hindus differed from region to region based on religion as expounded by authoritative law givers. Whereas Punjab, like Bombay, followed the Mithakshara School of Hindu Law, United Provinces and Bengal followed the Benares School of Hindu Law. As for the former, namely the Punjab, a Brahmin boy could be adopted even after the *Upanayana* ceremony (that is, the sacred thread marriage ceremony), whereas in the United Provinces, it was mandatory that a Brahmin boy should be adopted before the sacred thread ceremony. In the instant case, the adoptive father, Biru Maharaj, as stated earlier, adopted Ramachandra Pandey at Calcutta after the sacred thread marriage which, as per the Mithakshara School of Hindu Law by which he was governed, was valid. But the said adoption was invalid based on the boy's native place, namely the United Provinces, which followed the Benares School of Hindu Law.

If adoption be deemed a secular affair, the adoption that took place in Calcutta was perfectly valid as it fulfilled all the three required criteria, namely that (1) the person adopting was lawfully capable of taking in adoption, that (2) the person giving in adoption was lawfully capable of giving in adoption, and that (3) the person adopted was lawfully capable of being taken in adoption. However, from a religious standpoint, the said adoption was invalid, inasmuch as it failed to comply with the second and the third criteria required under the Benares School of Hindu Law.

The Calcutta High Court invalidated the adoption as it failed to comply with the required conditions of the Benares School of Hindu Law according to which, as stated earlier, neither the natural father giving his son in adoption nor the son adopted had the necessary legal qualification, as the adoption took place in Calcutta after the Upanayana ceremony.

This decision of the Calcutta High Court, it may respectfully be submitted, is not only contrary to the rules of conflict of laws but also unsound and unethical from a societal standpoint. It is contrary to the rules of conflict of laws for, an adoption duly completed with the participation of the natural father giving his son in adoption, the adoptive father taking the son in adoption and the adopted son who is given in adoption automatically secures for the adopted a home which is none other than that of the adoptive father, comparable to the concept of the intended matrimonial home in the case of a marriage. So it is from a societal standpoint, as any denial of the adoption defeats the expectations of the adopted to have a home with and to succeed to the estate of the adoptive father. It may not be inappropriate here to rely upon the pronouncement of the Privy Council in *Balusu Gurulingaswami* v. *Balusu Ramalakshnamma*[21] which considered a religious injuction as peremptory as in the instant case, such as that an one and only son cannot be given and taken in adoption, as no more than directory in nature. The said pronouncement of the Privy Council happens to endorse the view here taken by the author while reviewing related cases, Indian and foreign, as it (namely the view) is founded upon two unassailable norms of social justice and the legitimate expectations of the parties concerned. The said approach in the conflicts resolution process also meets the requirement that the validity of an adoption, as in the case of the validity of a marriage, must be determined in the light of the particular issue, namely the right or claim of the adopted son to inherit the property of the adoptive father that the court was called upon to determine.

NOTES

1. J.H.C. Morris, 'The Proper Law of a Tort', *Harvard Law Review*, Vol. 64 (1950), p. 881.
2. Willis L.M. Reese, 'Marriage in American Conflict of Laws', *The International and Comparative Law Quarterly*, Vol. 26 (1977), p. 952 (1977).
3. Ibid., p. 952
4. Ibid., pp. 953–4
5. 305 NY 486, 114 NE 2d 4 (1953)
6. Compare *Re May's Estate* with *Catalano* v. *Catalano*, 148 Conn. 288, 170 A. 2d 726 (1961), the latter of which also involved a marriage between uncle and niece. The marriage was held invalid by the application of the law of the New York State of the husband's domicile where the spouses set up

their matrimonial home. Accordingly, the wife was denied a widow's right of support from her husband's estate.

7. 26 NJ 370, 140 A. 2d 65 (1958)
8. 183 MINN 92, 235 NW 529 (1931)
9. 170 MINN 317, 213 NW 32 (1927)
10. 455 PA 225, 314 A. 2d 255 (1974)
11. See Note 2 Supra
12. (1868) LR 3 HL55
13. (1940) Ch. 46
14. (1948) Ch. 79 at 92, (1947) 2 ALL ER 830
15. (1990) 2 FLR 261
16. (1948) Ch. 79 at 92, (1947) 2 ALL ER 830
17. (1990) 2 FLR 261
18. *Ratan Shah* v. *Bomanji*, (1938) ILR BOM 238.
19. *Keshaji* v. *Khai Khusroo*, (1939) 41 BOM LR 478.
20. *Sukdeo Sahi and others* v. *Kapil Deo Sing and others*, AIR 1960 CAL 597.
21. Ind. App. 113 P.C.

10

Law of Property

The Law of Property is as interesting and complicated as the Law of Persons. In the present work, the Law of Persons, consisting of marriage, matrimonial causes, and orders as to children, has received a detailed and an incisive treatment. Likewise, it is proposed to treat the Law of Property by dividing the subject into the law relating to immovables and movables and the law relating to succession, the latter of which, again, being subdivided into administration of estates and beneficial distribution, inasmuch as they constitute an integral part of succession.

CLASSIFICATION AND *SITUS*

CLASSIFICATION: A MATTER OF SEMANTICS

Property is classified as movable or immovable in conflict of laws the world over.[1] The law that determines whether a property is movable or immovable is the law of the place where the property is situtated.[2] The same conflicts rules apply to choses in action and choses in possession.[3] All the same, when the property in issue is the subject matter of a contract, the intention of the parties thereto may, from a legal standpoint, assume importance in the ascertainment of the applicable law for determining the nature of the property and the other related transactions.[4]

IMMOVABLES: AN INCLUSIVE CONCEPT

Immovables not only mean lands but include all estates, interests, and charges in and over lands.[5] They include freehold[6] and leasehold[7] interests, freehold land subject to a trust for sale though the sale as yet has not taken place,[8] rent charges,[9] mineral rights,[10] and also the interests of a mortgagee.[11] However, rent charges arising out of an equitable claim based on a contract between the parties, partake of the character of a moveable property, which can be recovered by an action in an Indian court, the presence of the defendant within its jurisdiction being the condition precedent.

Proceeds of sale of land lose their original character as immovable and are normally treated as moveables, although an interest in partnership land retains its character as immovable property, albeit a right one may claim in the distribution of partnership assets or, as the case may be, in respect of payment out of the assets of the value of a share in the partnership, is moveable.[12]

Classification of issues such as title deeds, fixtures, or growing crops is for the law of the land to determine. However, harvested crops by virtue of being severed from the land become moveables. So is the case with interests in chattels subject, of course, to their being classified under the rules relating to interests in land, stated earlier in the sub-section titled 'Immovables: An Inclusive Concept'.[13]

Situs of Property: General Observations

Generally speaking, it is for the *lex fori* to determine the *situs* or location of property.[14] A property may be deemed to have different locations for different purposes. For example, a ship in the territorial waters of a state is considered having its location in that state.[15] On the contrary, a ship on the high seas may be deemed to be situated at her port of registry.[16] As for the location in respect of corporeal property, the general rule is that the property is situated where it is found.[17] Choses in action, too, have a *situs*.[18]

A simple contract debt is deemed to be situated at a place where it is recoverable by action.[19] Naturally, therefore, it is located at the place where the debtor has his residence.[20] The debtor may be resident in a number of countries depending upon the commercial transaction. For example, a debt due from a bank to a customer is located at the branch where the customer has his account.[21] In the case of a debt on a policy of insurance, it is at the place where the policy money is made payable under the policy.[22] Likewise, a debt due under a currency bill issued by a foreign government is situated in the country where payment is due on maturity.[23]

A specialty debt, which has a species of corporeal existence in the sealed instrument,[24] is located where the instrument is stituated.[25] This rule is also applied to mortgage debts[26] and to bonds issued by foreign governments under statutory authority.[27]

Negotiable Instruments and Other Transferable Documents: Their Location

Documents such as negotiable instruments, bonds and securities which are transferable by delivery[28] have their *situs* or location at the place where they are found.[29] Documents relating to choses in action such as shares, stocks, and bonds that are registered, have their *situs* where their registers are kept.[30] The *situs* of a beneficial interest under a trust will be the same as that of the property.[31] In case the trust merely creates a right of action against the trustees, the *situs* of that chose in action is where the trustees normally reside against whom it may be enforced.[32]

As has already been stated, a ship in the territorial waters of a state is considered as having its location in that state.[33] A ship on the high seas may be deemed to be located at the port of its registry.[34]

JURISDICTION IN RESPECT OF FOREIGN IMMOVABLES

General Rules of Conflict of Laws

It is a well known principle of conflict of laws that municipal courts refrain from exercising jurisdiction in respect of title to, or any kind of right or interest in, foreign immovables. An Indian court shall not entertain any action for a declaration of title to or division of foreign immovables or, as for that, possession of such immovables.[35] The same is the case with proceedings, if the issue involved is basically one of title of any kind in relation to the foreign immovable, such as a right to share in the annual allowances charged on the revenue of a foreign village,[36] or of a right to seek partition of a foreign land.[37]

Besides, an Indian court does not have the power to take such properties into calculation in adjusting the equities between the parties.[38] Nevertheless, courts have retained, in respect of the foreign immovables, a limited jurisdiction against persons within their jurisdiction, if there be an equity between the parties arising from contract, fraud or trust. In such cases, a court may choose to grant a declaration of title to a foreign land if otherwise there is no dispute as to its title.[39]

EQUITABLE JURISDICTION *IN PERSONAM*

In this area of exercise of equitable jurisdiction *in personam*, Indian law reports are replete with cases of resolution of local disputes by the application of local law, and not many involving conflicts resolution. The blame for this is not to be solely laid at the altar of courts of law in India. It is a painful reminder that the higher judiciary, namely the high courts and the Supreme Court of India, have not as yet come to grips with the conflicts resolution process and the nuances that have been inducted into it by a spate of juristic writings, particularly in the United States during the past seven decades or so, for the courts in those countries to draw from. The blame for this state of affairs may have to be equally borne by the legal community here in India, which has not so far come forward with provocative legal writings in this area of conflicts resolution which may educate and, at the same time, arouse the judiciary. This appraisal, the author candidly admits, may appropriately be characterized as introspective.

Courts in India, even as courts of equity in England and the common law world, assume jurisdiction in suits in respect of trusts affecting property situated in a foreign country, or for the preservation or protection of a trust fund situated in a foreign country, provided the trustee is in India. Even so, the Indian courts will not interfere with the administration of foreign trusts.[40] However, a court in India, in the exercise of its equitable jurisdiction, may order payment of mesne profits against a defendant who has been in wrongful possession of foreign land.[41]

APPLICATION OF EQUITABLE PRINCIPLES: SCOPE AND EFFECT

(i) A suit for specific performance of a contract of sale of immovable properties situated in India can be instituted against a non-resident foreigner, even if the contract was executed outside the country.[42] However, the absentee owner is amenable to the jurisdiction of an Indian court only if the court is otherwise competent; mere presence of property in India does not invest it with jurisdiction.

The Code of Civil Procedure, 1908, may confer upon the court requisite competence to pass a decree against an absent owner if, and only if, the cause of action has arisen within its jurisdiction.[43] Likewise, the jurisdictional competence of a court here in India extends to entertaining an action for mesne profits, arrears of rent or profits in respect of lands situated outside India, provided the defendant resides within its jurisdiction, but not against a non-resident foreigner.[44] The court's jurisdictional competence also extends to entertaining a claim for accounting based on a mortgage in respect of lands partly or wholly lying outside its jurisdiction.[45] To the said two categories, namely, mesne profits in respect of lands situated outside India and claim for accounting of mortgaged lands wholly or partly being outside India, we may add claim for arrears of rent, too, subject, of course, to the presence of the defendant within the jurisdiction of the concerned court in India.

(ii) A court in India exercises jurisdiction in a suit to enforce a trust in respect of foreign immovables, provided the trustee is within its jurisdiction.[46] Its jurisdictional competence includes the issue of the validity or otherwise of the administration of the trust.[47]

(iii) A common law court in the exercise of its jurisdiction *in personam*[48] is well within its jurisdictional competence to grant relief in cases of fraud or other inequitable dealings in respect of foreign immovables.[49] It, therefore, follows that its jurisdictional competence includes the power to set aside or otherwise provide relief against a conveyance of foreign immovables procured by fraud.[50]

A creditor who sets in motion execution proceedings and himself purchases foreign land belonging to his debtor may, by an order of a court in India, be compelled to hold the said land as a security for the debt subject, of course, to a right of redemption.[51]

This justifiably is an exception to the rule of conflict of laws that a law to govern foreign land is the *lex situs*, inasmuch as there is a contractual relationship between the parties to the case. Further, an Indian court, in the exercise of its jurisdiction *in personam*, can declare that a will in respect of properties situated outside its jurisdiction is a forgery.[52]

(iv) An Indian court, in exercise of its jurisdiction *in personam*,[53] can issue orders for foreclosure[54] or for redemption[55] if a legal or equitable mortgage of foreign immovables has been validly made according to the law of India. In such a case, the Indian court is well within its jurisdiction to compel the mortgagor to discharge the mortgage debt out of the sale proceeds of the sale of the land.[56] Likewise, an Indian court may, in pursuance of an order of redemption, grant an injunction against the mortgagee forbidding him from bringing an action for foreclosure in local courts.[57]

Besides, the court can also decree specific performance of a contract governed by the law of the land to grant a mortgage of foreign land and, accordingly, so interpret the contract of mortgage as requiring such equities and rights of redemption as per *lex fori*.[58]

(v) The jurisdictional competence of a court in India extends to entertaining an action for mesne profits in respect of lands situated outside India, provided the defendant resides within its jurisdiction, but not against a non-resident foreigner.[59] The court's jurisdictional competence also extends to entertaining a claim for accounting based on a mortgage in respect of lands partly or wholly lying outside its jurisdiction.[60]

If deemed appropriate, an Indian court may choose to appoint a receiver for enforcing rendition of accounts of foreign immovables.[61] However, the court should refrain from putting the receiver in possession of the foreign immovables. Accordingly, any party to the action in which the court's order for the appointment of a receiver is in place who prevents legitimate steps being taken in pursuance of the order to enable the receiver to take possession of the foreign immovables as per the *lex situs* may be found guilty of contempt of court.[62] However, there is no question of contempt of court if another person sets in motion proceedings in a court to obtain possession of the foreign immovables before the receiver takes proceedings.[63]

Administration of Estates and Trusts

A local court in India, as stated earlier, can assume jurisdiction in suits for the enforcement of express trusts in respect of land situated in a foreign country, or, as for that, pass such orders as may be appropriate to preserve or to protect a trust fund situated in a foreign country, provided the trustee is in India. All the same, the local court would refrain from interfering with the administration of a foreign trust.[64]

RULES OF CONFLICT OF LAWS IN RELATION TO IMMOVABLES

Introduction

It is a well established principle of conflict of laws that the rights over immovables are governed by the *lex situs*, that is, the law of the country where the immovable is situated.[65] This is the outcome of the doctrine of 'eminent domain', namely that the state is the superior owner of all lands situated within it and, as such, all rights relating to lands within its domain are for the state to regulate in the exercise of its sovereign rights. *Lex situs* means the local law of the country where the immovable is situated to the exclusion of the concerned country's rules of choice of law which may import into the Indian rules of choice of law the discredited *renvoi* doctrine, partial or total.[66]

Capacity

Issues relating to the capacity to assign[67] or to the acquisition of an immovable are governed by the *lex situs* of the immovable.[68]

Formalities

Any assignment of an immovable must conform to the formalities prescribed by the *lex situs* of the immovable.[69] Accordingly, a conveyance of land for its validity ought to comply with the required formalities of the *lex situs*.[70] Therefore, an assignment which fails to comply with the required formalities of the *lex situs* may give rise to an action in equity.[71]

According to the Rome Convention on the Law Applicable to Contractual Obligations, 1980, (vide Article 9, paragraph 6) the following rule is laid down. It reads as follows:

> If the subject matter of a contract pertains to a right in immovable property or, as may be, a right to use immovable property, the mandatory requirements of the *lex fori* of the country where the property is situated apply, irrespective of the country where the contract is concluded and irrespective of the law governing the contract.[72]

The above rule is well taken if kept within bounds and made applicable only to the parties to the Convention, their conflict rules notwithstanding. As stated in the preliminary chapter, the United Kingdom as a party to the Rome Convention was obliged to surrender the basic doctrine of the 'proper law of a contract' to the conventional rules vis-à-vis other parties to the Rome Convention, and could still retain it so far as non-parties are concerned. However, to impose on non-parties the rules of the Rome Convention in utter disregard of their peremptory rules of conflict of laws and in contravention of rules of equity and justice is nothing short of travesty of justice. If, for instance, a rule of the *lex situs* declares inadmissible a valid assignment or contract relating to immovables, it will surely be ignored as it contravenes the basic norm of conflict of laws, namely that procedural matters are for the *lex fori* to regulate, besides flying in the face of justice and equity.[73]

Material or Substantive or Essential Validity

It is a basic rule of conflict of laws that a material or essential validity of an assignment of immovable property is governed by the *lex situs* of the immovable.[74] This principle applies *proprio vigore* to such matters as the nature and incidents of the estates created in the immovable[75] and the restraints as well on alienation.[76]

Mortgage Debt: Currency for Measurement

The issue relating to the currency which serves as the unit of measurement of the debt is one of construction.[77] Usually it is the currency of the country where the immovables are situated that serves as the unit of account. However, in most of the cases it is the intention of the parties concerned that serves as the governing consideration.[78]

Likewise, the rate of interest payable on the mortgage debt will be that fixed by the *lex situs* of the immovable,[79] unless the intention of the parties concerned is to the contrary.[80]

Lex Situs and the Law of Limitation

The law of limitation of the country where the immovables are situated (*lex situs* of the immovables) will determine the effect of lapse of time upon the existence or enforcement of any right in respect of the immovables.[81] If according to the *lex situs* a person's title to immovables is extinguished, the court will simply put its *imprimatur* upon such extinguishment.[82] So is the case where an action for the recovery of land is time barred as per the *lex situs*.[83] Where the court is endowed with jurisdictional competence as per the *lex fori* to pronounce upon or enforce rights in respect of foreign immovables,[84] it will hold a right as time barred only if the law of limitation of the *situs* so ordains.[85]

RULES OF CONFLICT OF LAWS IN RELATION TO MOVABLES

When an assignment[86] of a chose in possession takes place, its validity and effect[87] are governed by the *lex situs*[88] of the chose. If by the *lex situs* an assignee acquires a good title,[89] it would be recognized the world over, and so will courts in India do. Applying the same yardstick, prior restrictions, if any, imposed on an assignee will receive due recognition everywhere.[90] As a corollary to the preceding proposition, it is immaterial if, by an assignment taking place abroad, the owner has lost his title to the chose to which he never gave his consent, not to talk of the chose being in the relevant foreign country against his will, and it is so even if he is a victim of a theft.[91] If the property happens to be in a country, a court in that country will apply its own law to govern the validity and effect of the assignment,[92] but not necessarily all the rules of its domestic law in view of the assignment taking place abroad.[93]

The title to a chose in possession remains unaltered due to a change in its location.[94] In other words, if the new *lex situs* does not recognize the validity or effect of an assignment that took place prior to the change of location, a court will, all the same, apply the old *lex situs* in respect thereof.[95] However, the validity and effect of an assignment made after such change of location will understandably be governed by the new *lex situs*.[96] Depending upon the issues that may arise, under the circumstances of the case, good title acquired under the old *lex situs* gets defeated.[97]

As in the case of assignment of choses in possession, the validity and effect of a pledge, too, are governed by the *lex situs* of the property pledged.[98] However, the relative rights of the pledgor and pledgee are governed by the proper law of their transaction which will help determine other connected issues such as, for example, whether the pledgee may redeliver the goods to the pledgor in certain circumstances without losing his security.[99]

The existence of a right of stoppage in transit and the manner of its exercise are also issues that are determined by *lex situs*.[100]

Law Relating to Negotiable Instruments and Documents of Title

As stated in the chapter devoted to negotiable instruments, in India the making and assignment of a negotiable instrument such as a bill of exchange, a promissory note, or a cheque is governed by the Negotiable Instruments Act, 1881.

In the absence of a contract to the contrary of a negotiable instrument, the ability of the maker or the drawer to assign the instrument is governed by the law of the place where he made the instrument and the respective liabilities of the acceptor and indorser by the law of the place where the instrument is made payable.[101]

Law Relating to Assignment of Bare Choses in Action

The mutual obligations arising between the assignor and the assignee under a voluntary assignment of a right against another person (namely the debtor) are governed by the law that applies to the contract between the assignor and the assignee.[102] The law that governs the said contract of assignment also determines issues relating to the extent to which it may be assigned,[103] the relationship between the assignor and the debtor, the conditions under which the assignment may be invoked against the debtor, and also whether the debtor's obligations have been discharged.[104]

GOVERNMENT DECREES OF SEIZURE OF PRIVATE PROPERTY: THEIR LEGAL EFFECTS (TERRITORIAL AND EXTRA-TERRITORIAL)

It is a well known principle of constitutional law that a state in the exercise of its right of eminent domain can, by a decree, acquire or requisition private property for public use, followed by a payment of compensation as *quid pro quo* to the person concerned whose property has been seized. This is so within the territorial limits of a state or a territory possessed or controlled by its government, whether he be a national[105] or a non-national[106] against whom the right has been exercised by the state. But when it comes to the acquisition or requisition of private property, whether of a national or of a foreigner extra-territorially, its legal consequences are far-reaching. Such decrees of seizure beyond the concerned state's territorial limits tantamount to infringement of the sovereignty of the other state or states within whose territorial limits the property or properties seized happen to be situated.[107] However, if the government somehow gets possession or control of the property, the owner will in vain attempt to recover the seized property by legal process in the country where the property is situated or brought, for the foreign government could then get the action stayed by successfully pleading sovereign immunity as a bar to the entertainment of the action by the court concerned.[108]

If, on the other hand, such decrees of acquisition or requisition of private property on the part of the concerned foreign state happen to be penal, not remedial, as interpreted and applied by courts in the foreign country or countries, it is equally a well know principle of private international law or conflict of laws, that a municipal court will not enforce a foreign penal law, either directly or indirectly.[109]

As it is left to the discretion of the municipal court concerned, before which the action for recovery is brought by the person whose property is seized, no one can hazard a guess as to whether or not the court would choose to characterize the decree as penal. However, if the decree is directed against the property of a particular individual,[110] of a particular company,[111] of persons of a particular race,[112] or of persons of a particular alien nationality,[113] the court will not hesitate to classify the action of the state as penal. A decree, however, cannot be construed as penal merely because no compensation or inadequate compensation is payable to the owner under it.[114]

Apolitical the institution of judiciary is, it will not give a decree requisitioning private property extra-territorial effect, even if the foreign government were an ally of its country during a war and the object of the decree was to prevent the property from falling into enemy hands.[115]

THE LAW RELATING TO TRUSTS

THE INDIAN TRUSTS AND APPLICABLE LAW

The Indian Trusts Act, 1882, even as any other Indian law, does not expressly provide for a choice of the applicable law.* Therefore, we are constrained to fall back upon the law relating to contracts such as the Indian Contract Act, 1872, and infer therefrom, by analogy, the law that governs a trust with a foreign element.[116]

The choice of law may be express if the settlor creating an instrument of trust chooses so to do. If that is not the case, we may have to, as aforesaid, go by the analogy of a contract having a foreign element, and ascertain by a parity of reasoning the proper law that governs the trust with a foreign element. The factors most closely connected with a trust and indicative of a proper law are as under:

(1) the place of administration of the trust designated by the settlor;

(2) the location of the assets of the trust;

(3) the place of residence or business of the trustee; and

(4) the stated objects of the trust and the place where they are to be fulfilled.[117]

The Scope and Ambit of the Applicable Law

The Indian Trusts Act, 1882 controls and regulates all aspects of a trust[118] such as its validity,[119] the mode of its creation,[120] the competence of the author to create a trust,[121] the duties and liabilities of the trustee or trustees,[122] the rights and powers of the trustee or trustees[123] and also their disabilities,[124] the rights and liabilities of the beneficiary or beneficiaries,[125] and, lastly, the process of extinction of a trust.[126]

The Governing Law

The law to govern a trust is the law chosen by the settlor. If such an exercise as to the choice of the governing law on the part of the settlor is absent, the law to govern a trust is that with which the trust is most closely connected.[127]

Recognition of Trusts

A trust that seeks recognition by implication is subject to, *inter alia*, the following conditions: that the trust property constitutes a separate fund, that a trustee may sue and be sued in his capacity as trustee, and that he may appear or act in his capacity as a trustee before a notary or any person acting in an official capacity. It needs to be emphasized, in this connection, that the rights and obligations of a trustee in respect of a trust are solely confined to the trust or the fund created under the trust. Accordingly, the personal assets of a trustee and the rights and obligations that arise therefrom are outside the purview of the trust or, as the case may be, the trust fund.[128]

SUCCESSION

Administration of Estates

Law Governing Administration

Choice of Law

Under the Indian Succession Act, 1925, the administration of the deceased person's movable assets is governed by the law of the country where the deceased was domiciled at the time of his death.[129] Administration of assets carries with it the dual function of collection of assets of the deceased and debts due to him[130] and payment to the creditors of their dues out of the assets.[131] With respect to the administration of the assets of the deceased, irrespective of whether the administration is principal or ancillary, the personal representative will be governed by the *lex fori*. In the matter of administration, India does not subscribe to the principle of 'unity of administration'. In this regard, it is the same as in England. Accordingly, a separate grant of letters of administration must be obtained from a court in India in respect of the property of the deceased left in India.[132] Under Indian law, letters of administration in respect of intestate succession are granted to those who are related to the deceased either through marriage or consanguinity in the order as specified under law, notwithstanding the fact that he had his domicile in a foreign country whose succession law, testate and intestate, differs from the law in India.[133]

Administration and Succession Distinguished

Administration, as stated above, is confined only to the collection of assets of the deceased and debts due to him, and the making of payments to creditors out of the assets. It does not include the distribution of the deceased's net assets after the payment of all debts, duties, and expenses.[134] Beneficial distribution is governed by separate rules.[135]

Administration of Estates: Role of the Judiciary

Admittedly, that while the local law in India in respect of judicial administration of the estates of the deceased is highly advanced, the same is not the case with the rules of choice of law in that area, as is generally the case with the Indian conflict of laws. One is, therefore, constrained to fall back upon English and American case law to illustrate the principles underlying the judicial role in the administration of the estates of the deceased.

An order of a court of the judicial administration of the estates of the deceased will normally extend to all his assets, wherever situated.[136] However, a local court lacks jurisdictional competence to provide for collection and/or administration of the foreign assets of the deceased.[137] The court will justifiably require all claims to be proved in the administration, and may restrain local creditors from proceeding against the estate in foreign courts.[138] An order of a local court for judicial administration does not render a foreign personal representative outside its jurisdiction accountable for his administration, except for assets of the deceased which are brought by him within its jurisdiction before they could be appropriated from out of the deceased's estate.[139]

However, if he is personally within the jurisdiction of a local court, he, like any local personal representative, is accountable to the court's order in his capacity as trustee of the will for the ultimate distribution of the deceased's net assets to the beneficiaries, wherever those assets are situated.[140]

Legal Status of Personal Representative

Legal Effect of Indian Grant

An Indian grant of representation vests in the personal representatives all the deceased's movable and immovable estate which, at the date of his death, are situated in India. It does not, however, vest in him assets situated outside India.[141] Such assets will be governed by the law of the country where they are situated.[142] However, there is an exception to the above conflicts rule, namely that if, for instance, the foreign assets are brought into the country before any person or persons have acquired a title to them under their *lex situs*, such assets will vest in the personal representative by virtue of his grant.[143]

Duties of the Executor

The primary duty of an executor or an administrator under an Indian grant is to collect the assets of the deceased wherever situated.[144]

Payment of Debts to Creditors

If the deceased was not in an Indian domiciliary, the application or appropriation of his movable property to the payment of his debts is still to be regulated by the law of India.[145] No creditor who has received payment of a part of his debt by virtue of the above mentioned rule is entitled to share in the proceeds of the immovable estate of the deceased, unless he brings such payment into account for the benefit of the other creditors.[146] No creditor has a right of priority over another, but the executor or administrator must pay all such debts of which he has knowledge, including his own, equally and rateably as far as the assets of the deceased will extend.[147]

Distribution and Remission of Net Assets

Where a person who is not an Indian domiciliary has died, leaving assets both in India and in the country in which he had his domicile at the time of his death, and there has been a grant of probate or letters of administration in India with respect to the assets and a grant of administration in the country of domicile with respect to the assets in that country, the executor or administrator in India, after having served the requisite notices[148] and after having discharged at the expiration of the time named in the notice, the lawful claims he knows of may transfer, with the consent of the executor or administrator in the country of domicile, the surplus or residue to him for distribution to those persons residing outside India.[149]

Right, Duties, and Legal Liabilities of Foreign Personal Representative

An Indian grant of representation is necessary to enable a foreign personal representative to make title to and to administer the property of a deceased person in India.[150] However, he can sue in his personal capacity if he has obtained a judgment against a debtor of the estate in a foreign country[151] or if he enforces his title to the assets of the deceased which he has reduced into his possession under the *lex situs*, even if the assets were brought to India a day after his death.[152]

Legal Liabilities of Foreign Personal Representatives

A foreign personal representative does not incur any liability in India for acts done or assets received by him by virtue of his authority as a foreign personal representative.[153] *A contrario*, only executors or administrators acting under the authority of an Indian law may administer the assets of the deceased situated in India.[154] *A priori*, a foreign personal representative who is not an executor or administrator under Indian law will be made liable as an executor *de son tort*[155] if he intermeddles with the assets of the deceased in India.[156]

Beneficial Distribution

Judicial Jurisdiction of an Indian Court

Indian courts have jurisdictional competence to determine any question relating to the succession[157] to a deceased person's estate, regardless of his domicile and whether or not it has exercised jurisdiction to make a grant of representation.[158] The jurisdiction is of an inclusive character so as to embrace all the movables and immovables of the deceased, wherever they are situated.[159] However, the court will not make an order with regard to the beneficial distribution of the estate unless the court is satisfied that the person before it is recognized by it as having the authorization to deal with the property in question.[160]

Judicial Jurisdiction of Foreign Courts

An Indian court will give effect to the decision of the court of domicile of the deceased at the date of his death on any question in respect of succession to his movables.[161] Likewise, in the matter of succession to immovables, an Indian court will follow the decision of the court of the country where the immovables are situated.[162]

Choice of Law

Succession to Movables and Immovables: The Governing Law

Subject to certain exceptions, namely the formal validity of a will, wills in foreign languages, and matters relating to construction of wills, (which are being dealt with, the first and the second under section 'Testate Succession' and the third under section 'Testamentary Exercise of Power of Appointment'), succession to movables of a deceased person is governed by the law of his domicile at the date of his death.[163] Again, subject to the same three exceptions as mentioned above, succession to his immovables is governed by *lex situs* (that is, the law of the place where the immovables are situated).[164]

Renvoi

The law that governs succession, testate or intestate, as per the choice of law rules, is the internal or the local law of the country concerned to the exclusion of the rules of choice of law of the forum (that is, doctrine of *renvoi*, partial or total).[165]

Succession: Changes in the Law of Domicile of the Deceased

Generally speaking, succession to movables is not affected by any changes in the law of the domicile of the deceased that are brought about after his death, whether or not retrospective.[166] However, in the case of succession to immovables such changes are taken into account.[167]

Legal Effects of Grant of Representation

The fact that a grant of letters of administration by a court stands unrevoked is conclusive evidence that the deceased died intestate (that is, without making a will).[168] Similarly, the fact that a grant of probate by a court remains unrevoked is conclusive evidence that the instrument admitted to probate is the last will of the testator.[169]

Intestate Succession

It is a well established principle of conflict of laws in the common law world that succession to movables intestate, wherever situated, is governed by the law of domicile at the date of his death.[170] The law of domicile is the governing law in matters of succession, including the devolution of the property of the deceased which, *inter alia*, takes into account issues such as the determination of the kindred of the deceased,[171] share of the widow,[172] and whether the deceased has left lineal descendants.[173]

Issues relating to succession to immovables of the deceased intestate are governed by the *lex situs*.[174]

Testate Succession

Capacity: Rules of Choice of Law

The personal capacity[175] (as distinguished from the proprietary capacity) of a testator to make a will of movables is governed by the law of his domicile.[176] Conflicts rules draw no distinction for this purpose between lack of capacity due to immaturity or status and incapacity arising from ill health.[177]

A beneficiary has the capacity to receive a legacy under a will if he has capacity either by the law of his domicile or by the law of the testator's domicile.[178] This conflicts rule relates only to movables. The *lex situs* governs capacity to make a will of immovables as well as to take under the will.[179]

Formal Validity under Common Law

A will of moveables is valid if it is in conformity with the formalities prescribed by the law of the testator's domicile at the date of his death.[180]

Lex domicilii, as interpreted and applied by courts in India, signifies reference to the internal law of India to the exclusion of rules of choice of law (that is, to the exclusion of *renvoi*.)[181]

A will of movables is valid if it is in conformity with the formal requirements of the *lex situs*.[182]

Formal Validity of a Will under the Indian Law of Succession

The formal validity of a will under the Indian law of succession is, as stated above, the same as it is under common law.[183]

Construction

The construction[184] of a will is governed by the law intended by the testator.[185] If it is a case of a will of movables, the presumption is that the law of the testator's domicile on the date of execution of the testament will be the governing law.[186] However, this presumption is rebuttable if there is sufficient indication that the testator intended his will to be construed according to the law of another country.[187] The intention of the testator may be expressed in the will,[188] or may be implied from the circumstances such as his use of a particular language,[189] or of expressions known only to a particular law.[190]

A will of immovables must, *prima facie*, be construed in accordance with the law of the testator's domicile on the date of execution of the will;[191] but this presumption may be rebutted if there is sufficient indication of the testator's intention to refer it to some other law,[192] such as where he uses the technical language of the country where the immovables are situtated.[193] A court, while construing a will of immovables in accordance with the laws of the testator's domicile, will so construe it as to enable the dispositions to operate to the fullest extent allowed by the *lex situs*.[194]

Wills in Foreign Languages

A will or a testament, even if it be purely local where there is no foreign element, brought before a local court for probate, will be liberally construed by it; or, so to say, the court will put itself into 'the arm chair of the testator', as the Privy Council in England once remarked. Such an attitude on the part of the court will go a long way in rendering justice to the testator and to the beneficiaries under the will. It is all the more so when a will written in a foreign language is brought before the concerned local court to be admitted to probate, translated into English or, as the case may be, into its (that is, court's) regional language. The court would then require, in keeping with the procedural due process, that the foreign will or a copy of it to be furnished, accompanied by an English translation or, as the case may be, a regional translation.[195] The court in its discretion may refer to the original will or a copy of it so as to adjudicate upon questions of construction.[196] In such of those cases where the will is to be construed according to the local law, the court's concern will be to look to the effect of the language in which it is written with a view to ascertain what the equivalent expressions are in the language of the concerned court.[197] Even if there be a need to construe the will or testament according to the law of the country in whose language it is written, the court will not refer to that law for the meaning of words which are not subject to any technical rules of construction under that law.[198]

Certain Indian Rules of Construction

The following are the rules of construction of a will under the Indian Succession Act, 1925:[199]

(i) It is not necessary that any technical words or terms of art be used in a will; but the wording must be such that the intentions of the testator may be derived from the will.[200]

(ii) If the thing which the testator intended to bequeath can be sufficiently identified from the description of it given in the will, but some parts of the description do not apply, such part of the description is rejected as erroneous, and the bequest takes effect.[201]

(iii) The intention of the testator cannot be set aside because it cannot take effect to the full extent; effect must be given to it as far as possible.[202]

(iv) A will or bequest that is not expressive of any definite intention is void for uncertainty.[203]

(v) Where a property is bequeathed to any person, that person is entitled to the whole interest of the testator in it, unless it appears from the will that only a restricted interest was intended for him.[204]

The material or essential validity of a will of movables is governed by the law of the testator's domicile on the date of his death.[205] The same rule of conflict of laws has been applied to issues such as whether the testator is legally obliged to leave a part of his movable estate to his widow or to his children,[206] or as *legitima portio* or *legitim*,[207] as a gift of movables to an attesting witness,[208] to a charity,[209] or for superstitious uses.[210]

As per choice of law rules, the material or essential validity is governed by the *lex situs*.[211] Similarly, the same principle of conflict of laws has also been applied to issues such as whether the testator is legally bound to leave a part of his immovable estate to his widow or children,[212] whether a gift of immovables to a charity is valid,[213] and to issues relating to the nature and incidents of the estates created in the immovables.[214]

Election

The question of election on the part of a beneficiary under a will arises only when the beneficiary chooses to take a benefit outside the will, but which is given to another person by the will, to the abandonment of a benefit given to him by the will. In such a case, as it has nothing to do with the intention of the testator, the question is not one of construction of the will but one of material or essential validity.[215] Accordingly, by the application of the rules of choice of law that, where the benefit under the will consists of movables, the issue whether the beneficiary is put to his election is governed by the law of the testator's domicile at the date of his death, irrespective of the fact that the *lex situs* of any immovables constituting the benefit happen to be outside the will.[216] Similarly, where the benefit under the will consists of immovables, *lex situs* of those immovables is the governing law as respects the question of election, irrespective, once again, of the *lex situs* of any immovables which may constitute the benefit outside the will, and irrespective of the law of the testator's domicile.[217]

Testamentary Revocation

This issue whether a will is revoked by a later will or codicil, in case the later will or codicil contains an express revocation clause, is one governed by the law that governs the validity of the later instrument.[218] As for its formality, it will be treated to have been properly executed, if its execution is in accordance with the rules of choice of law.[219]

Other testamentary modes of revocation[220] probably are governed by the law of the testator's domicile in the case of movables[221] and by the *lex situs* in the case of immovables.[222]

As in the case of testamentary revocation, in the case of subsequent marriage, too, the issue of whether the marriage would revoke a previous will of a movable[223] is governed by the law of the testator's domicile on the date of the marriage.[224] Any subsequent change of domicile is immaterial.[225] Similarly, the question of whether marriage revokes a previous will of immovables is governed by the *lex situs*.[226]

Testamentary Exercise of Power of Appointment

Logic and common sense would endorse the common law rule that a testator has capacity in conflicts cases to exercise by will a power of appointment over movables if he has the capacity to make the will by the law of his domicile, even if it be that he lacks such capacity by the law governing the instrument of creation.[227]

Likewise, a testator's capacity to exercise by will a power of appointment over immovables is governed by the *lex situs*.[228]Again, an exercise by will of a power of appointment in due compliance with the choice of law rules[229] or, in the alternative, in conformity with the law that governs the essential validity of the power[230] is deemed to have been properly executed. Such an exercise of the power of appointment under the will is not to be treated as improperly executed by reason only that its execution was not in accordance with any formal requirements contained in the instrument creating the power.[231]

The issue of whether a will exercises a power of appointment will be determined, *prima facie*, by the law of the testator's domicile at the date of execution of the will.[232] If it is evident that the testator intended the will to be construed in accordance with the law governing the instrument of creation,[233] or that powers of appointment are unknown to the law of the testator's domicile,[234] the issue will be determined by the law governing the instrument of creation.[235]

The material or essential validity of the exercise by will of a power of appointment over movables is governed by the law that governs that instrument of creation.[236] However, if the testator chooses to blend the appointed movables into one mass with his own estate, he would then be endowed with the right to exercise his general power, in which case the material or essential validity of the appointment is governed by the law of the testator's domicile at the date of his death.[237]

The material or essential validity of an appointment of immovables by will is governed by the *lex situs*.[238]

The issue of the revocation by will of the exercise of a power of appointment is governed by the choice of law rules.[239]

NOTES

1. See Sir Peter North and J.J. Fawcett, *Cheshire and North's Private International Law*, Thirteenth Edition (London, Edinburgh, Dublin: LexisNexis Butterworths, 1999), pp. 923–4. Strange as it may seem, courts in England, while acknowledging the universality of the classification of property as movable or immovable, would still cling to the domestic classification of property as realty or personalty. See *Macdonald* v. *Macdonald*, 1932 SC (H.L.) 79 p. 84, 1932 SLT 381; Re Cutcliffe's Will Trusts, *Brewer* v. *Cutcliffe*, (1940) Ch. 565, (1940) 2 ALL. ER 297. However, contrary to this welcome attitude of courts in England, we have, at the same time, the diehard attitude of judges in England as exhibited by Cozens-Hardy, M Rand Farwell, LJ in Re Hoyles, *Row* v. *Jagg*, (1911) 1 Ch. 179 p. 183, 185 CA where they declined to lend countenance to the universality of the classification of property as movable or immovable as against the domestic classification of property as realty and personalty, though they admitted the former classification as a valid principle to be applied in cases involving foreign jurisdictions.

2. For this proposition, namely that the character of the property, whether it is movable or immovable, is determined by the law of the place where the property is situated, there are numerous cases and almost all of them barring three of the twentieth century set out below are nineteenth century decisions. They are: Re Cutcliffe's Will Trusts, *Brewer* v. *Cutcliffe*, (1940) Ch.565, (1940) 2 ALL ER 297; Re Berchtold *Berchtold* v. *Capron*, (1923) 1 Ch.192; Re Hoyles, *Row* v. *Jagg*, (1911) 1 Ch.179, CA. For other cases, all of them of the nineteenth century, that would include *Drummond* v. *Drummond*, (1799) 6 BRO PARL CAS 601, 56 ER 780, HL.

3. Ibid. See for example, Re Hoyles, *Row* v. *Jagg*, (1911) 1 Ch. 179 p. 183, CA (for immovables); Re Hanziani, *Herbert* v. *Christopherson*, (1930) 1 Ch. 407 p. 424 (for movables). Also see for a general analysis, *Haque* v. *Haque*, (No. 2) (1965) 114 CLR 98 p. 107, (1966) ALR 553 p. 555, HC (Aust.) where choses in action, by which we mean movables, are described as 'intangible movables', as 'physical mobility is not the quality of the conceptual', which phrase is not generally employed.

4. Re Fitzgerald, *Surman* v. *Fitzgerald*, (1904) 1 Ch. 573, CA.

5. Re Hoyles, *Row* v. *Jagg*, (1911) 1 Ch. 179 p. 183, 186, CA.

6. *Freke* v. *Lord Carbery*, (1873) LR 16 Eq 461 p. 466.

7. *Freke* v. *Lord Carbery*, (1983) LR 16 Eq 461; *Duncan* v. *Lawson*, (1889) 41 Ch. D 394, 53 JP 532, 37 WR 524; *Pepin* v. *Bruyère*, (1902) 1 Ch.24, CA. Also See Re Gentili's Goods, (1875) 1 R 9 Eq 541; De *Fogassieras* v. *Duport*, (1881) 11 LR IR 123.

8. Re *Berchtold* v. *Capron*, (1923) 1 Ch. 192; *Murrary* v. *Champernowne*, (1901) 2 IR 232, 351 LT 68.

9. *Chatfield* v. *Berchtold*, (1872) 7 Ch. App 192. Also see *Whitaker* v. *Forbes*, (1985) LR 1OCP 583 (Austrian land).

10. Re Trepca Mines Ltd., (1960) 3 ALL ER 304n, (1960) 1 WLR 1273, CA.

11. Re Hoyles, *Row* v. *Jagg*, (1911) 1 Ch. 179 CA. We notice that courts in the Commonwealth of Australia, in cases concerning land within their jurisdictions, are divided as to the correctness of the principle laid down in this case: see authorities reviewed in *Haque* v. *Haque*, (No. 2) (1965) 114 CLR 98, pp. 118, 119, (1966) ALR 553 p. 555, HC (Aust), (the interest of an unpaid vendor of land could be equated with that of a mortgagee and was, therefore, in the court's view, movable); Re Greenfield (1985)) 2 NZLR 662.

12. See notes 10 and 11 supra.

13. *Haque* v. *Haque*, (No. 2) (1965) 114 CLR 98 pp. 122, 130, (1966) ALR 553 pp. 565–6; Re Berchtold, *Berchtold* v. *Capron*, (1923) 1 Ch. 192 p. 206.

14. Re Hoyles, *Row* v. *Jagg*, (1911) 1 Ch. 179 p. 186, CA.

15. *Rossano* v. *Manufacturers' Life Insurance Co. Ltd.*, (1963) 2 QB 352, pp. 379–80, (1962) 2 ALL ER 214 p. 230.

16. *Trustees Executors and Agency Co. Ltd.* v. *Inland Revenue Commissioners*, (1973) Ch. 254, (1973) 1 ALL ER 563.

17. *Trustees Executors and Agency Co. Ltd.* v. *Inland Revenue Commissioners*, (1973) Ch. 254 p. 263, (1973) 1 ALL ER 563 p. 568; Also see *Compania Naviera Vascongado* v. *SS Cristina*, (1938) AC 485, (1938) 1 ALL ER 619 p. 733, HL; the Jupiter (1924) p. 236 p. 239, CA.

18. *Associated Hotels of India Ltd.* v. *R.B. Jodha Mal Kothalia*, AIR 1957 PUNJ 291, 59 PUNJ LR 578 (The *situs* of a judgment debt is the place where the decree was passed),

19. *Nath Bank Ltd.* v. *Andhar Manick Tea Company Ltd.*, AIR 1960 CAL 779 p. 783, (1960) 64 CAL WN 161, (1960) 30 Com Cas 306 (original document creating the specialty debt being in Calcutta at the material time, the locality of the debt is deemed to be in Calcutta); *Associated Hotels of India Ltd.* v. *R.B. Jodha Mal Kothalia*, AIR 1957 PUNJ 201, 59 PUNJ LR 578

(As stated earlier, the *situs* of a judgment debt is the place where the decree was passed).

20. Until a debt is payable and recoverable, it has no *situs*; Re Helbert Waagg & Co. Ltd.'s Claim, (1956) Ch. 323 pp. 339–40, (156) 1 ALL ER 129 p. 135. Cf. *Kwok Chi Leung Karl* v. *Comr of Estate Duty*, (1988) 1 WLR 1035, PC (non-negotiable promissory note had a *situs* for purposes of estate duty. See North and Fawcett, *Cheshire and North's Private International Law*, Thirteenth Edition, p. 955.

21. Re Maudslay, Sons and Field, (1900) 1 Ch. 602; *Payne* v. *R.*, (1902) AC 552, PC; *Swiss Bank Corpn.* v. *Boehmische Industrial Bank*, (1923) 1 KB 673 p. 678, CA; English Scottish and *Austrian Bank Ltd.* v. *Inland Revenue Comrs.*, (1932) AC 238, HL.

22. *Martin* v. *Nadel*, (1906) 2 KB 26, C.A.; *Richardson* v. *Richardson*, (1927) p. 228; *Swiss Bank Corporation* v. *Boehmische Industrial Bank*, (1923) 1 KB 673 pp. 678–9, CA; *Joachimson* v. *Swiss Bank Corpn.*, (1921) 3 KB 110, CA; *Clare & Co.* v. *Dresdner Bank*, (1915) 2 KB 576; *R.* v. *Irwin A. Lovitt*, (1912) AC 212 pp. 218–19, PC; *Arab Bank Ltd.* v. *Barclays Bank (Dominion, Colonial and Overseas)*, (1954) AC 495, (1954) 2 ALL ER 226, HL, *Rabindra N. Maitra* v. *Life Insurance Corpn. of India*, AIR 1964 CAL 141.

23. Re Russo-Asiatic Bank, Re Russian Bank for Foreign Trade, (1934) Ch. 720 (In view of the fact that obligation was to pay in Sterling in London on maturity, it was held that the debt was located in London.

24. *Nath Bank Ltd.* v. *Andhar Manick Tea Company Ltd.*, AIR 1960 CAL 779, (1960) 64 CAL WN 161, (1960) 30 Com Cas 306.

25. Ibid.

26. *Toronto General Trusts Corpn.* v. *R.*, (1919) AC 679, PC.

27. *Royal Trust Co.* v. *A-G for Alberta*, (1930) AC 144, PC.

As was the case with foot notes 20 to 23, foot notes 29 to 33 infra are also drawn from Govindaraj, *Conflict of Laws*, Vol. 10 (New Delhi: LexisNexis Butterworths, 2001), p. 260.

28. That is, not requiring transfer on a register: Cf. note 30 infra.

29. *A-G* v. *Bouwens*, (1838) 7 LJ Ex 297; *Winans* v. *A-G*, (1910) AC 27, HL; *A-G* v. *Glendining*, (1904) 92 LT 87; Re Clark, *Mckechnie* v. *Clark*, (1904) 1 Ch. 294.

30. *A-G* v. *Higgins*, (1857) 2 H&N 339; *New York Brewery Co. Ltd.* v. *A-G*, (1899) AC 62, HL; *Inland Revenue Comrs.* v. *Maple & Co. (Paris) Ltd.*, (1908) AC 22, HL; *Brassard* v. *Smith*, (1925) AC 371, PC; *Baelz* v. *Public Trustee*, (1926) 1 Ch. 863; *London and South American Investment Trust Ltd.* v. *British Tobacco co. (Australia) Ltd.*, (1927) 1 Ch. 107; *Erie Beach Co. Ltd.* v. *A-G for Ontario*, (1930) AC 161, PC; *R.* v. *Williams*, (1942) AC 541, (1942) 2 ALL ER

95, PC. Shares allotment letters fall within the same principle: *Young* v. *Phillips (Inspector of Taxes)*, (1984) STC 520, 58 TC 232. See North and Fawcett, *Cheshire and North's Private International Law*, Thirteenth Edition (London, Edinburgh, Dublin: LexisNexis Butterworths, 1999), pp. 969, 973.

31. Re Berchtold, *Berchtold* v. *Capron*, (1913) 1 Ch.192; *Philipson–Stow* v. *Inland Revenue Comrs*, (1961) AC 727 p. 762, (1960) 3 ALL ER 814 p. 831 HL. See also the ratio in *Haque* v. *Haque*, (No. 2) (1965) 114 CLR 98 p. 107, HC (Aust). See also Section 5, The Indian Succession Act (1925) for the law regulating succession to deceased person's property.

32. Re Cigala's Settlement Trusts, (1878) 7 Ch. D 351; *Lord Sudeley* v. *A-G*, (1897) AC 11, HL; Re *Smyth Leach* v. *Leach*, (1898) 1 Ch. 89; *Favorke* v. *Steinkopff*, (1922) 1 Ch. 174; *A-G* v. *Johnson*, (1907) 2 KB 885; *Stamp Duties (Queensland) Comr.* v. *Livingston*, (1965) AC 694, (1964) 3 ALL ER 692 pp. 693–6, P.C. See also Section 20, The Code of Civil Procedure, 1908.

33. See note 15 supra.

34. See Note 16 supra.

35. *Nilkanth Balwant Natu* v. *Vidya Narsingh Bharathi Swami*, AIR 1930 PC 188, (1930) 34 CAL WN 854, (1930) 59 MAD LJ 379; *M.Y.A.A. Nachiappa Chettiar* v. *Muthu Karuppan Chettiar*, AIR 1946 MAD 398; *Krishnaji Pandurang Sathe* v. *Ganjanan Balwant Kulkarni*, 2 IC 489, (1909) ILR 33 BOM 373, (1909) 11 BOM LR352.

36. *Keshav* v. *Vinayak*, (1899) ILR 23 BOM 22.

37. *Pazhavakkath Madathil Gopala Pattar's Sons Subramanya Iyer* v. *Pazhavakkath Madathil Gopal Pattar's Sons Lakshmana Ayyar*, AIR 1951 MAD 742; *M.Y.A.A. Nachiappa Chettiar* v. *Muthu Karuppan Chettiar*, AIR 1946 MAD 398.

38. *M.Y.A.A. Nachiappa Chettiar* v. *Muthu Karuppan Chettiar*, AIR 1946 MAD 398.

39. *Kashinath Govind* v. *Anant Sitaramboa*, (1899) ILR 24 BOM 407, (1900) 2 BOM LR 47; *Dev Samaj Council, Lahore* v. *Amritlal Motilal*, AIR 1934 SIND 123; *Chidambaram Chettiar* v. *Subrahmanian Chettiar*, AIR 1953 MAD 492, 28 SIND LR 54. (It is open to an arbitrator or the court to record an admission of title to foreign properties by the parties and to record it in the award or in the decree; however, it was reiterated that the court cannot decide title to foreign property).

40. *Bilasrai Joharmal* v. *Shivnarayan Sarupchand*, AIR 1944 PC 39, 212 IC 433, (1944) ALL LJ 172, (1944) 48 CAL WN 448, (1944) 1 MAD LJ 466.

41. *Mahadev Govind Suktankar* v. *Ramachandra Govind Suktankar*, AIR 1922 BOM 188, 681C 510, (1922) ILR 46 BOM 108 (The defendant, in this case, failed to reconvey a foreign land in terms of an award).

42. *Muhammad Eusoof* v. *Subrahmanyam Chettiar*, AIR 1952 MAD 272.

43. Sections 19 and 20 of the Code of Civil Procedure, 1908. See *Karnataka Films Ltd.* v. *Official Receiver, Madras* and, as such, the Official Receiver of Chitrakala Movietone Ltd., AIR 1952 MAD 481, (1951) 2 MAD LJ 641.

44. *Debendra Chandra Saha* v. *Pramatha Chandra Roy*, AIR 1958 CAL 700.

45. *Prithi Singh* v. *Ganesh Pd. Singh*, AIR 1951 ALL 462, (1950) ALL LJ 431.

46. See note 6 relating to trusts generally.

47. Re Clinton, *Clinton* v. *Clinton*, (1903) WR 316; *Chellaram* v. *Chellaram*, (1985) Ch. 409, (1985) 1 ALL ER 1043 (Held that the court had jurisdiction to administer a foreign trust, even where the trust funds were outside the jurisdiction by ordering its trustee to fulfil their obligations under the trust and power; the court may if necessary, remove the trustees and appoint new trustees by orders *in personam* against the existing trustees). Cf. *Edinburg Corporation* v. *Aubery*, (1753) AMB-236, 27 ER 157; *A-G* v. *Lepine*, (1818) 2 SWANS 181, 36 ER 584. See section 'Recognition of Trusts'.

48. See section 'Equitable Jurisdiction *In Personam*'.

49. *Lord Comes Anglasse* v. *Muschamp*, (1682) 1 VERN 76, 23 ER 322; *British South Africa Co.* v. *Companhia de Moçambique*, (1893) AC 602, p. 626; *Jones* v. *Geddes*, (1845) 14 SIM 606, 60 ER 493; *Lord Portarlington* v. *Soulby*, (1834) 3 My&K 104, p. 108, 40 ER 40, pp. 41–2; *White* v. *Hall*, (1806) 12 VES 521, 33 ER 122; *Lord Cranstown* v. *Johnston*, (1796) 3 VES 170, 30 ER 952; *Angus* v. *Angus*, (1737) West Temp Hard 23, 25 ER 800; *Razelos* v. *Razelos*, (1969) 3 ALL ER 929, (1970) 1 SLR 392; *Cook Industries Inc.* v. *Galliber*, (1679) Ch. 439, (1978) 3 ALL ER 945.

50. *Lord Comes Anglasse* v. *Muschamp*, (1682) 1 VERN 76, 23 ER 800. See notes 45 and 46 under the subtitle 'Trusts', supra.

51. *Lord Cranstown* v. *Johnston*, (1796) 3 VES 170, 30 ER 952. It is otherwise if the local court ordered a judicial sale: See *White* v. *Hall*, (1806) 12 VES 321, 33 ER 122. See notes 45 and 46 under the subtitle Trusts, supra.

52. *Nittala Achayya* v. *Nittala Yellamma*, AIR 1923 MAD 109, 72 IC 920, (1922) MAD WN 834, 16 MAD LW 785. See also section 'Equitable Jurisdiction *In Personam*'.

53. See 'Equitable Jurisdiction *In Personam*', pp. 158–60.

54. *Toller* v. *Carteret*, (1705) 2 VERN 494, 23 ER 916l; *Earl of Derby* v. *Duke of Athol*, (1749) 1 VES SEN 202 p. 204, 27 ER 982 p. 983; *Lord Portarlington* v. *Soulby*, (1834) 3 My&K 104 p. 108; Cf. *Norris* v. *Chambers*, (1861) 29 BEAV 246 p. 255, 54 ER 621 p. 624; affd (1861) 3 De GF &J 583, 45 ER 1004; *Paget* v. *Ede*, (1874) LR 18 Eq 118; Re Hawthorne, *Graham* v. *Massey*, (1883) 23 Ch. D 743 pp. 747–8. See also *Bawtree* v. *Great North-West Central*

Railway Co., (1898) 14 TLR 448, CA. Where the local law does not permit foreclosure, a court cannot order the sale of foreign land; *Grey* v. *Maintoba and North Western Railway Co. of Canada*, (1897) AC 254, PC.

55. *Beckford* v. *Kemble*, (1822) 1 Sim & St 7, 57 ER 3.

56. *Earl of Derby* v. *Duke of Athol*, (1749) 1 VES SEN 202 p. 204, 27 ER 982 p. 983; Re Courtney, ex p Pollard, (1840) Mont & Ch. 239.

57. *Beckford* v. *Kemble*, (1822) 1 Sim & St 7, 57 ER 3.

58. *British South Africa Co.* v. *De Beers Consolidated Mines Ltd.*, (1910) 1 Ch. 354 p. 383; affd, (1910) 2 Ch. 502, CA; affd (1900) 1 Ch. 273, CA; Re Smith, *Lawrence* v. *Kitson*, (1916) 2 Ch. 206.

59. See note 44 supra.

60. See note 45 supra.

61. *Harrison* v. *Gurney*, (1821) 2 Jac & W563, 37 ER743; *Duder* v. *Amsterdamseh Trustees Kantoor*, (1902) 2 Ch. 132; Re Maudstay Sons and Field, *Maudstay* v. *Maudstay Sons and Field*, (1900) 1 Ch. 602, p. 611; *Mercantile Investment and General Trust Co.* v. *River Plate Trust, Loan and Agency Co.*, (1892) 2 Ch. 303; *Paget* v. *Ede*, (1874) LR 18 Eq 118, p. 126; *Houlditch* v. *Marquess of Donegall*, (1834) CI&Fin 470, 6 ER 1232, HL; *Clarke* v. *Earl of Ormonde*, (1821) Jac 108, pp. 116 and 121, 37 ER 791, p. 794.

62. Re Maudstay Sons and Field, *Maudstay* v. *Maudstay Sons and Field*, (1900) 1 Ch. 602, p. 611.

63. Ibid.

64. See section 'Equitable Jurisdiction *In Personam*', notes 40 and 41 supra.

65. *Chutta Veettil Puthu Perambil Muhammad Koya* v. *Ponmanichandakath Katheesa Bi*, (1944) 2 MAD LJ 305, p. 365.

66. *R. Viswanathan* v. *Rukn-ul-Mulk Syed Abdul Wajid (dead)*, AIR 1963 SC 1, (1963) SCR 22.

67. See sections 'Beneficial Distribution' and 'Testate Succession'.

68. *Bank of Africa, Ltd.* v. *Cohen*, (1909) 2 Ch. 129, C.A.

69. *Waterhouse* v. *Stansfield*, (1852) 10 Hare 254, 68 ER 921; *Adams* v. *Clutterbuck*, (1883) 10 QBD 403. As to the formal validity of wills, see note 3 supra.

70. Re Hernando, *Hernando* v. *Sawtell*, (1884) 27 Ch. D 284 pp. 293, 296, Cf. *Coppin* v. *Coppin*, (1725) 2 P WMS 291, 24 ER 735.

71. See notes 40 and 41 supra.

72. Note: India is not a party to the Convention.

73. *Hicks* v. *Powell*, (1869) 4 Ch. App. 741 p. 746.

74. See sub-section 'Testate Succession' under 'Beneficial Distribution'.

75. See *Earl Nelson* v. *Lord Bridport*, (1845) 8 Beav 527, 50 ER 215; Re Miller, *Bailie* v. *Miller*, (1914) 1 Ch. 511.

76. *Waterhouse* v. *Stansfield*, (1852) 10 Hare 254 p. 259, 68 ER 921 p. 923.

77. *Phipps* v. *Earl of Anglesea*, (1721) IP Wms 696, 24 ER 576 (Marriage Settlement and Will); *Cope* v. *Cope*, (1846) 15 Sim 118, 60 ER 562 (Marriage Settlement); *Macrae* v. *Goodman*, (1846) 5 Moo PCC 315; 13 ER 512, PC (mortgage); *Marquis of Landsdowne* v. *Dowager Marchioness of Lansdowne*, (1820) 2 BLI 60, 4 ER 250, HL (settlement).

78. *Marquis of Landsdowne* v. *Dowager Marchioness of Landsdowne*, (1820) 2 Bli 60, 4 ER 250; HL (settlement); *Northern Bank Ltd.* v. *Edwards*, (1985) IR 284.

79. *Balfour* v. *Cooper*, (1883) 23 Ch. D 472, CA; see *Stapleton* v. *Conway*, (1750) 1 VES SEN 427, 27 ER 1122.

80. *Phipps* v. *Earl of Anglesea*, (1721) 1 P Wms 696, 24 ER 576 (rate of interest was fixed by consent).

81. See Chapter on Procedure under section 'Limitation of Actions', Govindaraj, *Conflict of Laws*, Vol. 10 (New Delhi: LexisNexis Butterworths, 2001), p. 263.

82. *Beckford* v. *Wade*, (1805) 17 VES 87, 34 ER 34, PC (Prescriptive title by virtue of possession for a stated period).

83. See Re Peat's Trusts, (1869) LR 7 Eq302. (English action for proceeds of foreign land will fail as time barred if it be barred by the foreign statute of limitations).

84. See notes 1 to 18 under section 'Jurisdiction Relating to Foreign Immovables' of the chapter on law of property.

85. *Pitt* v. *Lord Dacre*, (1876) 3 Ch. D 295 (land in Jamaica; English statute of limitations inapplicable; Cf. *Colonial Investment and Load Co.* v. *Harry James Martin*, (1928) SCR 440, (1928) 3 DLR 784, SC. (Can). See Govindaraj, *Conflict of Laws*, Vol. 10 (New Delhi: LexisNexis Butterworths, 2001) for the principles and foot notes, p. 268.

86. As this chapter deals with particular assignment, as to assignment on bankruptcy, succession and recognition of foreign judgments, see the chapters on bankruptcy, succession and recognition of foreign judgments respectively.

87. As to documents of title see section 'Assignment of Negotiable Instruments and Documents of Title', and as to chose in action see section 'Assignment of Bare Choses in Action' (supra) respectively.

88. As to location of property see note 1: Location of Property in General—under section '*Situs* of Property' of the chapter on law of property.

89. *Inglis* v. *Usherwood*, (1801) 1 EAST 515, 102 ER 198; *Cammell* v. *Sewell*, (1860) 5 H&N 728 p. 744, 157 ER 1371, Ex ch; *Castrique* v. *Imrie*, (1870) LR, 4 HL 414 p. 429; *City Bank* v. *Barrow*, (1880) 5 App Cas 664, HL; *Alcock* v. *Smith*, (1892) 1 Ch. 338 p. 268, CA; *Inglis* v. *Robertson*, (1898) AC 616, HL;

Embiricos v. *Anglo-Austrian Bank*, (1905) 1 KB 677 p. 683, CA; Re Korvine's Trust, *Levashoff* v. *Block*, (1921) 1 Ch. 343 p. 348; Re Anziani, *Herbert* v. *Christopherson*, (1930) 1 Ch. 407 p. 420; *Bankvoor Handel en Sheepvart NV* v. *Statford*, (1953) 1 QB 248 p. 257; (1951) 2 ALL ER 779 p. 786; *Winkworth* v. *Christic Manson and Woods Ltd.*, (1980) Ch. 496, (1980) 1 ALL ER 1121. The principle that sales ordered or confirmed by courts of *situs* shall be recognized by foreign courts is well illustrated in the classic decision Cammell v. Sewell as also in Minna Craig v. Chartered Mercantile Bank of India, London and China, (1897) 1 QB 460, CA.

90. See *Hooper* v. *Gumm*, (1867) 2 Ch. App. 282.

91. *Winkworth* v. *Christie Manson and Woods Ltd.*, (1980) Ch. 496, (19800 1 ALL ER.1121.

92. Re Korvine's Trust, *Livashoff* v. *Block*, (1921) 1 Ch. 343 (*donatio mortis causa*, that is, gift in anticipation of death'). Cf. Re Craven's Estate, *Loyds bank* v. *Cockburn*, (Nos l and 2) 1937 CL.423, (1937) 3 ALL ER 33 (same question treated as one of administration of estates).

93. *Dulaney* v. *Merry & Sons*, (1901) 1 KB 536; Re Pilkington's Will Trusts, *Pilkington* v. *Harrison*, (1937) Ch. 571, 91937) 3 ALL ER 213 (Registration under the Deeds of Arrangement Act, 1914 (U.K.).

94. *Cammel* v. *Sewell*, (1860) 5 H&N 728 pp. 742–3; 157 ER 1371, Ex Ch.; *Winkworth* v. *Christie Manson and Woods Ltd.*, (1980) Ch. 496, (1980) 1 ALL ER 1121.

95. See in this connection, Dicey and Morris, *The Conflict of Laws*, 12th edn. (1993), pp. 972–6; *Simpson* v. *Fogo*, (1863) 1 Hem & M 195, 71 ER 85; *Hooper* v. *Gumm*, (1867) 2 Ch. App 282; *Industrial Acceptance Corpn. Ltd.* v. *La Flamme*, (1950) OR 311, (1950) 2 DLR 822; *Century Credit Corpn.* v. *Richard*, (1962) OR 815, (1962) 34 DLR (2d) 291, Ont CA.

96. See section 'Assignment of Bare Choses in Action', infra.

97. For the proposition that good title acquired under the old *lex situs* gets defeated we may advert to as an example rules of the new *lex situs* as to sales in market overt, sales by mercantile agents and judicial sales. *Cammel* v. *Sewell*, (1860) 5 H&N 728 p. 744, 157 ER 1371, Ex Ch; *Metha* v. *Sutton*, (1913) 108 LT 214; affd (1913) 109 LT 529, CA; *Embiricos* v. *Anglo-Austrian Bank*, (1905) 1 KB 677 p. 684, CA: *Winkwoth* v. *Christie Manson and Woods Ltd.*, (1980) Ch. 496, (1980) 1 ALL ER 1121.

98. *City Bank* v. *Barrow*, (1880) 5 App Cas 664, HL; *Inglis* v. *Robertson*, (1898) AC 616, HL; Cf. *North Western Bank Ltd.* v. *Poynter Son and Macdonalds*, (1895) AC 56 HL.

99. *North Western Bank Ltd.* v. *Poynter Son and Macdonalds*, (1895) AC 56 HL. See also *Inglis* v. *Robertson*, (1898) AC 616 pp. 626–7, HL. For the effect

of later transactions see *North Western Bank Ltd.* v. *Poynter Son and Macdonalds*, (1895) AC 56 HL.

100. *Inglis* v. *Usherwood*, (1801) 1 EAST 515, 102 ER 198.

101. The Negotiable Instruments Act, 1881, Section 134.

102. See Article 12(1) of the Convention on the Law Applicable to Contractual Obligations, (1980) (the Rome Convention, 1980). Note: India is not a party to the Convention.

103. See *Campbell Connelly & Co. Ltd.* v. *Noble*, (1963) 1 ALL ER 237 p. 239, (1963) WLR 252 p. 255; *Compania Colombiana de Seguros* v. *Pacific Steam Navigation Co.*, (1965) 1 QB 101 pp. 128–9, (1964) 1 ALL ER 216 p. 235; *Macmillan Inc.* v. *Bishopsgate Investment Trust Plc*, (No. 3) (1995) 3 ALL ER 747, (1995) 1 WLR 978, CA; on appeal (1996) 1 ALL ER 585, (1996) 1 WLR 387 CA.

104. Article 12 (2) of the Rome Convention, 1980. See for substantive treatment and foot notes Govindaraj, *Conflict of Laws*, Vol. 10 (New Delhi: LexisNexis Butterworths, 2001), pp. 267–70.

105. *A.M. Luther* v. *James Sagor & Co.*, (1921) 3 KB 532, CA; Re Helbert Wagg & Co. Ltd.'s Claim, (1956) Ch. 323 pp. 344–5, (1956) 1 ALL ER 129 p. 138 and many other cases of similar kind. The physical control by the sovereign of the property seized in pursuance of an expropriatory decree, coupled with the doctrine of retroactive effect of recognition, might render the grant of recognition otiose, even if it be that such recognition was not forthcoming until after the decree was made. See *A.M. Luther* v. *James Sagor & Co.*, (1921) 3 KB 532, CA; Cf. *Gdynia Ameryka Linie* v. *Boguslawski*, (1953) AC 11, (1952) 2 ALL ER 470 HL; *Civil Air Transport Inc.* v. *Central Air Trnasport Corpn.*, (1953) AC 70, (1952) 2 ALL ER 733, PC.

106. *Perry* v. *Equitable Life Assurance Society of United States of America*, (1929) 45 TLR 468; Re Helbert Wagg & Co. Ltd.'s claim, 1956 Ch. 323 pp. 3449.

107. *Folliott* v. *Ogden*, (1789) 1 Hy BI 123, 126 ER 75; affd sub nom *Ogden* v. *Folliott*, (1790) 3 Term Rep 726 on appeal (1792) Bro Parl Cas 111, H.L.; see also in this connection, *A.M. Luther* v. *James Sagor & Co.*, (1921) 3 KB 532 CA and many other cases endorsing the same principle.

108. *Compania Naviera Vascongado* v. *SS Christina*, (1938) AC 485, (1938) 1 ALL ER 719 HL; The Arantzazu Mendi, (1939) AC 256, (1939) 1 ALL ER 719, HL.

109. *R. Viswanathan* v. *Rukn-ul-Mulk Syed Abdul Wajid (dead)*, AIR 1963 SC 1 p. 16, (1963) 3 SCR 22.

See generally, cases on expropriation of private property to appreciate how courts define what is penal and what is not penal and the criteria they apply to characterize expropriatory decrees.

110. *Banco de Vizcaya* v. *Don Alfonso de Borbon y Austria*, (1955) 1 KB 140.
111. Rose Mary (1953) 1 WLR 246, Aden SC; as explained in Re Herbert Wagg & Co. Ltd.'s Claim, (1956) Ch. 323 p. 346, (1956) 1 ALL ER 129 p. 139.
112. *Frankfurther* v. *Exner Ltd.*, (1947) Ch. 629; *Novello & Co. Ltd.* v. *Hinrichsen Edition Ltd.*, (1951) Ch. 595, (1951) 1 ALL ER 779; affd (1951) Ch.1026, (1951) 2 ALL ER 457 CA.
113. *Wolff* v. *Oxholm*, (1817) GM&S 92, 105 ER 1177; Re Fried Krupp AG (1917) 2 Ch. 188; Re Herbert Wagg & Co. Ltd.'s Claim, (156) Ch. 323 pp. 345–6, (1956) 1 ALL ER 129 pp. 138–9.
114. *A.M. Luther* v. *James Sagor & Co.*, (1921) 3 KB 532 CA; *Princess Paley Olga* v. *Weisz*, (1929) 1 KB 718 CA; *Bank Voor Handel en Scheepvaart NV* v. *Statford*, (1953) 1 QB 248 pp. 258, 260–3, (1951) 2 ALL ER 779 pp. 787, 788–90; Re Herbert Wagg & Co. Ltd.'s Claim, (1456) Ch. 323 p. 349, (1956) 1 ALL ER 129 p. 140; Cf. *AS Tallina Laevauhisus* v. *Estonian State SS Line*, (1947) 80 1.11. Rep 99 p. 111, CA.
115. *Bank voor Handel en Scheepvaart NV* v. *Slatford*, (1953), 1 QB 248, (1951) 2 ALL ER 779 (not following *Lorentzen* v. *Lydden & Co. Ltd.*, (1942) 2 KB 202 (for this p. 272 Butterworths).
116. See The Indian Trusts Act, 1882, Sections 7, 11. As to choice of law in respect of a contract, see section 'Determination of the Proper Law of a Contract', where this issue is discussed in detail.
117. See the Convention on the Law Applicable to Trusts and Their Recognition, 1986 (The Hague Convention, 1986: The Hague, 10 January 1986) Schedule Art. 7(a)-(d). India, as of now, is not a party to the convention.
118. See section 'The Law relating to Trusts & Charities'.
119. Sections 4–10, Indian Trusts Act, 1882, Chapter II.
120. Section 6, Indian Trusts Act, 1882.
121. Section 7, Indian Trusts Act, 1882.
122. Sections 11–30, Indian Trusts Act, 1882, Chapter III.
123. Sections 31–43, Indian Trusts Act, 1882, Chapter IV.
124. Sections 46–54, Indian Trusts Act, 1882, Chapter V.
125. Sections 55–69, Indian Trusts Act, 1882, Chapter VI.
126. Sections 77–79, Indian Trusts Act, 1882, Chapter VIII.
127. See section: 'Indian Trusts and Applicable Law'.
128. See the Convention on the Law Applicable to Trusts and Their Recognition, 1986, (The Hague Convention, 1986) Schedule Art 11 para 2. India is not a party to the Convention.
129. See Section 324 (1) as read with Sections 319–23, The Indian Succession Act, 1925.

130. Section 319, The Indian Succession Act, 1925.
131. Section 324, The Indian Succession Act, 1925.
132. Section 218, The Indian Succession Act, 1925.
133. Section 219 (g), The Indian Succession Act, 1925.
134. Re Wilks, *Keefer* v. *Wilks*, (1935) Ch. 645 pp. 648, 650.
135. Section 5(1)(2), The Indian Succession Act, 1925: The rules embodied in Section 5 of the Act embody the well known rules of conflict of laws, namely that under intestate succession, distribution of immovables is governed by the *lex situs* and of movables by the *lex domicilii*.
136. See section 'Succession'.
137. *Blackwood* v. *R*, (1883) 8 App. Cas 82, PC.
138. *Bunbury* v. *Bunbury*, (1939) 8 LJ Ch. 297; *Graham* v. *Maxwell*, (1849) 1 Mac & G 71, 47 ER 1403; *Carron Iron Co.* v. *Maclaren*, (1855) 5 HL Cas 416, 10ER 961; *Maclaren* v. *Stainton*, (1885) 26 LJ Ch. 332; Re Boyse, *Crofton* v. *Crofton*, (1880) 15 Ch. D 591; *Hope* v. *Carnegie*, (1866) 1 Ch. App 320; *Baillie* v. *Baillie*, (1867) LR 5 Eq 175; Re Low, *Bland* v. *Low*, (1894) 1 Ch. 147, CA.
139. *Lowe* v. *Farlie*, (1817) 2 MADD 101, 56 ER 272; *Logan* v. *Fairlie*, (1825) 2 Sim&St 284, 57 ER 355; revised on another point, (1835) 1 My&Cr 59, 40 ER 298; *Sandilands* v. *Innes*, (1829) 3 SIM 263; *Tyler* v. *Bell*, (1837) 2 My&Cr 89, 40 ER 575; *Bond* v. *Graham*, (1842) 1 HARE 482, 66 ER 11; *Harvey* v. *Fitzpatrick*, (1854) KAY 421, 69 ER 14.
140. *Ewing* v. *Orr Ewing*, (1883) 9 App Cas 34 HL.
141. *Deputy Commissioner of Singhubhum* v. *Jagdish Chandra Deo Dhabal Deb*, AIR 1921 PAT 206, 62 IC 513, (1921) 6 PAT LJ 411, (1921) 2 PAT LT 683. See also *A-G* v. *Dimond*, (1831) 1 Cr&J 356, 148 ER 1458; *A-G* v. *Hope*, (1834) 1 Cr M&R 530, 5 ER 863, HL; *Blackwood* v. *R*, (1883) 8 App Cas 82, PC: Re Fitzpatrick, *Bennett* v. *Bennett*, (1952) Ch. 86, (1951) 2 ALL ER 949.
142. See sections 324(1)(2) and 325 of The Indian Succession Act, 1925. See also *Blackwood* v. *R*, (1883) 8 App Cas 82, PC.
143. See sections 360 and 367 of The Indian Succession Act, 1925. See also *Whyte* v. *Rose*, (1842) 3 QB 493 p. 506, 114 ER 596 p. 601, Ex Ch.
144. Sections 319, 325, and 326, The Indian Succession Act, 1925. See further section 'Succession'.
145. Section 324 (1), The Indian Succession Act, 1925.
146. Section 324 (2), The Indian Succession Act, 1925.
147. Section 323, The Indian Succession Act, 1925.
148. Section 360, The Indian Succession Act, 1925.

149. Section 367, The Indian Succession Act, 1925.
150. Section 219 (g) as read with Sections 212, 213, The Indian Succession Act, 1925.
151. *Vanquelin* v. *Bouard*, (1863) 15 CBNS 341, 143 ER 817, Re Macnichol, *Macnichol* v. *Macnichol*, (1874) LR 19 Eq. 81.
152. *Currie* v. *Bircham*, (1822) 1 Dow&Ry KB 35; Re Macnichol, *Macnichol* v. *Macnichol*, (1874) LR Eq 81; *Vanquelin* v. *Bouard*, (1863) 15 CBNS 341, 143 ER 817. However, even if he be entitled to the assets of the deceased which he has not reduced into his possession, the question whether he could still enforce his title to the assets is an open issue: *Whyte* v. *Rose*, (1842) 3 QB 493 p. 506, 114 ER 596, Ex Ch; See Dicey and Morris, *The Conflict of Laws*, p. 1011. See also notes 1, 2, and 3 supra under the subtitle 'Legal Effect of Indian grant'.
153. *Degazon* v. *Barclays Bank International Ltd.*, (1988) 1 FTLR 17, CA.
154. See notes 150–2 supra under the sub-section 'Rights and Duties of Foreign Personal Representatives'.
155. As to executors *de son tort*, see section 'Succession'.
156. Ibid.
157. That is, the beneficial distribution of the net estate, after all debts, duties, and expenses of the said estate have been met. In this connection, we may have to recall that administration does not include succession the latter of which is governed by separate rules. See notes 6 and 7 under section 'Administration and Succession Distinguished' of the chapter on succession.
158. See section 'Succession'.
159. See notes 1 to 3 under section, 'Classification: A Matter of Semantics' of the chapter on law of property.
160. A foreign grant of representation is not sufficient: *A-G* v. *Hope*, (1834) 1 Cr M&R 530 pp. 540, 562–4, 5 ER 863, HL; Cf. Lorillard, *Griffiths* v. *Catforth*, (1922) 2 Ch. 638, (1922) ALL ER 500, CA. *Ewing* v. *Orr Ewing*, (1883) 9 App. Cas 34 pp. 38–9, 46 HL; *Vanquelin* v. *Bouard*, (1863) 15 CNBS 341, 143 ER 817; *Enobin* v. *Wylie*, (1862) 10 HL Cas 1 pp. 14, 19, 11 ER 924.161. Section 5(2), The Indian Succession Act 1925. See for example, *Sankaran Govindan* v. *Lakshmi Bharathi*, AIR 1974 SC 1764.
162. *Nilkanth Balwant Natu* v. *Vidya Narasing Bharathi Swami*, AIR 1930 PC 188, 126 IC 417, 57 IA 194, (1930) 34 CAL WN 854; *Debendra Chandra Saha* v. *Pramatha Chandra Roy*, AIR 1958 CAL 700; *Puzhavakkath Maddathil Gopala Pattar's Sons Subramanya Iyer* v. *Puzhavakkath Madathil Gopal Pattar's Sons Lakshmana Ayyar*, AIR 1951 MAD 742, (1949) 2 MAD LJ 785.
163. The Indian Succession Act, 1925, Section 5 (2). See for case law illustration, *Sankaran Govindan* v. *Lakshmi Bharathi*, AIR 1974 SC 1764.

164. The Indian Succession Act, 1925, Section 5 (1). See also the following cases: *Sankaran Govindan* v. *Lakshmi Bharathi*, AIR 1974 SC 1764; *Debendra Chandra Saha* v. *Pramatha Chandra Roy*, AIR 1958 CAL 700; *Pazhavakkath Madathil Gopala Pattar's Sons Subramanya Iyer v. Pazhavakkath Madathil Gopal Pattar's Sons Lakshmana Ayyar*, AIR 1951 MAD 742, (1949) 2 MAD LJ 785; *M.Y.A.A. Nachiappa Chettiar* v. *Muthu Karuppan Chettiar*, AIR 1946 MAD 398; *Nilkanth Balwant Natu* v. *Vidya Narasinh Bharathi Swami*, AIR 1930 PC 188, 126 IC 417, 57 IA 194, (1930) 34 CAL WN 854; *Kewhav* v. *Vinayak*, (1899) ILR 23 BOM22.

165. *R. Viswanathan* v. *Rukn-ul-Mulk Syed Abdul Wajid (dead)*, AIR 1963 SC 1, (1963) 3 SCR 22.

166. *Lynch* v. *Paraguay Provisional Government*, (1871) LR 2 P&D 268; followed in Re Aganoor's Trusts, (1895) 64 LJ Ch.521; approved in *Adams* v. *National Bank of Greece SA*, (1961) AC 255, (1960) 2 ALL ER 121, HL; applied in Re Marshall *Barclays Bank Ltd.* v. *Marshall*, (1957) Ch. 507, (1957) 3 ALL ER 172, CA (Criticized by Dicey and Morris, *The Conflict of Laws* (12th Edn. 1993) pp. 60, 62).

167. *Earl Nelson* v. *Lord Bridport*, (1845) 8 Beav 527, 50 ER 215.

168. *Tourton* v. *Flower*, (1735) 3 P Wms 369.

169. *Thornton* v. *Curling*, (1824) 8 Sim 310; *Whicker* v. *Hume*, (1858) 7 HL Cas 124, 11 ER 50.

170. Section 5(2), The Indian Succession Act, 1925.

171. Section 32, The Indian Succession Act, 1925.

172. Section 33, The Indian Succession Act, 1925.

173. Part V, Chapter II (Sections 31–49), The Indian Succession Act, 1925.

174. Section 5 (1), The Indian Succession Act, 1925.

175. When we talk of incapacity with reference to a will or testament, it ordinarily means proprietary incapacity relatable to the nature of the bequest or devise, and which is deemed a question of material or essential validity dealt with under section 'Testate Succession'. The question of personal capacity, on the contrary, relates to restrictions which attach to the person rather than the property of the testator such as, for example, physical and mental capacity, capacity of minors and married women, and the like.

176. Section 59 of The Indian Succession Act, 1925, relates to property which means and includes movable as well as immovable property. Re Maraver's Goods (1828) 1 HAG ECC 498, 162 ER 650; Re Fuld's Estate (No. 3), *Hartley* v. *Fuld*, (1968) p. 675 p. 696, (1965) 3 ALL ER 776 p. 780; Re Gulliver's Goods, (1869) 17 WR 742: Where there has been a change of domicile after execution, it is uncertain whether the domicile at the date of execution or at the date of death governs. However, Re Lewal's Settlement Trusts, (1918) 2 Ch. 39, a case

on the exercise of a power of appointment by will, is that it was not a case of change of domcile.

177. Re Fuld's Estate (No. 3), *Hartley* v. *Fuld*, (1968) p. 675 p. 696, (1965) 3 ALL ER 776 p. 780.

178. Re Hellmann's Will (1866) LR 2 Eq 363, Re Schnapper (1928) Ch. 420; *Donoboe* v. *Donoboe*, (1887) 19 LR 1r 349; Cf. *Leslie* v. *Bailley*, (1843) 2 Y&C Ch. Cas 91.

179. *Ratan Shah* v. *Bomanji*, (1938) ILR BOM 238; *Keshaji* v. *Khai Khusroo*, (1939) 41 BOM Lr 478; see also *Philipson Stow* v. *Inland Revenue Comrs*, (1961) AC 727 p. 743, (1960) 3 ALL ER 814 p. 819, HL; *Bank of Africa Ltd.* v. *Cohen*, (1909) 2 Ch. 129 CA (capacity to transfer immovables *inter vivos*. See Govindaraj, *Conflict of Laws*, Vol. 10 (New Delhi: LexisNexis Butterworths, 2001), pp. 280–1.

180. The Indian Succession Act, 1925, Section 5(2).

181. *R. Viswanathan* v. *Rukn-ul-Mulk Syed Abdul Wajid (dead)*, AIR 1963 SC 1, (1963) 3 SCR 22.

182. The Indian Succession Act, 1925, section 5 (1). Insistence on a rigid compliance with the common law rule, as stated above, may cause hardship to the testator who, while being resident in a country other than the country where his immovable property is situated, will be disabled from making a will, as he cannot comply with the formal requirements of the *lex loci actus*.

183. See section 'Formal Validity of Common Law' as stated above. See also section 'Succession'.

184. For distinguishing questions of construction from questions of status, See Re Fergusson's Will, (1902) 1 Ch. 483 p. 487 (while meaning of gift to next of kin is a matter of construction, legitimacy of those entitled under the will is a matter of status). Similarly, construction or, so to say, meaning and interpretation of the will must be distinguished from the question of material or essential validity: the former determines the testator's intention, while the latter determines the effect to be given to the intention: see *Baring* v. *Ashburton*, (1886) 54 LT 463, where it was made clear that while *lex domicilii* governs matters of construction, *lex situs* governs material or essential validity; see also *Philipson-Stow* v. *Inland Revenue Comrs*, (1961) AC 727 p. 761, (1960) 3 ALL ER 814 p. 830, HL. The following cases illustrate what are matters that are deemed construction under testamentary dispositions: the question of whether a legacy is given in satisfaction of a previous obligation (*Campbell* v. *Campbell*, (1866) LR1Eq 383); the question of the applicability of the doctrine of *cy-près* to a charitable bequest (Re De Noailles, *Clouston* v. *Tufnell*, (1916) 85 LJ Ch. 807); the question of destination of lapsed legacies (*Anstruther* v. *Charmer*, (1835) 3 CI & Fin 544 p. 570, 6 ER 1541, HL).

185. *Bradford* v. *Young*, (1885) 29 Ch.D 617 p. 624, CA; *Philipson-Stow* v. *Inland Revenue Comrs*, (1961) AC 727 pp. 760–1, (1960) 3 ALL ER 814 p. 830, HL; *Di Sora* v. *Phillips*, (1863) 10 HL Cas 624, 11 ER 1168 (a case of contract); Cf. *Enohin* v. *Wylie*, (1862) 10 HL Cas 1 p. 24, 11 ER 924.

186. The meaning of the words employed by a person while framing an instrument can be inferred only under the assumption that he intended to use those words attributed to them by the law of the country he belonged to at the time of the making of the instrument: *Yates* v. *Thomson*, (1835) 3 CI& Fin 544 p. 588, 6 ER 1541, HL, per Lord Brougham; *Philipson-Stow* v. *Inland Revenue Comrs*, 1961 AC 727 p. 761, (1960) 3 ALL ER 814 p. 830, HL; Re Sillar, *Hurley* v. *Wimbush and Bavington*, (1956) IR 344; Re Cunnington, *Healing* v. *Webb*, (1924) 1 Ch. 68; Re Manners, *Manners* v. *Manners*, (1923) 1 Ch. 220; Re Fergusson's will, (1902) 1 Ch. 483; Re *Cliff* v. *Trusts*, (1892) 2 Ch. 229 p. 232; *Bradford* v. *Young*, (1885) 29 Ch.D 617, CA: *Ewing* v. *R. Ewing*, (1862) 10 HL Cas 1, 11 ER 924; *Bernal* v. *Bernal*, (19832) 3 My&Cr 559, 40 ER 1042; *Trotter* v. *Trotter*, (1828) BLi NS 502, 5 ER 179 HL.

187. The following two cases, namely *Bradford* v. *Young*, (1885) 29 Ch.D 617, CA and Re Cunnington, *Healing* v. *Webb*, (1924) 1 Ch. 68, are in accord with Dicey's statement that the maxim that the terms of a will should be construed with reference to the law of the testator's domicile 'is a mere canon of interpretation' (now 'merely a rebuttable presumption') which should not be adhered to when there is any reason, from the nature of the will, or otherwise, to suppose that testator wrote it with reference to the law of some other country': see now the slightly modified text in Dicey and Morris, *The Conflict of Laws*, pp. 1039–40).

188. *Rephael* v. *Boehm*, (1952) 22 1 JCh.299; Cf. Re Prince, *Tomlin* v. *Latter*, (1900) 1 Ch. 442 (Exercise by will of power of appointment); *Cockburn* v. *Raphael*, (1852) 1J Ch. 299 (express reference to Great Britain of inheritance).

189. However, the fact that the will was written in a language other than that of the domicile is not, *ipso facto*, a sufficient indication that it should be construed according to the law of the country in whose language it is written: *Reynolds* v. *Kortright*, (1854) 18 Beav 417, 52 ER 164 (English domicile; Spanish language); Re Manners, *Manners* v. *Manners*, (1923) 1 Ch. 220 (English domicile; Spanish language); Re Bonnefoi, *Surrey* v. *Perrin*, (1912) p. 233, CA (Italian domicile; English language) *Baring* v. *Ashburton*, (1886) 54 LT 463 (English domicile; French language).

190. *Studd* v. *Cook*, (1883) 8 App Cas 577 HL (will of immovables); Cf. Re *Cliff* v. *Trusts*, (1892) 2 Ch. 229; contrast *Bradford* v. *Young*, (1885) 29 Ch. D 617, CA (The presence of a few technical expressions was held to be insufficient indication of an intention that the will should be construed according to the

law of the country to which the expressions belonged); *Trotter* v. *Trotter*, (1828) 4 BLi NS 502, 5 ER 179 HL.

191. *Trotter* v. *Trotter*, (1828) 4 BLi NS 502, 5ER 179 HL: *Philipson–Stow* v. *Inland Revenue Comrs*, (1961) AC 727 p. 761, (1960) 3 ALL ER 814 pp. 830, 831, HL; *Baring* v. *Ashburton*, (1886) 54 LT 463; *Bradford* v. *Young*, (1885) 29 Ch. D 617 p. 623, CA *Studd* v. *Cook*, (1883) 8 App Cas 577 HL: *Maxwell* v. *Maxweill*, (1852) 16 BEAV 106, 42 ER 1048.

192. *Yates* v. *Thomson*, (1835) 3 CI & Fin 544 p. 588, 6 ER 1541, HL.

193. See *Bradford* v. *Young*, (1885) 29 Ch. D 617 p. 623, CA. The effect may be that, in so far as a will disposes of both movables and immovables, it is to be construed according to two different laws.

194. *Studd* v. *Cook*, (1883) 8 App Cas 577 p. 591, HL: Cf. Re Miller, *Bailie* v. *Miller*, (1914) 1 Ch. 511 (the question was one of essential validity rather than construction).

195. As to probate of foreign wills and their translations see section 'Succession'.

196. Re Cliff's Trusts, (1892) 2 Ch. 229 (Correcting the report in *L' Fit* v. *L' Batt*, (1718) IP Wms 526, 24 ER 500, Re *Manners* v. *Manners*, (1923) 1 Ch. 220.

197. *Reynolds* v. *Kortright*, (1854) 18 Beav 417 p. 426, 52 ER 164; Cf. *Baring* v. *Ashburton*, (1886) 54 LT 463.

198. *Bernal* v. *Bernal*, (1838) 3 My & Cr 559 p. 580, 40ER 1042.

199. The Indian Succession Act, 1925, Part VI Ch. VI (Sections 74–111). See also section 'Succession'.

200. The Indian Succession Act, 1925, Section 74. See also *Narasimhan* v. *Perumal (dead)*, AIR 1994 NOC 39, MAD (even though the document in the case was styled as settlement deed, it was held to be a will); *Rajrani Sehgal* v. *Purshottam Lal*, (1992) 46 DLT 263; *Nathu* v. *Devi Singh*, AIR 1966 PUNJ 266; *Lalit Mohun Singh Roy* v. *Chukkun Lal Roy*, (1897) 1 LR 24 CAL 834, 24 1 A 10, (1897) 1 CAL WN 387.

201. Section 78, The Indian Succession Act, 1925; see also *Sajanibai* v. *Surajmal*, (1985) MP LJ 227.

202. Section 87, The Indian Succession Act, 1925. See also *Pappoo* v. *Kuruvilla*, (1994) 2 Ker Lt 278.

203. Section 89, The Indian Succession Act, 1925. See also *Pappoo* v. *Kuruvilla*, (1994) 2 Ker LT 278.

204. Section 95, The Indian Succession Act, 1925. See also *Narayanan Anandan* v. *Rakesh*, (1994) 1 Ker LT 475. Note: see Govindaraj, *Conflict of Laws*, Vol. 10 (New Delhi: LexisNexis Butterworths, 2001), pp. 281–2.

205. See note 163 under section 'Choice of Law'. See also note 170.

206. *Thornton* v. *Curling*, (1824) 8 Sim 310; Re Adams, *Hutchings and Parker Bank of Ireland Trustee Co. Ltd.* v. *Adams*, (1967) IR 424; Re Ross, *Ross* v. *Waterfield*, (1930) 1 Ch. 377; Re Annesley, *Davidson* v. *Annesley*, (1926) Ch. 692; *Bartlett* v. *Bartlett*, (1925) AC 377 PC: Re Groos, *Groos* v. *Groos*, (195) 1 Ch. 572; Re Trufort, *Trafford* v. *Blane*, (1887) 36 Ch. D 600; *Campbell* v. *Beaufoy*, (1856) 1 J Ch. 645, 70 ER 445. *The Halsbury's Laws of England* is of the view that the cases set out above are more appropriately regarded as raising a question of material or essential validity rather than one of capacity, as the restrictions under the law of the domicile is attached in each case to the property rather than the person of the testator: see note 1 under sections 'Capacity: Basic Conflicts Rules' and 'Testate Succession' in Chapter 6. 'Analogous rights exist under English law by virtue of the English court's power to award reasonable financial provision out of the estate of a deceased person. The court's jurisdiction is limited to cases where the deceased died domiciled in England and Wales, whether the property is movable or immovable: Inheritance (Provision for Family and Dependants) Act, 1975, (U.K.) s.1.'—Halsbury's Law of England. The burden of proving an English domicile lies on the applicant: *Mastaka* v. *Midland Bank Executor and Trustee Co. Ltd.*, (1941) 1 ALL ER 236.

207. Legitim, in Scottish law, is the children's share of the father's movable property which he cannot otherwise dispose of by will. Legitima portio in some continental European systems like Italy means much the same thing.

208. Re Priest, *Belfield* v. *Duncan*, (1944) Ch. 58, (1944) 1 ALL ER 51.

209. *Macdonald* v. *Macdonald*, (1872) LR 14 Eq 60 (marshalling in favour of charity.)

210. Re Elliott, *Elliott* v. *Johnson*, (1891) 39 WR 297.

211. See note 163 under sub-section 'Choice of Law' under 'Beneficial Distribution' of section 'Succession'.

212. Re Hernando, *Hernando* v. *Sawtell*, (1884) 27 Ch. D 284; Re Ross, *Ross* v. *Waterfield*, (1930) 1 Ch. 377; *Bartlett* v. *Bartlett*, (1925) AC 377, PC.

213. *Whicker* v. *Hume*, (1858) 7 HL Cas 124, 11 ER 50; Re Hoyles, *Row* v. *Jagg*, (1911) 1 Ch. 179; Re Grassi, *Stubberfield* v. *Grassi*, (1905) 1 Ch. 584; *Duncan* v. *Lawson*, (1889) 41 Ch. D 394.

214. *Earl Nelson* v. *Lord Bridport*, (1846) 8 Beav 547, 50 ER 215 (Change in the nature of the estate from entailed to absolute interest; Re Miller, *Bailie* v. *Miller*, (1914) 1 Ch. 511 (disposability of entailed interests; Re Moses, *Moses* v. *Valentine*, (1908) 2 Ch. 235 (right to enjoy in specie).

215. See Re Mengel's Will Trusts, *Westminster Bank Ltd.* v. *Mengel*, (1962) Ch. 791 p. 797, (1962) 2 ALL ER 490 p. 492. For the proposition that

election has nothing to do with the intention of the testator and, as such, nothing to do with construction of the testator's will as well; Re Mengel's Will Trusts, *Westminster Bank Ltd.* v. *Mengel*, p. 800 Ch. p. 495 (ALL ER) (not following Re Allen's Estate, *Prescott* v. *Allen and Beaumont*, (1945) 2 ALL ER 264.

216. Re Ogilvie, *Ogilvie* v. *Ogilvie*, (1918) 1 Ch. 492 p. 498, Re Mengel's Will Trusts, *Westminster Bank Ltd.* v. *Mengel*, (1962) Ch. 791, (1962) 2 ALL ER 490. For case illustrations of this principle see also the following cases: *Balfour* v. *Scott*, (1793) 6 BRO PAL Cas 550, 2 ER 1259, HL; *Brown* v. *Gregson*, (1920) AC 860, HL (rule of the *lex situs* preventing a beneficiary from giving up foreign immovables taken outside the will exonerated him from the duty to elect under Scottish domestic law); *Baring* v. *Ashburton*, (1886) 54 LT 463, *Harrison* v. *Harrison*, (1873) 8 Ch. App 342; *Maxwell* v. *Maxwell*, (1852) 16 BEAV 106, 42 ER 1048; *Allen* v. *Anderson*, (1846) 5 Hare 163, 67 ER 870; *Dundas* v. *Dundas*, (1830) 2 Dow&CI 249, 6 ER 757, HL; *Trotter* v. *Trotter*, (1828) 4 Bli NS 502, 5 ER 179, HL; *Brodie* v. *Barry*, (1813) 2 VES & B 127, 35 ER 267. See also the Indian Succession Act, 1925, Part VI Chapter XXII (Sections 180–90).

217. For case illustrations of the principle see *Johnson* v. *Telford*, (1830) 1 Russ & M 244, 39 ER 94; *Orrell* v. *Orrell*, (1871) 6 Ch. App 302; *Dewar* v. *Maitland*, (1866) LR 2 Eq 834; *Maxwell* v. *Maxwell*, (1852) 16 Beav 106, 42 ER 1048.

218. *Cottrell* v. *Cottrell*, (1872) LR 2 P&D 397; Re Manifold, *Slater* v. *Chryssaffinis*, (1962) Ch.1, (1961) 1 ALL ER 710. Restating what has already been stated, a brief summary of the ratio employed in the above cases is as under: The principle depends on the choice of law rules for wills of movables so far as the instrument purports to revoke a will of movables, and on the choice of law rules for will of immovables so far as it purports to revoke a will of immovables. The question of validity must be distinguished from the question of construction of the revocation clause, which is governed, *prima facie*, by the law of the testator's domicile: Re *Wayland's Estate*, (1951) 2 ALL ER 1041; Re Manifold, *Slater* v. *Chryssaffinis* above (revocation clause in a will dealing with property in one country does not necessarily revoke will dealing with property in another country). The question of whether a later will impliedly revokes an earlier will is similarly one of construction governed, *prima facie*, by the law of the testator's domicile. As to construction see sub-section 'Construction' under section 'Beneficial Distribution' of Chapter 7.

219. See sub-sections 'Formal Validity Under Common Law' and 'Formal Validity of a Will' under section 'Beneficial Distribution' of the chapter on succession.

220. Sections 69, 70, and 72, The Indian Succession Act, 1925.

221. Eg. by destruction of the will.
222. *Velasco* v. *Coney*, (1934) p. 143 (a case on the power of appointment by will). For whether this is the domicile at the date revocation or at the date of death, see Dicey and Morris, *The Conflict of Laws*, (Twelfth Edition, 1993), pp. 1049–50. This would seem to follow from the principle: See under sub-section 'Succession to Movables and Immovables: the Governing Law' under 'Choice of law' of 'Beneficial Distribution' of the chapter on succession.
223. Section 69, The Indian Succession Act, 1925: The Indian conflicts rule which makes a will null and void on marriage is part of matrimonial law and not of testamentary law. See also Re Martin, *Loustalan* v. *Loustalan*, (1900) p. 211 p. 240, CA.
224. Re Reid's Goods (1866) LR IP&D 74; *Westerman's Executor* v. *Schwab*, (1905) 8F 132, 43 SLR 161, 13 SLT 584, Ct of Sess; Re Groos' Estate, (1904) p. 269; Re Von Faber's Goods, (1904) 20 TLR 640; Re Martin, *Loustalan* v. *Loustalan*, (1900) p. 211, CA.
225. Re Reid's Goods, (1866) LR IP&D 74; Re Groos' Estate, p. 269.
226. Re Earl Caithness (1891) 7 TLR 354; Re Martin, *Loustalan* v. *Loustalan*, (1900) p. 211 p. 234, CA. However, Dicey and Morris, *The Conflict of Laws*, p. 1051, hold a contrary view, citing *Davies* v. *Davies*, (1915) 31 WLR 396 p. 399, 24 DLR 737 p. 740; Re Howard, (1924) 54 DLR 109 p. 119, (1924) 1 DLR 1062 p. 1071.)
227. Re Lewal's Settlement Trusts, *Gould* v. *Lewal*, (1918) 2 Ch. 391. However, where the instrument of creation provided that the donee might exercise the power 'by will or codicil executed in such a manner as to be valid according to the law of her domicile': See Re Lewal's Settlement Trusts, *Gould* v. *Lewal* above p. 396. Wherever the law of domicile does not govern the essential validity of the appointment, probably the law governing the instrument of creation is also sufficient to govern capacity. See sub-section 'Material or essential validity' infra. The point was mooted but was not decided in Re Langley's Settlement Trusts, *Lloyd's Bank Ltd.* v. *Langley*, (1961) 1 ALL ER 78, (1961) 1 WLR 41; Affirmed (1962) Ch. 541, (1961) 3 ALL ER 803, CA (Power of withdrawal from fund. As to capacity to make a will see sub-section 'Capacity' under 'Testate Succession' supra.
228. Ibid.
229. See note 163 supra for choice of law rules. Compliance with the formal requirements of the law of the testator's domicile was a way of satisfying the common law rule for the formal validity of the exercise of a power: *D'Huart* v. *Harkness*, (1865) 34 BEAV 324, 55 ER 660; Re Wilkinson's Settlement, *Butler* v. *Wilkinson* (1917) 1 Ch. 620; Re Price, *Tomlin* v. *Latter*, (1900) 1 Ch. 442.

230. Section 2 (1) (d), The Indian Succession Act, 1925 confirming the rule of common law: *Tatnall* v. *Hankey*, (1938) 2 MOO PCC 342, 12 ER 1036; *Murphy* v. *Deichler*, (1909) AC 446, HL; Re Baker's Settlement Trusts, *Hunt* v. *Baker*, (1908) WN 161; Re Trefond's Goods, (1899) p. 247; Re Huber's Goods, (1896) p. 209; Re Hallyburton's Goods, (1866) LR1 P&D 90; Re Alexander's Goods, (1860) IJPM&A 93, 6 JUR NS 345, 8 WR 451, 2LT 50.
231. The Indian Succession Act, Section 2 (2).
232. Re Price, *Tomlin* v. *Latter*, (1900) 1 Ch. 442 p. 452; Durie's *Trustees* v. *Osborne*, (1960) SC 444, (1961) SLT 53; Re Mc Morran, *Mercantile Bank of India Ltd.* v. *Perkins*, (1958) Ch. 624, (1958) 1 ALL ER 186; Re Simpson, *Coutts & Co.* v. *Church Missionary Society*, (1916) 1 Ch. 502; Re D'Este's Settlement Trusts, *Poulter* v. *D'Este*, (1903) 1 Ch. 898 p. 905. See section 'Succession'.
233. Re Price, *Tomlin* v. *Latter*, (1900) 1 Ch. 442.
234. Re Price, *Tomlin* v. *Latter*, (1900) 1 Ch. 442; Re Fenston's Settlement, *Max-Muller* v. *Simonsen*, (1971) 3 ALL ER 1092 pp. 1095–96, (1971) WLR 1640 pp. 1644–5; Re Waite's Settlement Trusts, *Westminster Bank Ltd.* v. *Brouard*, (1958) Ch. 100, (1957) 1 ALL ER 629; Cf. Re McMorran, *Mercantile Bank of India Ltd.* v. *Perkins*, (1958) Ch. 624, (1958) 1 ALL ER 186; Re Strong, *Strong* v. *Meissner*, (1925) 95 IJ Ch. 22; Re Lewal's Settlement Trusts, *Gould* v. *Lewal*, (1981) 2 Ch. 391; Re Wilkinson's Settlement, *Butler* v. *Wilkinson*, (1917) 1 Ch. 620; Re Simpson *Coults & Co.* v. *Church Missionary Society*, (1916) 1 Ch. 502; Re Baker's Settlement Trusts, *Hunt* v. *Baker*, (1908) WN 161. See contrary view in the following two cases, which do not serve as precedent and not followed: Re D'Este's Settlement Trusts, *Poulter* v. *D'Este*, (1903) 1 Ch. 898; Re Scholefield, *Scholefield* v. *St. John*, (1905) 2 Ch. 408, CA.
235. Re Fenston's Settlement, *Max-Muller* v. *Simonsen*, (1971) 3 ALL ER 1092 p. 1095, (1971) 1 WLR 1640 p. 1644.
236. *Pouey* v. *Hordern*, (1900) 1 Ch. 492 (special power); Re Mégret, *Tweedie* v. *Maunder*, (1901) 1 Ch. 547 (general power) the underlying idea is that the testator has not disposed of by will his own property, but he only nominated the persons whose names are to be inserted in the settlement creating the power: Re Pryce, *Lawford* v. *Pryce*, (1911) 2 Ch. 286 p. 296, CA.
237. Re Pryce, *Lawford* v. *Pryce*, (1911) 2 Ch. 286, CA; Re Khan's Settlement, *Coutts & Co.* v. *Senior Dowager Begum of Bhopal*, (1966) 1 Ch. 567, (1966) 1 ALL ER 160; not following Re Walte's Settlement Trusts, *Westminster Bank Ltd.* v. *Brouard*, (1958) Ch. 100, (1957) 1 ALL ER 629, Cf. *Pouey* v. *Hordern*, (1900) 1 Ch. 492 p. 495. The reason is that by his disposition the testator has shown an intention to make the movables subject to the power, to be treated as

being and deemed to be part of his free estate: See Re Pryce, *Lawford* v. *Pryce* above; Re Khan's Settlement, *Coutts & Co.* v. *Senior Dowager Begum of Bhopal* above.

238. Re Hernando, *Hernando* v. *Sawtell*, (1884) 27 Ch. D 284.

239. See sub-sections 'Testamentary Revocation' and 'Revocation by Subsequent Marriage' under section 'Testate Succession' supra.

11

Insolvency and Corporations

INSOLVENCY

Insolvency Jurisdiction of an Indian Court

An Indian court[1] has jurisdiction to adjudicate any debtor as an insolvent where that debtor:

(1) is ordinarily resident;[2]
(2) carries on business;[3]
(3) personally works for gain; or
(4) if he has been arrested or imprisoned, where he is in custody, within the jurisdiction.[4]

Effect of an Indian Bankruptcy Order on Debtor's Property

On the making of an order of adjudication, the property[5] of the insolvent, wherever situated,[6] vests in the official assignee (or the 'trustee in bankruptcy', as he is known in England), and becomes divisible among the creditors; thereafter, as directed by the Presidency Towns Insolvency Act, 1909, or the Provincial Insolvency Act, 1920, no creditor to whom the insolvent is indebted in respect of any debt provable in insolvency, during the pendency of the insolvency proceedings, has any remedy against the property of the insolvent in respect of the debt. Further, no creditor may commence any suit or legal proceedings except with the leave of the court and on the terms that the court may impose.[7]

Choice of Law in an Indian Insolvency

An Indian court has the power to decide all questions of title, priority, or of any other nature, whether involving matters of law or of fact, which may arise in any case of insolvency within the cognizance of the court, or which the court may deem it expedient or necessary to decide for the purpose of doing justice or for the distribution of property in the case.[8] In other words, the Indian court will apply the law of the forum (that is, the *lex fori*) in all proceedings relating to insolvency from adjudication to discharge. The order of adjudication will relate back to, and take effect from, the date of the presentation of the petition.[9]

Discharge by Virtue of an Indian Order

An order of discharge releases the insolvent from all debts provable in insolvency[10] except the following:

(i) any debt due to the government;

(ii) any debt or liability incurred by means of any fraud or fraudulent breach of trust to which he was a party;

(iii) any debt or liability in respect of which he has obtained forbearance by any fraud to which he was a party; or

(iv) any liability under an order for maintenance made under the Code of Criminal Procedure, 1908.[11]

Further, an order of discharge does not release any person who, at the date of the presentation of the petition, was a partner or co-trustee with the insolvent, or was jointly bound or had made any joint contract with him or any person who was surety for him.[12]

An order of adjudication passed by a foreign court will not affect immovable property situated in India.[13] Subject to this exception, a valid discharge given by a foreign court in an insolvency proceeding is treated as a valid discharge of every debt incurred anywhere, including in India.[14]

Effect in India of Foreign Insolvencies

An Indian court recognizes a foreign adjudication in insolvency rendered by a court of competent jurisdiction, unless the foreign adjudication affects immovable property in India.[15] Domicile could be deemed to be a basis for the exercise of jurisdiction by a court in insolvency proceedings.[16]

CORPORATIONS

In the new millennium we have embarked upon, in which free trade and globalization are the watch words, the study of corporations and the legal controls they need be subjected to assume importance, comparable only to a study of international commercial arbitration. The format of the study consists of three parts, namely (1) the legal status, domicile and powers of corporations, (2) their jurisdictional controls and (3) the role of the judiciary in the winding up of corporations, national or multinational.

Legal Status, Domicile, and Powers

Recognition of Foreign Corporations

Indian corporate law recognizes the existence of corporate entities duly incorporated in foreign countries. Naturally, therefore, the Indian choice of law rules, which form part of the municipal law of India, come into play in the process of subjecting foreign corporations and multinationals to legal controls. In other words, foreign corporate entities will under Indian law be allowed to sue and be sued in India in their corporate capacity.[17] *Ipso jure*, whether a corporation has continued its existence, or has been dissolved or, as the case may be, has undergone a metamorphosis in the sense of its emergence as a new entity, either due to a merger or otherwise substituting for the original, it will likewise be governed by the law of its place of incorporation.[18]

The *lex fori* of the place of incorporation will determine issues such as who represents the corporation and acts on its behalf[19] and the extent of an individual member's liability for the corporation's debts.[20] Indian courts, in the exercise of their discretionary powers,[21] will be loathe to interfere in matters which are purely internal to foreign corporations such as the rights and obligations *inter se* between their members. Such matters which may be characterized as internal management and control of the affairs of the corporation ought, in principle, to be governed by the law of the place of incorporation.[22] By a parity of reasoning, an international organization incorporated under the domestic law of a foreign country, lacking as it does legal personality and, accordingly, denied the capacity to sue and be sued before local courts,[23] enjoys the legal status of a foreign corporation.[24] *A contrario*, an international organization which has earned the recognition of a number of foreign states and, as such, from a functional standpoint is on the domain of public international law, automatically earns the recognition of local courts; hence, by virtue of being clothed with a distinct legal personality, has also the capacity to sue and be sued before local courts.[25] By the same token, other bodies such as government corporations created under the law of a country earn the recognition of being endowed with legal personality.[26]

As for India, under the Companies Act, 1956, it is mandatory for a foreign company to comply with the prescribed conditions contained therein, requiring the company to furnish to the Registrar of Companies the full address of its office in India which is deemed its principal place of business and also the name or names and addresses of the person or persons authorized to accept service of process on behalf of such company in India.[27]

Amalgamation

If by the law of the place of incorporation a foreign corporation is amalgamated with another foreign corporation, the resultant corporate entity will be recognized in India. If the law further provides that the assets and liabilities of the predecessor corporations are to be borne by the new corporation that has emerged from the amalgamation, the same will receive due recognition in India.[28] However, the law of the place of incorporation cannot absolve the new company of the liabilities of the old except by the law applicable to the contract giving rise to those liabilities.[29]

Dissolution

Indian law relating to corporations based on the Companies Act, 1956, recognizes, as does the English law, a dissolution to which a foreign corporation has been subjected to in accordance with the law of its place of incorporation, based on the principle that the will of the sovereign authority which created it can also destroy it.[30] If the corporation is in the process of being wound up in accordance with the law of its place of incorporation, it can still sue and be sued;[31] but if the process of winding up has ended and the corporation has been dissolved, it is dead or non-existent as per English law which, in principle, is endorsed by the common law of India, subject to the (Indian) Companies Act, 1956, which provides for a functionally oriented brief revival under the winding up order of a court.[32] Neither a non-existing foreign corporation nor an unincorporated overseas subsidiary can sue or be sued in the courts of the overseas country.[33] The issue of whether a foreign corporation has been so dissolved is a question of fact that depends on the evidence of the foreign law concerned.[34]

Under the (Indian) Companies Act, 1956, when a body corporate incorporated outside India, which has been carrying on business in India, ceases to carry on business in India, it may be wound up as an unregistered company, notwithstanding the fact that the body corporate has been dissolved or has otherwise ceased to exist under or by virtue of the laws of the country under which it was incorporated.[35]

A bank or a corporate body incorporated in a foreign country is deemed an unregistered company in India[36] and winding up proceedings for that company may be filed in a court.[37] A court in India has jurisdiction to wind up a foreign company no matter how big the company is, provided it has assets and an office in India.[38] It would make no difference whatsoever if an order for winding up of a company has been made by a court invested with jurisdiction at the place where the company is domiciled.[39] A winding up order issued by a court of competent jurisdiction of the company's domicile does not as such bind an Indian court to entertain winding up proceedings in India; it may, however, decline to do so on practical considerations.[40] For the purpose of determining the jurisdiction of the court in respect of winding up, an unregistered company is deemed to be registered in the state where its principal place of business is situated or, if it has principal place of business in more than one state, then, in each state where it has a principal place of business; the principal place of business situated in that state in which proceedings are being instituted will, for all purposes of the winding up, be deemed to be the registered office of the company.[41]

No unregistered company may be wound up under the Companies Act, 1956, voluntarily or subject to the jurisdiction of the court.[42]

As per the Companies Act, 1956, an Indian court has power to direct that all or any part of a property, movable or immovable, belonging to a company or held by trustees on its behalf, will vest in the official liquidator by his official name.[43]

Domicile of Corporations

A corporation is domiciled in the country under the law of which it is incorporated.[44] Unlike an individual who can change his domicile at will, a corporation cannot change its domicile even if it carries on business elsewhere.[45]

Most of the reasons for attributing a domicile to individuals (such as, for example, legitimacy, legitimation, marriage, divorce, and succession on death) are inapplicable to corporations; but statutes occasionally refer to the domicile of corporations, thus making it necessary to decide where they are domiciled.[46]

Powers of Foreign Corporations

The powers of a foreign corporation are defined and governed by its constitution as interpreted by the law of its place of incorporation.[47] Its powers in relation to a particular transaction may also be limited by the law of the country which governs the transaction in question. It does not, however, follow that if the transaction is *ultra vires* the corporation, it must be void. The effect of this lack of capacity on the validity of the transaction is a matter for the law which governs the transaction in question.[48]

Jurisdiction over Corporations

Corporations and Local Courts' Jurisdiction

It is a basic jurisprudential principle that any person, natural or fictitious, has a standing before courts. A corporation, Indian or foreign, is deemed a person under law by virtue of which it may appear as a defendant to an action before Indian courts as any other, endowed with legal personality. Accordingly, well known jurisdictional rules that are in vogue in resolving commercial disputes in general do apply to companies as well.[49]

Corporations and Service of Summons

As per the (Indian) Code of Civil Procedure, 1908, service of summons on a corporation, Indian or foreign, is as set out below.[50]

Summons may be served:

1. on the secretary or on any director, or any other officer of the corporation; or

2. by leaving it or sending it by post addressed to the corporation at its registered office or, in the absence of a registered office, at the place where the corporation carries on business.

While sending the summons by registered post to the office of the corporation is healthy and acceptable, the same is not the case with leaving the summons at the office of the corporation. A mere handing over of the summons to an employee of the corporation not authorized to accept summons on its behalf does not constitute a valid service of summons to a corporation or a company.[51] Postal acknowledgment of summons served on the registered office of the company received by an employee is in accord with procedural due process for a good service of summons, as outlined in the Code of Civil Procedure, 1908.[52]

The (Indian) Companies Act, 1956, makes it obligatory for a foreign company to deliver to the Registrar for registration (1) the name and address or the names and addresses of some one or more persons resident in India, authorized to accept service of process and any notices or other documents required to be served on the company on behalf of the company; and (2) the full address of the office of the company in India which is deemed to be its principal place of business in India.[53]

Winding Up of Corporations

Indian Courts: Their Jurisdictional Competence

Under the (Indian) Companies Act, 1956, a High Court,[54] and not the subordinate courts, is invested with jurisdiction to order the winding up of any company registered in India, whether the company is solvent or insolvent, even if it was formed solely to carry on business abroad.[55]

A high court has also jurisdiction to set in motion winding up proceedings as against an unregistered company[56] subject to the conditions laid down in the Companies Act, 1956.[57]

The Scope and Ambit of an Indian Winding-up Order

From the date of the order of a court for the winding up of a company, all the property and effects of the company are deemed to be in the custody of the court.[58] The liquidator, on being authorized by the court, has the power to sell the immovable and movable property as also the actionable claims of the company by public auction or private contract, the power to transfer the whole of the property to any person or body corporate, or to sell in parcel and to do such other things as may be necessary and proper for winding up of the affairs of the company and distributing its assets.[59]

As the winding up of a company is comparable to insolvency,[60] assets collected in the winding up may be utilized to discharge liabilities, Indian and non-Indian. If there takes place a contemporaneous foreign liquidation, it is incumbent on the official liquidator to secure equal treatment for all claimants from out of the assets of the company, rather than reserve Indian assets for Indian creditors. Therefore, it becomes the responsibility of the court to restrain a claimant, subject to its personal jurisdiction, who is out to commence proceedings against the company in such circumstances that lay bare his intent to obtain an inequitable share of the assets overseas.[61] This common law principle, as highlighted in not so recent English cases, does not have any bearing on execution overseas, but that the court, to whose personal jurisdiction the claimant is subject may be required by it to surrender the fruits of his foreign execution for the benefit of all the creditors.[62] Similarly, as exemplified in old English cases, if a foreign company is being wound up in India and simultaneously in its country of incorporation, the surplus of assets left over after the creditors have been paid, that are at the disposal of the local liquidator, ought normally to be handed over to the foreign liquidator.[63]

The Scope and Ambit of a Foreign Winding-up order

As stated earlier, the law of the place of incorporation determines who is entitled to act on behalf of a company.[64] We may infer therefrom, based on the analogy of unity in bankruptcy proceedings, that the liquidator appointed under the law of the place of incorporation will be recognized by courts in India, as has been the practice of courts in England, too, with an unbroken continuity.[65] It is understandable that courts do recognize the authority of a liquidator appointed under another law.[66]

Multinational Insolvencies: the Norm of Judicial Cooperation

Based on the twin criteria that the ascertainment of the debts incurred are provable and that the distribution of the assets among the creditors, secured and unsecured, in the wake of the winding up of a corporation are governed by insolvency rules,[67] it is incumbent, in cases of multinational insolvencies, on the part of courts in the countries concerned to coordinate with each other with a view to securing equitable satisfaction of the creditors' claims and distribution of the assets.[68]

Receivership

From the foregoing analysis, it may be stated that a receiver duly appointed by a court of the country of incorporation of the company may, on being authorized here in India by a court of competent jurisdiction, exercise his powers in India.[69]

NOTES

1. Only a district court has insolvency jurisdiction. However, a state government may, by notification in the Official Gazette, invest any court subordinate to the district court with jurisdiction in any class of cases, giving that court concurrent jurisdiction with the district court: Section 3, Provincial Insolvency Act, 1920.
2. A place of residence is the place where the person intends to reside: *Dina Nath Vaidya* v. *Krishna Dutt*, AIR 1953 AJMER 8. Further, a person may have two permanent residences at one time and may reside in only one of them: *Mohan Singh* v. *Lajya Ram*, AIR 1956 PUNJ 188, (1956) ILR PUNJ1299, 58 PUNJ LR 312.
3. Carrying on business means commercial business: *Ellappa Naicker* v. *Sivasubramanian Mariagaran*, AIR 1937 MAD 293, 169 IC 244, (1936) 71 MAD LJ 609, (1936) 44 MAD LW 567.
4. Section 11, Provincial Insolvency Act.
5. The term 'property' includes the property of the insolvent over which he has the disposing powers, even though he does not have possession of the property: *Muktilal Agarwal* v. *Trustees of the Provident Fund of the Tin Plate Co.*, AIR 1956 SC 336, (1956) SCJ 406, (1956) 1 MAD LJ (SC) 183. Further, all property which is acquired by or devolves on the insolvent after the date of an order of adjudication and before his discharge vests in the court or the official assignee, and the provisions of Section 17 (2) Presidency-towns Insolvency Act, 1909, (corresponding to Section 28 (2), Provincial Insolvency Act, 1920,) apply.
6. Section 17 (2), The Presidency-towns Insolvency Act, 1909 and Section 28 (2), Provincial Insolvency Act, 1920 vest the whole of the property of the insolvent in the court or the official assignee. The phrase 'whole of the property'

employed in the Provincial Insolvency Act, 1920, presumably includes property wherever situate, as is made explicit in the Presidency-towns Insolvency Act, 1909; *Jayantilal Keshavlal Gajjar* v. *Kantilal Jesingbhai Dalal*, AIR 1955 BOM 170; BN *Lang* v. *Jasvantilal Hatichand*, AIR 1926 BOM 471, 94 IC 146, (1926) 50 BOM 439.

7. See Section 17 (2), The Presidency-towns Insolvency Act, 1909, and Section 28(2), the Provincial Insolvency Act, 1920.

8. Section 4 (1), The Provincial Insolvency Act, 1920.

9. Section 28 (7), The Provincial Insolvency Act, 1920.

10. Section 44 (2), The Provincial Insolvency Act, 1920.

11. Section 44(1) The Provincial Insolvency Act, 1920.

12. Section 44(3) The Provincial Insolvency Act, 1920.

13. *(Gummideli) Anantapadmanabhaswami* v. *Official Receiver of Secunderabad*, AIR 1933 PC 134 p. 135, 142 IC 552, 60 IC 167, (1933) 37 CAL WN 553; *Lakhpat Rai Sharma* v. *Atma Singh*, AIR 1962 PUNJ 228, (1961) ILR 2 PUNJ 166.

14. *Magadhu Pillai Rowther* v. *Asan Muhammadhu Rowther*, AIR 1920 MAD 934 p. 935, 51 IC 38, (1919) 9 MAD LW 535.

15. See note 13 supra.

16. See Section 11, The Provincial Insolvency Act, 1920,: Section 11, The Presidency-towns Insolvency Act, 1909.

17. *Lazard Bros & Co.* v. *Midland Bank Ltd.*, (1993) AC 280 p. 297 HL.

18. For dissolution of a company see section 'Dissolution' infra. See also *National Bank of Greece and Athens* v. *Metliss*, (1958) AC 509, (1957) 2 ALL ER 608, HL.

19. *Bank of Ethiopia* v. *National Bank of Egypt and Liguori*, (1937) Ch. 513, (1937) 3 ALL ER 8; *Damon Cia Naviera SA* v. *Hapag-Lloyd International SA, The Bankenstein, The Blankenstein, The Blankenstein*, (1985) 1 ALL ER 475, (1985) 1 WLR 435 CA; *Carl Zeiss Stiftung* v. *Rayner and Keeler Ltd.*, (No. 2) (1967) 1 AC 853 p. 919, 972, (1966) 2 ALL ER 536 p. 556, 586, HL; *Banco de Bilbao* v. *Sancha*, (1938) 2 KB 176, (1938) 2 ALL ER 253, CA.

20. *Risdon Iron and Locomotive Works* v. *Furness*, (1906) 1 KB 49, CA; *J.H. Rayner (Mining Lane) Ltd.* v. *Department of Trade and Industry*, (1990) 2 AC 418, (1989) 3 ALL ER 523, HL; *Kutchera* v. *Buckingham International Holdings Ltd.*, (1988) IR 61, 9 ILRM 501; Cf. *Bateman* v. *Service*, (1881) 6 App Cas 386, PC.

21. See Sudlow v. Dutch Rhenish Railway Co. (1855) 21 BEAV 43; contrary was the ruling in *Pickering* v. *Stephenson*, (1872) I.R 14 E 522, where the court restrained the application of a foreign corporation's funds by injunction in an

ultra vires transaction); *Pergamon Press Ltd.* v. *Maxwell*, (1970) 2 ALL ER 809, (1970) 1 WLR 1167; Re Schintz, *Schintz* v. *Warr*, (1926) Ch. 710 CA.

22. *Pergamon Press Ltd.* v. *Maxwell*, (1970) 2 ALL ER 809, (1970) 1 WLR 1167.

23. *J.H. Rayner (Mincing Lane) Ltd.* v. *Department of Trade and Industry*, (1990) 2 AC 418, (1989) 3 ALL ER 523, HL.

24. *Arab Monetary Fund* v. *Hashim*, (No. 3) (1991) 2 AC 114, (1991) 1 ALL ER 871, HL.

25. *Westland Helicopters Ltd.* v. *Arab Organisation for Industrialization*, (1995) QB 282, (1995) 2 ALL ER 387.

26. *Bumper Development Corpn. Ltd.* v. *Metropolitan Police Comr.*, (1991) 4 ALL ER 638, (1991) 1 WLR 1362, CA. See also sub-section 'Amalgamation' infra.

27. Section 592, Companies Act, 1956.

28. *National Bank of Greece and Athens SA* v. *Metliss*, (1958) AC 509, (1957) 3 ALL ER 608, HL; *RKO Pictures Inc.* v. *Cannon Screen Entertainment Ltd.*, (1990) BC LC 364; *Steel Authority of India Ltd.* v. *Hind Metals Inc.*, (1984) 1 Lloyd's Rep 405, 134 NIJ 204.

29. *Adams* v. *National Bank of Greece SA*, (1961) AC 255, (1960) 2 ALL ER 421, HL.

30. *Lazard Bros. & Co.* v. *Midland Bank Ltd.*, (1933) AC 289 p. 297, HL.

31. *Russian Commercial and Industrial Bank* v. *Comptoir d'Escompte de Mulhouse*, (1925) AC 112, HL; *First Russian Insurance Co.* v. *London and Lancashire Insurance Co. Ltd.*, (1928) Ch. 922; *Employers' Liability Assurance Corpn.* v. *Sedwick Collins & Co.*, (1927) AC 95, HL; *Banque internationale de Comerce de Petrograd* v. *Goukassow*, (1925) AC 150, (1923) 2 KB 682, HL.

32. *Russian and English Bank* v. *Baring Bros. Co. Ltd.*, (1932) 1 Ch. 435; *Lazard Bros. & Co.* v. *Midland Bank Ltd.*, (1933) AC 289, HL. However, as stated earlier in this work, Section 588 (2) of The (Indian) Companies Act, 1956, provides for a functionally oriented brief revival under the winding up order of a court, which would enable the official liquidator to bring or defend in his official name any suit or legal proceeding relating to the property or which is necessary to bring or defend for the purpose of effectually winding up the company or recovering its property.

33. *Russian and English Bank* v. *Baring Bros. Co. Ltd.*, (1932) 1 Ch. 435; *Lazard Bros. & Co. Ltd.* v. *Midland Bank Ltd.*, (1933) AC 289, HL; *Deutsche Bank and Disconto Gesellschaft* v. *Banque des Merchands de Moscou*, (1932) 158 LT 364, CA.

34. *Lazard Bros. & Co.* v. *Midland Bank Ltd.*, (1933) AC 289, HL; Re Russo-Asiatic Bank, (1934) Ch. 720.

35. Section 584, The Companies Act, 1956.

36. Section 582, The Companies Act, 1956.

37. Re Travancore National and Quilon Bank Ltd., AIR 1939 MAD 318, 183 IC 353, (1938) MAD WN 1313.

38. Re Travancore National and Quilon Bank Ltd., AIR 1939 MAD 318, 183 IC 353, (1938) MAD WN 1313; Re Frontier Bank Ltd., AIR 1951 PUNJ 145; Re Indian Companies Act VII of 1913 and Traders Bank Ltd., Labor 1913, AIR 1949 LAH 48.

39. Re Travancore National and Quilon Bank Ltd., AIR 1939 MAD 318, 183 IC 353, (1938) MAD WN 1313.

40. Ibid.

41. Section 583 (2), The Companies Act, 1956.

42. Section 583 (3), The Companies Act, 1956.

43. Section 588 (1), The Companies Act, 1956.

44. *Gasque* v. *Inland Revenue Comrs*, (1940) 2 KB 80, 23 TC 210; *Carl Zeiss Stiftung* v. *Rayner and Keeler Ltd.*, (No. 3) (1970) Ch. 506 p. 544, (1969) 3 ALL ER 897 p. 914.

45. *Gasque* v. *Inland Revenue Comrs*, (1940) 2 KB 80, 23 TC 210; *Carl Zeiss Stiftung* v. *Rayner and Keeler Ltd.*, (No. 3) (1970) Ch. 506 at 544, (1969) 3 ALL ER 897 at 914. This does not prevent a corporation from being dissolved in the country in which it is incorporated, and 'reincorporating' in another country.

46. Re Travancore National and Quilon Bank Ltd., AIR 1939 MAD 318, 183 IC 353, (1938) MAD WN 1313.

47. *Rison Iron and Locomotive Works* v. *Furness*, (1906) 1 KB 49, CA; *J.H. Rayner (Mincing Lane) Ltd.* v. *Department of Trade and Industry*, (1990) 2 AC 418, (1989) 3 ALL ER 523, HL; *Janred Properties Ltd.* v. *Ente Nazionale Italiano per il Tarismo*, (1989) 2 ALL ER 444, CA. However, a company may be estopped from a reliance upon the incapacity under the law of its place of incorporation, atleast if the particular transaction is governed by English law: *Janred Properties Ltd.* v. *Ente nazionale Italiano per il Tarismo*, (1989) 2 ALL ER 444, CA.

48. See the Saudi Princie, (1982) 2 Lloyd's Rep 255; *Janred Properties Ltd.* v. *Ente Nazionale Italiano per il Tarismo*, (1989) 2 ALL ER 444, CA.

49. See the Chapter on Jurisdictional Competence of Courts, supra as also, generally, the Law Relating to Business Associations (Companies and Corporations).

50. Order 29, rule 2, The Code of Civil Procedure, 1908. See also *Hyderabad Municipality* v. *Hakumal*, AIR 1928 SIND 111. (Note: The mode of service as laid down in the Code of Civil Procedure, 1908, (namely, order 29, rule 2)

may be availed of only in cases where there is no mode of service provided by any other statute).

51. *Shalimar Rope Works Ltd.* v. *Abdul Hussain*, AIR 1980 SC 1163, (1980) 3 SCC 595, (1980) 2 SCJ 324.

52. That is, in Compliance with order 29, rule 2 of the Code of Civil Procedure, 1908.

53. Section 596, The (Indian) Companies Act, 1956; *P.S. Anant Narayan* v. *Massey Ferguson Ltd.*, (1965) 1 MAD LJ 550; see also *Hyderabad Municipality* v. *Hakumal*, AIR 1928 SIND 111. See Govindaraj, Halsbury's Laws of India Series, *Conflict of Laws*, Vol. 10 (New Delhi: LexisNexis Butterworths, 2001), pp. 297–9.

54. Section 2 (11), The Companies Act, 1956

55. Section 433 (e), The Companies Act, 1956. See the Law Relating to Business Associations: Companies and Coporations.

56. Section 582, The Companies Act, 1956: A foreign company falls within the meaning of an unregistered company. Also, a bank incorporated in a foreign country is an unregistered company, and winding up proceedings can be filed in India: Re *Travancore National and Quilon Bank Ltd.* v. *Reghuraja Bharathi*, AIR 1939 MAD 318, 183 IC 353, (1938) Mad WN 1313; *Reghubar Dayal* v. *The Sarrafa Chamber*, AIR 1954 ALL 555: (Companies consisting of not more than 10 members in the case of banking companies, and not more than 20 members in the case of other companies can legitimately remain unregistered under the Companies Act, 1956, and may be wound up by a court.

57. The conditions are:
a. if the company is dissolved or has ceased to carry on business, or is carrying on business only for the purpose of winding up its affairs;
b. if the company is unable to pay its debts;
c. if the court is of the opinion that it is just and equitable that the company should be wound up: Section 583(4), The Companies Act, 1956.

58. Section 456 (2), The Companies Act, 1956.

59. Section 457 (1), The Companies Act, 1956.

60. Section 529, The Companies Act, 1956.

61. Re Vocalion (Foreign) Ltd., (1932) 2 Ch. 196; Re North Carolina Estate Co., (1889) 5 TLR 328. However, a secured creditor will not be impeded in the enforcement of his security: *Minna Craig SS Co.* v. *Chartered Mercantile Bank of India, London and China*, (1897) 1 QB 71.

62. Re Oriental Inland Steam Co., ex p Scinde Railway Co., (1874) 9 Ch. App 557; Re Vocalion (Foreign) Ltd., (1932) 2 Ch. 196.

63. The English precedent exemplified in Re Commercial Bank of South Australia, (1886) 33 Ch. D 174; Re Vocalion (Foreign) Ltd., (1932) 2

Ch. 196; the English common law rule as illustrated in the above mentioned cases presumably holds good in India.

64. In respect of persons who are entitled to act on behalf of a company see note 3 under sub-section 'Recognition of Foreign Corporations' under section 'Legal Status, Domicile, and Powers', supra.

65. *Bank of Ethiopia* v. *National Bank of Egypt and Ligouri*, (1937) Ch. 513; *Felixstowe Dock and Railway Co.* v. *United States Lines Inc.*, (1989) QB 360, (1988) 2 ALL ER 77; *Baden* v. *Société Général pour Favoriser le Développement du Commerce et de l'Industrie en France SA*, (1992) 4 ALL ER 161, (1993) 1 WLR 509n, affd, (1992) 4 ALL ER 279n, (1985) BCLC 258n, CA.

66. For a possible analogy see the following cases: Re A Company (No. 00359 of 1987), (1988) Ch. 210, (1987) 3 ALL ER 137; Re A Company (No. 003102 of 1991), ex p Nyckeln Finance Co. Ltd., (1991) BCLC 359.

67. The Companies Act, 1956, Section 529.

68. By a parity of reasoning, the principles contained in Section 529 of the Companies Act, 1956, may be extended to multinational insolvencies.

69. Sections 529, 600, The Companies Act, 1956. See also section 'Multinational Insolvencies: the Norm of Judicial Cooperation', notes 14 and 15 supra.

12

Foreign Judgments

RECOGNITION AND ENFORCEMENT

Section 13 of the Indian Civil Procedure Code, 1908 lays down a seven-fold criteria set out below, the fulfilment of which will impart to a foreign judgment, brought before an Indian court for recognition and enforcement, finality and conclusiveness. A word of caution is needed while recourse is had to Section 13 of the C.P.C. in that the section is just illustrative, not exhaustive. This is borne out by leading illustrations where *ex parte* judgments of foreign courts were obtained as in *Smt. Satya* v. *Teja Singh*[1] and *Y. Narasimha Rao* v. *Y. Venkatalakshmi*[2] to annul marriages duly performed in India as per Hindu law. To execute such make-belief *ex parte* decrees of divorce obtained by errant husbands in foreign courts here in India is, to say the least, travesty of justice. To counter such malady, Section 13 of the C.P.C. has to be suitably amended so as to effectively deal with the scope of jurisdiction exercised legally but invoked unjustly with a view to circumvent decrees obtained in violation of rules of conflict of laws.

According to the said Section 13 of the C.P.C., a foreign judgment shall be conclusive between the parties as to any matter directly adjudicated upon[3] as also their privies litigating under the same title. However, its conclusiveness can be challenged on the following grounds, namely

(a) where it has not been pronounced by a court of competent jurisdiction;

(b) where it has not been on the merits of the case;

(c) where it appears on the face of the proceedings to be founded on an incorrect view of international law or a refusal to recognize the law of India in cases in which such law is applicable;

(d) where the proceedings in which the judgment was obtained are opposed to natural justice;

(e) where it has been obtained by fraud;

(f) where it sustains a claim founded on a breach of any law in force in India.

Refusal to Recognize the Applicable Indian Law

For a refusal to recognize or, as the case may be, turning a blind eye to the applicable Indian law by the foreign court, we have the classic example in *Y. Narasimha Rao* v. *Y. Venkatalakshmi*,[4] where the Supreme Court of India, speaking through Sawant J., refused to recognize the *ex parte* decree of divorce given by a New Mexico court on the basis of the New Mexican law. The marriage between the parties had, in fact, been solemnized in India as per Hindu law. According to the Supreme Court, it could be dissolved only on the basis of that law, that is, Hindu law.

Judgment Opposed to Natural or Substantial Justice

What Constitutes Denial of Natural or Substantial Justice?

The defence of denial of natural or substantial justice is as vague as the defence based on infringement of public policy of a country. Denial of natural justice means flouting the due process of law. Due process of law is defined by Willis and Willoughby, two distinguished authorities on the Constitution of the United States, as under:

(i) notice;

(ii) opportunity of being heard;

(iii) fair and impartial tribunal; and

(iv) an orderly procedure according to Willis or a court of competent jurisdiction according to Willoughby.

What does not constitute denial of natural justice?

The following, *inter alia*, do not under common law constitute denial of natural justice, namely

(i) that the judgment is manifestly wrong;[5]

(ii) that the court admitted evidence which is inadmissible as per *lex fori*;[6]

(iii) that the court failed to admit evidence which is admissible as per *lex fori*.[7]

The second and the third relate to procedure and, as such, governed by the *lex fori*. Professor Morris holds a similar view.[8] As for the first, namely that the mere fact that the judgment is manifestly wrong as in *Godard* v. *Gray*, where a French court misconstrued a clause in a charter party relating to the issue of penalty for non-performance of the agreement, governed by English law as the proper law, was upheld by an English court on a suit filed by the plaintiffs, who were Frenchmen, on the strength of the French judgment, despite it being a mistaken view of the English law or, as for that matter, any other (factual) mistake, provided that the French judgment was rendered on merits.

Judgment Obtained by Fraud

In the memorable words of Grey, C.J., in the Duchess of Kingston's case[9] fraud is defined as: 'Fraud is an extrinsic, collateral act, which vitiates the most solemn proceedings of Courts of Justice.'

Fraud may be perpetrated by the plaintiff who may invoke the jurisdiction of a court unjustly, though the court's exercise of jurisdiction may be legal as per the *lex fori*, with a view to circumvent the decree obtained in violation of rules of conflict of laws. Indian cases such as *Smt. Satya* v. *Teja Singh*[10] and *Y. Narsimha Rao* v. *Y. Venkatalakshmi*[11] are instances of that kind. Accordingly, any foreign decree procured by fraud, though obtained in conformity with the *lex fori* as to the jurisdictional competence of the foreign court which issued the decree, can be impeached for fraud when a suit is instituted before a local court for its recognition and enforcement. If a foreign judgment can be so impeached for fraud, it entails reopening the merits of the case which have already been determined by the foreign court. Consequently, the basic principle of conflict of laws, namely that the merits cannot be reopened, suffers a setback.

The said principle is further eroded by the common law rule, namely that whereas a local judgment cannot be impeached for fraud in the absence of fresh evidence, a foreign judgment, on the contrary, can be impeached for fraud even without such evidence.

How, then, do we subscribe to the so-called common law rule, consistently vouched by courts in England, as we notice from the four decisions of the court of appeal, where foreign judgments rendered on merits were reopened on allegation of fraud,[12] to which we may add a fifth one, again a decision of the court of appeal where the very issue of fraud had been addressed in a separate action in the courts of the foreign country concerned?[13] The defence of, or the justification for, the ill-conceived and illogical common law rule, which strikes at the root of the well known doctrine as to the finality and conclusiveness of a foreign judgment rendered on merits, taking into consideration the alleged fraud, is forthcoming from a recent House of Lords decision.[14] Lord Bridge, speaking for the unanimous court, emphatically endorsed the common law rule of discriminating foreign judgments rendered on merits vis-à-vis local judgments in respect of their finality and conclusiveness where the defence of fraud received due judicial consideration on the part of the foreign courts. Lord Bridge, in the course of his judgment, observed that where there might be strong policy arguments for giving a foreign judgment the same finality as an English judgment, it was out of the question to alter the common law rule so that it was different from a statutory rule;[15] and to do so is to mock at the common law which has presumably received legislative endorsement. Section 13(e) of the Indian Civil Procedure Code is, arguably, cast in the same mould as Section 9(2)(d) of the Administration of Justice Act, 1920, and Section 4(1)(a)(iv) of the Foreign Judgments (Reciprocal Enforcement) Act, 1933. If a foreign judgment rendered on merits can be re-opened by courts in England, even if the allegation of fraud received due notice and consideration at the hands of the concerned foreign court, it strikes at the root of the science of conflict of laws and makes a mockery of the doctrine of comity born out of the impartiality and objectivity of courts of law of the civilized world.

Sustaining a Claim Founded on a Breach of Any Law in Force in India

This rule is obvious and therefore does not require any comment. There are cases where foreign courts, in deciding matrimonial disputes between Indians governed by the Hindu law, turned a blind eye to the personal law of the parties and chose to give *ex parte* decrees of divorce based on the so-called domicile acquired by the husband by a make-believe residence in the concerned states of six or twelve weeks, as is the case with the States of Nevada and New Mexico in the United States. To expect of Indian courts to honour such *ex parte* decrees of divorce granted by courts in Nevada and New Mexico in actions brought before them (namely the Indian courts) by the errant husbands for recognition and enforcement of such decrees is to reduce rules of conflict of laws to a mere rope of sand.[16] They are not, so to say, foreign judgments worth the name. Such instances, call them fraud or constructive fraud played by the plaintiff husband, are sure to bring about a divorce between law and morals or, as for that matter, between law and justice.

Justice Sawant, in the case *Y. Narasimha Rao* v. *Y. Venkatalakshmi*, bemoaned the employment by foreign courts of the archaic rule that the wife's domicile follows that of her husband and that it is the husband's domiciliary law which determines the jurisdiction and judges the merits of the case. However, he adds yet another observation, which presumably forms part of the ratio and puzzles a conflicts lawyer. It runs thus:

> *Since with regard to the jurisdiction of the forum as well as the ground on which it is passed the foreign decree in the present case is not in accordance with the Act under which the parties are married* and the respondent had not submitted to the jurisdiction of the court or consented to its passing, it cannot be recognized by the courts in this country and is, therefore, unenforceable. [Emphasis added].

Here it may be submitted, with respect, that while the exercise of jurisdiction, being a procedural matter, is for the *lex fori* to determine in conformity with the rules of conflict of laws, the grant of substantive relief, on the contrary, ought to be in accordance with matrimonial law of India. Obviously, there is a mix up of the procedural issue of exercise of jurisdiction and the substantive issue of granting relief, the latter alone being governable by the law under which the marriage took place, namely the Hindu law.

In the case *Neeraja Saraph* v. *Jayant Saraph*[17] R.M. Sahai, J. of the Supreme Court of India, in an action brought before the Court by a deserted wife of a non-resident Indian husband for maintenance, made a threefold recommendation addressed to the legislature for its thoughtful consideration which partake of the character of ratio. They are:

> (a) *no marriage between an NRI and an Indian woman which has taken place in India may be annulled by a foreign court* [emphasis added];

(b) provision may be made for adequate alimony to the wife in the property of the husband both in India and abroad; and
(c) the decree granted by Indian courts may be made executable in foreign courts both on principle of comity and by entering into reciprocal agreements like Section 44-A of the Civil Procedure Code which makes a foreign decree executable as it would have been a decree passed by that court.

While the second and the third recommendations are wholesome and appropriate, the same cannot be said of the first recommendation. Not only does it sound out of tune with the basic tenets of the science of conflict of laws governing assumption of jurisdiction by a foreign court, it, in fact, strikes at the very root of the doctrine of comity.

If an English court under the common law of England could re-open a foreign judgment rendered on merits if there be fraud on the part of the plaintiff, even if the issue of fraud had, as aforesaid, been judicially determined by the foreign court, the Supreme Court of India, speaking through Sahai, J., goes a step further by debarring altogether a foreign court from even entertaining the action!

FOREIGN ARBITRAL AWARDS AND FOREIGN JUDGMENTS BASED UPON SUCH AWARDS: A JURIDICAL INQUIRY

General Observations

The difference between a local judgment or, as the case may be, a local arbitral award vis-à-vis a foreign judgment or a foreign arbitral award is that, whereas a local judgment or a local arbitral award is *res judicata* in the sense of automatic merger of the original cause of action into the judgment or the award, the same is not the case with a foreign judgment or foreign arbitral award. Maybe in the case of an arbitral award, it has to be confirmed by a local higher judiciary if the procedural law of the country concerned so requires. Whether it be a foreign judgment or a foreign arbitral award, for it to be enforced in a country other than the country where the judgment was given or the award rendered, a suit may have to be instituted for its recognition and enforcement. However, from a legal standpoint in the case of a foreign judgment, it merely requires an institution of a suit in the concerned country by the successful party for its recognition and enforcement, in the case of a foreign arbitral award, on the other hand, the party concerned has the option either to sue on the basis of the foreign award or on the basis of the original cause of action that resulted in the award. But that does not, as we shall presently see, relegate a foreign arbitral award to an inferior legal status vis-à-vis a foreign judgment. The classic example to bring home this point is *Badat & Co., Bombay* v. *East India Trading Co.*, the first test case before the Supreme Court of India. The facts of the case are briefly as follows:

The plaintiff respondent, namely the East India Trading Co., which was incorporated in the State of New York, entered into a contract with the defendant–appellant company, a partnership firm carrying on import and export business in Bombay, upon the terms of the Amercian Spice Trade Association. One of the terms of the said Association was that all questions and controversies and all claims arising under the contract should be submitted and settled by arbitration and the award made by the arbitrators should be final and binding on the parties. Disputes having arisen between the parties on two contracts entered into by them, they were referred to arbitration which culminated in two *ex parte* awards against the appellant–defendant, which were confirmed by a judgment of the Supreme Court of New York in accordance with the procedural law of New York to facilitate their enforcement in a foreign court. Thereupon, the plaintiff–respondent filed a suit against defendant–appellant for the enforcement of the awards on the original side of the Bombay High Court on the basis of the judgment of the Supreme Court of New York or, alternatively, on the basis of the awards themselves. The defendant company which preferred an appeal before the Supreme Court of India succeeded in its action. The two grounds based on which the Supreme Court allowed the appeal were as follows:

(i) The cause of action for the plaintiff's suit on the original side of the Bombay High Court, inasmuch as it rested on the judgment of the New York Supreme Court, must be taken to have arisen outside the original jurisdiction of the Bombay High Court and the suit based upon that judgment to the exclusion of the original cause of action must be held to be beyond the jurisdiction of the High Court of Bombay.

(ii) The arbitral awards, lacking as they do, finality or conclusiveness as per *lex fori* (that is, the law of New York) till they actually culminate in a judgment, cannot furnish a valid cause of action for the suit before the Bombay High Court.

It may here be respectfully submitted that the ratio employed by the Supreme Court of India, set out above, is out of tune with the accepted norms of private international law as to the binding effect of foreign awards or judgments.

Ratio number one contradicts the 'doctrine of obligation'. Even if, for the sake of argument, the original cause of action does not in the case of a foreign arbitral award merge with the judgment confirming the award as per the *lex fori*, which provides a new cause of action, the question of lack of jurisdiction for the Bombay High Court to entertain the suit based upon the judgment does not arise, if Section 13 (a) and (b) of the Indian Civil Procedure Code, 1908, incorporating the said doctrine of obligation is understood aright, thus making the judgment *res judicata*. Besides, the technical procedural rule of nexus between jurisdiction and cause of action has no relevance whatsoever to actions brought before municipal courts for enforcement of foreign judgments.

Ratio number two of the Supreme Court of India, which relegates foreign awards to an inferior legal status as compared to foreign judgments, is equally fallacious. In fact, a foreign arbitral award is assimilable to a foreign judgment and may, by itself, like the latter, furnish a valid cause of action for a suit seeking its enforcement. The procedural formality, as in this case, requiring a further ratification or confirmation of the award by the Supreme Court of New York, could neither affect its validity nor make it any the less binding between the parties. Finality or conclusiveness of a foreign arbitral award may be presumed irrespective of the formality of a further ratification that may be required under the *lex fori*, provided that the award satisfies three conditions, namely submission of the parties to arbitration, conduct of arbitration in accordance with the submission and, finally, its validity by the law of the forum. As all the three elements happened to be present in the award in this case, the award itself could furnish a valid cause of action for the suit instituted in the Bomaby High Court for its enforcement. The view taken here is fortified by the decision of the Queen's Bench Division of the High Court of England, though repudiated by the Supreme Court of India, in *Union Nationale Des Cooperatives Agricoles* v. *Robert Catterall & Co. Ltd.*[18] Therein the high court aptly observed:

The fact that the award was not directly enforceable in Denmark until a judgment of the Danish courts had been obtained did not prevent the award being a final award within Section 37(1)(d) and, accordingly, Section 36(1) applied to it and it was enforceable in the same way as an English award.[19]

India is a party to both the Geneva Convention of 1937 and the New York Convention of 1958. The latter of the two conventions, namely the New York Convention, which is an improvement on the Geneva Convention, has substituted for the phrase 'the award has become final' in the country in which it was made the phrase 'the award has not yet become binding' on the parties. The change in phraseology has the desired effect of overcoming difficulties of what would constitute 'finality and conclusiveness' of an award rendered by an arbitration tribunal, duly constituted as per the terms of the arbitration agreement between the concerned parties. If the proper law happens to be in a country which is a party to the New York Convention, an award does not become final unless it has been confirmed by a judgment of the Supreme Court of New York. In the case *ONGC* v. *Western Co. of North America*, the Supreme Court of India reiterated the ratio it employed in the Badat Case by way of interpretation of Article V (1)(e) of the New York Convention, namely (i) that the enforceability must be determined *as per the law applicable to the award*. [emphasis added], or in other words, the proper law; (ii) French, German, and Indian courts have taken the view that the enforceability as per the law of the country which governs the award is essential (sic) precondition for asserting that it has become binding under Article V (1)(e).[20]

The above mentioned ratio of the Supreme Court of India is in consonance with Section 17 of the Indian Arbitration Act, 1940, according to which finality can be attributed to an award only on its being transformed into a judgment and decree of a court. This interpretative norm has been decorously dropped after the coming into force of the Arbitration and Conciliation Act, 1996, under (see Section 35) which an arbitration award shall be final and binding on the parties and persons claiming under it, respectively. Section 36 of the Act further provides that

> [w]here the time for making an application to set aside the arbitral award under Section 34 has expired, or such application having been made, it has been refused, the award shall be enforced under the Code of Civil Procedure, 1908 (5 of 1908) in the same manner as if it were a decree of the court.

The outcome of the Arbitration and Conciliation Act, 1996, is that the requirement of a judgment or a decree passed in terms of the award as a prerequisite for its enforcement has been done away with and, accordingly, an arbitral award becomes final and binding on the parties which could be enforced as if it is a decree of a court.[21]

Forum for Arbitration, Whether Irrevocable: Scope for the Operation of the Doctrine of Balance of *Conveniens*

If in a commercial contract the parties exercise their option as to the applicable law for conducting arbitration, the presumption is that the arbitration is to take place in the country of the applicable law, subject, of course, to balance of convenience determinable by the court exercising jurisdiction based on the legal status of the parties, such as that one of the parties cannot afford to go to the country of the applicable law, coupled with the availability of evidence, oral and documentary, at the place where the court exercises jurisdiction.[22]

NOTES

1 AIR 1975 SC 105

2. AIR 1991 SC 821

3. See *R. Viswanthan* v. *Rukn-ul-Mulk Syed Abdul Wajid (dead)*, AIR 1963 SC 1 p. 14; 1963 SCR 22.

4. AIR 1991 SC 821

5. *Godard* v. *Gray*, (1870) LR 6 QB 139. See *Castrique* v. *Imrie*, (1870) LR 4 HL 414; *Robinson* v. *Fenner*, (1913) 3 KB 835 p. 842.

6. *De. Cosse Brissac* v. *Rathbone*, (1861) 6. H&N 301 (the sixth plea).

7. *Scarpetta* v. *Lowenfeld*, (1911) 27 TLR 509; *Robinson* v. *Fenner*, supra.

8. J.H.C. Morris and David McClean, *Conflict of Laws*, Fourth Edition, p. 117.

9. (1776), 2 SLC 644

10. AIR 1975 SC 105

11. AIR 1991 SC 821

12. *Abouloff* v. *Oppenheimer*, (1882), 10 QBD 295; *Vadala* v. *Lawes*, (1890) 25 QBD 310; *Syal* v. *Heyward*, (1948) 2 KB 443; and *Jet Holdings Inc.* v. *Patel*, (1990) 1 KB 335.

13. *House of Spring Gardens Ltd.* v. *Waite*, (1991) 1 QB 241.

14. *Owens Bank Ltd.* v. *Bracco*, (1992) 2 ALL E.R. 193.

15. See Section 9(2)(d) of The Administration of Justice Act, 1920 and Section 4(1)(a)(iv) of The Foreign Judgments (Reciprocal Enforcement) Act, 1933.

16. See *Smt. Satya* v. *Teja Singh*, AIR 1975 SC 105 and *Y. Narasimha Rao* v. *Y. Venkata Lakshmi*, AIR (1991) SC 821.

17. (1994) 6 SCC 461

18. See V.C. Govindaraj, Note: *Badat & Co., Bombay* v. *East India Trading Co.*, AIR 1964 SC 538 `Foreign Arbitral Awards and Foreign Judgments Based Upon Such Awards', *The International and Comparative Law Quarterly (ICLQ)* (October 1964), p. 1465.

19. (1959) 2 QB 44

20. (1987) 1SCC496 p. 514

21. See Amal K. Ganguli, *India and International Law* (Martinus Nijhoff Publishers, 2005), 319 pp. 335–6.

22. *Black Sea SS UL Lastochkina Odessa USSR.* v. *Union of India*, AIR (1976) AP 103 p. 107.

13

Procedure

SUBSTANCE AND PROCEDURE: THE BASIC DISTINCTION

The jurisprudential distinction between substance and procedure is that whereas substance relates to rights and obligations of the parties to a dispute, procedure is the means employed to determine such rights and obligations. Matters of substantive law are governed by the *lex causae* (that is, the law that governs the cause of action), the law found applicable under the concerned country's rules for the choice of law. Matters of procedure, on the other hand, are governed by the *lex fori* (that is, the law of the forum), the law of country where the action is brought.[1] Often we come across matters which are characterized as procedure but, in reality, affect the substance such as the law relating to limitation and, for that matter, the law of evidence. Therefore, the classification of an issue as procedural or substantive is one of authority rather than principle depending upon how courts would choose to characterize the issue.[2] Likewise, matters relating to mode of trial of an action and the period within which an appeal can be preferred against a judgment in an action are for the *lex fori* to determine as matters of procedure.[3] Matters such as who can sue and be sued are equally for the *lex fori* to determine as, for example, a suit against a corporate entity,[4] an international organization,[5] a state,[6] an inanimate object,[7] et cetera. Issues relating to admissibility of evidence are for the *lex fori* to determine. Inadequacy or want of stamp which may render a document inadmissible as per *lex causae* may, nevertheless, be admissible as per *lex fori*, unless it be that the *lex causae* would render such a document wholly null and void for absence of the stamp.[8]

As per Indian law, a contract need not necessarily be in writing for it to be deemed valid and binding.[9] On the contrary, if it could be inferable from the terms of the contract that the execution of a written contract is a condition precedent for it to become binding on the parties, then in the absence of a written contract, the same cannot be deemed to have come into force between the parties.[10] Issues relating to the competence of witnesses to depose or, as the case may be, any privilege claim are, again, for the *lex fori* to determine. So is the case with issues relating to burden of proof including standard of proof.[11]

As regards presumptions under the law of evidence, those that may be classified as irrebuttable presumptions such as, for example, consummation of a marriage where both the husband and the wife ostensibly live together for a length of time are a matter of substance and, as such, governed by the *lex causae*.[12] On the contrary, it is uncertain whether rebuttable presumptions of law such as the legitimacy of a child born out of wedlock[13] or the operation of estoppel[14] are matters of substance or procedure to be governed by the *lex causae* or the *lex fori* respectively.

PROCEDURAL MATTERS OF INTERLOCUTORY CHARACTER

As stated above at the beginning of this chapter, certain procedural matters, not all, of interlocutory character are governed by the *lex fori*. Courts in India, and generally municipal courts all over the world, may choose to issue temporary injunctions either unconditionally or on condition that may seem to them to be reasonable and proper,[15] or, if deemed necessary, appoint receivers, too, in cases that may warrant such a course.[16]

In all such cases, the location of the assets within jurisdiction invests the concerned court with competence, notwithstanding the fact that the concerned party is or is not domiciled, resident, or present within jurisdiction.

At any stage of a suit, the court may, either of its own motion or on the application of any defendant, order the plaintiff, for reasons to be recorded, to give within the time fixed by it security for the payment of all costs incurred or likely to be incurred by a defendant.[17] However, the order must be made in all cases in which it appears to the court that a sole plaintiff is, or (when there are more plaintiffs than one) that all the plaintiffs are residing out of India and that the plaintiff does not possess or none of the plaintiffs possesses any sufficient immovable property within India other than the property in suit.[18]

REMEDIAL MEASURES FOR ENFORCING A RIGHT

All remedial measures for enforcing a right, such as an injunction, or an order for specific performance or for rendition of accounts of profits, being matters of procedure, are governed by the *lex fori*.[19] A plaintiff's action for enforcing a right will not be defeated merely because the remedies available under the *lex fori* are greater or less than, or otherwise different from, those in the foreign country.[20] If, on the contrary, the *lex fori* machinery by way of remedies is so different from that of the foreign country as to make the right sought to be enforced under the *lex fori* essentially different, the action for enforcing such a right is bound to fail.[21]

Under the common law, there remains a distinction in respect of assessment of damages for any breach of a contract between remoteness of damage such as damages for pain and suffering which, as matters of substance, are governed by the *lex causae* and the quantification of damages, such as determining the money value for any particular item or items of losses including making of adequate provision for future or prospective losses which, as matters of procedure, are governed by the *lex fori*.[22]

Damages for breach of contract or tort or restitution for breach of contract if awarded by a foreign court in the case of a liquidated debt, in foreign currency, the same shall be converted into domestic currency at the date on which the court authorizes enforcement.[23]

Matters relating to the liability to pay interest and the rate of interest thereon payable upon a contractual debt are, as matters of substance, governed by the proper law of the contract. Also, the interest rate made payable is on the basis of the currency in question at the time of judgment.[24]

For all the propositions set out in the three preceding paragraphs in respect of damages, Indian courts may, hopefully, when occasions arise, adopt them *mutatis mutandis*.

The question of whether matters relating to set-off and counter claim put forth by the defendant could be tried together with the plaintiff's is one of procedure and, as such, for the *lex fori* to determine. But the question of whether a set-off has the effect of discharging or extinguishing the plaintiff's claim, wholely or partly, is a matter of substance for the *lex causae* to determine.[25]

On the question of working out priorities among claimants upon a limited fund, such as in the case of creditors in a bankruptcy, winding up of a company, or administration of the assets, testate or intestate, or it be working out priorities among claimants against a ship in admiralty proceedings, the *lex fori* is the governing law.

If, on the contrary, it is a question of working out priorities in cases of competing assignments of a debt, it is probably the *lex loci contractus* to which the assignment relates; and if it be one of working out priorities of claims against immovables, it is probably the *lex situs* (namely the law of the place where they are situated) that is the governing law. The English conflicts rules on questions of priorities among claimants upon a limited fund may, in the absence of comparable statutory directives or Indian cases on the subject, be deemed to be also part of Indian conflict of laws.[26]

On the subject of wagering or gaming contracts, Section 30 of the Indian Contract Act, 1872, lays down the rule that agreements by way of wager are void, and that no suit can be brought for recovering anything alleged to have been won on any wager, or entrusted to any person to abide by the result of any game or any uncertain event on which any wager is made. As the above rule of the Indian Contract Act declaring void wagering contracts in one of procedure, no Indian court can entertain an action brought before it for money won upon a wager in a foreign country, even though the wager is lawful as per its proper law.[27]

CONFLICT OF LAWS AND THE LAW OF LIMITATIONS

It is a well known principle of conflict of laws that when execution is sought of a foreign decree, the law of the forum (that is, *lex fori*) will govern. The law of limitation, even as the law of evidence, by and large, is assimilated to the law relating to procedure, and hence part of the *lex fori*. Where an execution is sought in India of a foreign decree, the Indian law of limitation will apply in order to determine whether the execution application is within time or not.[28] As matters of procedure and questions of limitation are governed by the *lex fori*, issuance of a decree and the execution of a pending decree are governed by the *lex fori*.[29]

It is a well established conflicts rule that so much of the law that affects only the remedy and procedure is governed by the law of the country where the action is brought to the exclusion of the foreign law. Therefore, the court of the forum will not apply the foreign law of limitation which affects the remedy only as it is a matter of mere procedure. If, on the other hand, a right is extinguished or a title is created, the foreign law of limitation in question will be applied, as it ceases to be a matter of procedure.[30]

MATTERS OF ENFORCEMENT

As earlier stated, all matters that are classified as process generally, including interlocutory orders or mesne profits and execution subsequent to judgment are determined by the *lex fori*. Therefore, the law to govern questions such as whether a judgment debtor can be arrested for non-payment of debt,[31] or whether his property could be attached to realize the debt[32] is for the *lex fori* to determine.

STAY OF PROCEEDINGS: UNDERLYING NORMS AND PRINCIPLES

General Observations

Section 10 of the Indian Code of Civil Procedure, 1908, deals with the subject of a grant of stay. An Indian court, according to the Code of Civil Procedure, will not proceed with the trial of a suit if the matter in issue is also directly and substantially in issue in a previously instituted suit between the same parties, or between parties under whom they or any of them claim litigating under the same title where such suit is pending in the same or any other court in India having jurisdiction to grant the relief claimed, or in any other court beyond the limits of India established or continued by the Central Government or having like jurisdiction, or before the Supreme Court. Such a grant of stay by an Indian court as per the said Section 10 of the Code of Civil Procedure is mandatory, not discretionary, as in England. In a catena of Indian cases, courts have pronounced that the phrase 'directly and substantially in issue' conveys only the meaning that the matter in issue in the two suits should directly and substantially be the same, and not that the decision be identical in the two suits, nor is it necessary that the matter in issue in the two suits be entirely the same or identical.[33]

From a legal standpoint, staying of an action by a court facilitates due determination of the rights of the parties to a suit. Besides, it also highlights the court's concern that the same matter should not be allowed to be agitated more than once. Issuance of an injunction by a court of law, in contradistinction to stay, restrains a party from bringing, or threatening to bring, proceeding before a foreign court after having initiated legal proceedings in a local court based on the same cause of action. A local court may, at its discretion, grant a stay sought by the defendant based on the ground that the parties have, by contract, agreed that the courts of a foreign country are to have jurisdiction over a dispute and that the institution by the plaintiff of an action in India constitutes a breach of that contract.

Stay of Action: *Forum Non Conveniens*

Stay of action by an Indian court on the ground of forum *non conveniens* acts as a deterrent to forum shopping resorted to by a plaintiff to seek and obtain unfairly a decree from a court of his choice, adversely to the interests of the defendant. The doctrine of *forum non conveniens*, based on which stay is granted by a local court at its discretion, only promotes justice; but, discouraging repeated litigation on the same question, paves the way to securing uniformity of decision which in turn would strengthen conflict of laws and judicial comity.

However, if the plaintiff insists that in the interests of justice he be allowed to proceed in the same court, the burden of proof lies with the plaintiff. He should clearly establish that he would be at a disadvantage if he is compelled to submit to a foreign court due to various reasons, such as that the quality of justice available to him in a foreign forum would be inferior,[34] that if he establishes clearly[35] that he may not get a fair hearing before the designated foreign court,[36] that his action may before the foreign court be time barred,[37] that the costs of the action in the foreign forum may be so prohibitive as to deprive him of the fruits of victory,[38] or that he may lose his case before the foreign court which may not be the case with the present court, and so on.[39]

Other Causes for Stay of Proceedings

(i) Abuse of the process of a court of forum where action is brought, or, as the case may be, any vexatious action with intent to harass the defendant may be a ground for staying the action instituted by the plaintiff.[40]

(ii) If the plaintiff institutes action simultaneously in two courts which are substantially identical, he may be put to his election and be required to discontinue the proceedings with which he elects not to proceed.[41]

(iii) If a plaintiff brings an action before an Indian court in breach of a provision in a contract vesting in a foreign court exclusive jurisdiction to entertain such disputes, the Indian court has power to stay the proceedings.[42] However, the Indian court may choose to stay the proceedings on the defendant's application only on the condition that the plaintiff establishes, to the satisfaction of the court, that it is just and proper to allow the action to proceed. The onus in that case lies heavily on the plaintiff to make out a strong case before being allowed to break his contract.[43]

As per the English conflict of laws, as seen through English cases, a stay will be denied if the foreign jurisdiction clause is in contravention of a statutory provision forbidding ouster of the jurisdiction of the court in certain type of case,[44] or where the term, or the entire contract, is void or otherwise unenforceable.[45] Again, a stay will not be forthcoming where the court on which the contract purports to confer jurisdiction is no longer the same as was contemplated by the parties at the time of the making of the contract.[46]

It is for the proper law of the contract to determine whether the foreign jurisdiction clause is exclusive or non-exclusive acquiesced in by the parties to the exercise of jurisdiction by those courts.[47] The burden of proof in respect of the clause purporting to confer exclusive jurisdiction over the dispute in question, or obliges the plaintiff to sue in a nominated court, is on the defendant who relies on it.[48] If on a proper construction the clause relating to conferment of jurisdiction is of non-exclusive in character, an application for stay will be determined in accordance with the general principles governing stays on the ground of *forum non conveniens*.[49]

Breach of Jurisdiction Clause: Applicable Norms

A court, in the exercise of its discretion to grant or refuse a stay of proceedings, (albeit the discretion should be exercised in favour of the grant of stay unless there is a compelling reason not to do so), will have to consider, *inter alia*, the following circumstances:

(a) in which country the evidence on the issues is situated, or more readily available;[50]

(b) in which country the witnesses are available;[51]

(c) whether it is prejudicial or not for the plaintiff to sue in a foreign country;[52]

(d) whether the plaintiff would or would not be inconvenienced by the suit being instituted in a foreign court;[53]

(e) whether the amount of the claim is relatively small as compared to the expenses of a trial in a foreign country.[54]

Although the considerations set out above for grant of stay may be similar to what may be required for the grant of stay on the ground of *forum non conveniens*, both require separate treatment; and, in fact, the circumstances enumerated here are stronger as compared to those required for the grant of stay on the ground of *forum non conveniens* and, accordingly, the grant of stay here becomes compelling.

Grant of Injunction to Restrain Foreign Proceedings: Underlying Juridical Criteria

In the matter of granting injunction against a respondent who has either commenced or threatens to commence proceedings in a foreign court, an Indian court, on application to it, should satisfy itself that it has jurisdictional competence to issue such injunction to restrain the respondent from continuing with or commencing such proceedings.[55] The court will then issue an injunction to restrain the respondent if, and only if, it is convinced that the conduct of the respondent is inequitable.[56]

The injunction issued by an Indian court is directed not at the foreign court in entertaining the action of the respondent, but at the respondent restraining him from taking the matter to a foreign court.[57] The Indian court issuing such an injunction does so with great caution.[58]

The jurisdictional competence of the Indian court over the respondent ought necessarily to be in accordance with well known principles of exercise of jurisdiction *in personam*. The grant of injunction must in the circumstances of the case be lawful. In case the respondent has his defence against so being restrained by an injunction issued by an Indian court, he is well within his right to seek of it by an application,[59] to have the service of process set aside.[60]

As has already been stated, the court exercising jurisdiction over the respondent should satisfy itself that, in the circumstances of the case, it is equitable so to do.[61] There is, at the same time, no fixed categories of cases in respect of grant of injunction restraining the respondent from taking the matter, already being agitated before an Indian court, to a foreign court; but the ground on which the injunction is granted to the respondent is that his action against the applicant is oppressive or vexatious.[62] Also, the court granting the injunction does so on being convinced that the jurisdiction of the domestic court is the natural forum for the litigation of the respondent's claim against the applicant.[63] Such injunctions are resorted to sparingly; but in case the applicant seeking injunction can establish that the foreign proceedings constitute a breach of an exclusive jurisdiction clause, the court may be persuaded to grant an injunction based solely on that ground.[64]

PROOF OF FOREIGN LAW

Foreign Law Needs Proof

Foreign law needs to be proved to the satisfaction of the court as does a question of fact.[65] Courts are not expected to take cognizance of a foreign law *suo motu*. It needs to be specifically pleaded by the party or parties relying upon it.[66] It must, as aforesaid, be proved to the satisfaction of the court like any other plea set up by the concerned party or parties.[67] The onus of proof of a foreign law, therefore, lies on the party who relies on it. There are plenty of English authorities in support of this proposition such as *Mostyn* v. *Fabrigas*,[68] *Lloyd* v. *Guibert*[69] and *Earl Nelson* v. *Lord Bridport*[70] and the like. However, a foreign law need not be proved if it is admitted.[71] Also, a court may, in exceptional circumstances and, of course, with the consent of the parties, decide a question of foreign law without proof.[72] Evidence may have to be given if a question arises as to how a discretion would be exercised under a foreign law. Of course, this is a corollary to and a consequence of equating a foreign law with a question of fact.[73]

Mode of Proof of Foreign Law

An Indian court is not expected to do research into foreign law or the concepts which have foreign origin.[74] A foreign law, meaning concept(s) which have foreign origin, requires to be proved in civil proceedings by properly qualified witnesses—that is to say, by persons who are suitably qualified to do so by virtue of their knowledge or experience and who are competent to give expert evidence on questions of law of any country, irrespective of whether they have actually practised or are entitled to practise law in the country concerned. If the expert's evidence is not contradicted, the court will normally accept it,[75] unless his evidence is obviously unreliable or extravagant.[76] Where the witnesses deposit into court materials as part of their evidence, the court is entitled to examine those materials.[77] In case there is conflict of evidence as to the interpretation of the materials so deposited into the court, the court is obliged to scrutinize them and form its own conclusion on them.[78]

Inasmuch as a foreign law or concepts of a foreign origin are deemed questions of fact, courts at common law may not generally rely upon a previous Indian decision bearing on such foreign law or concepts of foreign origin.[79]

NOTES

1. *Nella Thambi* v. *Ponnuswami*, (1907) 1. LR 2 MAD 406; *Ramanathan* v. *Somasundaram*, AIR 1964 Mad 527 (personal relief sought against respondents in the country within whose jurisdiction the debtors reside and carry on business); *R.A. Dickie & Co. (Agencies) Ltd.* v. *Municipal Board, Benares*, AIR 1956 CAL 216. See also English landmark cases such as *Chaplin* v. *Boys*, (1971) AC 356 p. 378–9, 381–3, and 392–5, (1969) 2 ALL E.R. 1085 at 1092–3, 1095–6, and 1104–6; *Leroux* v. *Brown*, (1852) 12 CB 801; *General Steam Navigation Co.* v. *Guillou*, (1843) 11M & W 877 p. 895, 152 ER 1119.

2. For example, matters relating to the service of originating process are deemed procedural and, as such, determinable by the *lex fori*. So is the case with execution processes of a judgment, such as attachment of property, arrest of the defendant, et cetera, which are governed by the *lex fori*.

3. Sections 96–112, Code of Civil Procedure.

4. Code of Civil Procedure, 1908, Order 29.

5. United Nations and other International Organizations Act, 1947.

6. Code of Civil Procedure, Order 27.

7. However, the *lex fori* may choose to recognize the legal personality arising under a foreign law: *Development Corporation Ltd.* v. *Metropolitan Police Commissioner*, (1991) 4 ALL ER 638, (1991) 1 WLR 1362 CA (Hindu Temple).

8. See note 2 supra.

9. See Indian Contract Act, 1872.

10. *J.K. Industries Ltd.* v. *Mohan Industries and Properties Pvt. Ltd.*, AIR 1992 DEL 305.

11. *Wiedemann* v. *Walpole*, (1891) 2QB 534. See, in this connection Ratanlal and Dhirajlal, *The Law of Evidence* (19th Edn.) (Delhi: LexisNexis Butterworths), 1999, p. 3.

12. *Gitika Bagechi* v. *Subhabrota Bagechi*, AIR 1966 CAL 246.

13. Section 112, The Indian Evidence Act, 1872.

14. Section 115, The Indian Evidence Act, 1872. See also for commentary on Sections 112 and 115, Ratanlal and Dhirajlal, *The Law of Evidence*, (1999), pp. 330–4 and pp. 363–94 respectively.

15. *A. Batcha Saheb* v. *Nariman K. Irani*, AIR 1958 MAD 491.

16. *Prabhat Mishra* v. *Jai Shankar Tripathi*, (1978) ALL LJ 672; *Dipakar Naskar* v. *Rotary Village*, (1978) 82 CAL WN 44.

17. Order 25 rule 1Code of Civil Procedure, 1908.

18. Order 25 rule 1, proviso, Code of Civil Procedure, 1908.

19. See The Specific Relief Act, 1963 and, in particular, Sections 36 and 37, injunctions, and Ch. II (Specific Performance and Rendition of Accounts of Profits.)

20. *Phrantzes* v. *Argenti*, (1960) 2 QB 19 p. 35, (1960) 1 ALL ER 778 p. 784.

21. *Phrantzes* v. *Argenti*, (1960) 2 QB 19 p. 35–6, (1960) 1 ALL ER 778 p. 784; Cf. *Shanaz* v. *Rizwan*, (1965) 1 QB 390, (1964) 2ALL ER 995. See Butterworths, p. 316.

22. See Kohnke v. Karger, (1951) 2 KB 670, (1951) 2 All ER 179; Chaplin v. Boys, (1969) 2 All Er 1085 at 1093, 1095-1096.

23. Ibid.

24. Ibid.

25. See (Indian) Code of Civil Procedure, 1908. On the question of whether a set-off or a counter claim would amount to a discharge of the defendant's obligation towards the plaintiff, is a matter of substance for which the Code of Civil Procedure, 1908, provides approach to a superior court in revision

subject, of course, to local law stipulations based on pecuniary limits to the exercise of jurisdiction.

26. See Convention on the Law Applicable to Contractual Obligations Art. 12, paras 1 and 2; *Noton* v. *Florence Land and Public Works Co.*, (1877) 7 Ch D. 332.

27. *Moulis* v. *Owen*, (1907) 1 KB 746 at 753, CA: *Hill* v. *William Hill (Park Lane) Ltd.*, (1949) AC 530 at 579 (1949) 2 All ER 452 at 481-482.

28. Section 11, Limitation Act, 1963. *Lakhpat Rai Sharma* v. *Atma Singh*, AIR 1962 PUNJ 228, (1961) 2 PUNJ 166; *Dhanji Arjan* v. *Ramji Mavji*, AIR (1950) KUTCH 58; *Nabibhai Vazirbhai* v. *Dayabhai Amulakh*, AIR (1916) BOM 200, 36 1C 269, (1916) ILR 400 BOM 504.

29. *Jhumarlal* v. *Tansukraj*, AIR 1957 ASSAM 127.

30. Re *Ar Ar Rm Ar Ramanathan Chettiar* v. *K M Ol M Somasundaram Chettiar*, AIR 1964 MAD 527, (1964) ILR 1 MAD 611, (1964) 2 MAD LJ 256; *R.A. Dickie & Co. (Agencies) Ltd.* v. *Municipal Board Benares*, AIR (1956) CAL 216.

31. Section 151, Code of Civil Procedure, 1908, as read with Order 21 rule 11A.

32. Section 151, Code of Civil Procedure, 1908, as read with Order 21 rules 12, 13.

33. *Arun General Industries Ltd.* v. *Rishabh Manufacturers Pvt. Ltd.*, AIR 1972 CAL 128; *Challapalli Sugars Ltd.* v. *Swadeshi Sugar Supply Pvt. Ltd.*, 1983 CAL 199; *Brylal and Co.* v. *Madhya Pradesh Electricity Board*, AIR 1975 CAL 69; *Shaw Wallace & Co. Ltd.* v. *Bholanath Mandanlal Sherawala*, AIR 1975 CAL 411, (1975) 79 CAL WN 830.

34. The Abidin Daver, (1984) AC 398, (1984) 1 All ER 470 HL; *Spiliada Maritime Corpn.* v. *Cansulex Ltd.*, (1987) AC 460 at 482-483, (1986) 3 All ER 843 at 850-860 HL; *Mudurogla Ltd.* v. *T C Ziraat Bankasi*, (1986) QB 1225, (1986) 3 All Er 682, CA.

35. Abidin Daver (1984) AC 398 at 410, (1984) 1 All Er 470 at 475

36. *Purcell* v. *Khayat*, (1987) Times 23 November.

37. *Spiliada Maritime Corpn.* v. *Consulex Ltd.*, (1987) AC 460 at 483-484, (1986) 3 All ER 843 at 860-861, HL; *The Pioneer, KH Enterprise* v. *Pioneer Container*, (1994) 2AC 324 at 347, (1944)) 2 All ER 250 at 267-268 P.C.

38. The Vishva Ajay (1989) 2 Lloyd's Rep. 558; *Agrafax Public Relations Ltd.* v. *United Scottish Society Inc.*, (1995) ILPR 753, CA; The Al Battani, (1993) 2 Lloyd's Rep. 219; *Roneleigh Ltd.* v. *MII Exports Inc.*, (1989) 1 WLR 619, CA.

39. *Banco Atlantico SA* v. *British Bank of Middle*, (1990) 2 Lloyd's Rep. 504, CA; *Brittania SS Insurance Association Ltd.* v. *Ausonia Assicurazioni SPA*, (1984) 2 Lloyd's Rep. 98, CA.

40. The Christiansborg, (1885) 10 PD 141, CA; Re Norton's Settlement, *Norton* v. *Norton*, (1908) 1 Ch. 471, CA.

41. See Section 10, Code of Civil Procedure, 1908.

42. Section 151, Code of Civil Procedure, 1908.

43. *Union of India* v. *Navigation Maritime Bulgare*, AIR 1973 Cal 526; *Lakshmi Narayan Ramniwas* v. *Mannesman Export Gmb H*, AIR 1960 CAL 733.

44. The Hollandia, (1983) 1 AC 565, (1982) 3 All ER 1141, HL.

45. Re Jogia (1988) 2 All ER 328 at 335, (1988) 1 WLR 484 at 492; The Emre II (1989) 2 Lloyd's Rep. 183; *Mackender* v. *Feldia AG*, (1967) 2 QB 590, (1966) 3 All ER 847.

46. *Carvalho* v. *Hull Blyth (Angola) Ltd.*, (1979) 3 All ER 280, (1979) 1 WLR 1228, CA

47. See Chapter V dealing with contracts and, in particular, the common law doctrine of the proper law of a contract.

48. *Evans Marshall & Co.* v. *Bertola SA*, (1973) 1 WLR 349 at 361, (1973) 1 All ER 992.

49. *DSV Silo-und Verwaltungsgesellschaft mb H.* v. *Owners of the Sennar*, The Sennar (No. 2) (1973) All ER 992; *Evans Marshall & Co* v. *Bertola SA*, (1973) 1 WLR 349 at 361.

50. See section 'Stay of Proceedings: *Forum non Conveniens*'.

51. Black Sea SS UL Lastochkina Odessa, *USSR* v. *Union of India*, AIR 1976 AP 103, (1975) 2 Andh WR 339; *B.R. Herman and Mohatto (India) Pvt. Ltd.* v. *Swedish East India Co. Ltd.*, AIR 1967 Cal 24, (1960) ILR 2 Cal 85; *Lakshminarain Ramniwas* v. *N.V. Vereenigde Scheepraartmaatschappij*, AIR 1960 Cal 45, (1960) 64 Cal WN 269.

52. *B R Herman and Mohatto (India) Pvt. Ltd.* v. *Swedish East India Co. Ltd.*, AIR 1967 Cal 24, (1960) ILR 2 Cal WN 269.

53. Far East SS Line, Valdivostok, *USSR* v. *Union of India*, AIR 1973 Mad 169, (1972) 2 Mad LJ 578.

54. Black Sea SS UL Lastochkina Odessa, *USSR* v. *Union of India*, AIR 1976 AP 103, (1975) ILR AP 805, (1975) 2 Andh WR 339; Far East SS Line, Valdivostok, *USSR* v. *Union of India*, AIR 1973 Mad 169, (1972 2 Mad LJ 578.

55. See Chapter III dealing with the subject 'The Consecutive Stages of Conflict of Laws' in which the issue of judicial jurisdiction is dealt with elaborately.

56. *Nath Bank Ltd.* v. *Andhar Manick Tea Co. Ltd.*, AIR 1960 CAL779, (1960) CAL WN 161, (1960) Comp. Cas 306.

57. *Settlement Corpn.* v. *Hochshild*, (1966) Ch. 10, (1965) 3 All Er 486; *Société Nationale Industrielle Aérospatiale* v. *Lee Kui Jak*, (1987) AC 871, (1987) 3 ALL ER 510, PC: *British Airways Board* v. *Laker Airways Ltd.*, (1985) AC 58

(1984) 3 All ER 39, HL; *Castanho* v. *Brown and Root (UK) Ltd.*, (1981) AC 557, (181) 1 All ER 143, H.L.

58. See note 55 supra.

59. Order 39 rule 4, Code of Civil Procedure, 1908.

60. Ibid.

61. Nath Bank Ltd., ibid.

62. Ibid.

63. *Société Nationale Industrielle Aérospatielle* v. *Lee Kui Jak*, (1987) AC 871, (1987) 3 All ER 510 PC.

64. *Sohio Supply Co.* v. *Gatoil (United States of America) Inc.*, (1989) 1 Lloyd's Rep. 588, CA; *Continental Bank NA* v. *Aeakos Cia Naviera SA.*, (1944) 2 All ER 540, (1994) 1 WLr 588, CA. See further *Aggeliki Charis Compania Maritima SA* v. *Pagnan SPA*, The Angelic Grace (1995) 1 Lloyd's Rep. 87, CA Cf. *British Airways Board* v. *Laker Airways Ltd.*, (1985) AC 58, (1984) 3 All ER 39, HL; Cf. *Doherty* v. *Allman*, (1878) 3 App Cas 709.

65. *Khoday Gangadara Sah* v. *A. Swaminadha Mudali*, AIR 1926 Mad. 218 at 219, 92 1C 112, (1925) 22 MAD LW 679.

66. Ibid.

67. Section 103, The Indian Evidence Act, 1872.

68. (1774) 1 COWP 161

69. (1865) LR 1 QB 115, p. 129

70. (1845) 8 BEAV 527, 50 ER 215

71. *Moulis* v. *Owen*, (1907) 1 KB 746, CA.

72. *Beatty* v. *Beatty*, (1924) 1 KB 807 at 814–15; *Jabbour* v. *Custodian of Absentee's Property of State of Israel*, (1954) 1 ALL ER 145 at 153, (1954) 1 WLR 139 p. 147–8.

73. *National Mutual Holdings Pty Ltd.* v. *Sentry Corn*, (1889) 87 ALR 539. See in this connection, Govindaraj, *Conflict of Laws*, Vol. 10 (New Delhi: LexisNexis Butterworths, 2001), p. 328.

74. *Saklat* v. *Bella*, AIR 1925 PC 298, (1926) 28 BOM LR161.

75. *Buerger* v. *New York Life Assurance Co.*, (1927) 96 LJ KB 930 at 940, CA; *Sharif* v. *Azad*, (1967) 1 Qb 605 at 616, (1966) 3 all ER 785 at 788; *Rossano* v. *Manufacturers' Life Insurance Co. Ltd.*, (1963) 2 QB 352 at 381, (1962) 2 All ER 214 at 231.

76. *Buerger* v. *New York Life Assurance Co.*, (1927) 96 LJ KB 930 at 941.

77. *Earl Nelson* v. *Lord Bridport*, (1845) 8 Beav 527 at 541, 50ER 215; *Lazard Bros & Co.* v. *Midland Bank Ltd.*, (1933) AC 289 at 298, HL.

78. *Law Society of India* v. *Fertilizers and Chemicals Travancore Ltd.*, AIR 1994 KER 308.

79. *Jamshed A. Irani* v. *Banu J. Irani*, AIR (1966) BOM LR.798.

14

Hague Conventions on Private International Law

An Appraisal

INTRODUCTION

The world has to graciously acknowledge the contribution the Hague Conference on Private International Law has hitherto made and continues to make in its endeavour to obtain from the world community approval and acceptance of the outcome of its efforts to unify rules of conflict of laws. The task undertaken by the conference is challenging, but it is to be pursued relentlessly till the goal it has set for itself, namely unifying rules of conflict of laws, is fully accomplished. It augurs well for the conference that India, a vast subcontinent in Asia with a population of more than a billion, has become an active member of the Hague Conference. That the Government of India had acceded to four of the thirty nine conventions, namely Abolishing the Requirement of Legalisation for Foreign Public Documents, 1961, Service Abroad in Civil or Commercial Matters, 1965, Taking of Evidence Abroad in Civil or Commercial matters, 1970, and Protection of Children and Co-operation in Respect of Inter-country Adoption, 1993, is in itself gratifying. The fact that the United States, the United Kingdom, and Canada, among others, are parties to the Hague Convention of Service Abroad of Judicial and Extrajudicial Documents on Civil or Commercial Matters is a feather in the cap of the Hague Conference. With this prefatory note, a few of the vital conventions whose aim is to secure the interests of women and children and thereby enhance their welfare, call for scrutiny.

Justice Chandrachud, as he then was, in the leading case of *Smt. Satya* v. *Teja Singh*[1] passionately urged that the Indian Parliament may consider enacting a law akin to the Recognition of Divorces and Legal Separations Act, 1971, passed by the British Parliament (which has since been repealed by the Family Law Act, 1986, which contains in Part II provisions similar to the 1971 Act), and simultaneously enter into an agreement with the British Government to facilitate reciprocal enforcement of matrimonial decrees between the two countries, as envisaged in Section 44-A of the Indian Code of Civil Procedure, 1908. He further suggested that, in this regard, the Hague Convention on the Recognition of Divorces and Legal Separations, 1970, may serve as a model with a view to obviate the confusion caused by the differing systems of conflict of laws.

RECOGNITION OF DECREES OF DIVORCES AND JUDICIAL SEPARATION AND MAINTENANCE OBLIGATIONS

The conventions are laudable considering that they incorporate concepts aimed at accommodating countries governed by systems of law that seemingly defy unification, such as the common law countries which have adopted domicile as the test and countries on the continent of Europe which have adopted nationality as the test to govern personal law. The conventions, therefore, offer the concept of 'habitual residence' as a compromise between the concepts of domicile and nationality.

Undoubtedly the Hague Convention on the Recognition of Divorces and Legal Separations, 1970, as suggested by Justice Chandrachud, may, by and large, serve as a model. But there are certain clauses in the convention which are disturbing and which may dissuade states from ratifying or, as the case may be, acceding to it. For example, clause (a) of paragraph 2 of Article 6 reads as follows: 'The recognition of a divorce or legal separation shall not be refused—because the internal law of the state in which such recognition is sought would not allow divorce or, as the case may be, legal separation upon the same facts.' We may take, for example, the ground of irretrievable breakdown of the marriage based on which foreign courts may grant a decree of divorce. So long as the Indian Parliament does not choose to amend the personal laws of the various religious communities inhabiting the subcontinent, courts in India may not be persuaded to recognize and give effect to foreign decrees of divorce or, as the case may be, legal separation based on that ground. Much worse is clause (b) of paragraph 2 of Article 6 which reads: 'The recognition of a divorce or legal separation shall not be refused—because a law was applied other than that applicable under the rules of private international law of that state.' This clause, in particular, runs counter to the verdict of the Supreme Court of India in *Y. Narasimha Rao* v. *Y. Venkatalakshmi*.[2] Therein, Justice Sawant, speaking for the Supreme Court, turned down a decree of divorce granted by a court in New Mexico on an application made to it by the husband seeking divorce from his Indian wife, based on the so-called domiciliary status that he acquired by a three months residence in New Mexico. In the course of the judgment, after having made a fervent appeal to the Parliament of India to come forward with an enactment incorporating relevant rules of private international law in this area, the learned judge made the following significant observation which constitutes the pivotal ratio, if we may say so, leading to the decision in the case:

'The jurisdiction assumed by the foreign court as well as the grounds on which the relief is granted must be in accordance with the matrimonial law (namely Hindu law) under which the parties are married.'

The exceptions to the above rule may be the following:

(a) where the matrimonial action is filed in the forum where the respondent is domiciled or habitually and permanently resides and the relief is granted on a ground available in the matrimonial law under which the parties are married;

(b) where the respondent voluntarily and effectively submits to the jurisdiction of the forum as discussed above and contests the claim which is based on a ground available under the matrimonial law under which the parties are married; and

(c) where the respondent consents to the grant of relief *although the jurisdiction of the forum is not in accordance with the provisions of the matrimonial law of the parties* [emphasis added].

As for the Convention on the Law Applicable to Maintenance Obligations, concluded on 2 October 1973, not much need be said except that the norms set down therein in respect of maintenance obligations are helpful and efficacious.

The Convention on the Recognition and Enforcement of Decisions Relating to Maintenance Obligations, 1973, is cast in a mould making it acceptable to states which may be considering whether or not to ratify or accede to it. However, it is the considered opinion of lawyers and academics that the convention may have to be supplemented by appropriate administrative measures designed to effectuate enforcement processes. In this regard, it sounds helpful to take note of the suggestions and recommendations of the International Academy of Matrimonial Lawyers (IAML) which has been accorded the status of an Observer-cum-Special Commission on Maintenance Obligations, which are set out in its letter dated 2 April 2003.[3] The following are the measures recommended by the IAML:

> We need to establish and enforce child support and other family maintenance obligations through appropriate administrative proceedings, which are speedy, efficient, and at little or no cost to the obligee. As the present state of the law does not facilitate and promote the stated objective, the IAML suggests the conclusion of a new convention, which may contain detailed provisions for coordinating the efforts of those on the judicial side and of those on the administrative side to have support and maintenance orders established and enforced as efficiently and cost effectively as possible.

The above recommendations of the IAML, it is no exaggeration to say, are articulate, pragmatic, prudent, and wholesome. We may add that, over and above all these, it is but appropriate to enter into bilateral arrangements with countries so as to mutually facilitate enforcement of maintenance/alimony orders given by courts.

CHILD CUSTODY AND CHILD ABDUCTION

Introduction

Under chapter 'Law Relating to Children',[4] discussion was devoted exclusively to a case-oriented study of two aspects of welfare of children, namely custody and guardianship. The present one is in the nature of a prelude to a study of the Hague Convention on the Civil Aspects of International Child Abduction, 1980, and the feasibility of India becoming a party to it. Needless to say, child custody and child abduction are to be given the highest priority in the study of conflict of laws devoted to Law of Persons. It, in fact, ranks much above the subject of marriage and matrimonial causes which has received an exhaustive treatment in Chapter 7 of the present work. One has to appreciate the helplessness of the child when the parents get separated from each other on dissolution of their marriage or judicial separation. It gets further aggravated when the parents, living in two different countries, approach courts in their respective countries and obtain conflicting custody orders, resulting in the child being uprooted from its habitual residence. While granting child custody orders, courts make it a point to pass further orders vesting the right of custody in one spouse and the right to visit in the other. This the courts do for the welfare of the child which is for them of paramount consideration. As earlier stated, in *habeas corpus* petitions for child custody, high courts, as *parens patriae*, exercise their inherent jurisdiction in contradistinction to statutorily conferred jurisdiction. This is highlighted by the Kerala High Court in the leading case of *Marggarate* v. *Chacko*.[5]

Before turning our attention to Indian cases where custodial orders of courts are, in the main, based on one and only criterion, namely the welfare of the child which courts deem to be of paramount consideration, it serves as prerequisite to highlight pronouncements of courts in England and other countries as what serves as the yardstick to measure the concept of the welfare of the child.

The Privy Council in England in the oft quoted dictum that it employed relating to proceedings on child custody issue emphasizes that the welfare and happiness of the infant is of paramount consideration and that an order of a foreign court as to the child's custody ought to receive due weight *as only one of the facts to be taken into consideration* [emphasis added]. The meaning and content of the welfare of the child is brought out in bold relief by Lindley, L.J., of the Chancery Division in England in McGrath (Infants), Re[6] and by Hardy Boys, J., of the New Zealand court in *Walker* v. *Walker and Harrison*.[7] According to Lindley, L.J. '... the welfare of the child is not to be measured by money alone nor by physical comfort only. The word 'welfare' must be taken in its widest sense. The moral and religious welfare must be considered as well as its physical well-being nor can the ties of affection be disregarded.'[8]

Hardy Boys, J., of the New Zealand court by way of defining the welfare of the child observed:

Welfare is an all-encompassing word. It includes material welfare, both in the sense of adequacy of resources to provide a pleasant home and a comfortable standard of living and in the sense of an adequacy of care to ensure that good health and due personal pride are maintained. However, while material considerations have their place they are secondary matters. *More important are the stability and the security, the loving and the understanding care and guidance, the warm and compassionate relationships, that are essential for the full development of the child's own character, personality and talents* [emphasis added].

In the leading case *Dhanwanti Joshi* v. *Madhav Unde*,[9] the Supreme Court of India quoted with approval the decision of the Privy Council in *Mckee* v. *Mckee* and the ratio employed therein, namely *that in proceedings relating to child custody the welfare and happiness of the infant is of paramount consideration and that an order of a foreign court as to the child's custody ought to receive due weight as only one of the facts to be taken into account* [emphasis added]. It (namely the Supreme Court) went on to say that accordingly, it is the duty of the court to form an independent judgment as to the merits of the matter in respect of the welfare of the child, uninfluenced by any order of a foreign court as to custody which, of course, may have to receive due weight as the circumstances of the case may warrant.

In yet another case, namely *Santa Sharma, Appellant* v. *Sushil Sharma, Respondent*,[10] the Supreme Court held that a decree as to custody of minor children of a foreign court (in this case of an American Court), though a relevant factor, cannot override the consideration of the welfare of the minor children. In this connection, the court quoted with approval the Privy Council's dictum in *Mckee* v. *Mckee*, namely 'comity of courts demanded not its enforcement, but its grave consideration'. The court drew our attention to the fact that the House of Lords in England endorsed the above mentioned dictum of the Privy Counicil in *J.* v. *C.*[11] The same happens to be the view of courts in the United States[12] and Australia.[13]

We may, here, make a passing reference to two other decisions of the Supreme Court adverted to earlier, namely *Elizabeth Dinshaw (Mrs)* v. *Arvand M. Dinshaw and Another* and *Surinder Kaur Sandhu* v. *Harbax Singh Sandhu*,[14] in both of which the Supreme Court gave the custody of a minor to the mother in preference to the father based on the norm of the welfare of the child, even though Section 6 of the Hindu Minority and Guardianship Act, 1956, names the father as the natural guardian of a minor son. In this connection, we may draw the attention of the reader to two recent decisions of the Supreme Court and a decision of the High Court of Delhi—*Sahiba Ali* v. *State of Maharashtra*,[15] *Kumar V. Jagirdar* v. *Chethana Ramatheertha*,[16] and *Paul* v. *State of NCT of Delhi*[17]—which endorse the child's welfare as crucial to determining the choice of a guardian for a child. However, the Supreme Court, in a recent case, observed that the principle of vesting in the mother, the guardianship of a minor need not necessarily be considered an inflexible rule.

Reverting, once again, to Dhanwanti Joshi's case, the Supreme Court drew our attention to the state of the law as respects countries not parties to the Hague Convention on Civil Aspects of International Child Abduction, 1980. While endorsing the view held by the Court of appeal in England in L., Re[18] that the ruling of the Privy Council in *Mckee* v. *Mckee* still holds, the Supreme Court significantly observed that the requested state in child custody matters may have to form an independent judgment on the merits of the case based, of course, on the welfare of the child, which may in certain circumstances necessitate non-compliance with the order of a foreign court as to custody.

The Court further observed that whether to adopt a summary inquiry or an elaborate inquiry is left to the discretion of the court in the requested state. The Court may, depending on the circumstances of the case, choose to adopt a summary inquiry and return custody to the country from which the child was removed in the absence of proof of harmful consequences to the child by such return. It may, on the contrary, have recourse to an elaborate inquiry on merits and come to the conclusion of not returning the child to its native country having regard to the other facts and circumstances of the case, taking into consideration also the time factor since its removal, that may militate against the return of the child to its habitual residence. It is open to the court of the requested state to have recourse to either a summary inquiry or, in the alternative, an elaborate inquiry that would enable it to go into the merits of the case in response to a foreign custody order. This reflects the pre-1980 Hague Convention attitude or that of non-parties' attitude to the convention. The above option, admittedly, is not open to countries which choose to become parties to the convention. This issue will receive due consideration when we take up the topic of whether India should embrace the 1980 Hague Convention.

Whether India Should Embrace the 1980 Hague Convention on the Civil Aspects of International Child Abduction

Bearing in mind that a healthy child custody promotes the welfare of the child and that abduction disrupts and dislodges the child from its habitual residence, unless it be that any such removal is conducive to and in the interests of the child, and recalling to our mind the philosophy behind the concept of child welfare, devised and promoted by the judiciary that aroused legislators and world leaders to translate the said concept into action in the shape of municipal legislations and international instruments such as the Geneva Declaration of the Rights of the Child, 1924, and the Declaration of the Rights of Child adopted by the General Assembly of the United Nations on 20 November, 1959, the present 1980 Hague Convention on Child Abduction is to be evaluated.

To the reader, that this prefatory note itself sounds like a preamble and that it may render the preamble appended to the convention otiose, is misconceived. On the contrary, the above prefatory note only signifies the philosophy behind the baneful act of child abduction and the need to eradicate it, whereas the preamble to the convention is the expounded philosophy's translation into action.

The aim and objective of the convention, as set out in the Preamble, is '... to protect children internationally from the harmful effects of their wrongful removal or retention and to establish procedures to ensure their prompt return to the state of their habitual residence, as well as to secure protection for rights of access.' The said objective stems from the primordial consideration that 'the interests of children are of paramount importance in matters relating to their custody.'

Child custody and child abduction are antithetical or antagonistic to each other. While child custody promotes the welfare of the child if such custody is held by parents, by either one of them or, by a guardian duly appointed by a court of law, abduction disrupts or dislodges the child from its habitual residence, unless it be conclusively proved to the satisfaction of the concerned court of the requested state that the removal is in the child's best interests. Justifiably, the Hague Convention on the Civil Aspects of International Child Abduction, 1980, considers removal or retention of a child wrongful, provided that at the time of such removal or retention the child was in the lawful custody of either a natural or a legally authorized guardian or guardians and that the custodial right had actually been exercised at the time of the removal. Thus, Article 3 of the Convention contains the three elements that constitute abduction, namely the actual exercise of custodial right of the minor child by the natural guardian or guardians or by the legal guardian, the removal of the minor child from its habitual residence without the consent of such guardian or guardians, and the consequent breach of rights of custody that had taken place by such removal or retention, whether such rights of custody be the outcome of a judicial or administrative decision, or it be the outcome of the operation of law.

Article 12 of the convention lays down the condition or conditions as between the parties to the convention for the making of a request for the return of the minor child and the corresponding obligation on the part of the judicial or administrative authority of the requested state to return the minor child to the requesting state. It runs thus:

> If the request for the return of the minor child be made within a year, or even if it be beyond the period of one year, unless it be that the child has become assimilated in its new environment, the minor child has to be returned to the requesting state. The requested state may, however, stay the proceedings or dismiss the application for the return of the child, if the said authority has reason to believe that the child has been removed from the jurisdictional control of the requested state.

Article 13 of the convention which commences with a *non obstante* clause is in the nature of an exception to Article 12. The exceptions are as set out below:

(i) it would be deemed a removal only if the person, institution, or other body entrusted with the custody of the child were actually exercising the right of custody or, as the case may be, did not consent to or acquiesce in the removal or retention;

(ii) that the restoration of the custody of the minor child would expose it to physical or psychological harm or otherwise place the child in an intolerable situation; and

(iii) that the obligation to return the custody of the minor child on the part of the judicial or administrative authority no longer exists if in case the child objects to its being returned and the authority is satisfied that the child, based on age or maturity, is capable of exercising its option.

There are two exceptions to Article 12 of the convention, namely Articles 16 and 20 respectively. They are as under:

Article 16 of the convention denies to the judicial or administrative authority of the requested state in child custody matters the right to decide on the merits of the case in holding a detailed inquiry before it has been determined that the child is not to be returned under this convention or that the application under this convention has been inordinately delayed.

This exception negates the ruling of the Privy Council in *Mckee* v. *Mckee* and the ratio employed therein which was embraced by the Supreme Court of India, as aforesaid, in the two leading cases, namely Dhanwanti Joshi's case and Santa Sharma's case. The ratio, which no longer holds good in view of Article 16 of the convention, is set out below, namely that in proceedings relating to child custody, the welfare and happiness of the infant is of paramount consideration and that an order of the foreign court as to the child's custody ought to receive due weight as only one of the facts to be taken into consideration [emphasis added]. Accordingly, it is the duty of the court to form an independent judgment as to the merits of the matter in respect of the welfare of the child, uninfluenced by any order of a foreign court as to custody which, admittedly, may have to receive due weight as the circumstances of the case may warrant, as the Supreme Court ratiocinated in Dhanwanti Joshi's case. The Supreme Court in Santa Sharma's case further clarified its attitude to a custody order passed by a foreign court (here, in this case, a custodial order of an American court), namely that though it (that is, the custodial order) may serve as a relevant factor, it cannot override consideration relating to the welfare of the child. The court quoted with approval the Privy Council's dictum in *Mckee* v. *Mckee*, namely 'comity of courts demanded not its enforcement, but its grave consideration'.

Article 20 of the convention is yet another exception to Article 12 mandating return of custody, namely that it (that is, Article 20) permits refusal on the part of the requested state to return the child to the requesting state if such return would violate any fundamental principle relating to the protection of human rights and fundamental freedoms of that state.

It is of interest to note that the convention fixes sixteen as the age limit for a minor child. This age limit, however, is to be construed contextually in the sense that if the age limit for a minor child is, as is the case with India, eighteen, that accordingly is to be deemed the limit.

In the light of the foregoing discussion, adoption of or accession to the Hague Convention on the Civil Aspects of International Child Abduction, 1908, seems appropriate. Besides, we may also consider the option of entering into suitable bilateral agreements with the Commonwealth countries and also others, modelled on the UK–Pakistan Protocol of 17 January 2003.

The Hague Convention on Protection of Children and Cooperation in Respect of Inter-Country Adoption, 1993

Inter-Country Adoptions: Strategies for Eliminating Misuse[19]

The inter-country or transnational adoption process is highly complicated in the sense that it involves sensitive issues which are set out below:

(i) ensuring that the child is not given away in adoption in the country of origin based on monetary or other extraneous considerations;

(ii) ascertaining the qualifications and the fitness of the adoptive parents as well as seeking information as to whether the law of the receiving state permits such adoption; and

(iii) securing the overall interests of the child to be adopted by conforming to the spirit of the various international conventions touching and concerning the welfare of the child and, in particular, the norms and standards contained in Article 1 of the Convention on Protection of Children and Cooperation in Respect of Inter-Country Adoption, 1993 and Article 21 of the convention on the Rights of the Child of 20 November, 1989.

Over and above the norms and standards set out above, inter-country adoptions involve issues such as migration, citizenship, passport, visa, et cetera.

Hitherto, inter-country adoptions, in the absence of a law on the subject, were based on the Guardians and Wards Act, 1890, albeit improvised or contrived. Under that format, the adoptive parent/parents are the appointed guardians by the district court or family courts, after they comply with all the required formalities and in their capacity as duly appointed guardians, are allowed to take the child to the receiving state for adoption there. Now that India has become a party to the Hague Convention on Inter-Country Adoption, 1993, with effect from 1 October 2003, legislation is required incorporating the provisions of the Convention so as to make it part of the law of the land.

It is interesting, in this connection, to take note of the comprehensive guidelines set out by the Supreme Court of India in the leading case, *Lakshmi Kant Pandey, Petitioner* v. *Union of India, Respondent*, in respect of inter-country adoptions. In the absence of legislation on the subject, the guidelines spelt out by the Supreme Court in the abovementioned case, by virtue of Article 141 of the Constitution of India, will have the force of law. Based upon the Supreme Court's guidelines in Lakshmi Kant Pandey's case and in keeping with the letter and spirit of the Hague Convention on Protection of Children and Cooperation in Respect of Inter-Country Adoption, 1993, the Ministry of Social Welfare, Government of India, issued in the year 1995 revised guidelines on the subject. It is hoped that the Union Parliament will, at the earliest, bring out a comprehensive legislation on the subject of inter-country adoptions in keeping with the guidelines of the Supreme Court and the Revised Guidelines of the Ministry of Social Welfare, Government of India. Needless to say, parliamentary enactment on the subject of inter-country adoptions will render recourse to the Guardians and Wards Act, 1890, on the subject otiose. Besides, it has to be secular and so designed as to cater to the needs of all the communities in India.

The purported legislation on the subject of inter-country adoptions may have to be on the following lines:[20]

(i) That the adoption taking place here in India shall serve the best interests of the child as contemplated in the 1993 Hague Convention and other United Nations conventions.

(ii) The norm of the 'best interests of the child' shall best be served if such inter-country adoption results in a total integration of the child into the adoptive family.

(iii) The said legislation shall incorporate the procedural and substantive requirements of Articles 4 and 5 of the convention.

(iv) The enactment shall provide for the establishment of a central authority such as a Central Adoption Resource Agency (that is, CARA) as contemplated in the Revised Guidelines of the Ministry of Social Welfare, Government of India. As only one such authority at the seat of the Government of India may not be able to cope with the entire work involved in inter-country adoptions that take place in various parts of the country, there needs to be established such authorities in all the States and the Union Territories that constitute the Union of India.

(v) The composition of the CARA shall, as set out in the Revised Guidelines, be composed of a chairman and six other members, three of whom shall be women.

(vi) The contemplated legislation shall also incorporate the procedural requirements embodied in Articles 14 to 22 of the Hague Convention which are, at present, contained in the Revised Guidelines.

(vii) The proposed legislation shall incorporate penal provisions for countering any abuse of the adoption process such as abduction, sale of, or traffic in, children as visualized in Article (1)(b) of the Convention, and also make it obligatory for other contracting states through bilateral agreements.

(viii) As the Revised Guidelines cannot be a substitute for a statute on the subject, it is urged that a law be forthwith enacted on the above lines.

THE LAW RELATING TO SUCCESSION

General Rules of Conflict of Laws

Succession is of two kinds, namely intestate and testate. By intestate succession we mean succession to the property by the heirs of the deceased in the absence of a will or testament. By testamentary succession we mean succession to the property by the heirs of the deceased in accordance with the will or testament that the deceased had made prior to his death. The testator is at liberty to make subsequent wills superseding the earlier ones. Besides, he can, if he so chooses, make codicils which are in the nature of supplementaries or additions to a will, explaining, modifying, adding to, subtracting from, qualifying, altering, restraining, or revoking provisions in a will.[21] A will can be challenged before a court of law on grounds of lack of formal validity or, as the case may be, lack of substantive or essential validity. On the top of it all, it is a prerequisite that the testator possesses necessary capacity under the law to make a will or, so to say, that he enjoys under the law testamentary capacity.

Succession to movables, according to the common law, is governed by the *lex domicilii* of the testator. This principle is based upon the doctrine *mobilia sequunter personam* (namely movables follow the law of the person).[22] On the other hand, immovables are governed by the *lex situs* (namely the law of the place where the property is situated). This principle is based upon the doctrine *immobilia situm sequunter* (namely immovable things that follow their site or position are governed by the law of the place where they are fixed).[23]

As has been stated earlier, a testamentary disposition should fulfill requisite conditions under the law for its formal validity as well as for its substantive or essential validity. So far as the formal validity is concerned, prior to the passing of the Indian Succession Act, 1925, in India and the Wills Act of 1861 in England, the governing law was the *lex domicilii* at the time of testator's death both in India and in England. As for the substantive or essential validity of the instrument, the governing law as of now is the *lex domicilii* in respect of movables and *lex situs* in respect of immovables.

The present position with respect to the formal validity of a testamentary disposition is that it is governed by the *lex domcilii* of the testator at the time of making of the instrument or at the time of his death, as also by the *lex actus* (that is, the law of the place where the legal act takes place). In the United States, too, it is the same as in England.

Formal Validity under the Hague Convention on the Conflicts of Laws Relating to the Form of Testamentary Disposition

The convention on the conflict of laws relating to the Form of Testamentary Disposition, 1961, has liberalized and expanded the legal system that governs the form of a testamentary disposition, thus making it attractive for states to seriously consider becoming parties to it.

Article 1 of the convention validates testamentary dispositions as to form if they conform to one or other of the following laws:

(a) of the place where the testator made it, or

(b) of a nationality possessed by the testator, either at the time when he made the disposition, or at the time of his death, or

(c) of a place in which the testator had his domicile either at the time when he made the disposition, or at the time of his death, or

(d) of the place in which the testator had his habitual residence either at the time when he made the disposition, or at the time of his death, or

(e) so far as immovables are concerned, of the place where they are situated.

The world is moving fast and flexibility is the order of the day. India should not be found wanting as compared to other common law countries like the United Kingdom, the United States, Canada, Australia, and others, and should promptly enact a statute so as to facilitate admission to probate as to the form of testamentary dispositions. Bearing in mind this objective, we need to look into the salient features of the convention and ponder over them before we make up our mind whether or not India should become a party to it. They are as under:

(a) Article 1 offers various options relating to the formal validity of testamentary dispositions.

(b) Article 3 of the convention clarifies that the convention rules are *sui generis* and are in no way a hindrance to any other rules of law, present or future, the contracting states may choose to adopt as between them relating to the form of testamentary disposition.

(c) Article 6 declares that the rules of conflicts laid down in the convention are independent of any requirement as to reciprocity.

(d) Article 7 confers on states parties to the Convention the right to repudiate any of the applicable laws under the Convention on the ground of infringement of '*ordre public*' (that is, public order).

(e) Article 9 allows each contracting state to reserve the right, in derogation of Article 1, to determine in accordance with the *lex fori* the place where the testator had his domicile.

(f) Article 10 confers the right to contracting states not to recognize testamentary dispositions made orally, save in exceptional circumstances by one of its nationals possessing no other nationality.

(g) Article 11 confers upon states, parties to the Convention, the right to make reservation not to recognize, by virtue of provision of its own law relating thereto, forms of testamentary dispositions made abroad on conditions set out therein. However, the said reservation shall be deemed to be effective only in respect of property situated in the states making the reservation.

A thoughtful study of the provisions highlighted above would lead one to conclude that the Government of India may, without hesitation, become a party to the 1961 Hague Convention on the Conflicts of Laws Relating to the Form of Testamentary Dispositions.

The Hague Convention on the Law Applicable to Succession to the Estates of Deceased Persons

In the matter of succession to the estates of the deceased, testate or intestate, the common law world to which belong, namely the United Kingdom, the United States, and Commonwealth countries such as, *inter alia*, India, Canada, and the Commonwealth of Australia, have from time immemorial been following what is known as the scission system. Under this system, property is classified into two categories, namely movable and immovable, succession to the former being governed by *lex domicilii* and to the latter by *lex situs*. As opposed to the common law system of succession to property, countries on the continent of Europe and Latin America follow what is known as the unitary system under which property of any kind, movable or immovable, is treated as one single mass governed by one system of law, regardless of the *situs* of the property or parts thereof.

The Indian Succession Act, 1925, in keeping with the common law system of classifying property, in Section 5 (1) & (2) also classifies property into two categories, namely immovable and movable, governed respectively by *lex situs* and *lex domicilii* in matters of succession, testate or intestate.

Section 5 of the convention authorizes a person to designate the law of a particular state to govern succession to the whole of his estate. Such a designation will be effective only if, at the time of the designation or of his death, the person concerned was either a national of that state or had his habitual residence there. The concept of designation in matters of succession is alien to the common law system which India has embraced, which is deeply ingrained in our social fabric, and finds expression, too, in enactments such as the Indian Succession Act, as aforesaid. Besides, succession to property under the common law is by operation of law and not by an act of parties, the latter of which finds expression in the concept of designation by the testator of a particular state to govern succession to the whole of his estate.

Needless to say, Indian statutory enactments[24] and Indian case law[25] on the subject of succession to property, testate or intestate, exemplify the scission system of classification of property as immovable and movable.

In the final analysis, the Hague Convention on the Law Applicable to Succession to the Estates of the Deceased Persons, 1989, based on the two vital grounds set out above, without any further probe into it, simply becomes unacceptable.

THE LAW RELATING TO SERVICE OF SUMMONS ABROAD

The Existing Procedure for Service of Summons Under the (Indian) Code of Civil Procedure, 1908: Its Shortcomings

Service of summons abroad under the Indian Civil Procedure Code, 1908, takes place in pursuance of Section 29(c) as read with Order V Rule 26. Section 29(c) reads as follows:

Service of Summons

Summons and other processes are issued by:

(a) any other civil or revenue court outside India to which the Central Government has, by notification in the Official Gazette, declared the provisions of this Section to apply, may be sent to the courts in the territories to which this Code extends, and served as if they are summonses issued by such courts.

The Government of India in pursuance of Section 29(c) of the Civil Procedure Code, 1908, had notified the following countries to which the said section would extend: France, Spain, Belgium, Russia, Portugal, Japan, Kenya, Nepal, Iran, Egypt, Malaysia, Pakistan, Singapore, Sri Lanka, Burma, and Bangladesh.

The issuance of such a notification on the part of the government would facilitate foreign courts' summons to be treated as summons issued by courts in India and be served accordingly.

Reciprocity is established by virtue of the Government of India having entered into arrangement with the notified countries in pursuance of Section 29(c) as read with Order V Rule 26 (b) of the First Schedule to the Code of Civil procedure, 1908.[26] By virtue of such arrangement, summons issued by Indian courts would be treated by courts in the reciprocating countries as if the summons had been issued by them, and served accordingly on the concerned parties residing in those countries.

As regards countries with which the Government of India has no such reciprocal arrangement, Indian courts in pursuance of Order V Rule 25 of the Code of Civil Procedure, 1908, can send such summons, et cetera, in civil cases to parties residing abroad by registered post. Similar practice has to be followed by courts in those countries in the absence of reciprocal arrangement.[27]

Besides, there is yet another alternative course for serving summonses, as embodied in Order V Rule 26A of the Code of Civil Procedure, 1908, which reads as under:

Summons under 26A to be Sent to Officers of Foreign Countries

Where the Central Government has, by notification in the Official Gazette, declared in respect of any foreign territory that summons to be served on defendants actually and voluntarily residing or carrying on business, or personally working for gain in the foreign territory, may be sent to an officer of the Government of the foreign territory specified by the Central Government, the summonses may be sent to such officer, through the Ministry of the Government of India dealing with foreign affairs or in such other manner as may be specified by the Central Government and if such officer returns any such summons with an endorsement purporting to be done by him that the summons has been served on the defendant, such endorsement shall be deemed to be evidence of service.

The Limitations of the Existing State of the Law Relating to Service Abroad

Since an overwhelming majority of countries are outside the ambit of reciprocal arrangements, and since the alternative courses of serving summons such as through a designated officer of a foreign territory or through postal means do not seem to hold promise either, we may have to have recourse to a system hitherto not known to make service of summons abroad really efficacious. The prevailing system of service of summons abroad leaves much to be desired, particularly in respect of Non-resident Indians and their estranged spouses. *Ex parte* decrees granted by foreign courts more often than not may result in unpleasant consequences such as limping marriages, non-executed maintenance/alimony orders, denial of maintenance support to children, and the like. Considering all these, we have adopted the right course in becoming a party to the Hague Convention on the Service Abroad of Judicial and Extra Judicial Documents in Civil or Commercial Matters, 1965.

The Hague Convention on Service of Summons Abroad, 1965: A Review

The convention envisages the creation of a central authority in each of the contracting states, coupled with an obligation on their part to enact appropriate laws in respect thereof. The functioning of the Central Authority on the subject of service processes in civil or commercial matters ought necessarily to accord with the norms spelt out in Articles 3 to 6 of the convention. However, each contracting state has the discretion either to choose to serve summons processes through the Central Authority as envisaged in the convention, or have recourse to its own method as per its internal law, or even carry out summons process as requested by the applicant, unless it be that the method requested by the applicant is incompatible with its internal law. Article 8 of the Convention is flexible enough to allow the contracting states to effect service of judicial documents upon persons abroad even through their diplomatic or consular agents. This course, of course, is subject to the condition that the state where the service is to be effected may declare that it is opposed to such service within its territory, unless it be that the document is to be served on a national of the state where the documents originate from. Also the convention permits effecting service of documents through postal and other means subject, of course, to the state of destination not being opposed to such methods of service.

Article 13, however, introduces an exception by allowing the state addressed to refuse to comply with the request for serving of documents if it holds the view that such compliance would infringe its sovereignty or its security. It may not, however, do so solely on the ground that, as per its internal law it claims exclusive jurisdiction over the subject matter of the action or that its internal law would not permit the action upon which the application is based. The Central Authority shall, in case of such refusal, promptly inform the applicant stating the reasons for the refusal.

Articles 15 and 16 of the Convention extend further protection to the defendant from any avoidable adverse consequences in respect of service abroad of a writ of summons or an equivalent document. Article 15 lays down the rule that the non-appearance of the defendant before the designated court in a case, where a writ of summons or an equivalent document had to be transmitted abroad for the purpose of service under the provisions of the Convention, shall not lead to an *ex parte* judgment until it is established to the satisfaction of the court that,

(a) the document had actually been served in accordance with any prescribed method as per the internal law of the country concerned for the service of summons in domestic actions upon persons who are within the territory; or

(b) the document had actually been delivered to the defendant or to his residence by any other method provided for by this convention, and that in either of these cases the service or the delivery was effected affording the defendant sufficient time to defend his case.

However, the concerned contracting state may by a declaration seeking from the judge adjudicating the case a judgment even in the absence of a certificate of service or of the receipt of delivery, provided that all three of the following conditions are fulfilled: (a) that the document was transmitted by one of the methods contemplated in the convention, (b) a period of not less than six months, considered adequate by the judge for such transmission of the document, has elapsed and (c) no certificate of any kind has been received, despite every reasonable effort made on the part of the competent authorities of the state to obtain one.

Further, Article 16 deals with a case where despite the pronouncement of a judge *ex parte* against a defendant in a case where a writ of summons or an equivalent document had to be transmitted abroad for the purpose of service, the defendant is permitted to make an application within a reasonable time after getting to know of the judgment. The judge, in such an event, may relieve the defendant from the effects of the expiration of the time for appeal from the judgment, provided it is proved to the satisfaction of the court that: (a) the defendant for no fault of his had no timely knowledge about the document for him to defend his case or, as the case may be, no knowledge of the judgment in time to prefer an appeal and (b) the defendant had set out a *prima facie* defence to the action on merits.

However, the contracting states have the discretion to choose to declare the time limit within which the application has to be made which, in no case, is to be less than a year following the date of the judgment.

Article 16, however, clearly states that the above exemptions and time limit clauses shall have no application to judgments in respect of status or capacity of persons.

Considering that the Hague Convention on Service of Summons Abroad of Judicial and Extra-Judicial Documents in Civil or Commercial Matters, 1965, is so judiciously drafted, protecting the interests of the contracting states as well of the defendants, and also taking note of the fact that an overwhelming number of states, which include the United

States, the United Kingdom, and Canada among others, have become parties to the convention, the Government of India deserves due praise for acceding to the convention and thus help establish a world where due process of law reigns supreme.

HAGUE CONVENTION ABOLISHING THE REQUIREMENT OF LEGALIZATION FOR FOREIGN PUBLIC DOCUMENTS, 1961

The Indian accession to this Convention is yet another milestone in simplifying and systematizing the authentication of public documents. This convention, as stated in the preamble, abolishes the erstwhile requirement of public documents to be legalized for their authenticity by the diplomatic or consular agents of the country in which the document is to be produced.

Article 1 states that the Convention shall apply to public documents which have been executed in the territory of one contracting state and which have to be produced in the territory of another contracting state. It further states what, according to the Convention, are to be deemed public documents. They are as set out below:

(a) documents emanating from an authority or an official connected with the courts and tribunals of the state, including those emanating from a public prosecutor, a clerk of a court or a process server ('*huissier de justice*');

(b) administrative documents;

(c) notarial acts; and

(d) official certificates which are placed on documents signed by persons in their private capacity, such as those recording the registration of a document or the fact that it was in existence on a certain date and official and notarial authentications of signatures.

The Convention, however, excludes certain documents from its scope and ambit. They are:

(a) documents executed by diplomatic or consular agents; and

(b) administrative documents dealing directly with commercial or customs operations.

Article 2 of the Convention imposes an obligation on each contracting state to exempt from legalization of documents enumerated in the preceding Article 2, to which the present convention applies and which have to be produced in its territory, from the now obsolete practice, by virtue of this convention, of their getting certified by the diplomatic or consular agents of the country in which the documents have to be produced for their authenticity as to signature, capacity of the person/persons signing as well as the identity, where appropriate, of the seal or stamp which they bear.

Article 3 further clarifies that the only formality that is now required for a contracting state, after the coming into force of this convention, is a certificate as described in Article 4 issued by a competent authority of the state from which the document emanates as to the authenticity of the signature, the capacity in which the person signing the document has acted and, where appropriate, the identity of the seal or stamp which it bears.

A further exception is appended to in paragraph 2 of Article 3 which altogether dispenses with or, as the case may be, simplifies or exempts the document itself from legalization if either the laws, regulations, or practice in the state where the document is produced so ordain or an agreement to that effect is concluded between two or more contracting states.

Article 4 simply requires a certificate issued on the document itself or on an *allonge* in the form for which the model is provided in the annexe to the convention. Such a certificate, as per Article 5, shall be issued by the authorized concerned on a request made by the person who has signed the document or of any bearer. The certificate has to authenticate the signature, the capacity with which the person signing the document has acted and, where appropriate, the identity of the seal or stamp which the document bears. The said signature seal and stamp on the certificate shall stand exempted from all certification. Article 6 authorizes each contracting state to designate functionally qualified authorities to issue the certificate referred to in paragraph one of Article 3. Further, it shall be the duty of the designating state to give notice of it to the Ministry of Foreign Affairs of the Netherlands at the time of depositing its instrument of ratification or of accession or, as the case may be, of its declaration of extension. It shall also notify any change in the authorities designated.

Article 7 lays down the rule that each of the designated authorities shall be duty bound to keep a register or card index in which it shall record the certificates issued specifying:

(a) the number and date of the certificate; and

(b) the name of the person signing the public documents and the capacity with which he has acted or, in the case of unsigned documents, the name of the authority who has fixed the seal or stamp.

On being requested by any interested person, the authority who has issued the certificate shall verify whether the particulars contained therein are in accord with those in the register or card index.

Article 8 declares that if in a Convention or agreement concluded between two or more contracting states there are provisions subjecting the certification of a signature, seal or stamp to formalities more rigorous than those contained in Articles 3 and 4 of the Convention, the latter will prevail over or, so to say, override the former.

Article 9 which, in the nature of *ex abundante cautela*, imposes an obligation on each contracting state to take necessary steps to prevent the performance of legalizations by its diplomatic or consular agents in respect of public documents, enumerated under Article 1 of the Convention, which are exempted under this Convention.

The other provisions of the convention relating to ratification, accession, et cetera, follow the set pattern as enshrined in any other convention.

HAGUE CONVENTION ON TAKING OF EVIDENCE ABROAD IN CIVIL OR COMMERCIAL MATTERS, 1970

This Convention, read in conjunction with the other two conventions, namely the Convention on Service of Summons Abroad, 1965, and the Convention Abolishing the Requirement of Legalisation for Foreign Public Documents, 1961, may pave the way to establishing a global procedural due process that sounds appropriate in the global village in which we live in this, the twenty-first, millennium. The preamble, too, aptly describes the objective that the state signatories to the Convention seek to achieve, namely to facilitate transmission and execution of letters of request and to further the accommodation of the different methods which they use for this purpose, and also to improve mutual judicial cooperation in civil or commercial matters.

Chapter I: General Observations

Article 1 lays down the procedure for taking of evidence abroad among the contracting states. It emphasizes the fact that to obtain evidence abroad in civil or commercial matters, a letter of request has to be made by a judicial authority of a contracting state in accordance with the provisions of its law to the competent authority of another contracting state, requesting the latter to help obtain evidence or to perform some other judicial act intended for use in judicial proceedings, commenced or contemplated. It, however, clarifies that the phrase 'other judicial act' does not include the service of judicial documents or the issuance of any process by which judgments or orders are executed or enforced, or orders for provisional or protective measures for these categories of judicial processes are taken care of or, so to say, come within the purview of the Hague Convention on Service of Summons Abroad of Judicial and ExtraJudicial Documents in Civil or Commercial Matters, 1965.

Article 2 makes it mandatory for a contracting state to designate a central authority, in accordance with its own law, whose duty it is to receive letters of request sent by a judicial authority of another contracting state and transmit them to the authority competent to execute them. The said Article 2 further provides that it is incumbent upon the requesting authority to send letters of request directly to the central authority of the state of execution without channelizing them through any other authority of that state.

Article 3 sets out what a letter of request shall specify. They are:

(a) the authority requesting its execution and the authority requested to execute it, if known to the requesting authority;

(b) the names and addresses of the parties to the proceedings and their representatives, if any;

(c) the nature of the proceedings for which the evidence is required, giving all necessary information in regard thereto;

(d) the evidence to be obtained or other judicial act to be performed. Article 3 further states that, if deemed appropriate, the Letter shall specify, *inter alia*,

(e) the names and addresses of the persons to be examined;

(f) the questions to be put to the persons to be examined or a statement of the subject-matter about which they are to be examined;

(g) the documents or other property, real or personal, to be inspected;

(h) any requirement that the evidence is to be given on oath or affirmation, and any special form to be used;

(i) any special method or procedure to be followed under Article 9.

A letter of request may also mention information necessary for the application of Article 11 which exempts a person who may refuse to give evidence in the name of privilege or duty as also that no legalization or other like formality may be required.

Article 4 merely states that a letter of request shall be in the language of the authority requested to execute it or be accompanied by a translation into that language.

Paragraph 2, which is in the nature of an exception to paragraph 1, states that a contracting state shall accept a letter either in English or in French, or a translation into one of these languages, unless it enters a reservation against paragraph 2 as authorized by Article 33.

Further, if a contracting state has more than one official language and, for reasons of internal law, cannot accept letters in one of these languages for the whole of its territory, it shall, by declaration, specify the language in which the letter or translation thereof shall be expressed for execution in the specified parts of its territory. In case the requesting state fails to comply with the declaration, without justifiable excuse, the costs of translation into the required language shall be borne by the state of origin.

A contracting state may also, by declaration, specify the language or the languages other than those referred to in the preceding paragraphs, in which a letter may be sent to its central authority.

Any translation accompanying a letter shall be certified as correct either by a diplomatic officer or a consular agent or by a sworn translator or any other person so authorized in either state.

Articles 5 to 14 are in the nature of procedural due process that the convention has chosen to incorporate and, as such, they need only be highlighted and do not warrant any probing legal analysis.

Article 5 states that in case the central authority of the requested states considers that the request does not comply with the provisions of the convention, it shall promptly inform the state of origin which transmitted the letter of request, setting forth its objections to the letter. Article 6 simply states that if the letter of request has mistakenly been addressed to an authority not competent to execute it, the requesting state shall forthwith send it to the duly appointed competent authority in the same state for execution in accordance with the provisions of the convention.

Article 7 further states that the requesting state has a right to be informed, if it so desires, of the time and also the venue where the proceedings are to take place so that it may help the concerned parties and their representatives, if any, to make it convenient to be present. Alternatively, on being requested by the concerned authority of the state of origin, an obligation is cast on the requested state to directly inform the parties or their representatives of the time and the place where the proceedings will take place.

Article 8 sounds interesting in that it authorizes a contracting state to declare that members of the judicial personnel of the requesting authority of another contracting state may be allowed to be present at the execution of a letter of request. However, such a declaration requires prior authorization of the competent authority designated by the declaring state.

Article 9 makes it obligatory for the judicial authority executing a letter of request to apply its own law with regard to the methods and procedures to be followed. This is understandable, as procedural requirements of a country are governed by the *lex fori*. However, the said judicial authority may favourably respond to any request on the part of the requesting authority that a special method or procedure be followed, unless it be that following such a course is incompatible with the internal law of the state of execution or is impossible of performance by reason of its internal practice and procedure or by reason of practical difficulties.

Further, Article 9 mandates that a letter of request be expeditiously executed.

Article 10 authorizes the requested authority to apply appropriate measures of compulsion in executing a letter of request in keeping with its internal law for the execution of orders issued by the authorities of its own country or of requests made by parties in internal proceedings.

As adverted to in the concluding part of Article 3 of this Convention, in matters of execution of a letter of request the person concerned may refuse to give evidence in so far as he has a privilege or duty so to do (a) under the law of the state of execution; or (b) under the law of the state of origin and, that besides, the privilege or duty has been specified in the letter, or, at the instance of the requested authority, has otherwise been confirmed to that authority by the requesting authority.

Over and above what have already been stated, a contracting state may declare as to its willingness to respect the privileges and duties existing under the law of states other than the state of origin and the state of execution, to the extent specified in that declaration.

Article 12 is in the nature of an exception to the rule that a letter of request seeking its execution, under normal circumstances, should be honoured by the requested state. The two exceptions set out in Article 12 which may prompt the requested state to refuse to execute the letter are as under:

(a) in the state of execution the execution of the letter does not fall within the functions of the judiciary; or

(b) the state addressed considers that its sovereignty or security would be prejudiced thereby.

However, the executing state may not refuse execution solely on the ground that under its internal law it claims exclusive jurisdiction over the subject matter of the action or that its internal law would not admit of a right of action of it.

Article 13 deals with the subject of transmission of documents seeking execution of the letter of request on the part of the requesting state and return of the same of it (namely the requesting state) by the requested state.

It is as set out below:

The documents establishing the execution of the letter of request, according to Article 13, shall be sent by the requested authority to the requesting authority by the same channel which was used by the latter.

Whenever there is a failure in executing the letter wholely or partially, the requesting authority shall, in every instance, promptly be informed of the lapse through the same channel and also be assigned of the reasons therefore.

Article 14 is devoted to mundane matters such as reimbursement of the fees paid to experts and interpreters by the requesting authority, besides costs occasioned by the use of a special procedure requested by the state of origin under Article 9, paragraph 2.

The said Article 14 further states that the requested authority whose law obliges the parties themselves to secure evidence, and which itself is not able to execute the letter, may, after having obtained the consent of the requesting authority, appoint a suitable person to secure evidence. It further states that while seeking such consent the requested authority shall indicate the approximate costs which recourse to such procedure may entail. If the requesting authority gives its consent to the appointment of a suitable person to take evidence, it shall be obliged to reimburse any costs incurred. Without such consent on the part of the requesting authority, it shall not be liable for the costs incurred thereby.

Chapter II: Taking of Evidence by Diplomatic Officers, Consular Agents, and Commissioners

Article 15 authorizes a diplomatic officer or a consular agent of a contracting state to take evidence without compulsion in civil or commercial matters in the territory of another contracting state and within the area where he exercises his functions, of nationals of a state which he represents in aid of proceedings commenced in the courts of a state which he represents.

A contacting state may, however, declare that evidence may be taken by a diplomatic officer or a consular agent only if permission to that effect is given upon application made by him or on his behalf to the appropriate authority designated by the declaring state.

Article 16 is in the nature of a corollary to Article 15. Article 16 is hereby reproduced verbatim from the convention. The same reads as follows:

A diplomatic officer or a consular agent of a contracting state may, in the territory of another contracting state and within the area where he exercises his functions, also take evidence, without compulsion, of nationals of the state in which he exercises his functions or of a third state, in aid of proceedings commenced in the courts of a state which he represents, if

(a) a competent authority designated by the state in which he exercises his functions has given its permission either generally or in the particular case, and

(b) he complies with the conditions which the competent authority has specified in the permission.

A contacting state may declare that evidence may be taken under this Article (namely Article 16) without its prior permission.

Article 17 is a verbatim reproduction of Article 16 in the sense that the words '(a) diplomatic officer or a consular agent of a contracting state may' are substituted by the words 'a person duly appointed (by a contracting state) as a commissioner for the purpose may'.

Article 18 further states that a contracting state may declare that a diplomatic officer, a consular agent, or a commissioner, authorized to take evidence as per Articles 15, 16, and 17, may apply to the competent authority designated by the declaring state for appropriate assistance to obtain evidence by compulsion. The declaration may contain such conditions as the declaring state may see fit to impose.

If the authority chooses to grant the application, it shall apply such appropriate measures of compulsion as are prescribed by its law for use in internal proceedings.

Under Article 19 the said designated competent authority in giving permission as under Articles 15, 16 and 17, or in granting the application as under Article 18, may lay down such conditions as it deems fit, *inter alia*, as to the time and place of taking of the evidence. Similarly it may require that it may be given reasonable advance notice as to the time, date and place of the taking of the evidence; in such a case a representative of the authority shall be entitled to be present at the taking of the evidence. Article 20 further adds, that in the taking of evidence under any Article of this chapter, persons concerned may be legally represented.

Article 21 sets out the functional responsibilities of a diplomatic officer, a consular agent or a commissioner authorized to take evidence under Articles 15, 16 and 17. They are as under:

(a) he may take all kinds of evidence which are not incompatible with the law of the state where evidence is taken or contrary to any permission granted pursuant to the above Articles, and shall have power within such limits to administer an oath or take an affirmation;

(b) a request to a person to appear or to give evidence shall, unless the recipient is a national of the state where the action is pending, be drawn up in the language of the place where evidence is taken or be accompanied by a translation into such language;

(c) the request shall inform the person that he may be legally represented and, in any state that has not filed a declaration under Article 18, shall also inform him that he is not compelled to appear or to give evidence;

(d) the evidence may be taken in the manner provided by the law applicable to the court in which the action is pending provided that such manner is not forbidden by the law of the state where evidence is taken;

(e) a person requested to give evidence may invoke the privileges and duties to refuse to give the evidence contained in Article 11.

Article 22 is cast in the mould of a facilitating or enabling provision. It runs thus:

The fact that an attempt to take evidence under the procedure laid down in this chapter has failed, owing to the refusal of a person to give evidence, shall not prevent an application being subsequently made to take the evidence in accordance with Chapter I.

Chapter III: General Clauses

Article 23 requires that a contracting state may, at the time of signature, ratification or accession, declare that it will refrain from executing letters of request issued for the purpose of obtaining pre-trial discovery of documents known to common law countries.

Article 24 enables a contracting state to designate, in addition to the central authority, other authorities and also determine the extent of their competence. However, letters of request may in all cases be addressed to the central authority. Federal states may choose to designate more than one central authority.

As per Article 25, a contracting state having more than one legal system may have to designate authorities of one of such systems, which shall enjoy exclusive competence to execute letters of request pursuant to the Convention.

A contracting state may under Article 26, because of constitutional limitations, request the state of origin to reimburse fees and costs incurred in connection with execution of letters of request for the service of process necessary to compel the appearance of a person to give evidence, the costs of attendance of such persons, and the cost of any transcript of the evidence.

Any other contracting state may seek of that state, which had made a request pursuant to the above paragraph, reimbursement of similar fees and costs.

Articles 27 and 28 permit a contracting state or states to derogate from the norms and standards established under the present convention. For example, Article 27 states that the present convention shall not prevent a contracting state from:

(a) declaring that letters of request may be transmitted to its judicial authorities through channels other than those provided for in Article 2;

(b) permitting, by internal law or practice, any act provided for in this Convention to be performed upon less restrictive conditions;

(c) permitting, by internal law or practice, methods of taking evidence other than those provided for in this Convention.

Yet, again, Article 28 states that the present Convention shall not prevent an agreement between two or more contracting states to derogate from:

(a) the provisions of Article 2 with respect to methods of transmitting letters of request;

(b) the provisions of Article 4 with respect to the languages which may be used;

(c) the provisions of Article 8 with respect to the presence of judicial personnel at the execution of letters;

(d) the provisions of Article 11 with respect to the privileges and duties of witnesses to refuse to give evidence;

(e) the provisions of Article 13 with a request to the methods of returning executed letters to the requesting authority;

(f) the provisions of Article 14 with respect to fees and costs; and

(g) the provisions of Chapter II.

The sum and substance of Articles 29 to 32 is that the obligations arising under this Convention are supreme vis-à-vis any other obligations under any pre-existing convention or conventions; and that compatible provisions under conventions, subsisting or may be concluded in future among the contracting states, are non-derogable despite their [namely the contracting states] binding obligations to the rules of the present Convention.

Article 33 permits a state at the time of signature, ratification or accession to exclude, in whole or in part, the application of the provisions of paragraph 2 of Article 4 and of Chapter II, or, so to say, make reservations against them, as stated earlier. They may, nevertheless, at any time withdraw a reservation they had earlier made. The said Article further states that as between a state making a reservation, as aforesaid, and any other state that may be affected thereby, the latter is well within its right to apply the same rule against the former.

A state may, as per Article 34, at any time withdraw or modify a declaration.

The principle enunciated in Article 36 augurs well for the Convention. According to it, any difficulties which may arise between the contracting states in connection with the operation of this Convention shall be settled through diplomatic channels.

The rest of provisions of the Convention, namely Articles 35 to 42 barring Article 36, deal with ratification or accession, or other related matters that are germane to the convention.

NOTES

1. AIR 1975 SC 105
2. AIR 1991 SC 821
3. The Hague Convention on International Recovery of Child Support, IAML: As Observer-Cum-Special Commission on Maintenance Obligations.
4. Chapter 8: Law of Persons: Law Relating to Children.
5. AIR 1970. KER 1

6. (1893) 1 Ch. 143
7. 1981 New Ze Recent Law 257 (cited by British Law Commission, Working Paper No. 96 paragraphs 6–10).
8. Note 3 supra. See page 148.
9. (1998) 1 SCC 112
10. AIR 2000 SC 1019 p. 1023
11. 1970 AC 668, (1969) 1 ALL ER 788; (1964) 2 WLR 540
12. 24 American Jurisprudence, paragraph 1001.
13. *Khamis* v. *Khamis*, (1978) 4 Fam LR 410 (Full Court), Aus.
14. Chapter 7: Law of Persons—Part II and 'Law Relating to Children', Section titled 'Role of Courts as *Parens Patriae*', note 16.
15. (1974) 1 ALL ER 913, CA
16. 2004 (1) HLR SC 12
17. 2004 (1) HLR SC 468
18. 2005 (1) HLR DEL 428
19. See V.C. Govindaraj and C. Jayaraj, 'Non-Resident Indians and Private International Law'. *Indian Journal of International Law* of the Indian Society of International Law (Delhi: Hope India Publications, 2008), pp. 22–4.
20. Ibid.
21. *Black's Law Dictionary*, Revised Fourth Edition, (1968), p. 324.
22. Joseph Story, *Conflict of Laws*, p. 378.
23. 2 KENT Comm. 67; see *Black's Law Dictionary*, Revised Fourth Edition, p. 885.
24. See Section 5(1) &(2), The Indian Succession Act, 1925.
25. *R. Viswanathan* v. *Rukn-ul-Mulk Syed Abdul Wajid*, AIR 1963 SC; *Sankaran Govindan* v. *Lakshmi Bharathi*, AIR 1974 SC 1764.
26. See *The Consular Manual*, Revised Edition, (1983) issued by the Government of India, Ministry of External Affairs, p. 275.
27. Ibid.

15

The Trend-setting Developments in Conflict of Laws*

THE 'RULE SELECTION' RULE IN CONFLICT OF LAWS: A CRITIQUE OF THE SO-CALLED AMERICAN REVOLUTION

An attempt is made in this chapter to critically examine the 'vested or acquired rights' theory of Professor A.V. Dicey in England and Professor J.H. Beale in the United States, which is traceable to Ulrich Huber (1635–94), a Dutch jurist-cum-judge. Huber's formulations in respect of the binding force of law in general and conflict of laws in particular is derived from the sovereignty of states which, according to him, is unlimited and absolute. This view is in keeping with Hobbesian theory of sovereignty of states.

As laws are the dictates of states which enjoy absolute sovereignty, the inhabitants of states acquire rights in pursuance of the laws enacted by them and retain such rights wherever they go. The chief exponents of the vested or acquired rights theory are, as aforesaid, Professor Dicey in England and Professor Beale in the United States. Of the two, Professor Beale was a diehard adherent to the said vested or acquired rights theory in respect of contracts and torts. Justice Holmes and Justice Cordozo of the Supreme Court of the United States gave it a clean bill of health.

This doctrine suffered a setback in the recent past both in England and in the United States through the juristic writings of Professor Arminjon in France and Professors Cook and Lorenzen in the United States, all three of them virtually destroyed professor Beale's cherished vested rights theory.

* This chapter is a reproduction of the paper presented by the author to the *Indian Journal of International Law* and published in Volume 45, No. 4 (October–December 2005) of the journal.

Likewise, the traditional 'jurisdiction selection' rule was supplanted by the modern 'rule selection' rule, thanks to the proper law doctrine as applied by courts in England in respect of contracts, for which Professor Morris through his writings lent juristic support with a view to achieving, as he would put it, 'commercially sound and convenient' results in respect of contracts and 'socially sound and convenient' results in respect of torts. The 'rule selection' rule, originally piloted by Professor Cavers of the Harvard Law School obtained a categorical endorsement and a face lift, too, if I may say so, in the shape of the *Restatement, Second, the Conflict of Laws* (1971) of the American Law Institute, authored by the reporter, Professor Wills L.M. Reese of the Columbia Law School.

INTRODUCTION

I have chosen this topic with a view to impress upon the Indian legal fraternity that it is high time that we take it up as a mission, as did the Americans in a big way for the last seventy years or so, to reorient our attitude and approach to this area of legal discipline, namely conflict of laws or private international law, call it what you will.

With the onset of globalism, it is all the more imperative that we cut ourselves off from the umbilical cord, I mean to say the English conflicts rules as propounded by English publicists of the eminence of Dicey and Morris or, as for that, Professor Cheshire, and evolve our own conflicts rules, as did the Americans, to suit our needs based on our cultural and social environment.

It is of interest to note, in this connection, that the Supreme Court of India in a leading case of matrimonial dispute bemoaned the practice of our courts, in the absence of legislation, to fall back upon precedents which have taken their inspiration from English rules which resulted in conflicting decisions on a similar issue.[1]

As stated earlier, there are four distinct stages in the conflicts resolution process. They are:

(i) jurisdiction of the court of forum;

(ii) classification or characterization of the cause of action that calls for allocation of the issue involved to its correct legal category; say, for instance, whether the matter under litigation is one of breach of contract or of tort, or whether it is one of matrimonial rights between spouses or of succession or, again, whether it is one of administration of the assets of the deceased or of succession, the governing law in respect of the former relating to movables can only be *lex fori* as a matter of procedure or will be *lex domicilii* as a matter of substance;

(iii) identification by the court of forum of the *lex causae* (that is, the law that governs the cause of action) based on which judgment is rendered; and

(iv) recognition and enforcement of its judgment by the concerned foreign court.

The English conflict rules have a long history dating back to the third quarter of the eighteenth century; and, in this context, the judicial pronouncements of Lord Mansfield, rudimentary though they be, in respect of certain basic principles underlying the law of obligations can hardly be overemphasized. They are, to reiterate what has already been said, as under:

1. The law to govern a contract is the law of the place where the contract is made (that is, *lex loci contractus*), unless it be that the parties while concluding the contract had in their contemplation a law other than the *lex loci contractus* to govern their contract and made it explicit in their agreement.[2] He states, in yet another case, as a corollary to the above principle, that the law to govern a foreign contract is the law where the cause of action arose.[3]

2. Likewise, according to Lord Mansfield, the law to govern a foreign tort in a conflicts case is the law of the place where the tort occurred (that is, *lex loci delicti commissi*) and that, further, in his view, what would constitute a justification by the law of the place of the tort could be pleaded as a defence to an action in England.[4]

The second part of Lord Mansfield's enunciation in respect of a foreign tort, set out above, presumably led to the so-called 'double actionability' doctrine that is attributed to the eminent English Judge, Willis, J. in the leading case of *Phillips* v. *Eyre*.[5] The much maligned 'double actionability' doctrine has been given a seeming burial, so it appears, by the passing of an enactment by the British Parliament, namely Private International Law (Miscellaneous) Provisions Act, 1995.[6]

It is universally acknowledged as a basic principle of conflict of laws that the law to govern matters of procedure is the *lex fori* (that is, the law of the forum), whereas the law to govern matters of substance usually, though not necessarily, is the *lex causae* (that is, the law that govern the cause of action). A court called upon to resolve conflicts and determine the rights of the parties has to, first of all, characterize or classify the juridical acts in terms such as succession to movables or immovables, formal validity of marriage, capacity to marry or substantive or essential validity of marriage, breach of contract or tort and so on. Having done the said exercise, the court selects the *lex causae* on the basis of a connecting factor such as *lex domicilii* (that is, law of domicile), *lex patriae* (that is, law of nationality), *lex loci contractus* (that is, law of the place where the contract is made), *lex loci solutionis* (that is, law of the place of performace), *lex loci delicti commissi* (that is, law of place where a tortious act takes place).

The determination of the *lex causae* by a court leads automatically to its application by which we mean the internal law of the country or jurisdiction to the abandonment of, may we say, the fanciful or imaginary doctrine of *renvoi* (that is, remission), partial or total.

The English courts in conflicts cases till today have recourse to a mechanical selection of the country or jurisdiction on the basis of a connecting factor whose law or laws determine the rights of the parties. Presumably they do not examine the contents of the chosen law till they choose to apply it to determine the rights of the parties. For what we know, it may be a case of false conflict or, as the case may be, the application of the chosen law may lead to an injustice to the parties concerned or distort the rule of law which, needless to say, would undermine the role of courts as the upholders of the rule of law. English writers have formulated rules of conflict of laws based on such judicial dispensations. If the Indian courts, even as the courts in the Commonwealth countries, blindly follow the English judicial dispensations or the writings of English jurists based on a study by them of the case law of their country, it is not unlikely that justice may be miscarried and, consequently, those who seek resolution of their disputes on the basis of law and justice may meet with irreparable loss and hardship. I do not here suggest, let there be no mistake about it, that we adopt the policy of rendering justice in individual cases bereft of rules and principles that command universal respect, and without seeking guidance whatsoever from the thoughtful writings of eminent jurists whose works are the outcome as it were of their lifelong study and research of the subject under the present inquiry.

Morris and the Proper Law Theory

In this connection, it is no exaggeration to say that the contribution of the English jurist, Professor J.H.C. Morris, to the science of conflict of laws is significant. He not only had the unique distinction of mastering the English conflict of laws as expounded by Dicey and Cheshire, two great conflicts lawyers of the twentieth century, but also had the advantage of interacting with American conflicts lawyers during his stay at the the Harvard Law School as a Visiting Professor. The research paper that he contributed to *Harvard Law Review*, entitled 'The Proper Law of a Tort', begins with a poser which runs thus: 'English courts have reached results which, on the whole, seem *commercially convenient and sound* by applying the proper law doctrine to the question whether the defendant is liable for breach of contract. Why should we not reach results which are *socially convenient and sound* by applying the proper law doctrine to the question whether the defendant is liable for tort [emphasis added]?'[7]

Morris decries Professor Joseph Beale of the Harvard Law School, and rightly so, in respect of the governing principle applied to cases of foreign contract or foreign tort based on the discarded vested or acquired rights theory that held sway over courts and writers far too long. Beale, as the Reporter of the Original *Restatement*, *Conflict of Laws* of the American Law Institute, 1934 states as follows:

> that in respect of a foreign contract, 'issues of (its) validity are determined by the local law of the place of contracting', which was the place where occurred the last act necessary under the forum's rules of offer and acceptance to give the contract binding effect, assuming, hypothetically, that the local law of the place where the act occurred rendered the contract binding; and that in respect of 'issues of performance (they) are determined by the local law of the place of performace'.[8]

This simplistic enunciation by Beale as to the validity of a contract, namely that it is governed by the local law of the place of contracting, as stated above, is derived from the vested or acquired rights theory. By employing the same yardstick (namely the vested rights theory) to foreign torts in conflict cases, the *Restatement I, Conflict of Laws*, authored by Beale, declares: *'The place of wrong is the state where the last event necessary to make an actor liable for an alleged tort takes place'* [emphasis added].[9]

Morris emphatically recommends the application of the proper law doctrine to resolve disputes relating to the law of obligations, encompassing foreign contracts and foreign torts. He does, however, admit that the proper law theory appears to give a go-bye to principles relevant to the choice of the applicable rules of law such as 'protection of justified expectations of the parties', 'certainty, predictability and uniformity of result', and 'ease in the determination and application of the law to be applied', which factors are the virtue, if I may say so, of the mechanical rules of conflict of laws based on the 'jurisdiction selection' rule to the neglect, it appears, of the issue based 'rule selection' rule, which David Cavers of the Harvard Law School would urge courts to fall back upon that would help courts to avoid false conflicts, besides affording them an opportunity to take into consideration, in their judicial determination, the content of the law.

The proper law theory of Morris, thus conceived, when applied by courts to foreign contracts, would assuredly be 'commercially convenient and sound', and when applied to foreign torts would equally prove to be efficacious in the sense of its being 'socially convenient and sound.'

Critics may cavil at the 'proper law' theory of Morris or the 'rule selection' rule of Cavers as one that would vest in courts a discretion, untrammeled by judicial precedents, to resort to the practice of rendering justice in individual cases, so it appears, at the cost of norms like certainty, predictability and uniformity of results as also the justified expectations of parties. The 'rule selection' approach in conflicts cases that is in vogue in the United States for over four decades now, to the abandonment of the time-honoured 'jurisdiction selection' approach, incurred the wrath of Lord Wilberforce of the House of Lords in England who stigmatizes it in the following words: 'If one lesson emerges from the United States decisions—it is that the case to case decisions do not add upto a system of justice.'[10]

In the case of a foreign contract, if the parties to it seek certainty and definiteness, they could well achieve it by an express selection of the governing law, provided it be that the chosen law with respect to an issue in such a contract is most closely connected to the factual situation of the case for a court to put its *imprimatur* upon the parties' selection. If, on the contrary, such a selection by the parties as to the governing law in respect of an issue in a contract is absent, the court infers the applicable law from the nature of the contract and the surrounding circumstances of the case or, so to say, from an inquiry by it (namely the court) as to where the elements relating to that issue in a contract are densely grouped or where the centre of gravity lies.[11]

Morris endorses without reservation Walter Wheeler Cook's advice, presumably addressed to the courts, that 'the problems in the field under consideration [that is, contracts] need to be broken down into smaller groups and dealt with so as to meet the needs of society'.[12] That would enable courts, to recall the words of wisdom of Morris, 'to accord proper weight in a particular case to factors of constantly varying significance like the place of contracting, the place of performance, the nationality of the ship, the *situs* of the land, the domicile, residence and place of business of the parties, the reasonable expectations, the currency in which the obligation is expressed, and countless others'.[13] Also, in the second place, according to him, 'the rule enables attention to be concentrated not so much on the question, what law governs the validity of the contract, as on the question, what law governs the particular question before the court that would enable the court to give different answers to such questions as, for instance, 'offer and acceptance, reality of consent, formalities, necessity for consideration or 'cause', agency, capacity of the parties, essential validity, illegality, interpretation, scope, performance, discharge, remedies and so forth'.[14] The need to break down the problem into smaller groups and deal with them so as to meet the needs of the society may not ordinarily arise in the case of a tort as in a contract, inasmuch as cases relating to the former would attract mostly, allowing for possible exceptions, the *lex loci delicti commissi* (that is, the law of the place where the tort occurred), and that unlike the latter (namely contract), the former is prospective and pathological. Morris further states that to choose to apply the same conflicts rule of *lex loci delicti commissi* to resolving disputes relating to 'liability for automobile negligence, radio defamation, escaping animals, the seduction of women, economic conspiracies, and conversion' may not necessarily lead courts to achieve socially desirable results.[15] In that sense, those exceptional cases may call for breaking down the problem into smaller groups and dealing with them without being conditioned by the universally accepted rule of *lex loci deicti commissi*. In such exceptional cases, the *lex loci* may be fortuitous and, as such, inappropriate to apply, unless it be that the case belongs to the category that would attract the rule of 'conduct regulation' as opposed to 'loss allocation' or 'assessment of compensation' for the civil wrong.[16]

The Proper Law Doctrine: Case Illustations

Morris suggests, by illustrations, that in tort cases like conversion, it would be more appropriate to opt for the proper law doctrine in our search for good results than have recourse to *lex loci delicti commissi* as the governing law. More importantly, Beale's mechanistic 'last event' doctrine overlooks policy considerations altogether. Morris cites the case of a defendant who by his careless act in his own state causes injury to the plaintiff in another state. Rightly Goodrich holds that the law of the plaintiff's state, and not that of the defendant, governs the case, for the emphasis for the liability incurred is not on the defendant's negligence but on the harm that is caused to the plaintiff due to the defendant's negligence.[17]

Morris quotes, *inter alia*, American cases such as *Alabama Great Southern R.R.* v. *Carroll*[18] and *Levy* v. *Daniels' U-Drive Auto Renting Co.*,[19] to fortify his proper law doctrine in respect of tort cases, too, as in contract cases. The facts of the former case are as follows:

P, a resident of Alabama, was employed by D, an Alabama corporation, as a brakeman on freight trains operated by D and running between Birmingham, Alabama, and Meridian, Mississippi. P was injured in Mississippi due to the breaking of a link between two freight cars in that state. It was factually established that the link was defective when the train left Birmingham, and that the servants of D's corporation failed in their duty to inspect it in Alabama, and that the failure constituted negligence on their part. P failed in his action that he brought before an Alabama court on a mistaken application by it of the Mississippi common law fellow-servant rule, overlooking the Alabama Employers Liability Act under which P could have recovered damages for the injuries he sustained had the accident taken place in Alabama due to D's servants' negligence. The court denied recovery based on a faulty ratio, namely 'there can be no recovery in one state for injuries to the person sustained in another unless the infliction of the injuries is actionable under the law of the state in which they were received'. To say the least, this is a classic instance of a blind application of the *lex loci delicti commissi* doctrine based on the vested rights theory of Beale!

In the second case, namely *Levy* v. *Daniels' U-Drive Auto Renting Co.*,[20] the defendant company operating in the state of Connecticut rented a car to one Sack in Connecticut. One P happened to be a passenger in the car. The driver Sack parked the car so negligently on a Massachusetts highway that the defendant Meginn, who was no less negligent, ran into the car that resulted in injuries to P. All these facts, no doubt, namely the negligence of Sack and of the defendant Meginn and the injury that P sustained as a result of the negligence, occurred in Massachusetts. The State of Connecticut had a statute which provided that 'any person renting or leasing to another any motor vehicle owned by him shall be liable for any damage to any person or property caused by the operation of such motor vehicle while so rented or leased'. The court at Connecticut held the defendant company liable under the statute. The court, in the course of its judgment, did examine the purpose of the Connecticut statute which, according to it (namely the court), 'was not primarily to give the injured person a right of recovery against the tortious operator of the car, but to proctect the safety of traffic upon highways by providing an incentive to him who rented motor vehicles to rent them to competent and careful operators by making him liable for damages resulting from the tortious operation of the rented vehicles.' The decision, needless to say, strikes at the root of the 'last event' doctrine of Beale.

Morris quotes yet a couple of instances more to establish his thesis that Beale's 'last event' doctrine has lost its credibility in respect of foreign torts in conflicts cases yielding place to the 'proper law' doctrine which, as he says repeatedly, is 'socially convenient and sound'. One such case is *Scheer* v. *Rockne Motors Corp.*[21] which was a case of a New York bailor who was held liable in tort by a trial court in New York for his bailee's negligent act in Ontario in pursuance of an Ontario statute which provided that 'the owner of a motor vehicle shall be held liable for loss or damage sustained by any person by reason of negligence in the operation of such motor vehicle on a highway unless such motor vehicle was without owner's consent in the possession of some person other than the owner ...'[22]

Surprisingly, the court of appeals for the second circuit, presided over by Judge Learned Hand, reversed the trial court's judgment and ordered a new trial on the ground that bailor did not give the bailee permission to cross international border and go into Canada merely by virtue of giving the bailee possession of the car. As a matter of fact, there was no scope for rules of conflict of laws to come into play in this case for the reason that New York had a law similar to the law of Ontario imposing liability on the bailor for any accident occurring on a highway due to the negligence of the bailee. The New York law of bailment, entitled the New York Vehicle And Traffic Law, ran as follows: 'Every owner of a motor vehicle ... operated upon a public highway shall be liable... for injuries to person or property resulting from negligence in the operation of such motor vehicle. ...by any person...operating the same with the permission express or implied, of such owner.'[23]

Whether we apply the 'proper law' doctrine of Morris[24] or the 'rule selection' rule of Cavers[25] or even the 'local law' theory of Cook,[26] it would lead to the same result, making the New York bailor, the defendant in the case, liable in tort for the negligence of the bailee for causing injuries to the plaintiff in Ontario. The inference that is set out above as to the New York bailor's liability for the tort of negligence of the bailee in driving the vehicle entrusted to him by the bailor, resulting in injuries to the plaintiff in Ontario could be inferred by recourse, as aforesaid, to any of the three theories, namely the 'local law' theory of Cook, the 'rule selection' rule or 'the principle of preference' of Cavers and the proper law' theory of Morris.

Walter Wheeler Cook: The Local Law Theory

Cook's enunciation of the 'local law' theory is as under:

The forum, when confronted by a case involving foreign elements, always applies its own law to the case, but in doing so adopts and enforces as its own law a rule of decision found in the system of law in force in another state or country with which some or all of the foreign elements are connected, the rule so selected being in many groups of cases, and subject to the exceptions to be noted later, the rule of decision which the given foreign state or country would apply, not to this very group of facts now before the court of the forum, *but to a similar but purely domestic group of facts involving for the foreign court no foreign element* [emphasis added].

The rule thus incorporated into the law of the forum may for convenience be called the 'domestic rule' of the foreign state, as distinguished from its rule applicable to cases involving foreign elements. *The forum thus enforces not a foreign right but a right created by its own law.* [emphasis added].[27]

It is evident from Cook's enunciation of his 'Local Law' theory, that he denies to the foreign court the discretion to choose to employ choice of law rules or, so to say, exercise legislative jurisdiction so as to bestow on the plaintiff a right under its law. In other words, the foreign court's judicial jurisdiction is confined merely to its laying down a rule of decision based on its substantive law as if the dispute presented before it for its adjudication is purely local or domestic.

Justice Learned Hand: His, So-called, Local Law Theory

In this context, a passing reference needs to be made regarding the so-called 'Local Law' theory of Judge Learned Hand. It is, in fact, a variant of Cook's 'local law' theory, inasmuch as, unlike Cook, who insists that the court of forum enforces not a foreign right but a right created under its own law, but fashioned, to the extent possible, by reference to the domestic law of the concerned foreign country to the exclusion of the said foreign country's rules for the choice of law. Judge Hand, on the other hand, would look into the whole of the foreign law, including rules of choice of law that foreign country's court would employ in determining the right which, when found, as Professor Cavers remarks, 'should serve as the model for a right created by the forum'.[28] This is evident from Judge Hand's opinion in *Guinness* v. *Miller*.[29] For, in the course of his judgment in the said case, he observes: 'However, no court can enforce any law but that of his own sovereign, and, when a suitor comes to a jurisdiction foreign to the place of the tort, he can only invoke an obligation recognised by that sovereign. *A foreign sovereign imposes an obligation of its own as nearly as possible to that arising in the place where the tort occurs.*'[30] [emphasis added].

Cavers in his critique published in the year 1950 in the *Harvard Law Review* bearing the title, Comment: the Two 'Local Law' Theories, referred to earlier, lays bare the illusion that there are two local law theories attributed respectively to Professor Walter Wheeler Cook and Judge Learned Hand. In his view, the local law theory can be attributed only to Cook, and that the so-called local theory of Judge Hand calls for a different designation.

Both the theories of Professor Cook and Judge Hand, doubtless, reject the vested or acquired rights theory of Professor Beale. Cook's views, as one could see from the passage quoted above from his work, 'Logical and Legal Bases of the Conflict of Laws'[31] is that the court of forum enforces a right created by its own law; but, in doing so, also would consider a rule of decision of the concerned foreign court based on the substantive law of that state to the exclusion of its rules for the choice of law. On the contrary, Judge Hand, though he also insists, as is evident from his observation in the *Guinness case* quoted above, that the court of forum imposes an obligation arising under its own law and none other, and, while doing so, *moulds it in a manner as nearly homologous as possible to that arising in the place where the tort occurs* [emphasis added].

In the light of Judge Hand's utterance in the *Guinness case*, Cavers would choose to designate Judge Hand's so-called local law theory as the 'homologous right theory'.[32]

David F. Cavers: The 'Rule Selection' Rule

David Cavers of the Harvard Law School, in a pioneering article published in the *Harvard Law Review* in the year 1933,[33] forcefully advocated the employment by courts of what he would choose to call the 'rule selection' rule, in preference to the traditional 'jurisdiction selection' rule, in the conflicts resolution process. Therein he deprecated the traditional conflicts law system based, as it happened to be all along, on the mechanical 'jurisdiction selection' without turning attention to the content of the law which, more often than not, may lead to injustice to the parties and generate false conflicts.

He further contends that any mechanical application of the choice of law rules by recourse to the 'jurisdiction selection' method may result in miscarriage of justice, as he demonstrates by considering a hypothetical case based on *Milliken* v. *Pratt*[34] but with a reversal of the laws of the two states, namely Massachusetts and Maine. If, for instance, he argues, a married woman domiciled in Massachusetts entered into a contract of guarantee on behalf of her husband in the State of Maine for which she had the necessary capacity as per Massachusetts law, but not as per Maine law, it would be travesty of justice to declare the contract void based on the Maine law, namely the *lex loci contractus*. He asserts that the Maine law was intended to protect a married woman domiciled or resident in Maine, and certainly not a married woman domiciled or resident in Massachusetts. This case, according to him, is one of false conflict.

It took almost three decades for the 'rule selection' rule of Cavers to influence courts in the United States. In the case *Babcock* v. *Jackson*,[35] the New York court of appeals, speaking through Fuld, J., (as he then was), unreservedly embraced the 'rule selection' rule of Cavers by decreeing the suit for damages brought by the plaintiff, a gratuitous passenger in a motor vehicle driven by the defendant, the host driver, both being New Yorkers, aside the vehicle itself being registered and garaged in New York, for an accident that took place in Ontario, Canada, whose law denied a gratuitous passenger any right of recovery. Fuld, J., in his judgment categorically rejected the traditional choice of law rule of 'jurisdiction selection' based on the discredited vested rights theory of Professor Beale and incorporated in Section 384 of the original *Restatement of the Conflict of Laws*, despite the fact of its possessing the virtue of 'certainty, ease of application and predictability'.

The modern trend, in the opinion of Fuld, J., is to fall back upon the doctrine of 'center of gravity' or 'grouping of contacts', which courts adopt in contract cases which, *a fortiori*, can also be extended to tort cases with multi-state contacts. In this context, Fuld, J. observed: 'Justice, fairness and "the best practical result" may best be achieved by giving controlling effect to the law of the jurisdiction which, because of its relationship or contact with the occurrence or the parties, has the greatest concern with the specific issue raised in the litigation.'[36]

The above observation of Fuld, J. based on the 'rule selection' rule appears to meet the criticism of Morris who, while commending the English 'proper law' doctrine as worthy of serious consideration by courts in the United States, remarks: 'To a foreign observer, it seems extraordinary that there should be so much uncertainty in the United States as to what law governs the validity of a contract, and so much uncritical acceptance of the rule that tort liability is governed by the law of the place of wrong'.[37]

As irony would have it, Fuld, C.J., as he later became, ruefully admits in the subsequent cases that he decided cases involving guest statutes in conflicts setting with multi-state contacts, where the passenger and driver were domiciled or resident in different states, his grouping of contacts rule appears to be less categorical.[38]

It is of interest, in this connection, to advert to two other decisions of the Supreme Court of California, namely *Bernhard* v. *Harrah's Club*[39] and *Reich* v. *Purcell*,[40] where both the *lex fori* and the *lex loci* had a legitimate claim to seek application of their respective laws based on relevant policy considerations. In the first case, a reading of its factual situation revealed the presence of a true conflict. In the second case, however, the forum state happened to be a 'disinterested third state', to borrow Brainerd Currie's phrase, and the conflict centred round the laws of two other states.

Professor W.F. Baxter: The Comparative Impairment Theory

In the first case, quoted above, namely *Bernhard* v. *Harrah's Club*, the plaintiff, a Californian, was injured in a car accident caused by another Californian, who was inebriated due to overdrinking in the defendant's club in Nevada. As per the Californian law, a tavern keeper was liable for serving drinks to an intoxicated person. According to Nevada law no such liability was attached. The Supreme Court of California held the defendant, the Nevada tavern keeper, liable for the injury caused to the plaintiff, based not on the application of the *lex fori*, but on the application of the law of the state, namely that of California, 'whose interest would be most impaired if its law were not applied.' This ruling of the Californian Supreme Court seems to accord with Brainer Currie's 'governmental interest' theory. But, in reality, the decision was based on W.F. Baxter's 'comparative impairment' theory, an innovative approach to resolving conflicts.[41]

In the second case, namely *Reich* v. *Purcell*, a collision took place in Missouri between two cars, one owned by the defendant who was domiciled and resident in California and other driven by the wife of the plaintiff whose family was then resident in Ohio, as a result of which the plaintiff's wife and one of his children were killed. It so happened that the deceaseds' estates were administered in Ohio, though the plaintiff later acquired Californian domicile which could well be the intended matrimonial domicile of the deceased, as was argued. There happened to be as per Missouri law a limitation on damages recoverable for wrongful death actions, but not so under the laws of Ohio and California.

The court speaking through Traynor, C.J., applied the law of Ohio in granting damages for the wrongful death. The claims of the *lex fori* (that is, the law of California) or the *lex loci* (that is, the law of Missouri) to govern the case were rejected, inasmuch as the *lex fori* was obliged to consider all of the foreign and domestic elements and interests involved in the case to determine the law applicable, and the *lex loci*, which can be characterized as disinterested third state, had no interest whatsoever to apply its limitation provisions in wrongful death actions.

The decision in *Padula* v. *Lilarn Properties Corp.*,[42] a New York case, gives one the impression that the vested rights theory of Beale, as manifested by the *lex loci delicti commissi*, still rules the roost.

This was a case of a worker domiciled in New York who sustained injuries by a fall from a scaffold at a construction site in Massachusetts. The scaffold did not conform to the specifications promulgated under a New York labour law for the safety of the workers which prescribed 'strict and vicarious liability of the owner of the property' for any injury to a worker due to nonconformity with scaffold specifications. The court, affirming a summary judgment of the lower court in favour of the property owner, observed that as between the two competing laws, namely the New York law which was in the nature of 'conduct regulation' as against the Massachusetts law which was one of 'loss allocation' or 'assessment of compensation' for a tort liability, the latter was to be preferred. Reacting to this decision, Brochers sarcastically remarks: 'The great irony would be that, more than three decades after firing the first shot in the revolution that deposed territorialism, New York could well become the first state to return it to the throne'.[43]

Be that as it may. Apparently, the decision strikes one as a return to the discredited *lex loci* rule for tort liability. But, a careful look at it reveals that it (namely the decision) carries with it an innovative approach in tort liability cases of distinguishing competing applicable laws as one of 'conduct regulation' or 'loss allocation' which entails 'assessment of compensation'.

We may sum up our review of the 'rule selection' rule of Cavers as under:

Firstly, Professor Cavers himself admits that his thesis may have greater relevance to a federal union like the United States than the choice of law process in the international setting where the argument for certainty and uniformity based upon fear of local bias is patent.[44] In this connection, he observes:

'The application of mechanical rules of law in such a situation may, accordingly, be regarded as necessary to safeguard the alien litigant from xenophobia.'[45] Defending the central theme of his thesis based on choice of law rules or, more appropriately, 'principles of preference,' he remarks:

'Discretion is a safe tool only in the hands of the disinterested. Such a disinterestedness may readily be credited to courts within the bounds of a federal union. Its exercise by state courts in the United States may be welcomed, not feared, if and when courts restate not their rules but their problem.'[46]

Secondly, Professor Cavers asserts that his approach has for its aim the promotion of 'principles of preference', and, certainly not, as is attributed to him, 'justice in the individual case.' He further contends, as a rejoinder to his critics, that 'the application of a just rule should not be deemed incompatible with 'justice in individual case'.[47] In that context, he makes the following observation by way of clarification of his stand:

The court is not engaged (in a choice of law case) in an exercise in comparative jurisprudence, appraising the respective merits of the two rules of law. Rather the court is passing upon the conflicting claims of two parties, each of whom insists that the facts of the case justly require that one of the two rules, and not the other, be applied in its decision. It is therefore to the circumstances of the case that one must look for the problem.[48]

Thirdly, his objection to the 'jurisdiction selection' rule stems from the fact that it (namely the rule) makes the state the object of choice. 'In theory', he argues, 'it is only after the rule has selected the governing state by reference to the 'contact' prescribed in the rule that the court ascertains the contents of the state's law'.[49] However, basically he has no objection to a 'jurisdiction selection' rule, 'provided if it happens to be the product of two decisions chosen on policy grounds between competing rules in cases in which the law-fact patterns are reversed, provided that in the use of the rule thus synthesized its origin has not been lost sight of'.[50]

In fact, even in his original thesis published by the *Harvard Law Review* in 1933, referred to earlier in this work,[51] which has since been subjected to a good deal of criticism, he continued to advocate the same principle as reflected in his recent writings, set out above. For instance, he writes: 'The suggested approach would preclude the attainment of either certainty or uniformity in the conflict of laws because under it the decision of a case involving choice of law would depend on the content of the conflicting laws and the relative desirability of their application in the light of the facts of the controversy in litigation.'[52] He concedes; however, that 'certainty and uniformity are necessary as a curb on local bias which leads to the application of the *lex fori*, or a law similar thereto, in preference to a different law whose claims for consideration, objectively appraised, are superior.'[53]

The 'rule selection' rule of Cavers, as opposed to the traditional mechanical 'jurisdiction selection' rule, carries with it the virtue of empiricism and pragmatism. It, however, lacks, as Cavers himself would admit, qualities that go with the latter, namely 'certainty, predictability and uniformity of results'. All the same, Cavers hopes that over the years the 'rule selection' rule, too, dubbed by critics as 'justice in the individual case', may gradually acquire those very qualities that the 'jurisdiction selection' rule is endowed with. Also, we may have to agree with the critics that the 'rule selection' rule may at best be found workable in respect of contracts, torts and conveyances, and no others.

Interestingly enough, Professor Willis L.M. Reese, the Reporter of the *Restatement, Second, Conflict of Laws*, is of the view that, barring an action for annulment of a marriage or, as the case may be, seeking a declaratory judgment that a marriage does or does not exist, or launching a criminal prosecution for bigamy, the validity of a marriage in a great majority of situations may have to be treated merely as incidental to the determination of another issue and not, as courts do, treat marriage as 'an all-purpose concept', if our aim and objective is to achieve 'socially desirable results'. He, therefore, suggests that 'the validity of a marriage should be determined in the light of the particular issue involved'.[54] Such situations, according to him, which are manifold and which render the issue of the validity of a marriage incidental, are exemplified in instances such as a person, claiming to be a surviving spouse, asserts rights to testate or intestate succession, to pension, social security or workmen's compensation benefits, or to recover under the life insurance policy or for the wrongful death of the other spouse.[55] The same is the case when an alleged spouse seeks to recover for a loss of consortium resulting from injuries to the other spouse or for the alienation of the affections of the other spouse. He further quotes yet other instances wherein the issue of the validity of a marriage may be rendered incidental to a determination of the legitimacy of a child, of problems concerning matrimonial property, nationality, the rights to a name and of immigration and naturalization proceedings and countless others.[56]

Professor Brainerd Currie: The Governmental Interest Theory

It is interesting, in this connection, to briefly turn our attention to Brainerd Currie, the chief exponent of the governmental interest theory, who, in his endeavour to define and delimit judicial function in a democracy, observes:

> I do not know where to draw the line between judicial legislation that is 'molecular' or permissible, and that which is 'molar' or 'impermissible'. But the assessment of the respective values of the competing legitimate interests of two sovereign states, in order to determine which is to prevail, is a political function of a very high order. This is a function that should not be committed to courts

in a democracy. It is a function that courts cannot perform effectively, for they lack the necessary resources.'[57]

But this caveat that Currie administers does not deter courts, remarks Morris, citing the decision in *Bernhard* v. *Harrah's Club* in this regard, from resisting the temptation to weigh competing interests.[58]

Now turning to Morris and his proper law theory, which has been discussed *in extenso*, a comment or two is required since the said doctrine has received overwhelming approval in England in respect of cases on foreign contracts. The same, however, cannot be said of foreign torts. The classic instance of endorsement of the proper law doctrine in respect of foreign contracts is the decision of the House of Lords in England in the case *International Trustee for the Protection of Bond Holders* v. *R.*[59] This was a case of Great Britain floating a loan in the New York city, subscribed to by New Yorkers. The disputed issue related to the mode of repayment of the loan, whether the repayment was to be on the basis of the gold standard clause as per the terms of the contract or in terms of the American dollars in view of a congressional resolution forbidding repayment of loans in any mode other than in dollar terms. The House of Lords overruled the argument of the British Government based on sovereign immunity, thereby upholding the contention of the subscribers based on the proper law of the contract which, in this case, happened to be the law of New York where the loan was floated by the British Government and where the repayment had to take place.

In the case of foreign torts, however, Morris's proper law theory based on the postulate of its being 'socially convenient and sound', it appears, did not go well with courts in England. We may cite here the case of *Chaplin* v. *Boys*[60] which was one of claim for damages sought for by one British serviceman as against another British serviceman for the injuries sustained by the former in a road accident in Malta where they were temporarily stationed. The House of Lords unanimously decided that the plaintiff should recover the greater sum under the English law, the law of the forum, rather than a meager sum allowable under the Maltese law which, as per the factual situation, happened to be the proper law. Ironically enough, the unanimity in judgment was obscured by an astounding, inherently inconsistent, variety of ratio employed by Their Lordships, contrary to the basic tenet *ratio legis est anima legis* (that is, the reason of law is the soul of law). While Their Lordships, by and large, expressed sympathy for the Morris's proper law doctrine, which had taken deep roots in the United States, they would rather prefer to base their judgment on a flexible interpretation of Willis, J. formula in *Phillips* v. *Eyre* on grounds of public policy and in line with the American Restatement.[61] Lord Hodson in the company of Lord Wilberforce, in particular, would resist any inclination to give the American rule of the proper law of the tort a considered thought, based on the ground that, it (namely the proper law doctrine) has 'led to uncertain results and has not been fully developed in the United States.'[62]

Willis L.M. Reese's *Restatement (Second), Conflict of Laws*: 'A Holistic Approach to Conflict Resolution'

The Restatement (Second), Conflict of Laws, of the American Law Institute, which I choose to characterize as the 'Holistic Approach to Conflicts Resolution', can be traced to a thought provoking article authored jointly by Professors Elliott E. Cheatham and Willis L.M. Reese of the Columbia Law School.[63] The younger of the two, namely Professor Willes Reese, who was admired and respected as a conflicts lawyer *par excellence*, was chosen as the Reporter of the *Restatement (Second), Conflict of Laws*. The tentative drafts of the *Restatement*, which took thirteen years for its completion, was submitted by the council to the members of the American Law Institute in three parts for discussion successively at its forty-fourth, forty-fifth and forty-sixth annual meetings that were held in the years 1967, 1968 and 1969. The said final draft was approved and adopted on 23 May 1969.[64]

I may here hazard a guess that Professors Cheatham and Reese might have been influenced by Morris who brought out a year earlier his research paper in the *Harvard Law Review*, as aforesaid, entitled 'The Proper Law of a Tort', wherein he remarks: 'To a foreign observer, it seems extraordinary that there should be so much uncertainty in the United States as to what law governs the validity of a contract, and so much uncritical acceptance of the rule that tort liability is governed by the law of the place of the wrong.'[65]

The *Restatement (Second)* has virtually adopted the policy guidelines set down in the article of Professors Cheatham and Reese for the benefit of courts in resolving conflicts and in formulating issue-based rules of choice of law. It begins with a prefatory note which is reproduced hereunder for the benefit of the readers. It runs thus:

When an occurrence has substantial elements in two or more states having different local laws, it is necessary to determine which of these laws shall govern the rights of the parties. The problem of choice thus presented is the most difficult one in conflict of laws. The difficulty is primarily a consequence of the youth and fluidity of the subject. Not only is precedent relatively sparse in this area; that which exists is frequently misleading. Guidance therefore cannot be sought, as in many other branches of the law, from an accepted body of settled rules. Rather the judge frequently finds himself forced to pursue the inquiry into basic questions of policy and value.[66]

'The second source of difficulty', according to the learned professors,

stems from the belief, commonly held at an earlier time, that all aspects of choice of law could be handled satisfactorily by a relatively small number of simple rules derived logically from what was deemed to be a single overriding principle as, for example, power, sovereignty or vested rights. This view expressed by men of the greatest ability, [namely Justice Story, Professor Beale and Justice Holmes], had obvious appeal because it seemed to promise both certainty of result and ease of application. Its falsity is now generally recognized, but more than anything else it has retarded development in the field by inducing courts to look only to a simple, symmetrical system, unattuned to practical considerations.[67]

The *Restatement (Second)* has substantially adopted seven of the nine guidelines spelt out in the article to the abandonment of only two, namely that (1) the court should apply its own local law unless there is good reason for not doing so; and, that, (2) in choice of law, as in all laws, the attainment of justice in individual case is but one of many policies that is necessary to enable a court to distinguish a given case based on the presence of element or elements in its factual situation that calls for deviation from the normal rules in its (namely the court's) attempt to apply or interpret statutory directives or judicial precedents, if any.

The choice of law principles, as embodied in the *Restatement of the Law (Second), Conflict of Laws* read as follows:

'(1) A Court, subject to constitutional restrictions, will follow a statutory directive of its own state on choice of law.

(2) When there is no such directive, the factors relevant to the choice of the applicable rule of law include

(a) the needs of the interstate and international systems,
(b) the relevant policies of the forum,
(c) the relevant policies of other interested states and the relative interests of those states in the determination of the particular issue,
(d) the protection of justified expectations,
(e) the basic policies underlying the particular field of law,
(f) certainty, predictability and uniformity of result, and
(g) ease in the determination and application of the law to be applied.'[68]

In respect of the choice of law principles applicable to all contracts and to all issues in a contract, the *Restatement of the Law (Second)* has dealt with the subject broadly under three headings, namely

(1) general (Sections 187–8);

(2) various types of contracts requiring more precise rules for determining the state of the applicable law (Sections 189–99); and

(3) important issues relating to contracts such as capacity, formalities, substantial validity, misrepresentation, duress, undue influence and mistake, illegality, usury, construction, extent of contractual obligations, details of performance and measure of recovery (Sections 200–7).

Whatever may be the types of contract and the issues that arise thereunder, the norms that govern them are essentially based on the following formulae:

The law that governs a contract of the issue or issues that arise under the contract shall be in accordance with the choice exercised by the parties to the contract and made explicit in their agreement, unless it be that the law of the state the parties have chosen which is incorporated in their agreement:

(a) has no relationship to the parties or the transaction and there is no other reasonable basis for the parties' choice;

(b) that its application would be contrary to a fundamental policy of a state which has materially greater interest than the chosen state in the determination of the particular issue and which conforms to the rule laid down in the Restatement (Section 188) as to the applicable law in the absence of an effective exercise by the parties as to the choice of law, and, that the law of the state so chosen by the parties to govern their contract or, as the case may be, the issue or issues arising thereunder shall be the local law of the state to the exclusion of the rules for the choice of law (Section 187). It is evident, therefore, that the doctrine of *renvoi* is rejected.

In case the parties to a contract have failed to exercise their choice as to the applicable law, Section 188 of the *Restatement* provides that 'the rights and duties of the parties with respect to an issue in a contract are determined by the local law of the state which, as to that issue, has the most significant relationship to the transaction and the parties under the principles stated in Section 6'. The said Section 188 further lays down that 'in the absence of an effective choice of law by the parties', as per Section 187, 'the contracts to be taken into account in applying the principles of Section 6 to determine the law applicable to an issue include:

(a) The place of contracting,
(b) The place of negotiation of the contract,
(c) The place of performance,
(d) The location of the subject matter of the contract, and
(e) The domicile, residence, nationality, place of incorporation and place of business of the parties'.

A further rider is added to the law applicable to an issue, namely that 'these contacts are to be evaluated according to their relative importance with respect to the particular issue'. Yet another clause is added to the said Section 188, namely that 'if the place of negotiating the contract and the place of performance are the same state, the local law of this state will usually be applied, except as otherwise provided in Sections 189–99 and Section 203'.

Following the same pattern, (except that in a tort unlike that in a contract to talk of any exercise of choice as to the applicable law by the parties concerned is a misnomer), the *Restatement* has dealt with a tort giving rise to a civil liability in three parts, namely general principle applicable to all torts and to all issues in tort couched in terms of great generality (Section 145 of the *Restatement*), particular torts in respect of which the spelt out rules could be more precise (Sections 146–155) and particular issues that arise in tort (Section 156–174).

The general principle applicable to all torts and to all issues in tort is stated in Section 145 of the *Restatement* as follows:

(1) The rights and liabilities of the parties with respect to an issue in tort are determined by the local law of the state which, as to that issue, has the most significant relationship to the occurrence and the parties under the principles stated in Section 6.
(2) Contacts to be taken into account in applying the principles of Section 6 to determine the law applicable to an issue include:
(a) the place where the injury occurred;
(b) the place where the conduct causing the injury occurred;
(c) the domicile, residence, nationality, place of incorporation and the place of business of the parties; and
(d) the place where the relationship, if any, between the parties is centered.
These contacts are to be evaluated according to their relative importance with respect to that particular issue.

Having thus spelt out the issue-based general principles applicable to foreign contracts and foreign torts as stated in the *Restatement (Second)*, which I designated as 'A Holistic Approach to Conflicts Resolution', the scope of this monograph does not lend itself to any detailed inquiry, coupled with a critical appraisal, of the rules, general and specific, as embodied in the *Restatement*. But, one good thing that emerges from the *Restatement (Second)*, is that, unlike the original *Restatement* of Professor Beale in 1934, the *Restatement (Second)*, is realistic in its approach based, as to the choice of law rules, on case law 'open to re-examination as any other common law rules'. This is in sharp contrast to the original *Restatement* which as to the rules for the choice of law, to quote, yet again, Professors Cheatham and Reese, relied on 'a relatively small number of simple rules derived logically from that was deemed to be a single overriding principle as, for example, power sovereignty or vested rights'.

As we have already discussed in detail the various theories, doctrines and methods of publicists with illustrative cases, to me, it suggests, that there is no need *de novo* to test the holistic approach of *The Restatement (Second), Conflict of Laws* of the American Law Institute as to its credibility and worthiness, based on case law studies. *The Restatement (Second)*, I dare say, stood the test of time for over three decades. Even so, one would expect that legal scholars in the United States may be persuaded to give a fresh look at it, taking into consideration the march of law at a pace unimaginable which truly reflects changes in the structure, attitude and needs of the community verily, *Restatement (Third) of the American Law Institute* seeks to fulfil the expectation.

Strange as it may seem, with due respect to Morris, whose mastery over conflict of laws is unquestionably of the highest order, underwent a metamorphosis, so it appears, in the course of two decades, that is, from the year 1950 to the year 1970.

As has earlier been mentioned, Professor Morris as a Visiting Professor at the Harvard Law School wrote an article in the year 1951, entitled 'The Proper Law of a Tort'. Therein he defended the English proper law doctrine as applied by courts in England to contracts which, in his view, could also be extended to torts, aimed at producing results which could be characterized as 'commercially convenient and sound' in the case of contracts, and 'socially convenient and sound' in the case of torts. In contrast to the English proper law doctrine, according to him, the prevailing rules of choice of law in the United States in the areas of contracts[69] and torts,[70] under the influence of the vested rights theory of Beale, left much to be desired. He then wrote, I repeat, 'it seems extraordinary that there should be so much uncertainty in the United States as to what law governs the validity of a contract, and so much uncritical acceptance of the rule that liability is governed by the law of the place of wrong'.[71] But in the year 1971, in his book, *Conflict of Laws*, and again in the second edition of the same, published in the year 1980, he voiced an opinion eulogizing the choice of law process rendered innovatively and with sophistication by leading publicists of the United States, which runs thus:

> During the last fifty or sixty years there has been a spate of writing in the United States, some of it very vivid and some of it very sophisticated, on theories and methods in the conflicts of laws. *Nothing like it has been seen in any other country or in any other period of the centuries long history of our subject* [emphasis added.][72]

Conclusion

It is, indeed, a fascinating study in conflict of laws to view its growth and evolution during the past three hundred years or so. It is a movement from the primitive to the sophisticated. In other words, it is a movement from the writings of Ulrich Huber (1635–94), a Dutch jurist-cum-judge, among others, whose work entitled *De Conflictu Legum Diversarum in Diversis Imperiis*[73] which, according to Morris, is no more than 'a five quarto pages', had a pronounced influence on the Anglo–American conflicts lawyers of the eminence of Story, Beale and Dicey besides, of course, Justice Holmes.

Huber's formulation had for its basis sovereignty and power from which emerged the so-called 'vested or acquired rights' theory which he defined in the following terms: '"sovereigns will so act by way of comity that rights acquired within the limits of a government retain their force everywhere ...". The said formulation of Huber can, by no stretch of imagination, be characterized as primitive vis-à-vis modern formulations as to the choice of law in conflicts cases. It took a spate of writing on the part of American conflicts lawyers, dating back to the' thirties of the twentieth century, fortified further by Morris's contribution in the shape of the proper law doctrine in the area of contracts and torts, aimed at achieving results which are 'commercially and socially convenient and sound', to impart to their formulations realism and sophistication. This transformation in conflict of laws from the primeval to the modern bears a striking resemblance to the progression attained, be it the Roman private law, or the English law relating to persons, or the Hindu law after the recent codification, in all of which by legislation, or otherwise (by which I mean the common law), inequality of status or of opportunity is done away with, yielding place to equality and equal protection of the laws. Sir Henry Maine in his inimitable style aptly describes this movement of societies from the primitive to the modern in the following words:

'(T)he movement of the progressive societies has hitherto been a movement from Status to Contract'.[74]

I should say the credit goes to Professor Cavers to have drawn the attention of courts and the legal fraternity to choose to adopt the 'rule selection' rule or the 'principles of preference' to the abandonment of the traditional 'jurisdiction selection' rule, for the latter fails to look into the content of the conflicting laws before actually exercising the choice, which may not only result in injustice to the parties before the court but also likely to generate false conflicts. This, of course, was followed by the 'local law' theory of Professor Cook, the 'governmental interests' theory of Professor Brainerd Currie and Professor Baxter's theory of 'comparative impairment' of the interests of the competing states whose laws are in conflict and many more. In this context, Morris's contribution to the choice of law process through his proper law doctrine, as applied to contracts and torts, can hardly be overemphasized.

All these theories generated keen interest in the choice of law process, culminating in *The Restatement (Second), Conflict of Laws* which I choose to characterize as the Holistic Approach to Conflicts Resolution. It has set, as aforesaid, seven guidelines or criteria for the consideration of courts in resolving conflicts. It strongly advocated an issue-based approach to resolving conflicts.

After having critically reviewed the theories and methods and doctrines that have been emerging from time and time through the writings of jurists of repute, I may wind up this my piece on a note which may sound provocative. These theories and methods are comparable, if I may say so, to the many religions of the world which hold sway over their devout followers. The sacred scriptures are couched in different languages replete with attractive phrases. But, I dare say, that the sum and substance of all these scriptures are the unity of religions and universality of mankind. So is the case with these theories and methods. Am I wrong if I venture to pronounce a verdict, be it the 'rule selection' rule or the 'principles of preference' of Cavers, the 'governmental interests' theory based on policy considerations, whether molecular or molar, of Brainerd Currie, the 'proper law' theory of Morris, the 'holistic approach' to conflicts resolution of *The Restatement (Second), Conflict of Laws* of the American Law Institute, that all of them in substance converge and offer sense and direction to courts in their endeavour to resolve conflicts and render justice to the parties?

I may here draw an analogy from the world of sports. The players are the courts and these publicists are the coaches. The players on the field play their games adapting their moves as per exigencies, though conforming, by and large, to the strategies worked out by the coaches. So is the case with courts whose main goal is to appropriately resolve conflicts and render justice to the parties before them. Their guidelines in the conflicts resolution process are empiricism and pragmatism, and none other.

I may be failing in my duty if I omit to say appropriately a few words, addressed to the courts in India and the Indian legal fraternity, call them suggestions or a desire to share with them the little experience I gained over the years in my study and research of the subject under the present inquiry.

The Indian courts may have to adopt an issue-based approach to resolving conflicts, keeping in view at the same time our background as also the structure, the attitudes and the needs of our society. In this regard, we may have to remember the words of wisdom given to us by Professor Walter Wheeler Cook which, as stated earlier, runs thus: '... the problems in the field under consideration (namely contracts) need to be broken down into smaller groups and dealt with so as to meet the needs of society'.[75] The above suggestion would enable courts to accord proper weight in a particular case 'to factors of constantly varying significance like the place of contracting, the place of performance, the nationality of the ship, the *situs* of the land, the domicile, residence and place of business of the parties, their reasonable expectations, the currency in which the obligation is expressed and countless others'.[76] Also, the said rule would enable, as Morris puts it, to accord due attention to the question what law governs the particular question before the court, not so much as to what law governs the validity of the contract.[77]

There is no harm in quoting publicists of renown like Dicey, Morris and Cheshire on any aspect of the subject; but it should be confined to lending support to the conclusions that our courts reach, of course, with a touch of empiricism and pragmatism which, perforce, ought to be based on the needs, the requirements and the interest of our society.

I may conclude this manuscript by reproducing the observations of eminent Anglo–American jurists which, in my estimate, are basic to the science of conflict of laws. They are as under:

> In an interstate and international society, with a variety of local laws, a fairly uniform system of choice of law is needed to reduce the difficulties a person faces when he comes in contact with different legal systems. Were it otherwise, he would not know the permissible limits of his actions any more than he would in an intrastate transaction, if the local rules were unsettled. For this

reason, a court should hesitate long and hard before it departs from a widely accepted rule.[78]

'Private international law', writes Cheshire, 'is no more an exact science than in any other part of the law of England; it is not scientifically founded on the reasoning of jurists, but it is beaten out on the anvil of experience'.[79]

A COMPLEMENTARY RESUME

The growth and evolution of conflict of laws spread over three hundred years or so presents a fascinating study. The Anglo–American conflict of laws owes much to Ulrich Huber (1635–94), a Dutch jurist-cum-judge, among others, whose influence over leading publicists of eminence like story, Beale and Dicey besides, of course, Justice Holmes, is overwhelming. Huber's formulations had for their basis, to recall what has already been stated, sovereignty and power, which is evident from his three formulations, and in particular, the third, which is relevant for conflict of laws, which runs thus: 'Sovereigns will so act by way of comity that *rights acquired within the limits of a government retain their force everywhere* so far as they do not cause prejudice to the power or rights of such government or its subjects' [emphasis added].

The above formulation gave birth to the so-called vested or acquired rights theory for which A.V. Dicey in England and Joseph H. Beale in the United States are the votaries. In fact, Beale outclassed Dicey in his diehard adherence to the theory of 'vested' or 'acquired' rights.

According to Dicey, courts in England 'never in strictness enforce foreign law', and, that, 'when they are said to do so, they enforce not foreign laws, but rights acquired under foreign laws'.[80] Dicey's formulation of the so-called vested or acquired rights, which constitutes, according to him, General Principle No. I, reads as under: 'Every right which has been duly acquired under the law of any civilized country is recognized and, in general, enforced by English courts, and no right which has not been duly acquired is enforced, or, in general, recognized by English courts'.[81] He asserts that this maxim as to the recognition and enforcement of vested rights, which, according to him, constitutes General Principle No. II, 'lies at the foundation of the rules for determining the extra-territorial operation of law', and that the application of the principle, accordingly, is 'universally recognized', and that 'the recognition of rights acquired under foreign law is a leading principle of modern civilization'[82]

The vested or acquired rights theory finds its echo in the dicta of Justice Holmes and Justice Cordozo of the United States respectively in the leading cases *Slater* v. *Mexican National Railway*[83] and *Loucks* v. *Standard Oil Co. of New York.*[84] Justice Holmes, in fact, reiterated the principle he advocated in the Slater's case in the case *Mutual Life Insurance Co.* v. *Leibing,*[85] by asserting that, 'the constitution and the first principles of legal thinking allow the law of the place where a contract is made to determine the validity and the consequences of the act'.[86]

Professor J.H. Beale of the Harvard Law School and the Reporter of *The Restatement I, The Conflict of Laws*, American Law Institute, who, as stated earlier, outclassed Professor A.V. Dicey in his enunciation of the vested rights theory. In respect of a contract, he declares under section 'Rule of Place of Making', thus:

> The question whether a contract is valid ... can on general principles be determined by no other law than that which applies to the acts (of the parties), that is by the law of the place of contracting. *If the law of the place where the agreement is made annexes no legal obligation to it, there can be no other law which has power to do so* [emphasis added].[87]

Conversely, according to him, no other law, whether that of the place of performance, or any other, can avoid the effect of the law of the place where the contact is made.[88] To him the principle that contracts are governed as to their nature and validity by the law of the place where they are made is 'both sound theoretically and most practical'.[89]

In respect of tortious claims, too, according to him, it is the *lex loci delicti commissi* that is the governing law. 'It is impossible for a plaintiff', he observes, 'to recover in tort unless he has been given by some law a cause of action in tort, and this cause of action can be given only by the law of the place where the tort was committed'.[90]

The vested rights theory was shredded beyond recognition and thoroughly incinerated by the forceful and devastating writing of Arminjon[91] in France and Cook[92] and Lorenzen[93] in the United States.

Cook, in particular, pointing his finger towards the most regrettable decision in *Milliken* v. *Pratt*,[94] an instance, if I may say so, of a thoughtless translation into practice of the vested rights theory, comments that it is his concern 'to free the intellectual garden of the rank weeds in the shape of the vested rights theory of Beale so as to facilitate the planting and cultivation of useful vegetables'.[95]

Professor Cavers, commenting on Professor Cook's ruthless onslaught on Beale's vested rights theory observes: '(T)he author's technique has enabled him to destroy the intellectual foundation of the system to the erection of which Professor Beale devoted a lifetime.'[96] In contrast stands Professor Yntema's vitriolic comment which runs thus:

> It is regrettable that Cook did not take into account of the incisive criticisms to which the theory of sovereignty, on grounds of facts as well as principles, has been subjected to by political and juristic thinkers. Given his destructive intent to eliminate the weeds of current dogma from the garden of conflicts law, it would have enabled him to reduce them all—the garden, the principle of sovereignty and his own analysis included—to ashes from which a phoenix might in time arise.[97]

From the foregoing analysis, it is fair to comment that the vested rights theory is question begging, in the sense that, it is the factual situation and an issue-based inquiry into it by the concerned court as to the conflicting claims of the disputants that give rise to the applicable law, and not vice versa, if the aim and objective of the court is to render justice to the parties before it by recourse to appropriate choice of law process.

Professor Beale's vested rights theory, as articulated in Sections 332 and 377 of *The Restatement I, Conflict of Laws*, 1934 in respect of contracts and torts respectively was supplanted by the modern issue-based 'rule selection' rule, based on grounds of policy, value and interests, which is embodied in Sections 187 & 188 in respect of contracts and Section 145 in respect of torts of the *Restatement (Second), Conflict of Laws, 1971*. Likewise, the vested rights theory of Professor Dicey was decorously dropped in the eighth edition of Dicey's *The Conflict of Laws*, edited by J.H.C. Morris, in view of its having lost credibility with the courts and the juristic community in the contemporary choice of laws process.

More importantly, the traditional 'jurisdiction selection' rule had to yield place to the modern issue-based 'rule selection' rule which, by implication, means the abandonment of the time–honoured practice of treating legal transaction, be it contract, marriage, succession, or any as an 'all–purpose concept', to borrow Professor Willis Reese's phrase, instead of, as is deemed the right course, addressed to courts, as Professor Cook puts it, that 'the problems in the field under consideration (that is, contracts) need be broken down into smaller group and dealt with so as to meet the needs of society'.

Professor Cavers has chiefly been instrumental in ably advocating the 'rule selection' rule in preference to the traditional 'jurisdiction selection' rule in the conflicts resolution process in an article that he wrote, as stated earlier, in the *Harvard Law Review* in the year 1933, entitled 'A Critique of the Choice of Law Problem',[98] It took nearly four decades for the said 'rule selection' rule to be inducted into the choice of law process by courts. It is, therefore, no exaggeration to say that he revolutionized the whole approach to the choice of law process in conflicts cases. In that article, Cavers deprecated the traditional law system based, as it happened to be all along, on the mechanical jurisdiction selection without turning attention to the content of the law which, more often than not, may lead to injustice to the parties and generate false conflicts. He further contends that any mechanical application of the choice of law rules by recourse to the 'jurisdiction selection' method may result in miscarriage of justice as it happened in the leading case *Milliken* v. *Pratt*.[99]

It is of interest, in this connection, to take note of the observations of Professors Cheatham and Reese of the Columbia Law School with regard to the choice of law process which deserves reiteration. The choice of law process, according to them, is the most difficult one in conflict of laws in view of 'the youth and fluidity of the subject'. Unlike other branches of the law, precedents are relatively sparse in this area, besides they being misleading. In the absence of an accepted body of settled rules, courts are constrained to have recourse to basic questions such as policy and value in the determination of cases.

'The second source of difficulty, according to the learned professors, 'stems from the belief, commonly held at an earlier time, that all aspects of choice of law could be handled satisfactorily by a relatively small number of simple rules derived logically from what was deemed to be a single overriding principle as, for example, power, sovereignty or vested interests'. They further observe:

This view expressed by men of greatest ability, (namely Joseph Story, Professor Beale and Justice Holmes), had obvious appeal because it seemed to promise both certainty of result and ease of application. Its falsity is now generally recognised, but more than anything else it has retarded development in the field by inducing courts to look only to a simple, symmetrical system, unattuned to practical considerations.[100]

In reply to the critics of his 'rule selection' rule, Cavers admits that his thesis may have greater relevance to a federal union, like the United States, than to the choice of law process in the international setting, where the argument for certainty and uniformity based upon fear of local bias is patent.[101] While thus admitting the limitation in his 'rule selection' rule, as stated earlier, he observes: 'The application of mechanical rules of law in such a situation may, accordingly, be regarded as necessary to safeguard the alien litigant from xenophobia.'[102]

Secondly, Professor Cavers asserts that his approach has for its aim, the promotion of 'principles of preference', and certainly not, as is attributed to him, 'justice in the individual case'. He contends, as a rejoinder to his critics, that 'the application of a just rule should not be deemed incompatible with justice in individual case.'[103] In his view, the courts in conflicts cases is not engaged in an exercise in comparative jurisprudence, appraising the respective merits of the two rules of law. It (namely the court), on the other hand, passes judgment on a careful scrutiny of the conflicting claims of the two parties with a view to rendering justice. The emphasis, therefore, is on the circumstances of the case, and not on the conflicting laws of countries or jurisdiction that the problems present.[104]

This 'rule selection' rule of Cavers was followed by a spate of writing on conflicts law based on policy, value and interests, culminating in the *Restatement (Second), The Conflict of Laws*, 1971.

NOTES

1. *Y. Narasimha Rao* v. *Y. Venktalaskhmi*, AIR (1991) SC 821 p. 831.
2. Wim BI 234 p. 258–9.

3. 2 BURR 1077 p. 1078
4. *Mostyn* v. *Fabrigas*, (1774), I COWP 161.
5. (1870) LR 6 QBI
6. The abolition of the 'double actionability' doctrine, as per Section 10 of the Private International Law (Miscellaneous) Provision Act, 1995, applies to all torts committed after 1 May 1996 when the Act came into force, for no law can have retrospective operation. All the same, as per Section 13 of the Act, the said doctrine is preserved in respect of defamation.
7. J.H.C. Morris, 'The Proper Law of a Tort', *Harvard Law Review*, Vol. 64 (1951), pp. 881–3.
8. See Sections 332 and 358, *Restatement I, Conflict of Laws* of the American Law Institute, (1934).
9. Ibid, Section 377, (1934).
10. *Chaplin* v. *Boys*, (1965) 2 ALL ER1085 p. 1104.
11. See Sections 187 and 188, *Restatement (Second), Conflict of Laws*, American Law Institute (St. Paul Minnesota, American Law Institute Publishers, 1971).
12. Walter Wheeler Cook, Logical and Legal Bases of the Conflicts of Laws 431, (1942). See pp. 416–18.
13. Morris, 'The Proper Law of a Tort', p. 882.
14. Ibid.
15. Ibid: p. 884.
16. *Padula* v. *Lilarn Properties Corporation*, 84 NY 2d 519, 620; NYS. 2d 310; 644 NE 2d 1001 (1994). See also in this connection, *Babcock* v. *Jackson*, 12 NY 2d 473; 240 NY 2d 743; 191 NE 2d 279 (1963); *Tooker* v. *Lopez*, 24 NY 2d 584; 301 NYS 2d 532; 249 NE 2d 403 (1964); *Neumeier* v. *Kuchner*, 24 NY 2d 532; 301 NYS 2d 585; 301 NYS 2d 532; 249 NE 2d 434 (1972).
17. Goodrich, *Conflict of Laws*, p. 263.
18. 97 ALA 126, 11So. 803 (1892)
19. 108 CONN 333, 143 ATL 163 (1928)
20. Ibid.
21. 68F. 2d 942 (2nd Cir. 1934)
22. Ont. Highway Traffic Act Section 41-A (1930).
23. See Section 59, New York Vehicle and Traffic Law.
24. Morris, 'The Proper Law of a Tort', pp. 881–3.
25. David F. Cavers, 'A Critique of the Choice of Law Problem', *Harvard Law Review*, Vol. 47 (1933), p. 173.
26. Walter Wheeler Cook, *Logical and Legal Bases of the Conflict of Laws*, (1942), Ch.1, as also chapters 13 and 14. See also Walter Wheeler Cook, 'The

Logical and Legal Bases of Conflict of Laws', (1924) *Yale Law Journal*, Vol. 33 (1924), p. 457.

27. Ibid, pp. 21–2.

28. David F. Cavers, Comment: *The Two "Local Law" Theories*. Vol. 63 (1950), p. 822, at 824.

29. (1923) 291 Fed. 768

30. Ibid., p. 770.

31. Cook, see note 26 supra.

32. Cavers, see note 28 supra, p. 832.

33. Cavers, see note 25 supra, p. 173.

34. (1878) 125 MASS 374

35. 12 NY 2d 473 at 481; 191 NE 2d 279 at 283

36. Ibid.

37. Morris, 'The Proper Law of a Tort', p. 883.

38. *Tooker* v. *Lopez*, 24 NY 2d 569 p. 584; 249 NE 2d 394, p. 403 (1964); and, also see in particular, *Neumeier* v. *Kuchner*, 31 NY 2d 121; 286 NE 2d 454.

39. 16 CAL 3d 313; 546 p. 2d 719 (1976)

40. 67 CAL 2d 551; 432 p. 2d 727 (1967)

41. (1963) Stan. LR 1 p. 9

42. 84 NY 2d 519, 620; NYS 2d 310; 644 NE 2d 1001 (1994)

43. Brochers, 'The Return of the Territorialism to New York's Conflict of Law: *Padula* v. *Lilarn Properties Corpn.*', *Albany Law Review*, Vol. 58 (1995), p. 775.

44. David F. Cavers, *The Choice of Law: Selected Essays, 1933–83* (Durham: Duke University Press, 1985), p. 81.

45. Ibid.

46 David R. Cavers, *The Choice of Law Process*, (The University of Michigan Press, 1965), p. 78.

47. Ibid, p. 86.

48. Ibid, p. 86.

49. Cavers, 'A Critique of the Choice of Law Problem', *Merrill Law Review*.

50. Ibid.

51. Ibid.

52. Cavers, *Choice of Law—Selected Eassys, 1933–83*, p. 26.

53. Ibid., p. 27.

54. Willis L.M. Reese, '*Marriage in American Conflict of Laws*', *The International and Comparative Law Quarterly*, Vol. 26 (1977), p. 952.

55. Ibid., p. 953.

56. Ibid.

57. Brainerd Currie, *Selected Eassys on the Conflict of Laws*, p. 182.

58. J.H.C. Morris, *The Conflict of Laws*, Second Edition (London, Stevens and Sons, 1980), p. 513.

59. (1936) 3 ALL ER 407

60. (1969) 2 ALL ER 1085; (1971) AC 356

61. See Section 145 (1) of *The Restatement (Second), Conflict of Laws*, (1971).

62. Ibid, per Lord Hodson, p. 1092. See also in this connection, V.C. Govindaraj, 'Foreign Torts in Conflicts Cases: A Plea for a Viable Social Environmental Theory—The English Double Actionability Doctrine: Chaplin v. Boys,' (1971) AC 356, (1969) 2 ALL ER 1085, *Columbia Journal of Transnational Law*, Vol. 9 (1970), pp. 152–3.

63. Elliott E. Cheatham and Willis L.M. Reese, 'Choice of the Applicable Law', *Columbia Law Review*, Vol. 52 (1952), p. 959.

64. *Restatement (Second), The Conflict of Laws* (St. Paul Minnesota, American Law Institute Publishers, 1971).

65. Morris, *The Conflict of Laws*, Second Edition.

66. Cheatham and Reese, 'Choice of the Applicable Law', pp. 959–60.

67. Ibid.

68. Section 6, *Restatement of the Law (Second).*

69. Sections 332 and 358, *Restatement I, Conflict of Laws*, (1934).

70. Ibid, Section 377, (1934).

71. Morris, 'The Proper Law of a Tort' and *The Conflict of Laws*, Second Edition.

72. Morris, *The Conflict of Laws*, Second Edition, p. 499.

73. Huber, *De Conflictu legum Diversarum in Diversis imperiis*, Vol. III, Book 1, title 3.

74. Sir Henry Sumner Maine, *Ancient Law* (London: George Routledge & Sons, Limited, 1913), p. 141.

75. Cook, see note 26 supra, pp. 417–18.

76. Morris, *The Conflict of Laws*, Second Edition.

77. Ibid.

78. Cheatham and Reese, 'Choice of the Applicable Law', *Columbia Law Review*, pp. 969–70.

79. Sir Peter North and J.J. Fawcett, *Cheshire and North's Private International Law*, Thirteenth Edition (London, Edinburgh, Dublin: LexisNexis Butterworths, 1999), p. 32.

80. A.V. Dicey, *A Digest of the Law of England with Reference to The Conflict of Laws*, Third Edition, p. 11.

81. Ibid; pp. 23–4.

82. Ibid; p. 34: General Principle No. II.
83. (1904) 194 US 120, 126
84. 224 NY 99; 120 NE 198, 201 (1918)
85. (1922) 259 US 209
86. Ibid., p. 214.
87. J.H. Beale, *The Conflict of Laws*, Vol. 2, p. 1091.
88. Ibid; p. 1091.
89. Ibid; p. 1092.
90. Ibid; p. 1288.
91. P. Arminjon, *Recueil Des Cours, II* (1933), pp. 5–105.
92. Cook, 'The Logical and Legal Bases of Conflict of Laws', p. 457. See also Cook's major work, *Logical and Legal Bases of the Conflict of Laws*, Chapter 1 as also chapters 13 and 14.
93. Ernest N. Lorenzen, *Yale Law Journal*, Vol. 33 (1924) p. 736; reprinted in Lorenzen, *Selected Articles on the Conflict of Laws*, Chapter 1. See also pp. 104–11.
94. (1878) 125 MASS 374
95. See Preface to Walter Wheeler Cook's '*The Logical and Legal Bases of the Conflict of Laws*'.
96. David F. Cavers, 'Book Review of Cook', *Harvard Law Review*, (1943), pp. 1170–72; Reproduced in Cavers, see note 44 supra, pp. 41–2.
97. Yntema, Vol. 2, *American Journal of Comparative Law*, (1953), pp. 297–315.
98. Cavers, 'A Critique of the Choice of Law Problem', p. 173.
99. (1878) 125 MASS 374
100. Cheatham and Reese, 'Choice of the Applicable Law', *Columbia Law Review*, p. 959.
101. Ibid.
102. Cavers, note 44, p. 81.
103. David F. Cavers, *The Choice of Law Process*, p. 78.
104. Ibid; p. 86.

ANNEXURE 1

Convention Abolishing the Requirement of Legalisation for Foreign Public Documents

(Concluded 5 October 1961)
(Entered into force 24 January 1965)

The States signatory to the present Convention,

Desiring to abolish the requirement of diplomatic or consular legalisation for foreign public documents,

Have resolved to conclude a Convention to this effect and have agreed upon the following provisions:

Article 1

The present Convention shall apply to public documents which have been executed in the territory of one Contracting State and which have to be produced in the territory of another Contracting State.

For the purposes of the present Convention, the following are deemed to be public documents:

(a) documents emanating from an authority or an official connected with the courts or tribunals of the State, including those emanating from a public prosecutor, a clerk of a court or a process-server ('huissier de justice');

(b) administrative documents;

(c) notarial acts;

(d) official certificates which are placed on documents signed by persons in their private capacity, such as official certificates recording the registration of a document or the fact that it was in existence on a certain date and official and notarial authentications of signatures.

However, the present Convention shall not apply:

(a) to documents executed by diplomatic or consular agents;

(b) to administrative documents dealing directly with commercial or customs operations.

Article 2

Each Contracting State shall exempt from legalisation documents to which the present Convention applies and which have to be produced in its territory. For the purposes of the present Convention, legalisation means only the formality by which the diplomatic or consular agents of the country in which the document has to be produced certify the authenticity of the signature, the capacity in which the person signing the document has acted and, where appropriate, the identity of the seal or stamp which it bears.

Article 3

The only formality that may be required in order to certify the authenticity of the signature, the capacity in which the person signing the document has acted and, where appropriate, the identity of the seal or stamp which it bears, is the addition of the certificate described in Article 4, issued by the competent authority of the State from which the document emanates.

However, the formality mentioned in the preceding paragraph cannot be required when either the laws, regulations, or practice in force in the State where the document is produced or an agreement between two or more Contracting States have abolished or simplified it, or exempt the document itself from legalisation.

Article 4

The certificate referred to in the first paragraph of Article 3 shall be placed on the document itself or on an 'allonge', it shall be in the form of the model annexed to the present Convention.

It may, however, be drawn up in the official language of the authority which issues it. The standard terms appearing therein may be in a second language also. The title 'Apostille (Convention de La Haye du 5 octobre 1961)' shall be in the French language.

Article 5

The certificate shall be issued at the request of the person who has signed the document or of any bearer.

When properly filled in, it will certify the authenticity of the signature, the capacity in which the person signing the document has acted and, where appropriate, the identity of the seal or stamp which the document bears.

The signature, seal and stamp on the certificate are exempt from all certification.

Article 6

Each Contracting State shall designate by reference to their official function, the authorities who are competent to issue the certificate referred to in the first paragraph of Article 3.

It shall give notice of such designation to the Ministry of Foreign Affairs of the Netherlands at the time it deposits its instrument of ratification or of accession or its declaration of extension. It shall also give notice of any change in the designated authorities.

Article 7

Each of the authorities designated in accordance with Article 6 shall keep a register or card index in which it shall record the certificates issued, specifying:

(a) the number and date of the certificate,

(b) the name of the person signing the public document and the capacity in which he has acted, or in the case of unsigned documents, the name of the authority which has affixed the seal or stamp.

At the request of any interested person, the authority which has issued the certificate shall verify whether the particulars in the certificate correspond with those in the register or card index.

Article 8

When a treaty, convention or agreement between two or more Contracting States contains provisions which subject the certification of a signature, seal or stamp to certain formalities, the present Convention will only override such provisions if those formalities are more rigorous than the formality referred to in Articles 3 and 4.

Article 9

Each Contracting State shall take the necessary steps to prevent the performance of legalisations by its diplomatic or consular agents in cases where the present Convention provides for exemption.

Article 10

The present Convention shall be open for signature by the States represented at the Ninth Session of the Hague Conference on Private International Law and Iceland, Ireland, Liechtenstein and Turkey.

It shall be ratified, and the instruments of ratification shall be deposited with the Ministry of Foreign Affairs of the Netherlands.

Article 11

The present Convention shall enter into force on the sixtieth day after the deposit of the third instrument of ratification referred to in the second paragraph of Article 10.

The Convention shall enter into force for each signatory State which ratifies subsequently on the sixtieth day after the deposit of its instrument of ratification.

Article 12

Any State not referred to in Article 10 may accede to the present Convention after it has entered into force in accordance with the first paragraph of Article 11. The instrument of accession shall be deposited with the Ministry of Foreign Affairs of the Netherlands.

Such accession shall have effect only as regards the relations between the acceding State and those Contracting States which have not raised an objection to its accession in the six months after the receipt of the notification referred to in sub-paragraph *(d)* of Article 15. Any such objection shall be notified to the Ministry of Foreign Affairs of the Netherlands.

The Convention shall enter into force as between the acceding State and the States which have raised no objection to its accession on the sixtieth day after the expiry of the period of six months mentioned in the preceding paragraph.

Article 13

Any State may, at the time of signature, ratification or accession, declare that the present Convention shall extend to all the territories for the international relations of which it is responsible, or to one or more of them. Such a declaration shall take effect on the date of entry into force of the Convention for the State concerned.

At any time thereafter, such extensions shall be notified to the Ministry of Foreign Affairs of the Netherlands.

When the declaration of extension is made by a State which has signed and ratified, the Convention shall enter into force for the territories concerned in accordance with Article 11. When the declaration of extension is made by a State which has acceded, the Convention shall enter into force for the territories concerned in accordance with Article 12.

Article 14

The present Convention shall remain in force for five years from the date of its entry into force in accordance with the first paragraph of Article 11, even for States which have ratified it or acceded to it subsequently.

If there has been no denunciation, the Convention shall be renewed tacitly every five years.

Any denunciation shall be notified to the Ministry of Foreign Affairs of the Netherlands at least six months before the end of the five year period.

It may be limited to certain of the territories to which the Convention applies.

The denunciation will only have effect as regards the State which has notified it. The Convention shall remain in force for the other Contracting States.

Article 15

The Ministry of Foreign Affairs of the Netherlands shall give notice to the States referred to in Article 10, and to the States which have acceded in accordance with Article 12, of the following:

(a) the notifications referred to in the second paragraph of Article 6;

(b) the signatures and ratifications referred to in Article 10;

(c) the date on which the present Convention enters into force in accordance with the first paragraph of Article 11;

(d) the accessions and objections referred to in Article 12 and the date on which such accessions take effect;

(e) the extensions referred to in Article 13 and the date on which they take effect;

(f) the denunciations referred to in the third paragraph of Article 14.

In witness whereof the undersigned, being duly authorized thereto, have signed the present Convention.

Done at The Hague the 5th October 1961, in French and in English, the French text prevailing in case of divergence between the two texts, in a single copy which shall be deposited in the archives of the Government of the Netherlands, and of which a certified copy shall be sent, through the diplomatic channel, to each of the States represented at the Ninth Session of the Hague Conference on Private International Law and also to Iceland, Ireland, Liechtenstein and Turkey.

Annexure 2

Convention on the Service Abroad of Judicial and Extra-judicial Documents in Civil or Commercial Matters

(Concluded 15 November 1965)
(Entered into force 10 February 1969)

The States signatory to the present Convention,

Desiring to create appropriate means to ensure that judicial and extrajudicial documents to be served abroad shall be brought to the notice of the addressee in sufficient time,

Desiring to improve the organisation of mutual judicial assistance for that purpose by simplifying and expediting the procedure,

Have resolved to conclude a Convention to this effect and have agreed upon the following provisions:

Article 1

The present Convention shall apply in all cases, in civil or commercial matters, where there is occasion to transmit a judicial or extrajudicial document for service abroad.

This Convention shall not apply where the address of the person to be served with the document is not known.

Chapter I: Judicial Documents

Article 2

Each Contracting State shall designate a Central Authority which will undertake to receive requests for service coming from other Contracting States and to proceed in conformity with the provisions of Articles 3 to 6.

Each State shall organise the Central Authority in conformity with its own law.

Article 3

The authority or judicial officer competent under the law of the State in which the documents originate shall forward to the Central Authority of the State addressed a request conforming to the model annexed to the present Convention, without any requirement of legalization or other equivalent formality.

The document to be served or a copy thereof shall be annexed to the request. The request and the document shall both be furnished in duplicate.

Article 4

If the Central Authority considers that the request does not comply with the provisions of the present Convention it shall promptly inform the applicant and specify its objections to the request.

Article 5

The Central Authority of the State addressed shall itself serve the document or shall arrange to have it served by an appropriate agency, either—

(a) by a method prescribed by its internal law for the service of documents in domestic actions upon persons who are within its territory, or

(b) by a particular method requested by the applicant, unless such a method is incompatible with the law of the State addressed.

Subject to sub-paragraph *(b)* of the first paragraph of this Article, the document may always be served by delivery to an addressee who accepts it voluntarily.

If the document is to be served under the first paragraph above, the Central Authority may require the document to be written in, or translated into, the official language or one of the official languages of the State addressed.

That part of the request, in the form attached to the present Convention, which contains a summary of the document to be served, shall be served with the document.

Article 6

The Central Authority of the State addressed or any authority which it may have designated for that purpose, shall complete a certificate in the form of the model annexed to the present Convention.

The certificate shall state that the document has been served and shall include the method, the place and the date of service and the person to whom the document was delivered. If the document has not been served, the certificate shall set out the reasons which have prevented service.

The applicant may require that a certificate not completed by a Central Authority or by a judicial authority shall be countersigned by one of these authorities.

The certificate shall be forwarded directly to the applicant.

Article 7

The standard terms in the model annexed to the present Convention shall in all cases be written either in French or in English. They may also be written in the official language, or in one of the official languages, of the State in which the documents originate.

The corresponding blanks shall be completed either in the language of the State addressed or in French or in English.

Article 8

Each Contracting State shall be free to effect service of judicial documents upon persons abroad, without application of any compulsion, directly through its diplomatic or consular agents.

Any State may declare that it is opposed to such service within its territory, unless the document is to be served upon a national of the State in which the documents originate.

Article 9

Each Contracting State shall be free, in addition, to use consular channels to forward documents, for the purpose of service, to those authorities of another Contracting State which are designated by the latter for this purpose.

Each Contracting State may, if exceptional circumstances so require, use diplomatic channels for the same purpose.

Article 10

Provided the State of destination does not object, the present Convention shall not interfere with—

(a) the freedom to send judicial documents, by postal channels, directly to persons abroad,

(b) the freedom of judicial officers, officials or other competent persons of the State of origin to effect service of judicial documents directly through the judicial officers, officials or other competent persons of the State of destination,

(c) the freedom of any person interested in a judicial proceeding to effect service of judicial documents directly through the judicial officers, officials or other competent persons of the State of destination.

Article 11

The present Convention shall not prevent two or more Contracting States from agreeing to permit, for the purpose of service of judicial documents, channels of transmission other than those provided for in the preceding Articles and, in particular, direct communication between their respective authorities.

Article 12

The service of judicial documents coming from a Contracting State shall not give rise to any payment or reimbursement of taxes or costs for the services rendered by the State addressed.

The applicant shall pay or reimburse the costs occasioned by—

(a) the employment of a judicial officer or of a person competent under the law of the State of destination,

(b) the use of a particular method of service.

Article 13

Where a request for service complies with the terms of the present Convention, the State addressed may refuse to comply therewith only if it deems that compliance would infringe its sovereignty or security.

It may not refuse to comply solely on the ground that, under its internal law, it claims exclusive jurisdiction over the subject-matter of the action or that its internal law would not permit the action upon which the application is based.

The Central Authority shall, in case of refusal, promptly inform the applicant and state the reasons for the refusal.

Article 14

Difficulties which may arise in connection with the transmission of judicial documents for service shall be settled through diplomatic channels.

Article 15

Where a writ of summons or an equivalent document had to be transmitted abroad for the purpose of service, under the provisions of the present Convention, and the defendant has not appeared, judgment shall not be given until it is established that—

(a) the document was served by a method prescribed by the internal law of the State addressed for the service of documents in domestic actions upon persons who are within its territory, or

(b) the document was actually delivered to the defendant or to his residence by another method provided for by this Convention, and that in either of these cases the service or the delivery was effected in sufficient time to enable the defendant to defend.

Each Contracting State shall be free to declare that the judge, notwithstanding the provisions of the first paragraph of this Article, may give judgment even if no certificate of service or delivery has been received, if all the following conditions are fulfilled—

(a) the document was transmitted by one of the methods provided for in this Convention,

(b) a period of time of not less than six months, considered adequate by the judge in the particular case, has elapsed since the date of the transmission of the document,

(c) no certificate of any kind has been received, even though every reasonable effort has been made to obtain it through the competent authorities of the State addressed.

Notwithstanding the provisions of the preceding paragraphs the judge may order, in case of urgency, any provisional or protective measures.

Article 16

When a writ of summons or an equivalent document had to be transmitted abroad for the purpose of service, under the provisions of the present Convention, and a judgment has been entered against a defendant who has not appeared, the judge shall have the power to relieve the defendant from the effects of the expiration of the time for appeal from the judgment if the following conditions are fulfilled—

(a) the defendant, without any fault on his part, did not have knowledge of the document in sufficient time to defend, or knowledge of the judgment in sufficient time to appeal, and

(b) the defendant has disclosed a *prima facie* defence to the action on the merits.

An application for relief may be filed only within a reasonable time after the defendant has knowledge of the judgment.

Each Contracting State may declare that the application will not be entertained if it is filed after the expiration of a time to be stated in the declaration, but which shall in no case be less than one year following the date of the judgment.

This Article shall not apply to judgments concerning status or capacity of persons.

Chapter II: Extra-judicial Documents

Article 17

Extrajudicial documents emanating from authorities and judicial officers of a Contracting State may be transmitted for the purpose of service in another Contracting State by the methods and under the provisions of the present Convention.

Chapter III: General Clauses

Article 18

Each Contracting State may designate other authorities in addition to the Central Authority and shall determine the extent of their competence.

The applicant shall, however, in all cases, have the right to address a request directly to the Central Authority.

Federal States shall be free to designate more than one Central Authority.

Article 19

To the extent that the internal law of a Contracting State permits methods of transmission, other than those provided for in the preceding Articles, of documents coming from abroad, for service within its territory, the present Convention shall not affect such provisions.

Article 20

The present Convention shall not prevent an agreement between any two or more Contracting States to dispense with—

(a) the necessity for duplicate copies of transmitted documents as required by the second paragraph of Article 3,

(b) the language requirements of the third paragraph of Article 5 and Article 7,

(c) the provisions of the fourth paragraph of Article 5,

(d) the provisions of the second paragraph of Article 12.

Article 21

Each Contracting State shall, at the time of the deposit of its instrument of ratification or accession, or at a later date, inform the Ministry of Foreign Affairs of the Netherlands of the following—

(a) the designation of authorities, pursuant to Articles 2 and 18,

(b) the designation of the authority competent to complete the certificate pursuant to Article 6,

(c) the designation of the authority competent to receive documents transmitted by consular channels, pursuant to Article 9.

Each Contracting State shall similarly inform the Ministry, where appropriate, of—

(a) opposition to the use of methods of transmission pursuant to Articles 8 and 10,

(b) declarations pursuant to the second paragraph of Article 15 and the third paragraph of Article 16,

(c) all modifications of the above designations, oppositions and declarations.

Article 22

Where Parties to the present Convention are also Parties to one or both of the Conventions on civil procedure signed at The Hague on 17th July 1905, and on 1st March 1954, this Convention shall replace as between them Articles 1 to 7 of the earlier Conventions.

Article 23

The present Convention shall not affect the application of Article 23 of the Convention on civil procedure signed at The Hague on 17th July 1905, or of Article 24 of the Convention on civil procedure signed at The Hague on 1st March 1954.

These Articles shall, however, apply only if methods of communication, identical to those provided for in these Conventions, are used.

Article 24

Supplementary agreements between Parties to the Conventions of 1905 and 1954 shall be considered as equally applicable to the present Convention, unless the Parties have otherwise agreed.

Article 25

Without prejudice to the provisions of Articles 22 and 24, the present Convention shall not derogate from Conventions containing provisions on the matters governed by this Convention to which the Contracting States are, or shall become, Parties.

Article 26

The present Convention shall be open for signature by the States represented at the Tenth Session of the Hague Conference on Private International Law.

It shall be ratified, and the instruments of ratification shall be deposited with the Ministry of Foreign Affairs of the Netherlands.

Article 27

The present Convention shall enter into force on the sixtieth day after the deposit of the third instrument of ratification referred to in the second paragraph of Article 26.

The Convention shall enter into force for each signatory State which ratifies subsequently on the sixtieth day after the deposit of its instrument of ratification.

Article 28

Any State not represented at the Tenth Session of the Hague Conference on Private International Law may accede to the present Convention after it has entered into force in accordance with the first paragraph of Article 27. The instrument of accession shall be deposited with the Ministry of Foreign Affairs of the Netherlands.

The Convention shall enter into force for such a State in the absence of any objection from a State, which has ratified the Convention before such deposit, notified to the Ministry of Foreign Affairs of the Netherlands within a period of six months after the date on which the said Ministry has notified it of such accession.

In the absence of any such objection, the Convention shall enter into force for the acceding State on the first day of the month following the expiration of the last of the periods referred to in the preceding paragraph.

Article 29

Any State may, at the time of signature, ratification or accession, declare that the present Convention shall extend to all the territories for the international relations of which it is responsible, or to one or more of them. Such a declaration shall take effect on the date of entry into force of the Convention for the State concerned.

At any time thereafter, such extensions shall be notified to the Ministry of Foreign Affairs of the Netherlands.

The Convention shall enter into force for the territories mentioned in such an extension on the sixtieth day after the notification referred to in the preceding paragraph.

Article 30

The present Convention shall remain in force for five years from the date of its entry into force in accordance with the first paragraph of Article 27, even for States which have ratified it or acceded to it subsequently.

If there has been no denunciation, it shall be renewed tacitly every five years.

Any denunciation shall be notified to the Ministry of Foreign Affairs of the Netherlands at least six months before the end of the five year period.

It may be limited to certain of the territories to which the Convention applies.

The denunciation shall have effect only as regards the State which has notified it. The Convention shall remain in force for the other Contracting States.

Article 31

The Ministry of Foreign Affairs of the Netherlands shall give notice to the States referred to in Article 26, and to the States which have acceded in accordance with Article 28, of the following—

(a) the signatures and ratifications referred to in Article 26;

(b) the date on which the present Convention enters into force in accordance with the first paragraph of Article 27;

(c) the accessions referred to in Article 28 and the dates on which they take effect;

(d) the extensions referred to in Article 29 and the dates on which they take effect;

(e) the designations, oppositions and declarations referred to in Article 21;

(f) the denunciations referred to in the third paragraph of Article 30.

In witness whereof the undersigned, being duly authorised thereto, have signed the present convention.

Done at The Hague, on the 15th day of November, 1965, in the English and French languages, both texts being equally authentic, in a single copy which shall be deposited in the archives of the Government of the Netherlands, and of which a certified copy shall be sent, through the diplomatic channel, to each of the States represented at the tenth session of the Hague Conference on Private International Law.

On 25 October 1980 the Fourteenth Session adopted a Recommendation on information to accompany judicial and extra-judicial documents to be sent or served abroad in civil or commercial matters (Actes et documents de la Quatorzième session (1980), Tome I, *Matières diverses*, p. I-67; *idem*, Tome IV, *Entraide judiciaire*, p. 339; *Practical Handbook on the Operation of the Hague Convention of 15 November 1965 on the Service Abroad of Judicial and Extra-judicial Documents in Civil or Commercial Matters).*

Annexure 3

Convention on the Taking of Evidence Abroad in Civil or Commercial Matters

(Concluded 18 March 1970)
(Entered into force 7 October 1972)

The States signatory to the present Convention,

Desiring to facilitate the transmission and execution of Letters of Request and to further the accommodation of the different methods which they use for this purpose,

Desiring to improve mutual judicial co-operation in civil or commercial matters,

Have resolved to conclude a Convention to this effect and have agreed upon the following provisions:

Chapter I: Letters of Request

Article 1

In civil or commercial matters a judicial authority of a Contracting State may, in accordance with the provisions of the law of that State, request the competent authority of another Contracting State, by means of a Letter of Request, to obtain evidence, or to perform some other judicial act.

A Letter shall not be used to obtain evidence which is not intended for use in judicial proceedings, commenced or contemplated.

The expression 'other judicial act' does not cover the service of judicial documents or the issuance of any process by which judgments or orders are executed or enforced, or orders for provisional or protective measures.

Article 2

A Contracting State shall designate a Central Authority which will undertake to receive Letters of Request coming from a judicial authority of another Contracting State and to transmit them to the authority competent to execute them. Each State shall organize the Central Authority in accordance with its own law.

Letters shall be sent to the Central Authority of the State of execution without being transmitted through any other authority of that State.

Article 3

A Letter of Request shall specify—

(a) the authority requesting its execution and the authority requested to execute it, if known to the requesting authority;

(b) the names and addresses of the parties to the proceedings and their representatives, if any;

(c) the nature of the proceedings for which the evidence is required, giving all necessary information in regard thereto;

(d) the evidence to be obtained or other judicial act to be performed.

Where appropriate, the Letter shall specify, *inter alia*—

(e) the names and addresses of the persons to be examined;

(f) the questions to be put to the persons to be examined or a statement of the subject-matter about which they are to be examined;

(g) the documents or other property, real or personal, to be inspected;

(h) any requirement that the evidence is to be given on oath or affirmation, and any special form to be used;

(i) any special method or procedure to be followed under Article 9.

A Letter may also mention any information necessary for the application of Article 11.

No legalization or other like formality may be required.

Article 4

A Letter of Request shall be in the language of the authority requested to execute it or be accompanied by a translation into that language.

Nevertheless, a Contracting State shall accept a Letter in either English or French, or a translation into one of these languages, unless it has made the reservation authorized by Article 33.

A Contracting State which has more than one official language and cannot, for reasons of internal law, accept Letters in one of these languages for the whole of its territory, shall, by declaration, specify the language in which the Letter or translation thereof shall be expressed for execution in the specified parts of its territory. In case of failure to comply with this declaration, without justifiable excuse, the costs of translation into the required language shall be borne by the State of origin.

A Contracting State may, by declaration, specify the language or languages other than those referred to in the preceding paragraphs, in which a Letter may be sent to its Central Authority.

Any translation accompanying a Letter shall be certified as correct, either by a diplomatic officer or consular agent or by a sworn translator or by any other person so authorized in either State.

Article 5

If the Central Authority considers that the request does not comply with the provisions of the present Convention, it shall promptly inform the authority of the State of origin which transmitted the Letter of Request, specifying the objections to the Letter.

Article 6

If the authority to whom a Letter of Request has been transmitted is not competent to execute it, the Letter shall be sent forthwith to the authority in the same State which is competent to execute it in accordance with the provisions of its own law.

Article 7

The requesting authority shall, if it so desires, be informed of the time when, and the place where, the proceedings will take place, in order that the parties concerned, and their representatives, if any, may be present. This information shall be sent directly to the parties or their representatives when the authority of the State of origin so requests.

Article 8

A Contracting State may declare that members of the judicial personnel of the requesting authority of another Contracting State may be present at the execution of a Letter of Request. Prior authorization by the competent authority designated by the declaring State may be required.

Article 9

The judicial authority which executes a Letter of Request shall apply its own law as to the methods and procedures to be followed.

However, it will follow a request of the requesting authority that a special method or procedure be followed, unless this is incompatible with the internal law of the State of execution or is impossible of performance by reason of its internal practice and procedure or by reason of practical difficulties.

A Letter of Request shall be executed expeditiously.

Article 10

In executing a Letter of Request the requested authority shall apply the appropriate measures of compulsion in the instances and to the same extent as are provided by its internal law for the execution of orders issued by the authorities of its own country or of requests made by parties in internal proceedings.

Article 11

In the execution of a Letter of Request the person concerned may refuse to give evidence in so far as he has a privilege or duty to refuse to give the evidence—

(a) under the law of the State of execution; or

(b) under the law of the State of origin, and the privilege or duty has been specified in the Letter, or, at the instance of the requested authority, has been otherwise confirmed to that authority by the requesting authority.

A Contracting State may declare that, in addition, it will respect privileges and duties existing under the law of States other than the State of origin and the State of execution, to the extent specified in that declaration.

Article 12

The execution of a Letter of Request may be refused only to the extent that—

(a) in the State of execution the execution of the Letter does not fall within the functions of the judiciary; or

(b) the State addressed considers that its sovereignty or security would be prejudiced thereby.

Execution may not be refused solely on the ground that under its internal law the State of execution claims exclusive jurisdiction over the subject-matter of the action or that its internal law would not admit a right of action on it.

Article 13

The documents establishing the execution of the Letter of Request shall be sent by the requested authority to the requesting authority by the same channel which was used by the latter.

In every instance where the Letter is not executed in whole or in part, the requesting authority shall be informed immediately through the same channel and advised of the reasons.

Article 14

The execution of the Letter of Request shall not give rise to any reimbursement of taxes or costs of any nature.

Nevertheless, the State of execution has the right to require the State of origin to reimburse the fees paid to experts and interpreters and the costs occasioned by the use of a special procedure requested by the State of origin under Article 9, paragraph 2.

The requested authority whose law obliges the parties themselves to secure evidence, and which is not able itself to execute the Letter, may, after having obtained the consent of the requesting authority, appoint a suitable person to do so. When seeking this consent the requested authority shall indicate the approximate costs which would result from this procedure. If the requesting authority gives its consent it shall reimburse any costs incurred; without such consent the requesting authority shall not be liable for the costs.

Chapter II: Taking of Evidence by Diplomatic Officers, Consular Agents and Commissioners

Article 15

In civil or commercial matters, a diplomatic officer or consular agent of a Contracting State may, in the territory of another Contracting State and within the area where he exercises his functions, take the evidence without compulsion of nationals of a State which he represents in aid of proceedings commenced in the courts of a State which he represents.

A Contracting State may declare that evidence may be taken by a diplomatic officer or consular agent only if permission to that effect is given upon application made by him or on his behalf to the appropriate authority designated by the declaring State.

Article 16

A diplomatic officer or consular agent of a Contracting State may, in the territory of another Contracting State and within the area where he exercises his functions, also take the evidence, without compulsion, of nationals of the State in which he exercises his functions or of a third State, in aid of proceedings commenced in the courts of a State which he represents, if—

(a) a competent authority designated by the State in which he exercises his functions has given its permission either generally or in the particular case, and

(b) he complies with the conditions which the competent authority has specified in the permission.

A Contracting State may declare that evidence may be taken under this Article without its prior permission.

Article 17

In civil or commercial matters, a person duly appointed as a commissioner for the purpose may, without compulsion, take evidence in the territory of a Contracting State in aid of proceedings commenced in the courts of another Contracting State, if—

(a) a competent authority designated by the State where the evidence is to be taken has given its permission either generally or in the particular case; and

(b) he complies with the conditions which the competent authority has specified in the permission.

A Contracting State may declare that evidence may be taken under this Article without its prior permission.

Article 18

A Contracting State may declare that a diplomatic officer, consular agent or commissioner authorized to take evidence under Articles 15, 16 or 17, may apply to the competent authority designated by the declaring State for appropriate assistance to obtain the evidence by compulsion. The declaration may contain such conditions as the declaring State may see fit to impose.

If the authority grants the application it shall apply any measures of compulsion which are appropriate and are prescribed by its law for use in internal proceedings.

Article 19

The competent authority, in giving the permission referred to in Articles 15, 16 or 17, or in granting the application referred to in Article 18, may lay down such conditions as it deems fit, *inter alia*, as to the time and place of the taking of the evidence. Similarly it may require that it be given reasonable advance notice of the time, date and place of the taking of the evidence; in such a case a representative of the authority shall be entitled to be present at the taking of the evidence.

Article 20

In the taking of evidence under any Article of this Chapter persons concerned may be legally represented.

Article 21

Where a diplomatic officer, consular agent or commissioner is authorized under Articles 15, 16 or 17 to take evidence—

(a) he may take all kinds of evidence which are not incompatible with the law of the State where the evidence is taken or contrary to any permission granted pursuant to the above Articles, and shall have power within such limits to administer an oath or take an affirmation;

(b) a request to a person to appear or to give evidence shall, unless the recipient is a national of the State where the action is pending, be

drawn up in the language of the place where the evidence is taken or be accompanied by a translation into such language;

(c) the request shall inform the person that he may be legally represented and, in any State that has not filed a declaration under Article 18, shall also inform him that he is not compelled to appear or to give evidence;

(d) the evidence may be taken in the manner provided by the law applicable to the court in which the action is pending provided that such manner is not forbidden by the law of the State where the evidence is taken;

(e) a person requested to give evidence may invoke the privileges and duties to refuse to give the evidence contained in Article 11.

Article 22

The fact that an attempt to take evidence under the procedure laid down in this Chapter has failed, owing to the refusal of a person to give evidence, shall not prevent an application being subsequently made to take the evidence in accordance with Chapter I.

Chapter III: General Clauses

Article 23

A Contracting State may at the time of signature, ratification or accession, declare that it will not execute Letters of Request issued for the purpose of obtaining pre-trial discovery of documents as known in common law countries.

Article 24

A Contracting State may designate other authorities in addition to the Central Authority and shall determine the extent of their competence. However, Letters of Request may in all cases be sent to the Central Authority.

Federal States shall be free to designate more than one Central Authority.

Article 25

A Contracting State which has more than one legal system may designate the authorities of one of such systems, which shall have exclusive competence to execute Letters of Request pursuant to this Convention.

Article 26

A Contracting State, if required to do so because of constitutional limitations, may request the reimbursement by the State of origin of fees and costs, in connection with the execution of Letters of Request, for the service of process necessary to compel the appearance of a person to give evidence, the costs of attendance of such persons, and the cost of any transcript of the evidence.

Where a State has made a request pursuant to the above paragraph, any other Contracting State may request from that State the reimbursement of similar fees and costs.

Article 27

The provisions of the present Convention shall not prevent a Contracting State from—

(a) declaring that Letters of Request may be transmitted to its judicial authorities through channels other than those provided for in Article 2;

(b) permitting, by internal law or practice, any act provided for in this Convention to be performed upon less restrictive conditions;

(c) permitting, by internal law or practice, methods of taking evidence other than those provided for in this Convention.

Article 28

The present Convention shall not prevent an agreement between any two or more Contracting States to derogate from—

(a) the provisions of Article 2 with respect to methods of transmitting Letters of Request;

(b) the provisions of Article 4 with respect to the languages which may be used;

(c) the provisions of Article 8 with respect to the presence of judicial personnel at the execution of Letters;

(d) the provisions of Article 11 with respect to the privileges and duties of witnesses to refuse to give evidence;

(e) the provisions of Article 13 with respect to the methods of returning executed Letters to the requesting authority;

(f) the provisions of Article 14 with respect to fees and costs;

(g) the provisions of Chapter II.

Article 29

Between Parties to the present Convention who are also Parties to one or both of the Conventions on Civil Procedure signed at The Hague on the 17th of July 1905 and the 1st of March 1954, this Convention shall replace Articles 8–16 of the earlier Conventions.

Article 30

The present Convention shall not affect the application of Article 23 of the Convention of 1905, or of Article 24 of the Convention of 1954.

Article 31

Supplementary Agreements between Parties to the Conventions of 1905 and 1954 shall be considered as equally applicable to the present Convention unless the Parties have otherwise agreed.

Article 32

Without prejudice to the provisions of Articles 29 and 31, the present Convention shall not derogate from conventions containing provisions on the matters covered by this Convention to which the Contracting States are, or shall become Parties.

Article 33

A State may, at the time of signature, ratification or accession exclude, in whole or in part, the application of the provisions of paragraph 2 of Article 4 and of Chapter II. No other reservation shall be permitted.

Each Contracting State may at any time withdraw a reservation it has made; the reservation shall cease to have effect on the sixtieth day after notification of the withdrawal.

When a State has made a reservation, any other State affected thereby may apply the same rule against the reserving State.

Article 34

A State may at any time withdraw or modify a declaration.

Article 35

A Contracting State shall, at the time of the deposit of its instrument of ratification or accession, or at a later date, inform the Ministry of Foreign Affairs of the Netherlands of the designation of authorities, pursuant to Articles 2, 8, 24 and 25.

A Contracting State shall likewise inform the Ministry, where appropriate, of the following—

(a) the designation of the authorities to whom notice must be given, whose permission may be required, and whose assistance may be invoked in the taking of evidence by diplomatic officers and consular agents, pursuant to Articles 15, 16 and 18 respectively;

(b) the designation of the authorities whose permission may be required in the taking of evidence by commissioners pursuant to Article 17 and of those who may grant the assistance provided for in Article 18;

(c) declarations pursuant to Articles 4, 8, 11, 15, 16, 17, 18, 23 and 27;

(d) any withdrawal or modification of the above designations and declarations;

(e) the withdrawal of any reservation.

Article 36

Any difficulties which may arise between Contracting States in connection with the operation of this Convention shall be settled through diplomatic channels.

Article 37

The present Convention shall be open for signature by the States represented at the Eleventh Session of the Hague Conference on Private International Law.

It shall be ratified, and the instruments of ratification shall be deposited with the Ministry of Foreign Affairs of the Netherlands.

Article 38

The present Convention shall enter into force on the sixtieth day after the deposit of the third instrument of ratification referred to in the second paragraph of Article 37.

The Convention shall enter into force for each signatory State which ratifies subsequently on the sixtieth day after the deposit of its instrument of ratification.

Article 39

Any State not represented at the Eleventh Session of the Hague Conference on Private International Law which is a Member of this

Conference or of the United Nations or of a specialized agency of that Organization, or a Party to the Statute of the International Court of Justice may accede to the present Convention after it has entered into force in accordance with the first paragraph of Article 38.

The instrument of accession shall be deposited with the Ministry of Foreign Affairs of the Netherlands.

The Convention shall enter into force for a State acceding to it on the sixtieth day after the deposit of its instrument of accession.

The accession will have effect only as regards the relations between the acceding State and such Contracting States as will have declared their acceptance of the accession. Such declaration shall be deposited at the Ministry of Foreign Affairs of the Netherlands; this Ministry shall forward, through diplomatic channels, a certified copy to each of the Contracting States.

The Convention will enter into force as between the acceding State and the State that has declared its acceptance of the accession on the sixtieth day after the deposit of the declaration of acceptance.

Article 40

Any State may, at the time of signature, ratification or accession, declare that the present Convention shall extend to all the territories for the international relations of which it is responsible, or to one or more of them. Such a declaration shall take effect on the date of entry into force of the Convention for the State concerned.

At any time thereafter, such extensions shall be notified to the Ministry of Foreign Affairs of the Netherlands.

The Convention shall enter into force for the territories mentioned in such an extension on the sixtieth day after the notification indicated in the preceding paragraph.

Article 41

The present Convention shall remain in force for five years from the date of its entry into force in accordance with the first paragraph of Article 38, even for States which have ratified it or acceded to it subsequently.

If there has been no denunciation, it shall be renewed tacitly every five years.

Any denunciation shall be notified to the Ministry of Foreign Affairs of the Netherlands at least six months before the end of the five-year period.

It may be limited to certain of the territories to which the Convention applies.

The denunciation shall have effect only as regards the State which has notified it. The Convention shall remain in force for the other Contracting States.

Article 42

The Ministry of Foreign Affairs of the Netherlands shall give notice to the States referred to in Article 37, and to the States which have acceded in accordance with Article 39, of the following—

(a) the signatures and ratifications referred to in Article 37;

(b) the date on which the present Convention enters into force in accordance with the first paragraph of Article 38;

(c) the accessions referred to in Article 39 and the dates on which they take effect;

(d) the extensions referred to in Article 40 and the dates on which they take effect;

(e) the designations, reservations and declarations referred to in Articles 33 and 35;

(f) the denunciations referred to in the third paragraph of Article 41.

In witness whereof the undersigned, being duly authorized thereto, have signed the present Convention.

Done at Hague, on the 18th day of March, 1970, in the English and French languages, both texts being equally authentic, in a single copy which shall be deposited in the archives of the Government of the Netherlands, and of which a certified copy shall be sent, through the diplomatic channel, to each of the States represented at the Eleventh Session of the Hague Conference on Private International Law.

Annexure 4

Convention on the Recognition and Enforcement of Decisions Relating to Maintenance Obligations

(Concluded 2 October 1973)
(Entered into force 1 August 1976)

The States signatory to this Convention,

Desiring to establish common provisions to govern the reciprocal recognition and enforcement of decisions relating to maintenance obligations in respect of adults,

Desiring to coordinate these provisions and those of the Convention of the 15th of April 1958 on the Recognition and Enforcement of Decisions Relating to Maintenance Obligations in Respect of Children,

Have resolved to conclude a Convention for this purpose and have agreed upon the following provisions:

Chapter I: Scope of the Convention

Article 1

This Convention shall apply to a decision rendered by a judicial or administrative authority in a Contracting State in respect of a maintenance obligation arising from a family relationship, parentage, marriage or affinity, including a maintenance obligation towards an infant who is not legitimate, between—

(1) a maintenance creditor and a maintenance debtor; or

(2) a maintenance debtor and a public body which claims reimbursement of benefits given to a maintenance creditor.

It shall also apply to a settlement made by or before such an authority ('transaction') in respect of the said obligations and between the same parties (hereafter referred to as a 'settlement').

Article 2

This Convention shall apply to a decision or settlement however described.

It shall also apply to a decision or settlement modifying a previous decision or settlement, even in the case where this originates from a non-Contracting State.

It shall apply irrespective of the international or internal character of the maintenance claim and whatever may be the nationality or habitual residence of the parties.

Article 3

If a decision or settlement does not relate solely to a maintenance obligation, the effect of the Convention is limited to the parts of the decision or settlement which concern maintenance obligations.

Chapter II: Conditions for Recognition and Enforcement of Decisions

Article 4

A decision rendered in a Contracting State shall be recognized or enforced in another Contracting State—

(1) if it was rendered by an authority considered to have jurisdiction under Article 7 or 8; and

(2) if it is no longer subject to ordinary forms of review in the State of origin.

Provisionally enforceable decisions and provisional measures shall, although subject to ordinary forms of review, be recognized or enforced in the State addressed if similar decisions may be rendered and enforced in that State.

Article 5

Recognition or enforcement of a decision may, however, be refused—

(1) if recognition or enforcement of the decision is manifestly incompatible with the public policy ('ordre public') of the State addressed; or

(2) if the decision was obtained by fraud in connection with a matter of procedure; or

(3) if proceedings between the same parties and having the same purpose are pending before an authority of the State addressed and those proceedings were the first to be instituted; or

(4) if the decision is incompatible with a decision rendered between the same parties and having the same purpose, either in the State addressed or in another State, provided that this latter decision fulfils the conditions necessary for its recognition and enforcement in the State addressed.

Article 6

Without prejudice to the provisions of Article 5, a decision rendered by default shall be recognized or enforced only if notice of the institution of the proceedings, including notice of the substance of the claim, has been served on the defaulting party in accordance with the law of the State of origin and if, having regard to the circumstances, that party has had sufficient time to enable him to defend the proceedings.

Article 7

An authority in the State of origin shall be considered to have jurisdiction for the purposes of this Convention—

(1) if either the maintenance debtor or the maintenance creditor had his habitual residence in the State of origin at the time when the proceedings were instituted; or

(2) if the maintenance debtor and the maintenance creditor were nationals of the State of origin at the time when the proceedings were instituted; or

(3) if the defendant had submitted to the jurisdiction of the authority, either expressly or by defending on the merits of the case without objecting to the jurisdiction.

Article 8

Without prejudice to the provisions of Article 7, the authority of a Contracting State which has given judgment on a maintenance claim shall be considered to have jurisdiction for the purposes of this Convention if the maintenance is due by reason of a divorce or a legal separation, or a declaration that a marriage is void or annulled, obtained from an authority of that State recognized as having jurisdiction in that matter, according to the law of the State addressed.

Article 9

The authority of the State addressed shall be bound by the findings of fact on which the authority of the State of origin based its jurisdiction.

Article 10

If a decision deals with several issues in an application for maintenance and if recognition or enforcement cannot be granted for the whole of the decision, the authority of the State addressed shall apply this Convention to that part of the decision which can be recognised or enforced.

Article 11

If a decision provided for the periodical payment of maintenance, enforcement shall be granted in respect of payments already due and in respect of future payments.

Article 12

There shall be no review by the authority of the State addressed of the merits of a decision, unless this Convention otherwise provides.

Chapter III: Procedure for Recognition and Enforcement of Decisions

Article 13

The procedure for the recognition or enforcement of a decision shall be governed by the law of the State addressed, unless this Convention otherwise provides.

Article 14

Partial recognition or enforcement of a decision can always be applied for.

Article 15

A maintenance creditor, who, in the State of origin, has benefited from complete or partial legal aid or exemption from costs or expenses, shall be entitled, in any proceedings for recognition or enforcement, to benefit from the most favourable legal aid or the most extensive exemption from costs or expenses provided for by the law of the State addressed.

Article 16

No security, bond or deposit, however described, shall be required to guarantee the payment of costs and expenses in the proceedings to which the Convention refers.

Article 17

The party seeking recognition or applying for enforcement of a decision shall furnish—

(1) a complete and true copy of the decision;

(2) any document necessary to prove that the decision is no longer subject to the ordinary forms of review in the State of origin and, where necessary, that it is enforceable;

(3) if the decision was rendered by default, the original or a certified true copy of any document required to prove that the notice of the institution of proceedings, including notice of the substance of claim, has been properly served on the defaulting party according to the law of the State of origin;

(4) where appropriate, any document necessary to prove that he obtained legal aid or exemption from costs or expenses in the State of origin;

(5) a translation, certified as true, of the above-mentioned documents unless the authority of the State addressed dispenses with such translation.

If there is a failure to produce the documents mentioned above or if the contents of the decision do not permit the authority of the State addressed to verify whether the conditions of this Convention have been fulfilled, the authority shall allow a specified period of time for the production of the necessary documents.

No legalisation or other like formality may be required.

Chapter IV: Additional Provisions Relating to Public Bodies

Article 18

A decision rendered against a maintenance debtor on the application of a public body which claims reimbursement of benefits provided for a maintenance creditor shall be recognised and enforced in accordance with this Convention—

(1) if reimbursement can be obtained by the public body under the law to which it is subject; and

(2) if the existence of a maintenance obligation between the creditor and the debtor is provided for by the internal law applicable under the rules of private international law of the State addressed.

Article 19

A public body may seek recognition or claim enforcement of a decision rendered between a maintenance creditor and maintenance debtor to the extent of the benefits provided for the creditor if it is entitled *ipso jure*, under the law to which it is subject, to seek recognition or claim enforcement of the decision in place of the creditor.

Article 20

Without prejudice to the provisions of Article 17, the public body seeking recognition or claiming enforcement of a decision shall furnish any document necessary to prove that it fulfils the conditions of sub-paragraph 1, of Article 18 or Article 19, and that benefits have been provided for the maintenance creditor.

Chapter V: Settlements

Article 21

A settlement which is enforceable in the State of origin shall be recognised and enforced subject to the same conditions as a decision so far as such conditions are applicable to it.

Chapter VI: Miscellaneous Provisions

Article 22

A Contracting State, under whose law the transfer of funds is restricted, shall accord the highest priority to the transfer of funds payable as maintenance or to cover costs and expenses in respect of any claim under this Convention.

Article 23

This Convention shall not restrict the application of an international instrument in force between the State of origin and the State addressed or other law of the State addressed for the purposes of obtaining recognition or enforcement of a decision or settlement.

Article 24

This Convention shall apply irrespective of the date on which a decision was rendered.

Where a decision has been rendered prior to the entry into force of the Convention between the State of origin and the State addressed, it shall be enforced in the latter State only for payments falling due after such entry into force.

Article 25

Any Contracting State may, at any time, declare that the provisions of this Convention will be extended, in relation to other States making a declaration under this Article, to an official deed ('acte authentique') drawn up by or before an authority or public official and directly enforceable in the State of origin insofar as these provisions can be applied to such deeds.

Article 26

Any Contracting State may, in accordance with Article 34, reserve the right not to recognise or enforce—

(1) a decision or settlement insofar as it relates to a period of time after a maintenance creditor attains the age of twenty-one years or marries, except when the creditor is or was the spouse of the maintenance debtor;

(2) a decision or settlement in respect of maintenance obligations

(a) between persons related collaterally;

(b) between persons related by affinity;

(3) a decision or settlement unless it provides for the periodical payment of maintenance.

A Contracting State which has made a reservation shall not be entitled to claim the application of this Convention to such decisions or settlements as are excluded by its reservation.

Article 27

If a Contracting State has, in matters of maintenance obligations, two or more legal systems applicable to different categories of persons, any reference to the law of that State shall be construed as referring to the legal system which its law designates as applicable to a particular category of persons.

Article 28

If a Contracting State has two or more territorial units in which different systems of law apply in relation to the recognition and enforcement of maintenance decisions—

(1) any reference to the law or procedure or authority of the State of origin shall be construed as referring to the law or procedure or authority of the territorial unit in which the decision was rendered;

(2) any reference to the law or procedure or authority of the State addressed shall be construed as referring to the law or procedure or authority of the territorial unit in which recognition or enforcement is sought;

(3) any reference made in the application of sub-paragraph 1 or 2 to the law or procedure of the State of origin or to the law or procedure of the State addressed shall be construed as including any relevant legal rules and principles of the Contracting State which apply to the territorial units comprising it;

(4) any reference to the habitual residence of the maintenance creditor or the maintenance debtor in the State of origin shall be construed as referring to his habitual residence in the territorial unit in which the decision was rendered.

Any Contracting State may, at any time, declare that it will not apply any one or more of the foregoing rules to one or more of the provisions of this Convention.

Article 29

This Convention shall replace, as regards the States who are Parties to it, the Convention on the Recognition and Enforcement of Decisions Relating to Maintenance Obligations in Respect of Children, concluded at The Hague on the 15th of April 1958.

Chapter VII: Final Clauses

Article 30

This Convention shall be open for signature by the States which were Members of the Hague Conference on Private International Law at the time of its Twelfth Session.

It shall be ratified, accepted or approved and the instruments of ratification, acceptance or approval shall be deposited with the Ministry of Foreign Affairs of the Netherlands.

Article 31

Any State which has become a Member of the Hague Conference on Private International Law after the date of its Twelfth Session, or which is a Member of the United Nations or of a specialised agency of that Organisation, or a Party to the Statute of the International Court of Justice may accede to this Convention after it has entered into force in accordance with the first paragraph of Article 35.

The instrument of accession shall be deposited with the Ministry of Foreign Affairs of the Netherlands.

Such accession shall have effect only as regards the relations between the acceding State and those Contracting States which have not raised an objection to its accession in twelve months after the receipt of the notification referred to in sub-paragraph 3 of Article 37.

Such an objection may also be raised by Member States at the time when they ratify, accept or approve the Convention after an accession. Any such objection shall be notified to the Ministry of Foreign Affairs of the Netherlands.

Article 32

Any State may, at the time of signature, ratification, acceptance, approval or accession, declare that this Convention shall extend to all the territories for the international relations of which it is responsible, or to one or more of them. Such a declaration shall take effect on the date of entry into force of the Convention for the State concerned.

At any time thereafter, such extensions shall be notified to the Ministry of Foreign Affairs of the Netherlands.

The extension shall have effect as regards the relations between the Contracting States which have not raised an objection to the extension in the twelve months after the receipt of the notification referred to in sub-paragraph 4 of Article 37 and the territory or territories for the international relations of which the State in question is responsible and in respect of which the notification was made.

Such an objection may also be raised by Member States when they ratify, accept or approve the Convention after an extension.

Any such objection shall be notified to the Ministry of Foreign Affairs of the Netherlands.

Article 33

If a Contracting State has two or more territorial units in which different systems of law apply in relation to the recognition and enforcement of maintenance decisions, it may, at the time of signature, ratification, acceptance, approval or accession, declare that this Convention shall extend to all its territorial units or only to one or more of them, and may modify its declaration by submitting another declaration at any time thereafter.

These declarations shall be notified to the Ministry of Foreign Affairs of the Netherlands, and shall state expressly the territorial unit to which the Convention applies.

Other Contracting States may decline to recognise a maintenance decision if, at the date on which recognition is sought, the Convention is not applicable to the territorial unit in which the decision was rendered.

Article 34

Any State may, not later than the moment of its ratification, acceptance, approval or accession, make one or more of the reservations referred to in Article 26. No other reservation shall be permitted.

Any State may also, when notifying an extension of the Convention in accordance with Article 32, make one or more of the said reservations applicable to all or some of the territories mentioned in the extension.

Any Contracting State may at any time withdraw a reservation it has made. Such a withdrawal shall be notified to the Ministry of Foreign Affairs of the Netherlands.

Such a reservation shall cease to have effect on the first day of the third calendar month after the notification referred to in the preceding paragraph.

Article 35

This Convention shall enter into force on the first day of the third calendar month after the deposit of the third instrument of ratification, acceptance or approval referred to in Article 30.

Thereafter the Convention shall enter into force

– for each State ratifying, accepting or approving it subsequently, on the first day of the third calendar month after the deposit of its instrument of ratification, acceptance or approval;

– for each acceding State, on the first day of the third calendar month after the expiry of the period referred to in Article 31;

– for a territory to which the Convention has been extended in conformity with Article 32, on the first day of the third calendar month after the expiry of the period referred to in that Article.

Article 36

This Convention shall remain in force for five years from the date of its entry into force in accordance with the first paragraph of Article 35, even for States which have ratified, accepted, approved or acceded to it subsequently.

If there has been no denunciation, it shall be renewed tacitly every five years.

Any denunciation shall be notified to the Ministry of Foreign Affairs of the Netherlands, at least six months before the expiry of the five-year period. It may be limited to certain of the territories to which the Convention applies.

The denunciation shall have effect only as regards the State which has notified it. The Convention shall remain in force for the other Contracting States.

Article 37

The Ministry of Foreign Affairs of the Netherlands shall notify the States Members of the Conference, and the States which have acceded in accordance with Article 31, of the following—

(1) the signatures and ratifications, acceptances and approvals referred to in Article 30;

(2) the date on which this Convention enters into force in accordance with Article 35;
(3) the accessions referred to in Article 31 and the dates on which they take effect;
(4) the extensions referred to in Article 32 and the dates on which they take effect;
(5) the objections raised to accessions and extensions referred to in Articles 31 and 32;
(6) the declarations referred to in Articles 25 and 32;
(7) the denunciations referred to in Article 36;
(8) the reservations referred to in Articles 26 and 34 and the withdrawals referred to in Article 34.

In witness whereof the undersigned, being duly authorised thereto, have signed this Convention.

Done at Hague, on the 2nd day of October, 1973, in the English and French languages, both texts being equally authentic, in a single copy which shall be deposited in the archives of the Government of the Netherlands, and of which a certified copy shall be sent, through the diplomatic channel, to each of the States Members of the Hague Conference on Private International Law at the date of its Twelfth Session.

Annexure 5

Convention of 29 May 1993 on Protection of Children and Co-operation in Respect of Intercountry Adoption

The States signatory to the present Convention,

Recognizing that the child, for the full and harmonious development of his or her personality, should grow up in a family environment, in an atmosphere of happiness, love and understanding,

Recalling that each State should take, as a matter of priority, appropriate measures to enable the child to remain in the care of his or her family of origin,

Recognizing that intercountry adoption may offer the advantage of a permanent family to a child for whom a suitable family cannot be found in his or her State of origin,

Convinced of the necessity to take measures to ensure that intercountry adoptions are made in the best interests of the child and with respect for his or her fundamental rights, and to prevent the abduction, the sale of, or traffic in children,

Desiring to establish common provisions to this effect, taking into account the principles set forth in international instruments, in particular the United Nations Convention on the Rights of the Child, of 20 November 1989, and the United Nations Declaration on Social and Legal Principles relating to the Protection and Welfare of Children, with Special Reference to Foster Placement and Adoption Nationally and Internationally (General Assembly Resolution 41/85, of 3 December 1986),

Have agreed upon the following provisions—

Chapter I: Scope of the Convention

Article 1

The objects of the present Convention are—

(a) to establish safeguards to ensure that intercountry adoptions take place in the best interests of the child and with respect for his or her fundamental rights as recognized in international law;

(b) to establish a system of co-operation amongst Contracting States to ensure that those safeguards are respected and thereby prevent the abduction, the sale of, or traffic in children;

(c) to secure the recognition in Contracting States of adoptions made in accordance with the Convention.

Article 2

(1) The Convention shall apply where a child habitually resident in one Contracting State ('the State of origin') has been, is being, or is to be moved to another Contracting State ('the receiving State') either after his or her adoption in the State of origin by spouses or a person habitually resident in the receiving State, or for the purposes of such an adoption in the receiving State or in the State of origin.

(2) The Convention covers only adoptions which create a permanent parent-child relationship.

Article 3

The Convention ceases to apply if the agreements mentioned in Article 17, sub-paragraph *(c)*, have not been given before the child attains the age of eighteen years.

Chapter II: Requirements for Intercountry Adoptions

Article 4

An adoption within the scope of the Convention shall take place only if the competent authorities of the State of origin—

(a) have established that the child is adoptable;

(b) have determined, after possibilities for placement of the child within the State of origin have been given due consideration, that an intercountry adoption is in the child's best interests;

(c) have ensured that

(1) the persons, institutions and authorities whose consent is necessary for adoption, have been counselled as may be necessary and

duly informed of the effects of their consent, in particular whether or not an adoption will result in the termination of the legal relationship between the child and his or her family of origin;

(2) such persons, institutions and authorities have given their consent freely, in the required legal form, and expressed or evidenced in writing;

(3) the consents have not been induced by payment or compensation of any kind and have not been withdrawn;

(4) the consent of the mother, where required, has been given only after the birth of the child; and

(d) have ensured, having regard to the age and degree of maturity of the child; that

(1) he or she has been counselled and duly informed of the effects of the adoption and of his or her consent to the adoption, where such consent is required;

(2) consideration has been given to the child's wishes and opinions;

(3) the child's consent to the adoption, where such consent is required, has been given freely, in the required legal form, and expressed or evidenced in writing; and

(4) such consent has not been induced by payment or compensation of any kind.

Article 5

An adoption within the scope of the Convention shall take place only if the competent authorities of the receiving State—

(a) have determined that the prospective adoptive parents are eligible and suited to adopt;

(b) have ensured that the prospective adoptive parents have been counselled as may be necessary; and

(c) have determined that the child is or will be authorized to enter and reside permanently in that State.

Chapter III: Central Authorities and Accredited Bodies

Article 6

(1) A Contracting State shall designate a Central Authority to discharge the duties which are imposed by the Convention upon such authorities;

(2) Federal States, States with more than one system of law or States having autonomous territorial units shall be free to appoint more than one Central Authority and to specify the territorial or personal extent of their functions. Where a State has appointed more than one Central Authority, it shall designate the Central Authority to which any communication may be addressed for transmission to the appropriate Central Authority within that State.

Article 7

(1) Central Authorities shall co-operate with each other and promote co-operation amongst the competent authorities in their States to protect children and to achieve the other objects of the Convention.
(2) They shall take directly all appropriate measures to—

(a) provide information as to the laws of their States concerning adoption and other general information, such as statistics and standard forms;

(b) keep one another informed about the operation of the Convention and, as far as possible, eliminate any obstacles to its application.

Article 8

Central Authorities shall take, directly or through public authorities, all appropriate measures to prevent improper financial or other gain in connection with an adoption and to deter all practices contrary to the objects of the Convention.

Article 9

Central Authorities shall take, directly or through public authorities or other bodies duly accredited in their State, all appropriate measures, in particular to—

(a) collect, preserve and exchange information about the situation of the child and the prospective adoptive parents, so far as is necessary to complete the adoption;

(b) facilitate, follow and expedite proceedings with a view to obtaining the adoption;

(c) promote the development of adoption counselling and post-adoption services in their States;

(d) provide each other with general evaluation reports about experience with intercountry adoption;

(e) reply, in so far as is permitted by the law of their State, to justified requests from other Central Authorities or public authorities for information about a particular adoption situation.

Article 10

Accreditation shall only be granted to and maintained by bodies demonstrating their competence to carry out properly the tasks with which they may be entrusted.

Article 11

An accredited body shall—

(a) pursue only non-profit objectives according to such conditions and within such limits as may be established by the competent authorities of the State of accreditation;

(b) be directed and staffed by persons qualified by their ethical standards and by training or experience to work in the field of intercountry adoption; and

(c) be subject to supervision by competent authorities of that State as to its composition, operation and financial situation.

Article 12

A body accredited in one Contracting State may act in another Contracting State only if the competent authorities of both States have authorized it to do so.

Article 13

The designation of the Central Authorities and, where appropriate, the extent of their functions, as well as the names and addresses of the accredited bodies shall be communicated by each Contracting State to the Permanent Bureau of the Hague Conference on Private International Law.

Chapter IV: Procedural Requirements in Intercountry Adoption

Article 14

Persons habitually resident in a Contracting State, who wish to adopt a child habitually resident in another Contracting State, shall apply to the Central Authority in the State of their habitual residence.

Article 15

(1) If the Central Authority of the receiving State is satisfied that the applicants are eligible and suited to adopt, it shall prepare a report including information about their identity, eligibility and suitability to adopt, background, family and medical history, social environment, reasons for adoption, ability to undertake an intercountry adoption, as well as the characteristics of the children for whom they would be qualified to care.

(2) It shall transmit the report to the Central Authority of the State of origin.

Article 16

(1) If the Central Authority of the State of origin is satisfied that the child is adoptable, it shall—

(a) prepare a report including information about his or her identity, adoptability, background, social environment, family history, medical history including that of the child's family, and any special needs of the child;

(b) give due consideration to the child's upbringing and to his or her ethnic, religious and cultural background;

(c) ensure that consents have been obtained in accordance with Article 4; and

(d) determine, on the basis in particular of the reports relating to the child and the prospective adoptive parents, whether the envisaged placement is in the best interests of the child.

(2) It shall transmit to the Central Authority of the receiving State its report on the child, proof that the necessary consents have been obtained and the reasons for its determination on the placement, taking care not to reveal the identity of the mother and the father if, in the State of origin, these identities may not be disclosed.

Article 17

Any decision in the State of origin that a child should be entrusted to prospective adoptive parents may only be made if—

(a) the Central Authority of that State has ensured that the prospective adoptive parents agree;

(b) the Central Authority of the receiving State has approved such decision, where such approval is required by the law of that State or by the Central Authority of the State of origin;

(c) the Central Authorities of both States have agreed that the adoption may proceed; and

(d) it has been determined, in accordance with Article 5, that the prospective adoptive parents are eligible and suited to adopt and that the child is or will be authorized to enter and reside permanently in the receiving State.

Article 18

The Central Authorities of both States shall take all necessary steps to obtain permission for the child to leave the State of origin and to enter and reside permanently in the receiving State.

Article 19

(1) The transfer of the child to the receiving State may only be carried out if the requirements of Article 17 have been satisfied.

(2) The Central Authorities of both States shall ensure that this transfer takes place in secure and appropriate circumstances and, if possible, in the company of the adoptive or prospective adoptive parents.

(3) If the transfer of the child does not take place, the reports referred to in Articles 15 and 16 are to be sent back to the authorities who forwarded them.

Article 20

The Central Authorities shall keep each other informed about the adoption process and the measures taken to complete it, as well as about the progress of the placement if a probationary period is required.

Article 21

(1) Where the adoption is to take place after the transfer of the child to the receiving State and it appears to the Central Authority of that State that the continued placement of the child with the prospective adoptive parents is not in the child's best interests, such Central Authority shall take the measures necessary to protect the child, in particular—

(a) to cause the child to be withdrawn from the prospective adoptive parents and to arrange temporary care;

(b) in consultation with the Central Authority of the State of origin, to arrange without delay a new placement of the child with a view to adoption or, if this is not appropriate, to arrange alternative long-term care; an adoption shall not take place until the Central Authority of the State of origin has been duly informed concerning the new prospective adoptive parents;

(c) as a last resort, to arrange the return of the child, if his or her interests so require.

(2) Having regard in particular to the age and degree of maturity of the child, he or she shall be consulted and, where appropriate, his or her consent obtained in relation to measures to be taken under this Article.

Article 22

(1) The functions of a Central Authority under this chapter may be performed by public authorities or by bodies accredited under Chapter III, to the extent permitted by the law of its State.

(2) Any Contracting State may declare to the depositary of the Convention that the functions of the Central Authority under Articles 15 to 21 may be performed in that State, to the extent permitted by the law and subject to the supervision of the competent authorities of that State, also by bodies or persons who—

(a) meet the requirements of integrity, professional competence, experience and accountability of that State; and

(b) are qualified by their ethical standards and by training or experience to work in the field of intercountry adoption.

(3) A Contracting State which makes the declaration provided for in paragraph 2 shall keep the Permanent Bureau of the Hague Conference on Private International Law informed of the names and addresses of these bodies and persons.

(4) Any Contracting State may declare to the depositary of the Convention that adoptions of children habitually resident in its territory may only take place if the functions of the Central Authorities are performed in accordance with paragraph 1.

(5) Notwithstanding any declaration made under paragraph 2, the reports provided for in Articles 15 and 16 shall, in every case, be prepared under the responsibility of the Central Authority or other authorities or bodies in accordance with paragraph 1.

Chapter V: Recognition and Effects of the Adoption

Article 23

(1) An adoption certified by the competent authority of the State of the adoption as having been made in accordance with the Convention shall be recognized by operation of law in the other Contracting States. The certificate shall specify when and by whom the agreements under Article 17, sub-paragraph *(c)*, were given.

(2) Each Contracting State shall, at the time of signature, ratification, acceptance, approval or accession, notify the depositary of the Convention of the identity and the functions of the authority or the authorities which, in that State, are competent to make the certification. It shall also notify the depositary of any modification in the designation of these authorities.

Article 24

The recognition of an adoption may be refused in a Contracting State only if the adoption is manifestly contrary to its public policy, taking into account the best interests of the child.

Article 25

Any Contracting State may declare to the depositary of the Convention that it will not be bound under this Convention to recognize adoptions made in accordance with an agreement concluded by application of Article 39, paragraph 2.

Article 26

(1) The recognition of an adoption includes recognition of

(a) the legal parent-child relationship between the child and his or her adoptive parents;

(b) parental responsibility of the adoptive parents for the child;

(c) the termination of a pre-existing legal relationship between the child and his or her mother and father, if the adoption has this effect in the Contracting State where it was made.

(2) In the case of an adoption having the effect of terminating a pre-existing legal parent-child relationship, the child shall enjoy in the receiving State, and in any other Contracting State where the adoption is recognized, rights equivalent to those resulting from adoptions having this effect in each such State.

(3) The preceding paragraphs shall not prejudice the application of any provision more favourable for the child, in force in the Contracting State which recognizes the adoption.

Article 27

(1) Where an adoption granted in the State of origin does not have the effect of terminating a pre-existing legal parent-child relationship, it may, in the receiving State which recognizes the adoption under the Convention, be converted into an adoption having such an effect—

(a) if the law of the receiving State so permits; and

(b) if the consents referred to in Article 4, sub-paragraphs *(c)* and *(d)*, have been or are given for the purpose of such an adoption.

(2) Article 23 applies to the decision converting the adoption.

Chapter VI: General Provisions

Article 28

The Convention does not affect any law of a State of origin which requires that the adoption of a child habitually resident within that State take place in that State or which prohibits the child's placement in, or transfer to, the receiving State prior to adoption.

Article 29

There shall be no contact between the prospective adoptive parents and the child's parents or any other person who has care of the child until the requirements of Article 4, sub-paragraphs *(a)* to *(c)*, and Article 5, sub-paragraph *(a)*, have been met, unless the adoption takes place within a family or unless the contact is in compliance with the conditions established by the competent authority of the State of origin.

Article 30

(1) The competent authorities of a Contracting State shall ensure that information held by them concerning the child's origin, in particular information concerning the identity of his or her parents, as well as the medical history, is preserved.

(2) They shall ensure that the child or his or her representative has access to such information, under appropriate guidance, in so far as is permitted by the law of that State.

Article 31

Without prejudice to Article 30, personal data gathered or transmitted under the Convention, especially data referred to in Articles 15 and 16, shall be used only for the purposes for which they were gathered or transmitted.

Article 32

(1) No one shall derive improper financial or other gain from an activity related to an intercountry adoption.
(2) Only costs and expenses, including reasonable professional fees of persons involved in the adoption, may be charged or paid.
(3) The directors, administrators and employees of bodies involved in an adoption shall not receive remuneration which is unreasonably high in relation to services rendered.

Article 33

A competent authority which finds that any provision of the Convention has not been respected or that there is a serious risk that it may not be respected, shall immediately inform the Central Authority of its State. This Central Authority shall be responsible for ensuring that appropriate measures are taken.

Article 34

If the competent authority of the State of destination of a document so requests, a translation certified as being in conformity with the original must be furnished. Unless otherwise provided, the costs of such translation are to be borne by the prospective adoptive parents.

Article 35

The competent authorities of the Contracting States shall act expeditiously in the process of adoption.

Article 36

In relation to a State which has two or more systems of law with regard to adoption applicable in different territorial units—

(a) any reference to habitual residence in that State shall be construed as referring to habitual residence in a territorial unit of that State;

(b) any reference to the law of that State shall be construed as referring to the law in force in the relevant territorial unit;

(c) any reference to the competent authorities or to the public authorities of that State shall be construed as referring to those authorized to act in the relevant territorial unit;

(d) any reference to the accredited bodies of that State shall be construed as referring to bodies accredited in the relevant territorial unit.

Article 37

In relation to a State which with regard to adoption has two or more systems of law applicable to different categories of persons, any reference to the law of that State shall be construed as referring to the legal system specified by the law of that State.

Article 38

A State within which different territorial units have their own rules of law in respect of adoption shall not be bound to apply the Convention where a State with a unified system of law would not be bound to do so.

Article 39

(1) The Convention does not affect any international instrument to which Contracting States are Parties and which contains provisions on matters governed by the Convention, unless a contrary declaration is made by the States Parties to such instrument.

(2) Any Contracting State may enter into agreements with one or more other Contracting States, with a view to improving the application of the Convention in their mutual relations. These agreements may derogate only from the provisions of Articles 14 to 16 and 18 to 21. The States which have concluded such an agreement shall transmit a copy to the depositary of the Convention.

Article 40

No reservation to the Convention shall be permitted.

Article 41

The Convention shall apply in every case where an application pursuant to Article 14 has been received after the Convention has entered into force in the receiving State and the State of origin.

Article 42

The Secretary General of the Hague Conference on Private International Law shall at regular intervals convene a Special Commission in order to review the practical operation of the Convention.

Chapter VII: Final Clauses

Article 43

(1) The Convention shall be open for signature by the States which were Members of the Hague Conference on Private International Law at the time of its Seventeenth Session and by the other States which participated in that Session.
(2) It shall be ratified, accepted or approved and the instruments of ratification, acceptance or approval shall be deposited with the Ministry of Foreign Affairs of the Kingdom of the Netherlands, depositary of the Convention.

Article 44

(1) Any other State may accede to the Convention after it has entered into force in accordance with Article 46, paragraph 1.
(2) The instrument of accession shall be deposited with the depositary.
(3) Such accession shall have effect only as regards the relations between the acceding State and those Contracting States which have not raised an objection to its accession in the six months after the receipt of the notification referred to in sub-paragraph *(b)* of Article 48. Such an objection may also be raised by States at the time when they ratify, accept or approve the Convention after an accession. Any such objection shall be notified to the depositary.

Article 45

(1) If a State has two or more territorial units in which different systems of law are applicable in relation to matters dealt with in the Convention, it may at the time of signature, ratification, acceptance, approval or accession declare that this Convention shall extend to all its territorial units or only to one or more of them and may modify this declaration by submitting another declaration at any time.
(2) Any such declaration shall be notified to the depositary and shall state expressly the territorial units to which the Convention applies.

(3) If a State makes no declaration under this Article, the Convention is to extend to all territorial units of that State.

Article 46

(1) The Convention shall enter into force on the first day of the month following the expiration of three months after the deposit of the third instrument of ratification, acceptance or approval referred to in Article 43.
(2) Thereafter the Convention shall enter into force—

(a) for each State ratifying, accepting or approving it subsequently, or acceding to it, on the first day of the month following the expiration of three months after the deposit of its instrument of ratification, acceptance, approval or accession;

(b) for a territorial unit to which the Convention has been extended in conformity with Article 45, on the first day of the month following the expiration of three months after the notification referred to in that Article.

Article 47

(1) A State Party to the Convention may denounce it by a notification in writing addressed to the depositary.
(2) The denunciation takes effect on the first day of the month following the expiration of twelve months after the notification is received by the depositary. Where a longer period for the denunciation to take effect is specified in the notification, the denunciation takes effect upon the expiration of such longer period after the notification is received by the depositary.

Article 48

The depositary shall notify the States Members of the Hague Conference on Private International Law, the other States which participated in the Seventeenth Session and the States which have acceded in accordance with Article 44, of the following—

(a) the signatures, ratifications, acceptances and approvals referred to in Article 43;

(b) the accessions and objections raised to accessions referred to in Article 44;

(c) the date on which the Convention enters into force in accordance with Article 46;

(d) the declarations and designations referred to in Articles 22, 23, 25 and 45;

(e) the agreements referred to in Article 39;

(f) the denunciations referred to in Article 47.

In witness whereof the undersigned, being duly authorized thereto, have signed this Convention.

Done at The Hague, on the 29th day of May 1993, in the English and French languages, both texts being equally authentic, in a single copy which shall be deposited in the archives of the Government of the Kingdom of the Netherlands, and of which a certified copy shall be sent, through diplomatic channels, to each of the States Members of the Hague Conference on Private International Law at the date of its Seventeenth Session and to each of the other States which participated in that Session.

Annexure 6

Convention on the International Recovery of Child Support and Other Forms of Family Maintenance

(Concluded 23 November 2007)

The States signatory to the present Convention,

Desiring to improve co-operation among States for the international recovery of child support and other forms of family maintenance,

Aware of the need for procedures which produce results and are accessible, prompt, efficient, cost-effective, responsive and fair,

Wishing to build upon the best features of existing Hague Conventions and other international instruments, in particular the United Nations *Convention on the Recovery Abroad of Maintenance* of 20 June 1956,

Seeking to take advantage of advances in technologies and to create a flexible system which can continue to evolve as needs change and further advances in technology create new opportunities,

Recalling that, in accordance with Articles 3 and 27 of the United Nations *Convention on the Rights of the Child* of 20 November 1989,

– in all actions concerning children the best interests of the child shall be a primary consideration;

– every child has a right to a standard of living adequate for the child's physical, mental, spiritual, moral and social development;

– the parent(s) or others responsible for the child have the primary responsibility to secure, within their abilities and financial capacities, the conditions of living necessary for the child's development; and

– States Parties should take all appropriate measures, including the conclusion of international agreements, to secure the recovery of maintenance for the child from the parent(s) or other responsible persons, in particular where such persons live in a State different from that of the child.

Have resolved to conclude this Convention and have agreed upon the following provisions—

Chapter I: Object, Scope, and Definitions

Article 1 Object

The object of the present Convention is to ensure the effective international recovery of child support and other forms of family maintenance, in particular by—

(a) establishing a comprehensive system of co-operation between the authorities of the Contracting States;

(b) making available applications for the establishment of maintenance decisions;

(c) providing for the recognition and enforcement of maintenance decisions; and

(d) requiring effective measures for the prompt enforcement of maintenance decisions.

Article 2 Scope

(1) This Convention shall apply—

(a) to maintenance obligations arising from a parent-child relationship towards a person under the age of 21 years;

(b) to recognition and enforcement or enforcement of a decision for spousal support when the application is made with a claim within the scope of sub-paragraph *(a)*; and

(c) with the exception of Chapters II and III, to spousal support.

(2) Any Contracting State may reserve, in accordance with Article 62, the right to limit the application of the Convention under sub-paragraph 1 *(a)*, to persons who have not attained the age of 18 years. A Contracting State which makes this reservation shall not be entitled to claim the application of the Convention to persons of the age excluded by its reservation.

(3) Any Contracting State may declare in accordance with Article 63 that it will extend the application of the whole or any part of the Convention to any maintenance obligation arising from a family relationship, parentage, marriage or affinity, including in particular obligations in respect of vulnerable persons. Any such declaration shall give rise to obligations between two Contracting States only in so far as their declarations cover the same maintenance obligations and parts of the Convention.

(4) The provisions of this Convention shall apply to children regardless of the marital status of the parents.

Article 3 Definitions

For the purposes of this Convention—

(a) 'creditor' means an individual to whom maintenance is owed or is alleged to be owed;

(b) 'debtor' means an individual who owes or who is alleged to owe maintenance;

(c) 'legal assistance' means the assistance necessary to enable applicants to know and assert their rights and to ensure that applications are fully and effectively dealt with in the requested State. The means of providing such assistance may include as necessary legal advice, assistance in bringing a case before an authority, legal representation and exemption from costs of proceedings;

(d) 'agreement in writing' means an agreement recorded in any medium, the information contained in which is accessible so as to be usable for subsequent reference;

(e) 'maintenance arrangement' means an agreement in writing relating to the payment of maintenance which—

(i) has been formally drawn up or registered as an authentic instrument by a competent authority; or

(ii) has been authenticated by, or concluded, registered or filed with a competent authority, and may be the subject of review and modification by a competent authority;

(f) 'vulnerable person' means a person who, by reason of an impairment or insufficiency of his or her personal faculties, is not able to support him or herself.

Chapter II: Administrative Co-operation

Article 4 Designation of Central Authorities

(1) A Contracting State shall designate a Central Authority to discharge the duties that are imposed by the Convention on such an authority.
(2) Federal States, States with more than one system of law or States having autonomous territorial units shall be free to appoint more than one Central Authority and shall specify the territorial or personal extent of their functions. Where a State has appointed more than one Central Authority, it shall designate the Central Authority to which any communication may be addressed for transmission to the appropriate Central Authority within that State.
(3) The designation of the Central Authority or Central Authorities, their contact details, and where appropriate the extent of their functions as specified in paragraph 2, shall be communicated by a Contracting State to the Permanent Bureau of the Hague Conference on Private International Law at the time when the instrument of ratification or accession is deposited or when a declaration is submitted in accordance with Article 61. Contracting States shall promptly inform the Permanent Bureau of any changes.

Article 5 General functions of Central Authorities

Central Authorities shall—

(a) co-operate with each other and promote co-operation amongst the competent authorities in their States to achieve the purposes of the Convention;

(b) seek as far as possible solutions to difficulties which arise in the application of the Convention.

Article 6 Specific functions of Central Authorities

(1) Central Authorities shall provide assistance in relation to applications under Chapter III. In particular they shall—

(a) transmit and receive such applications;

(b) initiate or facilitate the institution of proceedings in respect of such applications.

(2) In relation to such applications they shall take all appropriate measures—

(a) where the circumstances require, to provide or facilitate the provision of legal assistance;

(b) to help locate the debtor or the creditor;

(c) to help obtain relevant information concerning the income and, if necessary, other financial circumstances of the debtor or creditor, including the location of assets;

(d) to encourage amicable solutions with a view to obtaining voluntary payment of maintenance, where suitable by use of mediation, conciliation or similar processes;

(e) to facilitate the ongoing enforcement of maintenance decisions, including any arrears;

(f) to facilitate the collection and expeditious transfer of maintenance payments;

(g) to facilitate the obtaining of documentary or other evidence;

(h) to provide assistance in establishing parentage where necessary for the recovery of maintenance;

(i) to initiate or facilitate the institution of proceedings to obtain any necessary provisional measures that are territorial in nature and the purpose of which is to secure the outcome of a pending maintenance application;

(j) to facilitate service of documents.

(3) The functions of the Central Authority under this Article may, to the extent permitted under the law of its State, be performed by public bodies, or other bodies subject to the supervision of the competent authorities of that State. The designation of any such public bodies or other bodies, as well as their contact details and the extent of their functions, shall be communicated by a Contracting State to the Permanent Bureau of the Hague Conference on Private International Law. Contracting States shall promptly inform the Permanent Bureau of any changes.

(4) Nothing in this Article or Article 7 shall be interpreted as imposing an obligation on a Central Authority to exercise powers that can be exercised only by judicial authorities under the law of the requested State.

Article 7 Requests for specific measures

(1) A Central Authority may make a request, supported by reasons, to another Central Authority to take appropriate specific measures under Article 6(2) *(b)*, *(c)*, *(g)*, *(h)*, *(i)*, and *(j)* when no application under

Article 10 is pending. The requested Central Authority shall take such measures as are appropriate if satisfied that they are necessary to assist a potential applicant in making an application under Article 10 or in determining whether such an application should be initiated.
(2) A Central Authority may also take specific measures on the request of another Central Authority in relation to a case having an international element concerning the recovery of maintenance pending in the requesting State.

Article 8 Central Authority costs

(1) Each Central Authority shall bear its own costs in applying this Convention.
(2) Central Authorities may not impose any charge on an applicant for the provision of their services under the Convention save for exceptional costs arising from a request for a specific measure under Article 7.
(3) The requested Central Authority may not recover the costs of the services referred to in paragraph 2 without the prior consent of the applicant to the provision of those services at such cost.

Chapter III: Applications through Central Authorities

Article 9 Application through Central Authorities

An application under this Chapter shall be made through the Central Authority of the Contracting State in which the applicant resides to the Central Authority of the requested State. For the purpose of this provision, residence excludes mere presence.

Article 10 Available applications

(1) The following categories of application shall be available to a creditor in a requesting State seeking to recover maintenance under this Convention—

(a) recognition or recognition and enforcement of a decision;

(b) enforcement of a decision made or recognised in the requested State;

(c) establishment of a decision in the requested State where there is no existing decision, including where necessary the establishment of parentage;

(d) establishment of a decision in the requested State where recognition and enforcement of a decision is not possible, or is refused,

because of the lack of a basis for recognition and enforcement under Article 20, or on the grounds specified in Article 22 *(b)* or *(e)*;

(e) modification of a decision made in the requested State;

(f) modification of a decision made in a State other than the requested State.

(2) The following categories of application shall be available to a debtor in a requesting State against whom there is an existing maintenance decision—

(a) recognition of a decision, or an equivalent procedure leading to the suspension, or limiting the enforcement, of a previous decision in the requested State;

(b) modification of a decision made in the requested State;

(c) modification of a decision made in a State other than the requested State.

(3) Save as otherwise provided in this Convention, the applications in paragraphs 1 and 2 shall be determined under the law of the requested State, and applications in paragraphs 1 *(c)* to *(f)* and 2 *(b)* and *(c)* shall be subject to the jurisdictional rules applicable in the requested State.

Article 11 Application contents

(1) All applications under Article 10 shall as a minimum include—

(a) a statement of the nature of the application or applications;

(b) the name and contact details, including the address and date of birth of the applicant;

(c) the name and, if known, address and date of birth of the respondent;

(d) the name and date of birth of any person for whom maintenance is sought;

(e) the grounds upon which the application is based;

(f) in an application by a creditor, information concerning where the maintenance payment should be sent or electronically transmitted;

(g) save in an application under Articles 10(1) *(a)* and (2) *(a)*, any information or document specified by declaration in accordance with Article 63 by the requested State;

(h) the name and contact details of the person or unit from the Central Authority of the requesting State responsible for processing the application.

(2) As appropriate, and to the extent known, the application shall in addition in particular include—

(a) the financial circumstances of the creditor;

(b) the financial circumstances of the debtor, including the name and address of the employer of the debtor and the nature and location of the assets of the debtor;

(c) any other information that may assist with the location of the respondent.

(3) The application shall be accompanied by any necessary supporting information or documentation including documentation concerning the entitlement of the applicant to free legal assistance. In the case of applications under Articles 10(1) *(a)* and (2) *(a)*, the application shall be accompanied only by the documents listed in Article 25.

(4) An application under Article 10 may be made in the form recommended and published by the Hague Conference on Private International Law.

Article 12 Transmission, receipt and processing of applications and cases through Central Authorities

(1) The Central Authority of the requesting State shall assist the applicant in ensuring that the application is accompanied by all the information and documents known by it to be necessary for consideration of the application.

(2) The Central Authority of the requesting State shall, when satisfied that the application complies with the requirements of the Convention, transmit the application on behalf of and with the consent of the applicant to the Central Authority of the requested State. The application shall be accompanied by the transmittal form set out in *Annex 1*. The Central Authority of the requesting State shall, when requested by the Central Authority of the requested State, provide a complete copy certified by the competent authority in the State of origin of any document specified under Articles 16(3), 25(1) *(a)*, *(b)* and *(d)* and (3) *(b)* and 30(3).

(3) The requested Central Authority shall, within six weeks from the date of receipt of the application, acknowledge receipt in the form set out in *Annex 2*, and inform the Central Authority of the requesting State what initial steps have been or will be taken to deal with the application, and may request any further necessary documents and information. Within

the same six-week period, the requested Central Authority shall provide to the requesting Central Authority the name and contact details of the person or unit responsible for responding to inquiries regarding the progress of the application.

(4) Within three months after the acknowledgement, the requested Central Authority shall inform the requesting Central Authority of the status of the application.

(5) Requesting and requested Central Authorities shall keep each other informed of—

(a) the person or unit responsible for a particular case;

(b) the progress of the case,

and shall provide timely responses to enquiries.

(6) Central Authorities shall process a case as quickly as a proper consideration of the issues will allow.

(7) Central Authorities shall employ the most rapid and efficient means of communication at their disposal.

(8) A requested Central Authority may refuse to process an application only if it is manifest that the requirements of the Convention are not fulfilled. In such case, that Central Authority shall promptly inform the requesting Central Authority of its reasons for refusal.

(9) The requested Central Authority may not reject an application solely on the basis that additional documents or information are needed. However, the requested Central Authority may ask the requesting Central Authority to provide these additional documents or information. If the requesting Central Authority does not do so within three months or a longer period specified by the requested Central Authority, the requested Central Authority may decide that it will no longer process the application. In this case, it shall inform the requesting Central Authority of this decision.

Article 13 Means of communication

Any application made through Central Authorities of the Contracting States in accordance with this Chapter, and any document or information appended thereto or provided by a Central Authority, may not be challenged by the respondent by reason only of the medium or means of communication employed between the Central Authorities concerned.

Article 14 Effective access to procedures

(1) The requested State shall provide applicants with effective access to procedures, including enforcement and appeal procedures, arising from applications under this Chapter.

(2) To provide such effective access, the requested State shall provide free legal assistance in accordance with Articles 14 to 17 unless paragraph 3 applies.

(3) The requested State shall not be obliged to provide such free legal assistance if and to the extent that the procedures of that State enable the applicant to make the case without the need for such assistance, and the Central Authority provides such services as are necessary free of charge.

(4) Entitlements to free legal assistance shall not be less than those available in equivalent domestic cases.

(5) No security, bond or deposit, however described, shall be required to guarantee the payment of costs and expenses in proceedings under the Convention.

Article 15 Free legal assistance for child support applications

(1) The requested State shall provide free legal assistance in respect of all applications by a creditor under this Chapter concerning maintenance obligations arising from a parent-child relationship towards a person under the age of 21 years.

(2) Notwithstanding paragraph 1, the requested State may, in relation to applications other than those under Article 10(1) *(a)* and *(b)* and the cases covered by Article 20(4), refuse free legal assistance if it considers that, on the merits, the application or any appeal is manifestly unfounded.

Article 16 Declaration to permit use of child-centred means test

(1) Notwithstanding Article 15(1), a State may declare, in accordance with Article 63, that it will provide free legal assistance in respect of applications other than under Article 10(1) *(a)* and *(b)* and the cases covered by Article 20(4), subject to a test based on an assessment of the means of the child.

(2) A State shall, at the time of making such a declaration, provide information to the Permanent Bureau of the Hague Conference on

Private International Law concerning the manner in which the assessment of the child's means will be carried out, including the financial criteria which would need to be met to satisfy the test.
(3) An application referred to in paragraph 1, addressed to a State which has made the declaration referred to in that paragraph, shall include a formal attestation by the applicant stating that the child's means meet the criteria referred to in paragraph 2. The requested State may only request further evidence of the child's means if it has reasonable grounds to believe that the information provided by the applicant is inaccurate.
(4) If the most favourable legal assistance provided for by the law of the requested State in respect of applications under this Chapter concerning maintenance obligations arising from a parent-child relationship towards a child is more favourable than that provided for under paragraphs 1 to 3, the most favourable legal assistance shall be provided.

Article 17 Applications not qualifying under Article 15 or Article 16

In the case of all applications under this Convention other than those under Article 15 or Article 16—

(a) the provision of free legal assistance may be made subject to a means or a merits test;

(b) an applicant, who in the State of origin has benefited from free legal assistance, shall be entitled, in any proceedings for recognition or enforcement, to benefit, at least to the same extent, from free legal assistance as provided for by the law of the State addressed under the same circumstances.

Chapter IV: Restrictions on Bringing Proceedings

Article 18 Limit on proceedings

(1) Where a decision is made in a Contracting State where the creditor is habitually resident, proceedings to modify the decision or to make a new decision cannot be brought by the debtor in any other Contracting State as long as the creditor remains habitually resident in the State where the decision was made.
(2) Paragraph 1 shall not apply—

(a) where, except in disputes relating to maintenance obligations in respect of children, there is agreement in writing between the parties to the jurisdiction of that other Contracting State;

(b) where the creditor submits to the jurisdiction of that other Contracting State either expressly or by defending on the merits of the case without objecting to the jurisdiction at the first available opportunity;

(c) where the competent authority in the State of origin cannot, or refuses to, exercise jurisdiction to modify the decision or make a new decision; or

(d) where the decision made in the State of origin cannot be recognised or declared enforceable in the Contracting State where proceedings to modify the decision or make a new decision are contemplated.

Chapter V: Recognition and Enforcement

Article 19 Scope of the Chapter

(1) This Chapter shall apply to a decision rendered by a judicial or administrative authority in respect of a maintenance obligation. The term 'decision' also includes a settlement or agreement concluded before or approved by such an authority. A decision may include automatic adjustment by indexation and a requirement to pay arrears, retroactive maintenance or interest and a determination of costs or expenses.

(2) If a decision does not relate solely to a maintenance obligation, the effect of this Chapter is limited to the parts of the decision which concern maintenance obligations.

(3) For the purpose of paragraph 1, 'administrative authority' means a public body whose decisions, under the law of the State where it is established—

(a) may be made the subject of an appeal to or review by a judicial authority; and

(b) have a similar force and effect to a decision of a judicial authority on the same matter.

(4) This Chapter also applies to maintenance arrangements in accordance with Article 30.

(5) The provisions of this Chapter shall apply to a request for recognition and enforcement made directly to a competent authority of the State addressed in accordance with Article 37.

Article 20 Bases for recognition and enforcement

(1) A decision made in one Contracting State ('the State of origin') shall be recognised and enforced in other Contracting States if—

(a) the respondent was habitually resident in the State of origin at the time proceedings were instituted;

(b) the respondent has submitted to the jurisdiction either expressly or by defending on the merits of the case without objecting to the jurisdiction at the first available opportunity;

(c) the creditor was habitually resident in the State of origin at the time proceedings were instituted;

(d) the child for whom maintenance was ordered was habitually resident in the State of origin at the time proceedings were instituted, provided that the respondent has lived with the child in that State or has resided in that State and provided support for the child there;

(e) except in disputes relating to maintenance obligations in respect of children, there has been agreement to the jurisdiction in writing by the parties; or

(f) the decision was made by an authority exercising jurisdiction on a matter of personal status or parental responsibility, unless that jurisdiction was based solely on the nationality of one of the parties.

(2) A Contracting State may make a reservation, in accordance with Article 62, in respect of paragraph 1 *(c)*, *(e)* or *(f)*.

(3) A Contracting State making a reservation under paragraph 2 shall recognise and enforce a decision if its law would in similar factual circumstances confer or would have conferred jurisdiction on its authorities to make such a decision.

(4) A Contracting State shall, if recognition of a decision is not possible as a result of a reservation under paragraph 2, and if the debtor is habitually resident in that State, take all appropriate measures to establish a decision for the benefit of the creditor. The preceding sentence shall not apply to direct requests for recognition and enforcement under Article 19(5) or to claims for support referred to in Article 2(1) *(b)*.

(5) A decision in favour of a child under the age of 18 years which cannot be recognised by virtue only of a reservation in respect of paragraph 1 *(c)*, *(e)* or *(f)* shall be accepted as establishing the eligibility of that child for maintenance in the State addressed.

(6) A decision shall be recognised only if it has effect in the State of origin, and shall be enforced only if it is enforceable in the State of origin.

Article 21 Severability and partial recognition and enforcement

(1) If the State addressed is unable to recognise or enforce the whole of the decision, it shall recognise or enforce any severable part of the decision which can be so recognised or enforced.

(2) Partial recognition or enforcement of a decision can always be applied for.

Article 22 Grounds for refusing recognition and enforcement

Recognition and enforcement of a decision may be refused if—

(a) recognition and enforcement of the decision is manifestly incompatible with the public policy ('ordre public') of the State addressed;

(b) the decision was obtained by fraud in connection with a matter of procedure;

(c) proceedings between the same parties and having the same purpose are pending before an authority of the State addressed and those proceedings were the first to be instituted;

(d) the decision is incompatible with a decision rendered between the same parties and having the same purpose, either in the State addressed or in another State, provided that this latter decision fulfils the conditions necessary for its recognition and enforcement in the State addressed;

(e) in a case where the respondent has neither appeared nor was represented in proceedings in the State of origin—

(i) when the law of the State of origin provides for notice of proceedings, the respondent did not have proper notice of the proceedings and an opportunity to be heard; or

(ii) when the law of the State of origin does not provide for notice of the proceedings, the respondent did not have proper notice of the decision and an opportunity to challenge or appeal it on fact and law; or

(f) the decision was made in violation of Article 18.

Article 23 Procedure on an application for recognition and enforcement

(1) Subject to the provisions of the Convention, the procedures for recognition and enforcement shall be governed by the law of the State addressed.

(2) Where an application for recognition and enforcement of a decision has been made through Central Authorities in accordance with Chapter III, the requested Central Authority shall promptly either—

(a) refer the application to the competent authority which shall without delay declare the decision enforceable or register the decision for enforcement; or

(b) if it is the competent authority take such steps itself.

(3) Where the request is made directly to a competent authority in the State addressed in accordance with Article 19(5), that authority shall without delay declare the decision enforceable or register the decision for enforcement.

(4) A declaration or registration may be refused only on the ground set out in Article 22 *(a)*. At this stage neither the applicant nor the respondent is entitled to make any submissions.

(5) The applicant and the respondent shall be promptly notified of the declaration or registration, made under paragraphs 2 and 3, or the refusal thereof in accordance with paragraph 4, and may bring a challenge or appeal on fact and on a point of law.

(6) A challenge or an appeal is to be lodged within 30 days of notification under paragraph 5. If the contesting party is not resident in the Contracting State in which the declaration or registration was made or refused, the challenge or appeal shall be lodged within 60 days of notification.

(7) A challenge or appeal may be founded only on the following—

(a) the grounds for refusing recognition and enforcement set out in Article 22;

(b) the bases for recognition and enforcement under Article 20;

(c) the authenticity or integrity of any document transmitted in accordance with Article 25(1) *(a)*, *(b)* or *(d)* or (3) *(b)*.

(8) A challenge or an appeal by a respondent may also be founded on the fulfilment of the debt to the extent that the recognition and enforcement relates to payments that fell due in the past.

(9) The applicant and the respondent shall be promptly notified of the decision following the challenge or the appeal.

(10) A further appeal, if permitted by the law of the State addressed, shall not have the effect of staying the enforcement of the decision unless there are exceptional circumstances.

(11) In taking any decision on recognition and enforcement, including any appeal, the competent authority shall act expeditiously.

Article 24 Alternative procedure on an application for recognition and enforcement

(1) Notwithstanding Article 23(2) to (11), a State may declare, in accordance with Article 63, that it will apply the procedure for recognition and enforcement set out in this Article.

(2) Where an application for recognition and enforcement of a decision has been made through Central Authorities in accordance with Chapter III, the requested Central Authority shall promptly either—

(a) refer the application to the competent authority which shall decide on the application for recognition and enforcement; or

(b) if it is the competent authority, take such a decision itself.

(3) A decision on recognition and enforcement shall be given by the competent authority after the respondent has been duly and promptly notified of the proceedings and both parties have been given an adequate opportunity to be heard.

(4) The competent authority may review the grounds for refusing recognition and enforcement set out in Article 22 *(a)*, *(c)* and *(d)* of its own motion. It may review any grounds listed in Articles 20, 22 and 23(7) *(c)* if raised by the respondent or if concerns relating to those grounds arise from the face of the documents submitted in accordance with Article 25.

(5) A refusal of recognition and enforcement may also be founded on the fulfilment of the debt to the extent that the recognition and enforcement relates to payments that fell due in the past.

(6) Any appeal, if permitted by the law of the State addressed, shall not have the effect of staying the enforcement of the decision unless there are exceptional circumstances.

(7) In taking any decision on recognition and enforcement, including any appeal, the competent authority shall act expeditiously.

Article 25 Documents

(1) An application for recognition and enforcement under Article 23 or Article 24 shall be accompanied by the following—

(a) a complete text of the decision;

(b) a document stating that the decision is enforceable in the State of origin and, in the case of a decision by an administrative authority, a document stating that the requirements of Article 19(3) are met unless that State has specified in accordance with Article 57 that decisions of its administrative authorities always meet those requirements;

(c) if the respondent did not appear and was not represented in the proceedings in the State of origin, a document or documents attesting, as appropriate, either that the respondent had proper notice of the proceedings and an opportunity to be heard, or that the respondent had proper notice of the decision and the opportunity to challenge or appeal it on fact and law;

(d) where necessary, a document showing the amount of any arrears and the date such amount was calculated;

(e) where necessary, in the case of a decision providing for automatic adjustment by indexation, a document providing the information necessary to make the appropriate calculations;

(f) where necessary, documentation showing the extent to which the applicant received free legal assistance in the State of origin.

(2) Upon a challenge or appeal under Article 23(7) *(c)* or upon request by the competent authority in the State addressed, a complete copy of the document concerned, certified by the competent authority in the State of origin, shall be provided promptly—

(a) by the Central Authority of the requesting State, where the application has been made in accordance with Chapter III;

(b) by the applicant, where the request has been made directly to a competent authority of the State addressed.

(3) A Contracting State may specify in accordance with Article 57—

(a) that a complete copy of the decision certified by the competent authority in the State of origin must accompany the application;

(b) circumstances in which it will accept, in lieu of a complete text of the decision, an abstract or extract of the decision drawn up by the competent authority of the State of origin, which may be made in the form recommended and published by the Hague Conference on Private International Law; or

(c) that it does not require a document stating that the requirements of Article 19(3) are met.

Article 26 Procedure on an application for recognition

This Chapter shall apply *mutatis mutandis* to an application for recognition of a decision, save that the requirement of enforceability is replaced by the requirement that the decision has effect in the State of origin.

Article 27 Findings of fact

Any competent authority of the State addressed shall be bound by the findings of fact on which the authority of the State of origin based its jurisdiction.

Article 28 No review of the merits

There shall be no review by any competent authority of the State addressed of the merits of a decision.

Article 29 Physical presence of the child or the applicant not required

The physical presence of the child or the applicant shall not be required in any proceedings in the State addressed under this Chapter.

Article 30 Maintenance arrangements

(1) A maintenance arrangement made in a Contracting State shall be entitled to recognition and enforcement as a decision under this Chapter provided that it is enforceable as a decision in the State of origin.

(2) For the purpose of Article 10(1) *(a)* and *(b)* and (2) *(a)*, the term 'decision' includes a maintenance arrangement.

(3) An application for recognition and enforcement of a maintenance arrangement shall be accompanied by the following—

(a) a complete text of the maintenance arrangement; and

(b) a document stating that the particular maintenance arrangement is enforceable as a decision in the State of origin.

(4) Recognition and enforcement of a maintenance arrangement may be refused if—

(a) the recognition and enforcement is manifestly incompatible with the public policy of the State addressed;

(b) the maintenance arrangement was obtained by fraud or falsification;

(c) the maintenance arrangement is incompatible with a decision rendered between the same parties and having the same purpose, either in the State addressed or in another State, provided that this

latter decision fulfils the conditions necessary for its recognition and enforcement in the State addressed.

(5) The provisions of this Chapter, with the exception of Articles 20, 22, 23(7) and 25(1) and (3), shall apply *mutatis mutandis* to the recognition and enforcement of a maintenance arrangement save that—

(a) a declaration or registration in accordance with Article 23(2) and (3) may be refused only on the ground set out in paragraph 4 *(a)*;

(b) a challenge or appeal as referred to in Article 23(6) may be founded only on the following—

(i) the grounds for refusing recognition and enforcement set out in paragraph 4;

(ii) the authenticity or integrity of any document transmitted in accordance with paragraph 3;

(c) as regards the procedure under Article 24(4), the competent authority may review of its own motion the ground for refusing recognition and enforcement set out in paragraph 4 *(a)* of this Article. It may review all grounds listed in paragraph 4 of this Article and the authenticity or integrity of any document transmitted in accordance with paragraph 3 if raised by the respondent or if concerns relating to those grounds arise from the face of those documents.

(6) Proceedings for recognition and enforcement of a maintenance arrangement shall be suspended if a challenge concerning the arrangement is pending before a competent authority of a Contracting State.

(7) A State may declare, in accordance with Article 63, that applications for recognition and enforcement of a maintenance arrangement shall only be made through Central Authorities.

(8) A Contracting State may, in accordance with Article 62, reserve the right not to recognise and enforce a maintenance arrangement.

Article 31 Decisions produced by the combined effect of provisional and confirmation orders

Where a decision is produced by the combined effect of a provisional order made in one State and an order by an authority in another State ('the confirming State') confirming the provisional order—

(a) each of those States shall be deemed for the purposes of this Chapter to be a State of origin;

(b) the requirements of Article 22 *(e)* shall be met if the respondent had proper notice of the proceedings in the confirming State and an opportunity to oppose the confirmation of the provisional order;

(c) the requirement of Article 20(6) that a decision be enforceable in the State of origin shall be met if the decision is enforceable in the confirming State; and

(d) Article 18 shall not prevent proceedings for the modification of the decision being commenced in either State.

Chapter VI: Enforcement by the State Addressed

Article 32 Enforcement under internal law

(1) Subject to the provisions of this Chapter, enforcement shall take place in accordance with the law of the State addressed.

(2) Enforcement shall be prompt.

(3) In the case of applications through Central Authorities, where a decision has been declared enforceable or registered for enforcement under Chapter V, enforcement shall proceed without the need for further action by the applicant.

(4) Effect shall be given to any rules applicable in the State of origin of the decision relating to the duration of the maintenance obligation.

(5) Any limitation on the period for which arrears may be enforced shall be determined either by the law of the State of origin of the decision or by the law of the State addressed, whichever provides for the longer limitation period.

Article 33 Non-discrimination

The State addressed shall provide at least the same range of enforcement methods for cases under the Convention as are available in domestic cases.

Article 34 Enforcement measures

(1) Contracting States shall make available in internal law effective measures to enforce decisions under this Convention.

(2) Such measures may include—

(a) wage withholding;

(b) garnishment from bank accounts and other sources;

(c) deductions from social security payments;

(d) lien on or forced sale of property;

(e) tax refund withholding;

(f) withholding or attachment of pension benefits;

(g) credit bureau reporting;

(h) denial, suspension or revocation of various licenses (for example, driving licenses);

(i) the use of mediation, conciliation or similar processes to bring about voluntary compliance.

Article 35 Transfer of funds

(1) Contracting States are encouraged to promote, including by means of international agreements, the use of the most cost-effective and efficient methods available to transfer funds payable as maintenance.

(2) A Contracting State, under whose law the transfer of funds is restricted, shall accord the highest priority to the transfer of funds payable under this Convention.

Chapter VII: Public Bodies

Article 36 Public bodies as applicants

(1) For the purposes of applications for recognition and enforcement under Article 10(1) *(a)* and *(b)* and cases covered by Article 20(4), 'creditor' includes a public body acting in place of an individual to whom maintenance is owed or one to which reimbursement is owed for benefits provided in place of maintenance.

(2) The right of a public body to act in place of an individual to whom maintenance is owed or to seek reimbursement of benefits provided to the creditor in place of maintenance shall be governed by the law to which the body is subject.

(3) A public body may seek recognition or claim enforcement of—

(a) a decision rendered against a debtor on the application of a public body which claims payment of benefits provided in place of maintenance;

(b) a decision rendered between a creditor and debtor to the extent of the benefits provided to the creditor in place of maintenance.

(4) The public body seeking recognition or claiming enforcement of a decision shall upon request furnish any document necessary to establish its right under paragraph 2 and that benefits have been provided to the creditor.

Chapter VIII: General Provisions

Article 37 Direct requests to competent authorities

(1) The Convention shall not exclude the possibility of recourse to such procedures as may be available under the internal law of a Contracting State allowing a person (an applicant) to seize directly a competent authority of that State in a matter governed by the Convention including, subject to Article 18, for the purpose of having a maintenance decision established or modified.

(2) Articles 14(5) and 17 *(b)* and the provisions of Chapters V, VI, VII and this Chapter, with the exception of Articles 40(2), 42, 43(3), 44(3), 45 and 55, shall apply in relation to a request for recognition and enforcement made directly to a competent authority in a Contracting State.

(3) For the purpose of paragraph 2, Article 2(1) *(a)* shall apply to a decision granting maintenance to a vulnerable person over the age specified in that sub-paragraph where such decision was rendered before the person reached that age and provided for maintenance beyond that age by reason of the impairment.

Article 38 Protection of personal data

Personal data gathered or transmitted under the Convention shall be used only for the purposes for which they were gathered or transmitted.

Article 39 Confidentiality

Any authority processing information shall ensure its confidentiality in accordance with the law of its State.

Article 40 Non-disclosure of information

(1) An authority shall not disclose or confirm information gathered or transmitted in application of this Convention if it determines that to do so could jeopardise the health, safety or liberty of a person.

(2) A determination to this effect made by one Central Authority shall be taken into account by another Central Authority, in particular in cases of family violence.

(3) Nothing in this Article shall impede the gathering and transmitting of information by and between authorities in so far as necessary to carry out the obligations under the Convention.

Article 41 No legalisation

No legalisation or similar formality may be required in the context of this Convention.

Article 42 Power of attorney

The Central Authority of the requested State may require a power of attorney from the applicant only if it acts on his or her behalf in judicial proceedings or before other authorities, or in order to designate a representative so to act.

Article 43 Recovery of costs

(1) Recovery of any costs incurred in the application of this Convention shall not take precedence over the recovery of maintenance.
(2) A State may recover costs from an unsuccessful party.
(3) For the purposes of an application under Article 10(1) *(b)* to recover costs from an unsuccessful party in accordance with paragraph 2, the term 'creditor' in Article 10(1) shall include a State.
(4) This Article shall be without prejudice to Article 8.

Article 44 Language requirements

(1) Any application and related documents shall be in the original language, and shall be accompanied by a translation into an official language of the requested State or another language which the requested State has indicated, by way of declaration in accordance with Article 63, it will accept, unless the competent authority of that State dispenses with translation.
(2) A Contracting State which has more than one official language and cannot, for reasons of internal law, accept for the whole of its territory documents in one of those languages shall, by declaration in accordance with Article 63, specify the language in which such documents or translations thereof shall be drawn up for submission in the specified parts of its territory.
(3) Unless otherwise agreed by the Central Authorities, any other communications between such Authorities shall be in an official language of the requested State or in either English or French. However, a Contracting State may, by making a reservation in accordance with Article 62, object to the use of either English or French.

Article 45 Means and costs of translation

(1) In the case of applications under Chapter III, the Central Authorities may agree in an individual case or generally that the translation into an official language of the requested State may be made in the requested State from the original language or from any other agreed language. If there is no agreement and it is not possible for the requesting Central Authority to comply with the requirements of Article 44(1) and (2), then the application and related documents may be transmitted with translation into English or French for further translation into an official language of the requested State.

(2) The cost of translation arising from the application of paragraph 1 shall be borne by the requesting State unless otherwise agreed by Central Authorities of the States concerned.

(3) Notwithstanding Article 8, the requesting Central Authority may charge an applicant for the costs of translation of an application and related documents, except in so far as those costs may be covered by its system of legal assistance.

Article 46 Non-unified legal systems: interpretation

(1) In relation to a State in which two or more systems of law or sets of rules of law with regard to any matter dealt with in this Convention apply in different territorial units—

(a) any reference to the law or procedure of a State shall be construed as referring, where appropriate, to the law or procedure in force in the relevant territorial unit;

(b) any reference to a decision established, recognised, recognised and enforced, enforced or modified in that State shall be construed as referring, where appropriate, to a decision established, recognised, recognised and enforced, enforced or modified in the relevant territorial unit;

(c) any reference to a judicial or administrative authority in that State shall be construed as referring, where appropriate, to a judicial or administrative authority in the relevant territorial unit;

(d) any reference to competent authorities, public bodies, and other bodies of that State, other than Central Authorities, shall be construed as referring, where appropriate, to those authorised to act in the relevant territorial unit;

(e) any reference to residence or habitual residence in that State shall be construed as referring, where appropriate, to residence or habitual residence in the relevant territorial unit;

(f) any reference to location of assets in that State shall be construed as referring, where appropriate, to the location of assets in the relevant territorial unit;

(g) any reference to a reciprocity arrangement in force in a State shall be construed as referring, where appropriate, to a reciprocity arrangement in force in the relevant territorial unit;

(h) any reference to free legal assistance in that State shall be construed as referring, where appropriate, to free legal assistance in the relevant territorial unit;

(i) any reference to a maintenance arrangement made in a State shall be construed as referring, where appropriate, to a maintenance arrangement made in the relevant territorial unit;

(j) any reference to recovery of costs by a State shall be construed as referring, where appropriate, to the recovery of costs by the relevant territorial unit.

(2) This Article shall not apply to a Regional Economic Integration Organisation.

Article 47 Non-unified legal systems: substantive rules

(1) A Contracting State with two or more territorial units in which different systems of law apply shall not be bound to apply this Convention to situations which involve solely such different territorial units.

(2) A competent authority in a territorial unit of a Contracting State with two or more territorial units in which different systems of law apply shall not be bound to recognise or enforce a decision from another Contracting State solely because the decision has been recognised or enforced in another territorial unit of the same Contracting State under this Convention.

(3) This Article shall not apply to a Regional Economic Integration Organisation.

Article 48 Co-ordination with prior Hague Maintenance Conventions

In relations between the Contracting States, this Convention replaces, subject to Article 56(2), the *Hague Convention of 2 October 1973 on the Recognition and Enforcement of Decisions Relating to Maintenance Obligations* and the Hague Convention of 15 April 1958 concerning the recognition and enforcement of decisions relating to maintenance obligations towards children in so far as their scope of application as between such States coincides with the scope of application of this Convention.

Article 49 Co-ordination with the 1956 New York Convention

In relations between the Contracting States, this Convention replaces the United Nations *Convention on the Recovery Abroad of Maintenance* of 20 June 1956, in so far as its scope of application as between such States coincides with the scope of application of this Convention.

Article 50 Relationship with prior Hague Conventions on service of documents and taking of evidence

This Convention does not affect the Hague Convention of 1 March 1954 on civil procedure, the *Hague Convention of 15 November 1965 on the Service Abroad of Judicial and Extrajudicial Documents in Civil or Commercial Matters* and the *Hague Convention of 18 March 1970 on the Taking of Evidence Abroad in Civil or Commercial Matters.*

Article 51 Co-ordination of instruments and supplementary agreements

(1) This Convention does not affect any international instrument concluded before this Convention to which Contracting States are Parties and which contains provisions on matters governed by this Convention.

(2) Any Contracting State may conclude with one or more Contracting States agreements, which contain provisions on matters governed by the Convention, with a view to improving the application of the Convention between or among themselves, provided that such agreements are consistent with the objects and purpose of the Convention and do not affect, in the relationship of such States with other Contracting States, the application of the provisions of the Convention. The States which have concluded such an agreement shall transmit a copy to the depositary of the Convention.

(3) Paragraphs 1 and 2 shall also apply to reciprocity arrangements and to uniform laws based on special ties between the States concerned.

(4) This Convention shall not affect the application of instruments of a Regional Economic Integration Organisation that is a Party to this Convention, adopted after the conclusion of the Convention, on matters governed by the Convention provided that such instruments do not affect, in the relationship of Member States of the Regional Economic Integration Organisation with other Contracting States, the application of the provisions of the Convention. As concerns the recognition or enforcement of decisions as between Member States of the Regional Economic Integration Organisation, the Convention shall not affect the rules of the Regional Economic Integration Organisation, whether adopted before or after the conclusion of the Convention.

Article 52 Most effective rule

(1) This Convention shall not prevent the application of an agreement, arrangement or international instrument in force between the requesting State and the requested State, or a reciprocity arrangement in force in the requested State that provides for—

(a) broader bases for recognition of maintenance decisions, without prejudice to Article 22 *(f)* of the Convention;

(b) simplified, more expeditious procedures on an application for recognition or recognition and enforcement of maintenance decisions;

(c) more beneficial legal assistance than that provided for under Articles 14 to 17; or

(d) procedures permitting an applicant from a requesting State to make a request directly to the Central Authority of the requested State.

(2) This Convention shall not prevent the application of a law in force in the requested State that provides for more effective rules as referred to in paragraph 1 *(a)* to *(c)*. However, as regards simplified, more expeditious procedures referred to in paragraph 1 *(b)*, they must be compatible with the protection offered to the parties under Articles 23 and 24, in particular as regards the rights of the parties to be duly notified of the proceedings and be given adequate opportunity to be heard and as regards the effects of any challenge or appeal.

Article 53 Uniform interpretation

In the interpretation of this Convention, regard shall be had to its international character and to the need to promote uniformity in its application.

Article 54 Review of practical operation of the Convention

(1) The Secretary General of the Hague Conference on Private International Law shall at regular intervals convene a Special Commission in order to review the practical operation of the Convention and to encourage the development of good practices under the Convention.

(2) For the purpose of such review, Contracting States shall co-operate with the Permanent Bureau of the Hague Conference on Private International Law in the gathering of information, including statistics and case law, concerning the practical operation of the Convention.

Article 55 Amendment of forms

(1) The forms annexed to this Convention may be amended by a decision of a Special Commission convened by the Secretary General of the Hague Conference on Private International Law to which all Contracting States and all Members shall be invited. Notice of the proposal to amend the forms shall be included in the agenda for the meeting.

(2) Amendments adopted by the Contracting States present at the Special Commission shall come into force for all Contracting States on the first day of the seventh calendar month after the date of their communication by the depositary to all Contracting States.

(3) During the period provided for in paragraph 2 any Contracting State may by notification in writing to the depositary make a reservation, in accordance with Article 62, with respect to the amendment. The State making such reservation shall, until the reservation is withdrawn, be treated as a State not Party to the present Convention with respect to that amendment.

Article 56 Transitional provisions

(1) The Convention shall apply in every case where—

(a) a request pursuant to Article 7 or an application pursuant to Chapter III has been received by the Central Authority of the requested

State after the Convention has entered into force between the requesting State and the requested State;

(b) a direct request for recognition and enforcement has been received by the competent authority of the State addressed after the Convention has entered into force between the State of origin and the State addressed.

(2) With regard to the recognition and enforcement of decisions between Contracting States to this Convention that are also Parties to either of the Hague Maintenance Conventions mentioned in Article 48, if the conditions for the recognition and enforcement under this Convention prevent the recognition and enforcement of a decision given in the State of origin before the entry into force of this Convention for that State, that would otherwise have been recognised and enforced under the terms of the Convention that was in effect at the time the decision was rendered, the conditions of that Convention shall apply.

(3) The State addressed shall not be bound under this Convention to enforce a decision or a maintenance arrangement, in respect of payments falling due prior to the entry into force of the Convention between the State of origin and the State addressed, except for maintenance obligations arising from a parent-child relationship towards a person under the age of 21 years.

Article 57 Provision of information concerning laws, procedures and services

(1) A Contracting State, by the time its instrument of ratification or accession is deposited or a declaration is submitted in accordance with Article 61 of the Convention, shall provide the Permanent Bureau of the Hague Conference on Private International Law with—

(a) a description of its laws and procedures concerning maintenance obligations;

(b) a description of the measures it will take to meet the obligations under Article 6;

(c) a description of how it will provide applicants with effective access to procedures, as required under Article 14;

(d) a description of its enforcement rules and procedures, including any limitations on enforcement, in particular debtor protection rules and limitation periods;

(e) any specification referred to in Article 25(1) *(b)* and (3).
(2) Contracting States may, in fulfilling their obligations under paragraph 1, utilise a country profile form recommended and published by the Hague Conference on Private International Law.
(3) Information shall be kept up to date by the Contracting States.

Chapter IX: Final Provisions

Article 58 Signature, ratification and accession

(1) The Convention shall be open for signature by the States which were Members of the Hague Conference on Private International Law at the time of its Twenty-First Session and by the other States which participated in that Session.
(2) It shall be ratified, accepted or approved and the instruments of ratification, acceptance or approval shall be deposited with the Ministry of Foreign Affairs of the Kingdom of the Netherlands, depositary of the Convention.
(3) Any other State or Regional Economic Integration Organisation may accede to the Convention after it has entered into force in accordance with Article 60(1).
(4) The instrument of accession shall be deposited with the depositary.
(5) Such accession shall have effect only as regards the relations between the acceding State and those Contracting States which have not raised an objection to its accession in the 12 months after the date of the notification referred to in Article 65. Such an objection may also be raised by States at the time when they ratify, accept or approve the Convention after an accession. Any such objection shall be notified to the depositary.

Article 59 Regional Economic Integration Organisations

(1) A Regional Economic Integration Organisation which is constituted solely by sovereign States and has competence over some or all of the matters governed by this Convention may similarly sign, accept, approve or accede to this Convention. The Regional Economic Integration Organisation shall in that case have the rights and obligations of a Contracting State, to the extent that the Organisation has competence over matters governed by the Convention.
(2) The Regional Economic Integration Organisation shall, at the time of signature, acceptance, approval or accession, notify the depositary in

writing of the matters governed by this Convention in respect of which competence has been transferred to that Organisation by its Member States. The Organisation shall promptly notify the depositary in writing of any changes to its competence as specified in the most recent notice given under this paragraph.

(3) At the time of signature, acceptance, approval or accession, a Regional Economic Integration Organisation may declare in accordance with Article 63 that it exercises competence over all the matters governed by this Convention and that the Member States which have transferred competence to the Regional Economic Integration Organisation in respect of the matter in question shall be bound by this Convention by virtue of the signature, acceptance, approval or accession of the Organisation.

(4) For the purposes of the entry into force of this Convention, any instrument deposited by a Regional Economic Integration Organisation shall not be counted unless the Regional Economic Integration Organisation makes a declaration in accordance with paragraph 3.

(5) Any reference to a 'Contracting State' or 'State' in this Convention shall apply equally to a Regional Economic Integration Organisation that is a Party to it, where appropriate. In the event that a declaration is made by a Regional Economic Integration Organisation in accordance with paragraph 3, any reference to a 'Contracting State' or 'State' in this Convention shall apply equally to the relevant Member States of the Organisation, where appropriate.

Article 60 Entry into force

(1) The Convention shall enter into force on the first day of the month following the expiration of three months after the deposit of the second instrument of ratification, acceptance or approval referred to in Article 58.

(2) Thereafter the Convention shall enter into force—

(a) for each State or Regional Economic Integration Organisation referred to in Article 59(1) subsequently ratifying, accepting or approving it, on the first day of the month following the expiration of three months after the deposit of its instrument of ratification, acceptance or approval;

(b) for each State or Regional Economic Integration Organisation referred to in Article 58(3) on the day after the end of the period during which objections may be raised in accordance with Article 58(5);

(c) for a territorial unit to which the Convention has been extended in accordance with Article 61, on the first day of the month following the expiration of three months after the notification referred to in that Article.

Article 61 Declarations with respect to non-unified legal systems

(1) If a State has two or more territorial units in which different systems of law are applicable in relation to matters dealt with in the Convention, it may at the time of signature, ratification, acceptance, approval or accession declare in accordance with Article 63 that this Convention shall extend to all its territorial units or only to one or more of them and may modify this declaration by submitting another declaration at any time.

(2) Any such declaration shall be notified to the depositary and shall state expressly the territorial units to which the Convention applies.

(3) If a State makes no declaration under this Article, the Convention shall extend to all territorial units of that State.

(4) This Article shall not apply to a Regional Economic Integration Organisation.

Article 62 Reservations

(1) Any Contracting State may, not later than the time of ratification, acceptance, approval or accession, or at the time of making a declaration in terms of Article 61, make one or more of the reservations provided for in Articles 2(2), 20(2), 30(8), 44(3) and 55(3). No other reservation shall be permitted.

(2) Any State may at any time withdraw a reservation it has made. The withdrawal shall be notified to the depositary.

(3) The reservation shall cease to have effect on the first day of the third calendar month after the notification referred to in paragraph 2.

(4) Reservations under this Article shall have no reciprocal effect with the exception of the reservation provided for in Article 2(2).

Article 63 Declarations

(1) Declarations referred to in Articles 2(3), 11(1) *(g)*, 16(1), 24(1), 30(7), 44(1) and (2), 59(3) and 61(1), may be made upon signature,

ratification, acceptance, approval or accession or at any time thereafter, and may be modified or withdrawn at any time.
(2) Declarations, modifications and withdrawals shall be notified to the depositary.
(3) A declaration made at the time of signature, ratification, acceptance, approval or accession shall take effect simultaneously with the entry into force of this Convention for the State concerned.
(4) A declaration made at a subsequent time, and any modification or withdrawal of a declaration, shall take effect on the first day of the month following the expiration of three months after the date on which the notification is received by the depositary.

Article 64 Denunciation

(1) A Contracting State to the Convention may denounce it by a notification in writing addressed to the depositary. The denunciation may be limited to certain territorial units of a multi-unit State to which the Convention applies.
(2) The denunciation shall take effect on the first day of the month following the expiration of 12 months after the date on which the notification is received by the depositary. Where a longer period for the denunciation to take effect is specified in the notification, the denunciation shall take effect upon the expiration of such longer period after the date on which the notification is received by the depositary.

Article 65 Notification

The depositary shall notify the Members of the Hague Conference on Private International Law, and other States and Regional Economic Integration Organisations which have signed, ratified, accepted, approved or acceded in accordance with Articles 58 and 59 of the following—

(a) the signatures, ratifications, acceptances and approvals referred to in Articles 58 and 59;

(b) the accessions and objections raised to accessions referred to in Articles 58(3) and (5) and 59;

(c) the date on which the Convention enters into force in accordance with Article 60;

(d) the declarations referred to in Articles 2(3), 11(1) *(g)*, 16(1), 24(1), 30(7), 44(1) and (2), 59(3) and 61(1);

(e) the agreements referred to in Article 51(2);

(f) the reservations referred to in Articles 2(2), 20(2), 30(8), 44(3) and 55(3), and the withdrawals referred to in Article 62(2);

(g) the denunciations referred to in Article 64.

In witness whereof the undersigned, being duly authorised thereto, have signed this Convention.

Done at The Hague, on the 23rd day of November 2007, in the English and French languages, both texts being equally authentic, in a single copy which shall be deposited in the archives of the Government of the Kingdom of the Netherlands, and of which a certified copy shall be sent, through diplomatic channels, to each of the Members of the Hague Conference on Private International Law at the date of its Twenty-First Session and to each of the other States which have participated in that Session.

ANNEX 1

Transmittal form under Article 12(2)

Confidentiality and Personal Data Protection Notice

Personal data gathered or transmitted under the Convention shall be used only for the purposes for which it was gathered or transmitted. Any authority processing such data shall ensure its confidentiality, in accordance with the law of its State.

An authority shall not disclose or confirm information gathered or transmitted in application of this Convention if it determines that to do so could jeopardise the health, safety or liberty of a person in accordance with Article 40.

☐ *A determination of non-disclosure has been made by a Central Authority in accordance with Article 40.*

(1) Requesting Central Authority	(2) Contact person in requesting State
(a) Address	(a) Address (if different)
(b) Telephone number	(b) Telephone number (if different)
(c) Fax number	(c) Fax number (if different)
(d) E-mail	(d) E-mail (if different)
(e) Reference number	(e) Language(s)

(3) Requested Central Authority ....
Address ....
....
(4) Particulars of the applicant
(a) Family name(s): ....
(b) Given name(s): ....
(c) Date of birth: .... (dd/mm/yyyy)

or

(a) Name of the public body: ....
....

(5) Particulars of the person(s) for whom maintenance is sought or payable

(a) ☐ The person is the same as the applicant named in point 4
(b) (i) Family name(s): .... Given name(s): ......
....
Date of birth: .... (dd/mm/yyyy)
(ii) Family name(s): ....
Given name(s): ....
Date of birth: .... (dd/mm/yyyy)
(iii) Family name(s): ....
Given name(s): ....
Date of birth: .... (dd/mm/yyyy)

(6) Particulars of the debtor

(a) ☐ The person is the same as the applicant named in point 4
(b) Family name(s): ....
(c) Given name(s): ....
(d) Date of birth: .... (dd/mm/yyyy)

(7) This transmittal form concerns and is accompanied by an application under:

☐ Article 10(1) *(a)*
☐ Article 10(1) *(b)*
☐ Article 10(1) *(c)*
☐ Article 10(1) *(d)*
☐ Article 10(1) *(e)*
☐ Article 10(1) *(f)*
☐ Article 10(2) *(a)*

☐ Article 10(2) *(b)*

☐ Article 10(2) *(c)*

(8) The following documents are appended to the application:

(a) For the purpose of an application under Article 10(1) *(a)* and:

In accordance with Article 25:

☐ Complete text of the decision (Art. 25(1) *(a)*)

☐ Abstract or extract of the decision drawn up by the competent authority of the State of origin (Art. 25(3) *(b)*) (if applicable)

☐ Document stating that the decision is enforceable in the State of origin and, in the case of a decision by an administrative authority, a document stating that the requirements of Article 19(3) are met unless that State has specified in accordance with Article 57 that decisions of its administrative authorities always meet those requirements (Art. 25(1) *(b)*) or if Article 25(3) *(c)* is applicable

☐ If the respondent did not appear and was not represented in the proceedings in the State of origin, a document or documents attesting, as appropriate, either that the respondent had proper notice of the proceedings and an opportunity to be heard, or that the respondent had proper notice of the decision and the opportunity to challenge or appeal it on fact and law (Art. 25(1) *(c)*)

☐ Where necessary, a document showing the amount of any arrears and the date such amount was calculated (Art. 25(1) *(d)*)

☐ Where necessary, a document providing the information necessary to make appropriate calculations in case of a decision providing for automatic adjustment by indexation (Art. 25(1) *(e)*)

☐ Where necessary, documentation showing the extent to which the applicant received free legal assistance in the State of origin (Art. 25(1) *(f)*)

In accordance with Article 30(3):

☐ Complete text of the maintenance arrangement (Art. 30(3) *(a)*)

☐ A document stating that the particular maintenance arrangement is enforceable as a decision in the State of origin (Art. 30(3) *(b)*)

☐ Any other documents accompanying the application (*e.g.*, if required, a document for the purpose of Art. 36(4)):

....

....

(b) For the purpose of an application under Article 10(1) *(b)*, *(c)*, *(d)*, *(e)*, *(f)* and (2) *(a)*, *(b)* or *(c)*, the following number of supporting documents (excluding the transmittal form and the application itself) in accordance with Article 11(3):

☐ Article 10(1) *(b)* ....
☐ Article 10(1) *(c)* ....
☐ Article 10(1) *(d)* ....
☐ Article 10(1) *(e)* ....
☐ Article 10(1) *(f)* ....
☐ Article 10(2) *(a)* ....
☐ Article 10(2) *(b)* ....
☐ Article 10(2) *(c)* ....

Name: .... (in block letters)
Date: ....
Authorised representative of the Central Authority ....
.... (dd/mm/yyyy)

ANNEX 2

ACKNOWLEDGEMENT FORM UNDER ARTICLE 12(3)

Confidentiality and Personal Data Protection Notice

Personal data gathered or transmitted under the Convention shall be used only for the purposes for which it was gathered or transmitted. Any authority processing such data shall ensure its confidentiality, in accordance with the law of its State.

An authority shall not disclose or confirm information gathered or transmitted in application of this Convention if it determines that to do so could jeopardise the health, safety or liberty of a person in accordance with Article 40.

☐ *A determination of non-disclosure has been made by a Central Authority in accordance with Article 40.*

(1) Requesting Central Authority	(2) Contact person in requesting State
(a) Address	(a) Address (if different)
(b) Telephone number	(b) Telephone number (if different)

(c) Fax number	(c) Fax number (if different)
(d) E-mail	(d) E-mail (if different)
(e) Reference number	(e) Language(s)

(3) Requesting Central Authority ....
Contact person ....
Address ....
....

(4) The requested Central Authority acknowledges receipt on .... (dd/mm/yyyy) of the transmittal form from the requesting Central Authority (reference number ....; dated .... (dd/mm/yyyy)) concerning the following application under:

☐ Article 10(1) *(a)*
☐ Article 10(1) *(b)*
☐ Article 10(1) *(c)*
☐ Article 10(1) *(d)*
☐ Article 10(1) *(e)*
☐ Article 10(1) *(f)*
☐ Article 10(2) *(a)*
☐ Article 10(2) *(b)*
☐ Article 10(2) *(c)*

Family name(s) of applicant: ....

Family name(s) of the person(s) for whom maintenance is sought or payable: ....
....
....

Family name(s) of debtor: ....

(5) Initial steps taken by the requested Central Authority:

☐ The file is complete and is under consideration
☐ See attached status of application report
☐ Status of application report will follow
☐ Please provide the following additional information and/or documentation:

....
....

☐ The requested Central Authority refuses to process this application as it is manifest that the requirements of the Convention are not fulfilled (Art. 12(8)). The reasons:

☐ are set out in an attached document

☐ will be set out in a document to follow

The requested Central Authority requests that the requesting Central Authority inform it of any change in the status of the application.

Name: .... (in block letters)

Date: ....

Authorised representative of the Central Authority ....
.... (dd/mm/yyyy)

ANNEXURE 7

Protocol on the Law Applicable to Maintenance Obligations

(Concluded 23 November 2007)

The States signatory to this Protocol,

Desiring to establish common provisions concerning the law applicable to maintenance obligations,

Wishing to modernise the *Hague Convention of 24 October 1956 on the law applicable to maintenance obligations towards children* and the *Hague Convention of 2 October 1973 on the Law Applicable to Maintenance Obligations*,

Wishing to develop general rules on applicable law that may supplement the *Hague Convention of 23 November 2007 on the International Recovery of Child Support and Other Forms of Family Maintenance*,

Have resolved to conclude a Protocol for this purpose and have agreed upon the following provisions—

Article 1 Scope

(1) This Protocol shall determine the law applicable to maintenance obligations arising from a family relationship, parentage, marriage or affinity, including a maintenance obligation in respect of a child regardless of the marital status of the parents.

(2) Decisions rendered in application of this Protocol shall be without prejudice to the existence of any of the relationships referred to in paragraph 1.

Article 2 Universal application

This Protocol applies even if the applicable law is that of a non-Contracting State.

Article 3 General rule on applicable law

(1) Maintenance obligations shall be governed by the law of the State of the habitual residence of the creditor, save where this Protocol provides otherwise.

(2) In the case of a change in the habitual residence of the creditor, the law of the State of the new habitual residence shall apply as from the moment when the change occurs.

Article 4 Special rules favouring certain creditors

(1) The following provisions shall apply in the case of maintenance obligations of—

(a) parents towards their children;

(b) persons, other than parents, towards persons who have not attained the age of 21 years, except for obligations arising out of the relationships referred to in Article 5; and

(c) children towards their parents.

(2) If the creditor is unable, by virtue of the law referred to in Article 3, to obtain maintenance from the debtor, the law of the forum shall apply.

(3) Notwithstanding Article 3, if the creditor has seized the competent authority of the State where the debtor has his habitual residence, the law of the forum shall apply. However, if the creditor is unable, by virtue of this law, to obtain maintenance from the debtor, the law of the State of the habitual residence of the creditor shall apply.

(4) If the creditor is unable, by virtue of the laws referred to in Article 3 and paragraphs 2 and 3 of this Article, to obtain maintenance from the debtor, the law of the State of their common nationality, if there is one, shall apply.

Article 5 Special rule with respect to spouses and ex-spouses

In the case of a maintenance obligation between spouses, ex-spouses or parties to a marriage which has been annulled, Article 3 shall not apply if one of the parties objects and the law of another State, in particular the State of their last common habitual residence, has a closer connection with the marriage. In such a case the law of that other State shall apply.

Article 6 Special rule on defence

In the case of maintenance obligations other than those arising from a parent-child relationship towards a child and those referred to in Article 5, the debtor may contest a claim from the creditor on the ground that there is no such obligation under both the law of the State of the habitual residence of the debtor and the law of the State of the common nationality of the parties, if there is one.

Article 7 Designation of the law applicable for the purpose of a particular proceeding

(1) Notwithstanding Articles 3 to 6, the maintenance creditor and debtor for the purpose only of a particular proceeding in a given State may expressly designate the law of that State as applicable to a maintenance obligation.

(2) A designation made before the institution of such proceedings shall be in an agreement, signed by both parties, in writing or recorded in any medium, the information contained in which is accessible so as to be usable for subsequent reference.

Article 8 Designation of the applicable law

(1) Notwithstanding Articles 3 to 6, the maintenance creditor and debtor may at any time designate one of the following laws as applicable to a maintenance obligation—

(a) the law of any State of which either party is a national at the time of the designation;

(b) the law of the State of the habitual residence of either party at the time of designation;

(c) the law designated by the parties as applicable, or the law in fact applied, to their property regime;

(d) the law designated by the parties as applicable, or the law in fact applied, to their divorce or legal separation.

(2) Such agreement shall be in writing or recorded in any medium, the information contained in which is accessible so as to be usable for subsequent reference, and shall be signed by both parties.

(3) Paragraph 1 shall not apply to maintenance obligations in respect of a person under the age of 18 years or of an adult who, by reason of an impairment or insufficiency of his or her personal faculties, is not in a position to protect his or her interest.

(4) Notwithstanding the law designated by the parties in accordance with paragraph 1, the question of whether the creditor can renounce his or her right to maintenance shall be determined by the law of the State of the habitual residence of the creditor at the time of the designation.
(5) Unless at the time of the designation the parties were fully informed and aware of the consequences of their designation, the law designated by the parties shall not apply where the application of that law would lead to manifestly unfair or unreasonable consequences for any of the parties.

Article 9 'Domicile' instead of 'nationality'

A State which has the concept of 'domicile' as a connecting factor in family matters may inform the Permanent Bureau of the Hague Conference on Private International Law that, for the purpose of cases which come before its authorities, the word 'nationality' in Articles 4 and 6 is replaced by 'domicile' as defined in that State.

Article 10 Public bodies

The right of a public body to seek reimbursement of a benefit provided to the creditor in place of maintenance shall be governed by the law to which that body is subject.

Article 11 Scope of the applicable law

The law applicable to the maintenance obligation shall determine *inter alia*—

(a) whether, to what extent and from whom the creditor may claim maintenance;

(b) the extent to which the creditor may claim retroactive maintenance;

(c) the basis for calculation of the amount of maintenance, and indexation;

(d) who is entitled to institute maintenance proceedings, except for issues relating to procedural capacity and representation in the proceedings;

(e) prescription or limitation periods;

(f) the extent of the obligation of a maintenance debtor, where a public body seeks reimbursement of benefits provided for a creditor in place of maintenance.

Article 12 Exclusion of renvoi

In the Protocol, the term 'law' means the law in force in a State other than its choice of law rules.

Article 13 Public policy

The application of the law determined under the Protocol may be refused only to the extent that its effects would be manifestly contrary to the public policy of the forum.

Article 14 Determining the amount of maintenance

Even if the applicable law provides otherwise, the needs of the creditor and the resources of the debtor as well as any compensation which the creditor was awarded in place of periodical maintenance payments shall be taken into account in determining the amount of maintenance.

Article 15 Non-application of the Protocol to internal conflicts

(1) A Contracting State in which different systems of law or sets of rules of law apply to maintenance obligations shall not be bound to apply the rules of the Protocol to conflicts solely between such different systems or sets of rules of law.

(2) This Article shall not apply to a Regional Economic Integration Organisation.

Article 16 Non-unified legal systems: territorial

(1) In relation to a State in which two or more systems of law or sets of rules of law with regard to any matter dealt with in this Protocol apply in different territorial units—

(a) any reference to the law of a State shall be construed as referring, where appropriate, to the law in force in the relevant territorial unit;

(b) any reference to competent authorities or public bodies of that State shall be construed as referring, where appropriate, to those authorised to act in the relevant territorial unit;

(c) any reference to habitual residence in that State shall be construed as referring, where appropriate, to habitual residence in the relevant territorial unit;

(d) any reference to the State of which two persons have a common nationality shall be construed as referring to the territorial unit designated by the law of that State or, in the absence of relevant rules,

to the territorial unit with which the maintenance obligation is most closely connected;

(e) any reference to the State of which a person is a national shall be construed as referring to the territorial unit designated by the law of that State or, in the absence of relevant rules, to the territorial unit with which the person has the closest connection.

(2) For the purpose of identifying the applicable law under the Protocol in relation to a State which comprises two or more territorial units each of which has its own system of law or set of rules of law in respect of matters covered by this Protocol, the following rules apply—

(a) if there are rules in force in such a State identifying which territorial unit's law is applicable, the law of that unit applies;

(b) in the absence of such rules, the law of the relevant territorial unit as defined in paragraph 1 applies.

(3) This Article shall not apply to a Regional Economic Integration Organisation.

Article 17 Non-unified legal systems: inter-personal conflicts

For the purpose of identifying the applicable law under the Protocol in relation to a State which has two or more systems of law or sets of rules of law applicable to different categories of persons in respect of matters covered by this Protocol, any reference to the law of such State shall be construed as referring to the legal system determined by the rules in force in that State.

Article 18 Co-ordination with prior Hague Maintenance Conventions

As between the Contracting States, this Protocol replaces the *Hague Convention of 2 October 1973 on the Law Applicable to Maintenance Obligations* and the *Hague Convention of 24 October 1956 on the law applicable to maintenance obligations towards children.*

Article 19 Co-ordination with other instruments

(1) This Protocol does not affect any other international instrument to which Contracting States are or become Parties and which contains provisions on matters governed by the Protocol, unless a contrary declaration is made by the States Parties to such instrument.

(2) Paragraph 1 also applies to uniform laws based on special ties of a regional or other nature between the States concerned.

Article 20 Uniform interpretation

In the interpretation of this Protocol, regard shall be had to its international character and to the need to promote uniformity in its application.

Article 21 Review of practical operation of the Protocol

(1) The Secretary General of the Hague Conference on Private International Law shall as necessary convene a Special Commission in order to review the practical operation of the Protocol.

(2) For the purpose of such review Contracting States shall co-operate with the Permanent Bureau of the Hague Conference on Private International Law in the gathering of case law concerning the application of the Protocol.

Article 22 Transitional provisions

This Protocol shall not apply to maintenance claimed in a Contracting State relating to a period prior to its entry into force in that State.

Article 23 Signature, ratification and accession

(1) This Protocol is open for signature by all States.

(2) This Protocol is subject to ratification, acceptance or approval by the signatory States.

(3) This Protocol is open for accession by all States.

(4) Instruments of ratification, acceptance, approval or accession shall be deposited with the Ministry of Foreign Affairs of the Kingdom of the Netherlands, depositary of the Protocol.

Article 24 Regional Economic Integration Organisations

(1) A Regional Economic Integration Organisation which is constituted solely by sovereign States and has competence over some or all of the matters governed by the Protocol may equally sign, accept, approve or accede to the Protocol. The Regional Economic Integration Organisation shall in that case have the rights and obligations of a Contracting State, to the extent that the Organisation has competence over matters governed by the Protocol.

(2) The Regional Economic Integration Organisation shall, at the time of signature, acceptance, approval or accession, notify the depositary in writing of the matters governed by the Protocol in respect of which competence has been transferred to that Organisation by its Member

States. The Organisation shall promptly notify the depositary in writing of any changes to its competence as specified in the most recent notice given under this paragraph.

(3) At the time of signature, acceptance, approval or accession, a Regional Economic Integration Organisation may declare, in accordance with Article 28, that it exercises competence over all the matters governed by the Protocol and that the Member States which have transferred competence to the Regional Economic Integration Organisation in respect of the matter in question shall be bound by the Protocol by virtue of the signature, acceptance, approval or accession of the Organisation.

(4) For the purposes of the entry into force of the Protocol, any instrument deposited by a Regional Economic Integration Organisation shall not be counted unless the Regional Economic Integration Organisation makes a declaration under paragraph 3.

(5) Any reference to a 'Contracting State' or 'State' in the Protocol applies equally to a Regional Economic Integration Organisation that is a Party to it, where appropriate. In the event that a declaration is made by a Regional Economic Integration Organisation under paragraph 3, any reference to a 'Contracting State' or 'State' in the Protocol applies equally to the relevant Member States of the Organisation, where appropriate.

Article 25 Entry into force

(1) The Protocol shall enter into force on the first day of the month following the expiration of three months after the deposit of the second instrument of ratification, acceptance, approval or accession referred to in Article 23.

(2) Thereafter the Protocol shall enter into force—

(a) for each State or each Regional Economic Integration Organisation referred to in Article 24 subsequently ratifying, accepting or approving the Protocol or acceding to it, on the first day of the month following the expiration of three months after the deposit of its instrument of ratification, acceptance, approval or accession;

(b) for a territorial unit to which the Protocol has been extended in accordance with Article 26, on the first day of the month following the expiration of three months after notification of the declaration referred to in that Article.

Article 26 Declarations with respect to non-unified legal systems

(1) If a State has two or more territorial units in which different systems of law are applicable in relation to matters dealt with in this Protocol, it may at the time of signature, ratification, acceptance, approval or accession declare in accordance with Article 28 that the Protocol shall extend to all its territorial units or only to one or more of them and may modify this declaration by submitting another declaration at any time.

(2) Any such declaration shall be notified to the depositary and shall state expressly the territorial units to which the Protocol applies.

(3) If a State makes no declaration under this Article, the Protocol is to extend to all territorial units of that State.

(4) This Article shall not apply to a Regional Economic Integration Organisation.

Article 27 Reservations

No reservations may be made to this Protocol.

Article 28 Declarations

(1) Declarations referred to in Articles 24(3) and 26(1) may be made upon signature, ratification, acceptance, approval or accession or at any time thereafter, and may be modified or withdrawn at any time.

(2) Declarations, modifications and withdrawals shall be notified to the depositary.

(3) A declaration made at the time of signature, ratification, acceptance, approval or accession shall take effect simultaneously with the entry into force of this Protocol for the State concerned.

(4) A declaration made at a subsequent time, and any modification or withdrawal of a declaration, shall take effect on the first day of the month following the expiration of three months after the date on which the notification is received by the depositary.

Article 29 Denunciation

(1) A Contracting State to this Protocol may denounce it by a notification in writing addressed to the depositary. The denunciation may be limited to certain territorial units of a State with a non-unified legal system to which the Protocol applies.

(2) The denunciation shall take effect on the first day of the month following the expiration of 12 months after the date on which the

notification is received by the depositary. Where a longer period for the denunciation to take effect is specified in the notification, the denunciation shall take effect upon the expiration of such longer period after the date on which the notification is received by the depositary.

Article 30 Notification

The depositary shall notify the Members of the Hague Conference on Private International Law, and other States and Regional Economic Integration Organisations which have signed, ratified, accepted, approved or acceded in accordance with Articles 23 and 24 of the following—

(a) the signatures and ratifications, acceptances, approvals and accessions referred to in Articles 23 and 24;

(b) the date on which this Protocol enters into force in accordance with Article 25;

(c) the declarations referred to in Articles 24(3) and 26(1);

(d) the denunciations referred to in Article 29.

In witness whereof the undersigned, being duly authorised thereto, have signed this Protocol.

Done at The Hague, on the 23rd day of November 2007, in the English and French languages, both texts being equally authentic, in a single copy which shall be deposited in the archives of the Government of the Kingdom of the Netherlands, and of which a certified copy shall be sent, through diplomatic channels, to each of the Members of the Hague Conference on Private International Law at the date of its Twenty-First Session and to each of the other States which have participated in that Session.

Case Index

Index

About the Author

V.C. Govindaraj is a former Professor at the Faculty of Law, University of Delhi, India, where he taught Constitutional Law, Public and Private International Law, Law of International Institutions, Law of the Sea, and Roman Law. He is a former Vice President, Life Time Achievement Award winner, and Life Member of the Indian Society of International Law. He has been a Visiting Professor at the Jawaharlal Nehru University, New Delhi, India, the National Law School, Bengaluru, India, the Indian Academy of International Law and Diplomacy, New Delhi, India, and the National Institute of Criminology and Forensic Science, New Delhi, India. He was Senior Fellow and Visiting Scholar at the Ford Foundation, Columbia University School of Law, New York, USA. He has worked for the Asian-African Legal Consultative Committee, New Delhi, India, has practiced law at the Madras High Court, Chennai, India, and has been a legal consultant for members of the Bar of the Supreme Court of India and the High Court of Delhi. He has served as a member of the Board of Examiners for the Union and Andhra Pradesh Public Service Commissions, India, and an examiner for many Indian universities. He has authored a number of scholarly articles and books in the areas of Public and Private International Law, Human Rights, and the Law of the Sea, and was a member of the editorial board of the *Indian Journal of International Law*.